BEATRICE WEBB'S DIARIES

1924–1932

The Earlier Life of Beatrice Webb

My Apprenticeship (to 1892)

Our Partnership (1892–1911)
Edited by Barbara Drake and Margaret Cole

Beatrice Webb's Diaries (1912–1924)
Edited by Margaret Cole

*Sidney and Beatrice Webb in the
garden at Passfield Corner*

BEATRICE WEBB'S DIARIES

1924 - 1932

Edited and with an Introduction by
MARGARET COLE

LONGMANS, GREEN AND CO
LONDON · NEW YORK · TORONTO

LONGMANS, GREEN AND CO LTD
6 & 7 CLIFFORD STREET LONDON W I
BOSTON HOUSE STRAND STREET CAPE TOWN
531 LITTLE COLLINS STREET MELBOURNE

LONGMANS, GREEN AND CO INC
55 FIFTH AVENUE NEW YORK 3

LONGMANS, GREEN AND CO
20 CRANFIELD ROAD TORONTO 16

ORIENT LONGMANS LTD
CALCUTTA BOMBAY MADRAS
DELHI VIJAYAWADA DACCA

First published 1956

PRINTED IN GREAT BRITAIN
BY WESTERN PRINTING SERVICES LTD., BRISTOL

INTRODUCTION

T H I S is the fourth of the autobiographical books of Beatrice Webb to appear. The first, *My Apprenticeship* (1926), was composed and published by herself; and covered her life up to the time of her marriage in 1892. Almost as soon as it had come out, it was recognised as going well beyond the scope of an autobiography; it was a penetrating series of essays on the social history of the nineteenth century, seen through the experience of a member of the "order-giving" classes who became intellectually "déclassée". It was based, of course, largely on the diaries which she had begun to keep in the 'seventies; but of direct quotation there was comparatively little, much less, in fact, than many students of social history would have wished, who delighted in the accounts of the working classes of Bacup, the grim picture of "philanthropy" as exemplified in St. Katherine's Building, and in the vivid portraits of Mitchell the Co-operative leader, the ageing Herbert Spencer, and many others, including, even, the young Sidney Webb.

The second volume, *Our Partnership*, was also prepared by Beatrice, almost completely, before her death; all that it required was a small amount of editing and arrangement. In this volume, which took the story up to 1912, when the Webbs followed the failure of their campaign to break up the Poor Law by a year's travel round the world, the diary material bulked much larger; the book, though divided by subjects rather than strictly by chronology, in contrast to its predecessor consisted mainly of short essays introducing the diary material. This made easy the transition, after her death, to the pure diary form.

In the third volume, 1912 to 1924, the material showed some trace that the author had made a beginning of editing it; there were a certain number of notes, explanatory or "second thoughts", which had been added, sometimes some

v

years after the date of the original entries; these were reproduced in the published text. In the present book, however,
revision by the author has reached the minimum; there are
only some half-dozen notes, all of which appear to have
been added almost immediately. These *Diaries*, therefore,
appear in print (subject to the corrections mentioned later)
exactly as they left their author's hand.

This volume ends in the spring of 1932, when the Webbs
left England for the U.S.S.R., a convenient stopping-point,
since, though the MS. continues until ten days before her
death in 1943, their part in public life in effect ceased after
that date. They were living retired in the country, entertaining many visitors, it is true, but intensely preoccupied,
for several years after their return, with the writing of their
enormous book on *Soviet Communism* (published in 1935)
and with controversy arising therefrom. For some years, the
British, or any other political system provided little more
than a "side-interest"; the rise of the Nazis, for example,
finds no mention. The *Diaries*, therefore, cease to be in any
way a first-hand account of politics and social life; fascinating as they are to read, they are purely a personal journal.
Furthermore, the editorial difficulties of length, references
to living persons, etc., which are mentioned later in this
introduction, increase in geometrical progression as time
goes on. For all these reasons their publication cannot be
immediate.

The book runs from 1924 to 1932—a period, as every
reader of it will find, of intense and continuous interest, both
in Beatrice's own life and in the events covered—there is no
melancholy "sag", such as was so apparent in the first part
of the preceding volume, when the political failure of the
Poor Law campaign and the depression of the First World
War combined to produce a nervous breakdown in its author
—here there is nothing of the sort, only occasional sensations
of exhaustion, not astonishing in one who had had doubtful
health all her life and was sixty-five years old at the date of
the first entry. As in the previous case, it is divided simply
by years; but it is interesting to observe how nearly this
division corresponds to actual divisions of interests and
events.

1924 begins with the formation of the first Labour Government—which fell in October, not November, as Beatrice prophesied with such near-accuracy at its birth; and Labour's first experience of office is its theme. Now that nearly all who took active part in that Cabinet are dead without leaving intimate records behind them, it may well be that Beatrice Webb's *Diaries* will prove to be (apart from the highly individual account of Viscount Snowden in his own *Autobiography*) the most considerable first-hand source for the inner history of the experiment. Those who think immediately of its brief life with its unheroic end in the muddle of the Campbell prosecution and the "Zinoviev Letter", who remember the second Labour Government with its more tragic but no more edifying fall, and the third with its strong programme strongly carried out, may perhaps wonder a little at the attention paid to those nine months: they forget, however, that only seven years earlier the Labour Party had been a loose federal group without individual membership and without a declared policy of any kind, and that less than six years had elapsed since its candidates were overwhelmed in the "coupon" election of 1918. Poy, the cartoonist of the *Evening News*, depicted Winston Churchill as wearing a peculiar governmental hat and saying to Labour, "*You* couldn't wear this Hat: you'd look So Silly in it"; and the thought that Labour could ever be "Fit to Govern" was to most middle-class publicists the height of absurdity. Hence the feeling that Baldwin and Asquith were taking a great gamble with the future of Britain in allowing MacDonald to form a government even under the most hampering minority conditions; hence the emphasis Beatrice lays on the initial competence of the incoming Ministers, and the fact that the Civil Service seems to respect them; and hence, too, her appreciation—perhaps prompted by Sidney the realist—of the value of MacDonald's physical assets as Prime Minister. There is much, in this section and later, of description and discussion of MacDonald, which may form material for final appraisement of the "boneless wonder"; but I do not think that any readers will think that Beatrice, any more than most of his contemporaries, succeeded in making him an intelligible personality; she could not understand his mental processes—if indeed anybody could—and she was not temperamentally conditioned to grasp the charismatic qualities which (however disastrous in the end) persuaded the unromantic Sidney and Arthur Henderson that "Mac" was the only possible leader for the Party.

MacDonald apart, however, the reader of to-day will find traces of a good many controversies and discussions which arose acutely when Labour first entered governing circles and which were not settled, if settled they now are, for some considerable time: the question of Ministerial salaries, for example, *vis-à-vis* the standard of living of the ordinary voter, the question of Court dress and Court ceremonial, etc. (The further question whether Labour Ministers should be responsible to the Party leader or to the Party's Executive Committee, which had been hotly debated at many early conferences, is not mentioned; it may be assumed that "the tradition of Parliament" smothered it easily as soon as Labour was in office.) Beatrice and Sidney both held firmly to the opinion that Labour Cabinets should set a tradition of modesty and refrain from "conspicuous waste"; but there was the additional problem of creating, particularly among lesser Ministers and valuable supporters and the wives of both, a core of self-confident responsibility which would eventually measure up to the *salons* of the past. Beatrice's own contribution to this very real necessity was the Half-Circle Club (which was not without its critics) and the Parliamentary Labour Club. Whether or not she succeeded is a matter of opinion; but there is no doubt that, with Sidney comfortably and on the whole successfully occupied at the Board of Trade, she worked very hard at the social side of the first Labour Government.

Too hard, perhaps, for her own capacity. For the record of 1925 begins with a confession of weariness with political life—except for the women of Seaham, whom she always found restful and refreshing until the connection with the division was terminated. The handing over of 41 Grosvenor Road to Susan Lawrence—"Farewell, little house by the Thames," as she wrote later—is accepted with scarcely a pang, for it means that she can now live in peace among the

pleasures of Passfield Corner and get on with "The Book"
—*My Apprenticeship*.

The Book is, in fact, the subject of Part II; and the entries
concerning it clearly show how nervous Beatrice was about
this, her first venture into lone authorship since her marriage.
She is afraid that it will not be good, nor find favour with
reviewers; she thinks Bernard Shaw does not like it, and,
worse still, she fears that Sidney does not. He seems to
think that the quotations from the *Diaries* are over-numerous
and not really worth including—a shocking and revealing
view, if her impression was correct. In sum, The Book is
costing her more effort than anything that she has done for
some time; and with surprising modesty she cannot feel sure
of its real value. So great was her preoccupation that the
rest of the year's entries are rather shadowy, though there
are a few vigorous character-sketches, of the Snowdens, for
example, and Graham Wallas; and the prophecy, remarkable
for 1925, that China will eventually go the way of Russia
and embrace the Communist creed.

Part III—1926—is, as one would expect, in the main
the story of the miners and the General Strike. On the
whole, it is an unsympathetic account: the Webbs, while
recognising, ever since Sidney's membership of the Sankey
Commission, the stupidity and obstinacy of the coal-owners
and the impossibility of doing anything to reform the mining
industry so long as they were in control, were generally in
favour of compromise and negotiation rather than strike
action, and violently opposed to anything that savoured of
syndicalism and "workers' control"; and in the General
Strike and particularly in the speeches of Arthur Cook, the
"inspired idiot", they found an echo of the doctrines they
had fought so fiercely in the Fabian Society more than a
dozen years before. What Beatrice says in criticism of the
movement of 1926 and its leadership was mostly quite true;
the strike was an impossible venture from the outset, an
attempt to coerce the Government by people who wanted
nothing less than a political revolution of any kind; the
leaders did not want it and had no idea what to do with the
genie when they had called it out of its bottle and saw to
their astonishment, not to say consternation, the rank and

file in town after town solidly marching out to their Unions' command; the leadership of the Miners' Federation was as bad, both before the strike and during the long months before surrender, as any leadership could have been; and the defeat did finally end the hopes of syndicalists, "Direct Actionists", and all who pinned their hopes of change to militant industrial action. But granted all this, one yet feels that Beatrice could have shown more sympathy with the emotions behind the strike, the sense of having been tricked into battle by the Government, and of working-class solidarity, of standing fast against a deliberate attack on the miner's standard of life.

She could not show the sympathy, because she did not feel it. In 1926, as earlier during the South African War and in the 1906 elections, and again later in 1931, the Webbs displayed their inability to understand the surges of non-rational emotion which play so great a part in most people's political attitudes; the passages in the *Diaries* in which Beatrice argues with herself about contributing to the Miners' Relief Funds and finally gives a hundred pounds to Seaham, not because they are convinced but as a return for the loyalty of the division to its member, reveal the conflict between the representative and those whom he represented.

One interesting fact emerges from her observations and discussions—the absence of real suffering, in the nineteenth-century sense, during the 1926 dispute. Even by that date, the beginnings of the Welfare State and the workings of the social conscience had softened the stark results of industrial strife in comparison with the days of the Chartists and the great Dock Strike. The miners surrendered in November because their battle was evidently lost; they were not starved into submission through their wives and children. (The malnutrition, the bankruptcy, and the hopelessness, which conditioned the outlook in the coalfields for a generation developed, for the most part, in the dreary years after the strike was over.) Under the circumstances, the gift of a hundred pounds well represented the Webbs' attitude; reading between the lines, one can sense that it was accepted as "payment in lieu of support". Sidney's resignation of his candidature, however natural at his age, was the obvious sequel.

After 1926, 1927 begins in an atmosphere of anti-climax, or at the least, of "marking time". *My Apprenticeship* has been published and received its reviews; and the work for the last volume of the *Poor Law History* is only just getting under way. The Trade Union movement is slowly struggling to its feet again in a chastened and cautious mood, holding talks with the opposite side (the Mond-Turner negotiations), and only feebly resisting the passage of the vindictive Trade Union Act; and though Beatrice presciently observed that the industrial defeat and its aftermath were improving the prospects of the political Labour movement, the Webbs were in process of dissociating themselves from active participation and did not expect to return. Up to the middle of 1928, the main interest of the *Diaries* is the beginning of the "pattern of living-in-retirement" which became so much a feature of Passfield Corner during the later years of the Partnership. Here we can see the week-end visitors and their entertainment, the brisk walks and the no less brisk discussions which have been so often described; it is no accident that so many of the best pen-portraits of politicians etc. are to be found in this section. The eager interest which Beatrice, to the end of her life, displayed in the character and opinions of those who would carry on after her death here begins to be apparent—and alongside therewith, a more personal interest in the varied descendants of the Potter sisters, which led up to the great family party at Passfield Corner in 1937.

By the middle of 1928, however, this pattern of meditation-cum-visits is pushed aside by the claims of the *Poor Law History*. Once again, after many years, the authors of *Methods of Social Study* betake themselves to the field-work so lovingly described therein; and for about twelve months, up to the time of the General Election, the paramount interest is the interviewing of Guardians, M.O.H.s, etc. in South Wales, the writing-up of the book, and the progress of Chamberlain's Derating Act, which at long last accomplished the "break-up"—though not the abolition—of the Poor Law. Much of the *Diary* here is field-worker's notes pure and simple; the jerky style, the many abbreviations—even, be it added, the more-than-usual illegibility of the written MS.—

give an impression of raw material which the author, had she lived, would probably have re-written in essay form. One might add that a later revision might possibly have softened some of the judgments; the Webbs were at the time still under the influence of the angry controversy over "Poplarism"—in which, it will be remembered, many of the leaders of the Labour Party were resentful of the way in which Lansbury had forced their hands; and they did not appear even to consider the possibility that the burden of unemployment and poverty (which, of course, became much more acute with the slump of the 'thirties) should be spread over the country as a whole. Hence, no doubt, the unusual acrimony of the sketch of George Lansbury on p. 183; even the completion of the book, and their satisfaction with Sidney's contributions to the Derating debates, did not persuade them that the social problem was solved—or that the Labour Party knew how to solve it.

The middle of 1929 sees another abrupt change, and from then until August 1931, the *Diaries*—with the important exception mentioned below—return to being a journal of the British political scene. After the General Election, and after some devious manoeuvring by MacDonald, Sidney was recalled to political life as Lord Passfield, Secretary of State for the Dominions and Colonies, and Beatrice willy-nilly resumed, in an expensive rented flat, the duties of a political hostess. I do not think, however, that I shall be alone in finding the "inner history" of the second Labour Government, notwithstanding the amusing vignettes of "high society" and the sketches of Dominion and other politicians, less intimate and less revealing than that of 1924.

For this there is more than one reason. First, Beatrice was five years older and by that much less inclined to endure cheerfully the wearisome details of political life; she yearned all the time for Passfield Corner, and admitted it. Secondly, the glamour which attended Labour's first trial of strength had departed, and the interval had not been long enough for new blood to make its appearance. The Ministers, for the most part—MacDonald, Snowden, Henderson, Thomas, Clynes—were the same as those who had gone down to defeat in 1924, and there was little reason to suppose that they would make a much more impressive showing than on the previous occasion. (Nor did they, even allowing for their exceedingly bad luck in economic events.) Disillusioned, as she had said, with the Party in 1924, Beatrice was not likely to be re-inspired in 1929.

The main reason, however, seems to have been the failure of Sidney as a Minister. At the Board of Trade he had done well; the curious congeries of duties which that assignment entailed suited him and, though not a good Parliamentary debater, his easy grasp of any brief commanded respect. The Colonial Secretaryship, however, was another matter altogether. Beatrice's *Diary* is very discreet; though she says that "Sidney shows me important dispatches"[1] she gives no hint of their contents or even of the major happenings within the Colonial Office. It is clear, however, that Sidney was as a Minister too much in the hands of his officials. On policy as a whole he was sound enough; his pronouncement on Paramountcy was a good if not a great State Paper; and in general his intention was to put into effect the main lines of Labour's colonial policy. But in a department like the Colonial Office, "main lines" are not enough; policy has to be implemented by thousands of small decisions in hundreds of different areas; and here Sidney's innate trust in the "expert" served him ill. "He would have made an excellent Civil Servant," says his wife (p. 230). So he would; so he did, in the short period before his marriage when he was a servant in the very department he was now called upon to control. But a Civil Servant is not the same as the Minister who has to reject or accept his advice, and it does not seem to have occurred to Sidney that the "expert"—whether departmental officer, colonial governor, or "on the spot" administrator—might be both perfectly competent and quite wrong. Hence he clashed at times with Labour men like Norman Leys in Kenya, who had hoped for a real change, involving the upset of many "competent administrators", in a Labour Colonial Office.

This gave cause for criticism and complaint; the outstanding failure was, however, in Palestine. It is true, of

---

[1] But she also writes "S. tells me little of what goes on in Cabinets."

course, that the Colonial Secretary had little freedom of action in Palestine, where policy was, then as thereafter, dictated mainly by Foreign Office and military considerations; nevertheless, Webb undoubtedly failed to grasp the situation which began with the riots at the Wailing Wall, and as a result, had to suffer the humiliation not only of having Dominion affairs removed from his hands (which may have been a domestic political necessity) but of seeing Palestine also taken out of them and put under a Committee of the Cabinet. A man less loyal to the committee system of government would probably have resigned under the latter rebuff, and some of his colleagues regretted that he did not; the only reference in the *Diaries* is the single remark that "people will say that your husband has not been a success as a Minister". That is a melancholy admission from anyone naturally so buoyant of temperament; it goes far to account for Beatrice's manifest lack of interest in the closing months of the Labour administration.

These closing months, however, are enlivened—if that be the word—by the day-to-day account of the last few weeks. Much has been written, by many hands, of the Great Betrayal of 1931; nor can it be said that the *Diaries* throw very much new light, other than the letter of MacDonald printed on p. 276, which in the light of later events seems to indicate that he was "exploring every avenue" in a sense unsuspected by his colleagues. What the *Diaries* do show, however, is the suddenness of the crisis. On August 4th appears the first sign that all is not well; a "jolly and cordial" meeting of the Cabinet is nevertheless perturbed by the report of the May Economy Committee set up by the Chancellor. By the 24th, less than three weeks later, all is over. MacDonald has kissed hands as Prime Minister of a National Government, the Gold Standard has been preserved from American attack in order to be abandoned within a month, and the Labour Party has proudly closed its ranks for all but a handful, only to meet, in October, the greatest electoral disaster in its history. No matter how often it is told, the story remains fantastic.

By October, however, and even before it, Beatrice had in effect ceased to care whether the British Labour Party lived or died. The last part of this volume can be best described in Browning's words

> "Look East, where whole new thousands are—
> In Vishnu-land what Avatar?"

It is fascinating to trace, through the later entries, the process of conversion—a process, it will be seen, which was practically complete before ever the Webbs set foot on Soviet soil. The speculations of those who, unlike G. D. H. Cole, had not been following their mental processes, as to what they would think of the U.S.S.R. when they got there, were quite beside the mark; the conversion took place well within the limits of this book.

When it opens, the Webbs are as anti-Soviet as any opponent could wish; they are indignant with the Trades Union Congress of the mid-'twenties for its pro-Russian sympathies, and scornful of the Russian contribution to the miners' funds in 1926. Beatrice writes (as so often in life she talked) of "creed-autocracies", equating the Soviets with Mussolini and deploring Shaw's championship of the latter. Thereafter there is for some time a gap in the references; she was either uninterested, or thinking of other things.

Early in 1930, however, when the troubles of the Palestine Report were at their height, she mentions meeting Sokolnikov (the Ambassador) and his wife at dinner, and obviously finds them interesting. By June she is reading about the U.S.S.R., books by W. H. Chamberlin and Maurice Hindus, is hearing from Sidney about Sir Esmond Ovey's dispatches from Moscow—which cause her to meditate on an historical comparison between Communism and Islam—and in early August the Sokolnikovs are week-end guests at Passfield Corner.

The insidious process has begun; later in the same month the *Diaries* record a defence of the U.S.S.R. against the visiting Snowdens, and without pin-pointing any passage, there are suggestions that the public morality of Soviet Russia is inclining to the kind of ideas which Beatrice would have liked to implant in the Half-Circle Club and the Labour Party. The first suggestion of a visit was apparently made in November; in January, 1931, Beatrice records that Mme. Sokolnikov sent her flowers on her birthday; a month later she doubts "the inevitability of gradualism"—i.e. inclines to accept the physical revolution which had made her so angry in 1917; and by July, a month before the crisis, she notes that "we are now on intimate terms" with the Soviet Embassy.

The ignominious end of the Labour Government—and possibly the enthusiasm of Bernard Shaw, who returned from Russia in August to lecture to the Fabian Summer School —hastened conversion. Under the date September 10th Beatrice writes: "Without doubt we are on the side of Russia"; by the end of the year the visit was fixed, and early in 1932 she was describing it as a "pilgrimage to Mecca"— adding that on further study the constitution of the U.S.S.R. appeared very much to resemble that which she and Sidney had advocated for Great Britain a dozen years before. Thereafter the Partnership was "immersed in Soviet litera-ture" to the date of departure for Russia, pausing only to set out (on 17th May) "our hypothetical conclusions" about the Soviet system. Some readers may be interested to com-pare this passage with the actual conclusions set out in the big book published in 1935.

There is, of course, much more in the *Diaries* than has been mentioned here. There is, in particular, a great deal of pungent portraiture of Beatrice's contemporaries in the political world—and here I must give special thanks to those living persons who permitted me to reproduce "can-did-camera" studies of themselves. Besides the Big Five of the Labour Cabinet and others already mentioned, many pictures stand out in the memory—of Haldane, Austen Chamberlain, Arthur Cook, Keynes, the Countess of War-wick, Ellen Wilkinson, Sankey; and sometimes even a single memorable phrase, such as Clynes in the 1924 Parliament "drooping like a snowdrop in an icy wind", of Susan Lawrence, "a woman chieftain", of MacDonald in 1926, "a magnificent substitute for a leader", and of Sidney, who "dislikes unnecessary communications" even with his wife! Long, long before, as recorded in *My Apprenticeship*,

Beatrice's diary revealed that she had considered, with Auberon Herbert, the possibility of writing a novel. This novel never eventuated; but these *Diaries* show that, so far as description of character goes, she would have been well qualified, if Sidney could have been induced to refrain from discouragement. (Description of *place* is another matter; it is curious that with all Beatrice's love of natural scenery, she seems so little capable of describing it. Even of her beloved Passfield, we learn little but that there were many song-birds. Their "travel diaries" proper were almost entirely written by Sidney and are, as might be expected, monu-mentally dull.) It must be realised, further, that the book is a *journal*, not a diary in the strict sense of the word. Written up at intervals varying according both to the state of her health and to what she was doing at the time—while on holiday, for example, she wrote practically nothing—it con-cerns itself with what interested her at any given moment; and, as Lord Beveridge complained in his introduction to the previous volume, "much goes unnoticed" of what others would have thought of first importance. It is not a history of the times, nor does it pretend to be; it is the immediate impression, unrevised and necessarily on occasion inaccurate in detail, made upon an individual powerful mind by the events and the personalities of her day; and it is, as she herself said, to some extent a safety-valve for her own emo-tional reactions. In anger or despair (or even in jubilation) she wrote herself out on paper rather than brood or trouble Sidney with "unnecessary communications"; but she would have been the first to protest against her diary being regarded as a work of historical research on a par with the Webb *corpus*.

Withal, there can be no doubt that it is a remarkable book and the book of a remarkable personality. What Beatrice in 1930 refers to as "the Webb myth" is a little less in evidence, and their joint reputation a little less high, than it was even a few years ago. This is partly the result of success. So much of the policy for home affairs which the Webbs worked out over fifty years is now accomplished fact—the Break-up of the Poor Law, the National Minimum of Civilised Life, Measurement and Publicity, a National Health Service—

*b**

these are no longer slogans, but commonplaces. Nationalised mines and railways, planning, State secondary education, the *New Statesman* and the London School of Economics—to take only a few examples of the causes to which the Webbs devoted themselves—are here to stay and are taken for granted. No one can possibly maintain that the London of to-day is not a far better place for the mass of its citizens than the London in which Sidney Webb wandered as a little boy—and that largely owing to Sidney's own exertions. But it is not Utopia, and those who have discovered this fact (which would hardly have caused the Webbs surprise) and who have also wearied of the long-drawn-out scarcities and drabness of the war and the post-war years, have in some measure joined in the nostalgic lamentations of the groups whose financial and social superiority has been threatened by modern conditions, in their outcry against approach to equalitarianism and their demand for colour, feasting and historic ritual—all things with which the Webbs were fundamentally out of sympathy. At the same time, the fact that their last great book committed them deeply—in common with a large number of their compatriots of the 'thirties—to whole-hearted support of the Soviet Union, even though this support was at the outset much less uncritical than was believed by many who had not taken the trouble actually to read *Soviet Communism*, discredited them in the eyes of those who were disillusioned by the cold war and the later phases of Stalinism.

These, however, are the fluctuations of reputation which are the lot of all who have figured greatly in their country's history; the unshakable fact remains that a large part of the conditions of living in the Britain of to-day is due directly to the life-work of the Partnership, that that life-work was carried out with a steadiness of application, an absence of rancour and recrimination, and an appreciation of the claims and interests of younger fellow-workers which is rare in any age, and that—by what some will find a paradox—of all allocations of "unearned income" few have paid in sum a higher social dividend than the thousand pounds a year which Richard Potter bequeathed to his eighth daughter.

MARGARET COLE

CONTENTS

CONTENTS

PLATES

Editorial Note

T H E principal difficulty offered by the present volume to its editor has been the sheer question of length. As Beatrice grew older and as her active life grew less, she wrote more and more in her diary; not only do the entries grow more frequent and more numerous, but their average length steadily increases. One single volume—not, it is true, in the period covered here—contains on a rough computation fifty thousand words. It was therefore impossible to contemplate publishing anything like the whole of the material, or even a selection on the scale of 1912–24; something much more drastic had to be attempted.

Some categories of omission are obvious. Passages which relate to persons now living or recently dead and which, whether correct or not, are too uninhibited to be publishable as yet—these occur more often, naturally, here than in earlier volumes: passages which deal with purely private or family concerns: passages which are concerned with her own state of health, which I am certain she would never have wished put upon record. I have also omitted most, though not quite all, of the many accounts of books which she had been reading, e.g. the memoirs of Colonel House, in the first place because these generally run to great length, and secondly because it is Beatrice as an observer, not a reviewer, whom I am concerned to show. I have also eliminated a very great deal of repetitiveness—there are, for example, half-a-dozen character-sketches of Haldane, not differing very greatly one from another, from which I have selected two only; and I have removed a few portions of narrative which seem to have been written from hearsay and which, according to my own knowledge or that of others, contain so many errors of fact that it would be misleading to print them. As Beatrice moved deeper into retirement, it followed as a matter of course that she got her information less at first-hand and more through others; and it is a matter of common experience among those who visited her at Passfield that she did not invariably listen to what was said to her, but gave accounts of her own which were received with polite absence of contradiction. Entries which begin "X was here for the week-end; he told me . . ." must therefore be received with caution; in some cases I have been able to check the facts, but in others I have had either to let the text stand with this warning, or if I felt serious doubt, to leave it out.

When all this was done, however, a problem of selection, within the limits imposed by a tolerable length, still remained; and here I must admit to arbitrary choice. I have retained what seemed to me of lasting interest, either historically or socially or for the development of Beatrice's character or frame of thought, and left out passages—including some reflections on general politics—whose interest seemed to me secondary. Certainly, if and when the full gigantic text is available, there will be critics to say, "Why was this left out? or that kept in?" This is inevitable; I would only add that, as on the previous occasion, I have printed the chosen extracts as they were written (with corrections of obvious minor errors), cutting out only sentences which would be libellous or painful reading: this is a volume of selections, not of snippets.

* * * * * *

It was fairly clear that the typescript prepared currently during Beatrice's lifetime had not been corrected, possibly not even read, by the author—both spelling and punctuation prove that. I have corrected obvious slips without drawing attention to them; but I have not attempted to make the punctuation logical, and have only altered it where to have left it alone would have made nonsense.

Beatrice's own few footnotes I have retained, marked with a * and signed B.W. The other footnotes are intended to provide the necessary explanation of the persons and incidents mentioned or referred to. I have not, however, in general repeated biographical information given in previous volumes.

M.I.C.

ACKNOWLEDGEMENTS

My thanks are due to Colonel Terence Maxwell and the Chamberlain Trustees for permission to quote the letter from Joseph Chamberlain in the Appendix.

Also to all who assisted with biographical and other information: my husband, Mr. S. K. Ratcliffe, Mr. Sydney Elliott of the *Daily Herald*, Mr. William Noble, Mr. J. S. Maywood, Librarian of *The Times*, Dr. Colston Williams and Mr. Roger Colston Williams, Mr. T. P. Holmes-Watkins of Pontypool, Mr. Richard John, Clerk to the Glamorgan County Council, Mr. Vernon Lawrence, Clerk to the Monmouthshire Archives Committee, and the Establishment Branches of the Ministry of Health and the Colonial Office.

Also to all those who gave permission for their own portraits to be included, and to Sylvia Mulvey for making a labour of love out of the typing.

HENDON, November 1955

PART I

1924

JANUARY 1924—DECEMBER 1924

January 8th.[1]—I had hoped to have the time and the brains to give some account of the birth of the Labour Cabinet. There was a pre-natal scene—the Embryo Cabinet—in J.R.M.'s room on Monday afternoon immediately after the defeat of the Government when the whole of the prospective Ministers were summoned to meet the future P.M. But the future P.M. did not arrive until half an hour after the time—so they all chatted and introduced themselves to each other. Lord Chelmsford, the one complete stranger, came up to Sidney and reminded him of the time when we stayed with them in Dorsetshire in the old L.C.C. days when S. was consorting with progressive L.C.C. Conservatives over the Education Bill of 1902–3. Whereupon S. introduced him to many of his future colleagues. Haldane meanwhile was beaming and telling anecdotes about the C.B.[2] and Asquith and other Cabinets: our old friend is literally revelling in his Heavy Father's part! He carried off Walsh, the ex-miner and present War Minister, to dine with him in order to instruct him how to behave with his Generals, also to see whether he could fit him out with a frock coat for the ceremony at B.P. next day: but Walsh's figure proved impracticable even for Haldane's ample coat. On Tuesday J.R.M. submitted to the King the twenty members of the Cabinet and there was a formal meeting at 10 Downing Street that afternoon of the Ministers designate. Haldane gave useful advice about procedure: Wheatley and Tom Shaw[3] orated somewhat, but for the most part the members were silent, and what remarks were made were businesslike. The consultation concerned the P.M.'s statement to Parliament. Committees were appointed, and a communiqué sent to the Press about the business done—which is an innovation and was not continued. Sidney was appointed chairman of the Committee to draw up a scheme for Unemployment and Housing.

On Wednesday the twenty Ministers designate, in their best suits (S. in the frock coat and tall hat he had brought from Japan and which had not been looked at since we returned in 1912—fortunately it fitted and was not moth-eaten) went to Buckingham Palace to be

---

[1] Date as in MS.—should probably read 19*th*.   [2] Campbell-Bannerman.
[3] Tom Shaw (1872–1938), textile Trade Unionist and M.P. for Preston. Minister of Labour, 1924; and Secretary for War, 1929–31.

sworn in; having been previously drilled by Hankey. Four of them came back to our weekly M.P.'s lunch to meet the Swedish Minister[1] —a great pal of ours. Uncle Arthur was bursting with childish joy over his H.O. seals in the red leather box which he handed round the company; Sidney was chuckling over a hitch in the solemn ceremony in which he had been right and Hankey wrong; they were all laughing over Wheatley—the revolutionary—going down on both knees and actually kissing the King's hand; and C. P. Trevelyan was remarking that the King seemed quite incapable of saying two words to his new Ministers: "he went through the ceremony like an automaton!"

Palmstierna and his wife—the only strangers among the Labour M.P.s—were expansively sympathetic and delighted at being asked to take part in this birth feast. Altogether we were a jolly party—all laughing at the joke of Labour in Office. On Thursday we had a more serious lunch—the P.M. to meet Thomas, the French head of the I.L.O. at Geneva, who had come to London straight from Poincaré (the other members of the party being Sanders, and [blank in M.S] of the I.L.O., and Margaret Bondfield, now Under-Secretary of the Ministry of Labour and the Government representative at Geneva). The dramatic event was the P.M.'s broad hint to Thomas—which made the Frenchman turn pale and gesticulate—"If the British Government was *not* to renew the French Treasury Bills the franc would go down to 250, would it not?" When he came up to the drawing-room Thomas was still muttering and gesticulating—a protest against any mention of such a horrible occurrence! According to Sanders, they went straight back to St. Aulaire,[2] the French Ambassador: "How can I get into touch with those Labour men?" asked plaintively the French aristocrat of his plebeian emissary.

The same evening there appeared to consult Sidney, Lunn (Overseas Department), Tom Shaw (Labour Ministry), Wheatley (M. of H.), and Short,[3] Under-Secretary for Scotland. The three latter stayed on till midnight—Wheatley and Shaw orating at each other, and Sidney and I intervening—trying to persuade each of them that their proposals were complementary, not mutually exclusive. The next morning C.P.T. appears: he impresses us with his terseness in expressing concrete proposals (largely derived from R. H. Tawney) and modest anxiety to learn. On Sunday evening comes our old acquaint-

---

[1] Baron Erik Kule Palmstierna (b. 1877). Entered the Swedish Coalition Government in 1917. Swedish Ambassador to Britain, 1920–37.

[2] August Felix, Comte de St. Aulaire (1866–1954). French diplomat; Ambassador to Britain, 1920–4.

[3] Alfred Short (1882–1938). Boilermaker, subsequently Trade Union Secretary and Labour M.P. for Wednesbury, 1918–31. He did not, however, hold any office in the 1924 Government, though he was Parliamentary Secretary to the Home Office in 1929. The Under-Secretary for Scotland in 1924 was James Stewart (1863–1943), hairdresser and M.P. for St. Rollox.

ance Sir Hubert Llewellyn Smith, who has fought shy of the Webbs all these thirty years only to find himself at the end of his career Sidney Webb's "Economic Adviser". I welcomed him so affectionately as my lost son that he unbent and became quite sentimentally reminiscent of our rambles together on The Argoed hill before my marriage. He is a remarkably able man who was marooned by Lloyd George. "You must rope him in," I said to Sidney, "he may like to return to the limelight as one of the big permanent officials who made the success of the Labour Movement and kept Lloyd George out in the cold. A grain of malice to an ounce of public spirit and constructive zeal is not a bad mixture—if you *must* have mixed motive!" So he becomes the economic adviser to Sidney's Committee on Unemployment.

Meanwhile I am living a distracted life which does not please me. I have taken over S.'s unofficial correspondence and dictated forty letters yesterday in twice as many minutes. What is far more troublesome is acting as the "Doyenne" among Ministers' wives, in the organisation of their social intercourse within the Party and with outsiders like the Court. Just at present there are two questions—clothes and curtseys. A sort of underground communication is going on between Grosvenor Road and Buckingham Palace which is at once comic and tiresome. However, it is one job like any other and has to be gone through. I hope to get the whole business fixed up in a few weeks; it is clear that until all these outstanding trivialities are settled once and for all, I shall not have a free fraction of energy over for anything else. The very most I can do is to dictate my letters and write up my diary from day to day. But oh! for the cottage and the book. And will my strength stand this irritating tangle of issues, each insignificant in itself but important as one among many which make up the Web of Destiny! My latest job has been to help Mrs. Clynes to get her establishment fixed up at 11 Downing Street. I have provided her with housekeeper, cook and butler; no, I forgot, the *very* latest task has been to soothe the feelings of Mrs. Snowden, deeply offended at being excluded from occupying the usual residence of the Chancellor of the Exchequer in favour of the wife of the Leader of the House. But the whole of the Labour world would have revolted at the bare idea of "Ethel" established in an official residence. She is a "climber" of the worst description, refusing to associate with the rank and file and plebeian elements in the Labour Party. Hence every "class-conscious" Labour man or woman listens for the echoes of Ethel—climbing, climbing, climbing, night and day! out of the Labour world into that of plutocrats and aristocrats. There is so little climbing in the Labour Party that one climber stands out in morbid prominence. The only other climbers are Thomas and his wife and daughters; but

3

Thomas drops his "h's" defiantly; and Mrs. Thomas is a retiring and discreet climber and has never pretended to be specifically Labour, and the daughters are so far removed from Labour circles that one of them when asked by a partner at a Half Circle Club[1] dance whether she was a "Fabian" retorted indignantly "No: I am a 'Thomas'"! . . .

February 8th.—Sidney is liking his work at the Board of Trade, finds his officials polished instruments, waiting on him hand and foot, seemingly acquiescent in any practicable policy. Fabians who are in the office report that after the first meeting of the General Council of the Board of Trade over which Sidney presided, and the subordinate Ministers—Gosling, Shinwell and Alexander—attended, the Permanent Heads remarked to each other that "these new men are very good"—"we have at last a business government"—"these men have trained minds"—"a long and complicated agenda has been disposed of in a single sitting".

Wheatley of the Ministry of Health startled and, on the whole, pleased his several Heads of Departments by requiring each of them to give him a lecture describing the work of his special department, which was taken down verbatim and afterwards carefully studied by the Minister and further questions asked. Of course these Labour men are new brooms and they have no "silly pleasures", and, on the whole, they are aware of their own ignorance and desperately anxious to "make good". Their almost naïve anxiety to learn, and complete lack of any "side", as official superiors, is pleasing to the Civil Servant, and I think the old bureaucracy is inclined to be well content with the new democracy. And after all is said and done, the great majority of the new Ministers have been themselves officials, Trade Union, Co-operative, and in some cases, like Sidney, Olivier and Snowden, actually Civil Servants, accustomed to public business—which has not been the case with the members of Liberal and Conservative Governments. The peculiar characteristic of this Government is, in fact, that every member, except perhaps Wheatley, has been a public servant and not a profiteer; and even Wheatley has spent most of his time and energy on municipal administration. Whether its policy is right or wrong, Labour will prove itself emphatically fit for *administration*—and that is what the Civil Service likes. It hates to be abused for slackness and inefficiency in carrying out a given policy (the direction of the policy is not its affair) because Ministers won't work at their jobs. I am inclined to think that before the Labour Government goes out there will be a great strengthening of the ties between the Parliamentary Party and the Civil Service world. The whole "social intercourse"

[1] The club founded by Mrs. Webb in order to groom Labour women and Labour men's wives for social life. See *Diaries*, 1912-24.

energy of the Labour Ministers and Labour Party generally will be devoted to increasing the solidarity within the Labour Movement and opening the door to all ranks of Civil Servants—not excluding the Heads—to enter in, the lower ranks formally and the Heads informally; and to co-operate in building up a new social order.

February 7th. [sic]—At the suggestion of the Half Circle Club E.C., Ishbel MacDonald summoned a meeting at 10 Downing Street of Ministers' wives, Cabinet and Under-Secretaries, to discuss whether or not there should be any organised effort to get acquainted with the wives of Labour members and to start a common-room for the Parliamentary Party and their womenkind near the H.C.C., pending the establishment of a permanent Labour Club. The stately formality of the Prime Minister's residence, with its messengers, menservants and private secretaries moving to and fro with an odd combination of secretiveness and solemnity, with its inhospitable hall where a dozen of us were kept waiting, and grand reception rooms through which we were ushered like a deputation, is not a homely surrounding! But 10 Downing Street, and respect for the Prime Minister's daughter, attracted some twenty of the wives, including Mrs. Snowden and Mrs. Patrick Hastings, who are seldom seen in the homes of the humbler members of the Labour Party! Ishbel is an attractive creature; charming to look at, in a pretty new frock, simple and direct in speech and manner; to-day she is a little puritan. How she will develop under the glare and glamour of official splendour and power remains to be seen. She herself is against anything that is "organised"; she announced her intention of being "at home" one day a week and asking the Labour Members' wives to visit her and have a "homely cup of tea" and suggested that other Ministers' wives might do likewise. Mrs. Snowden also thought that the matter could be left to individuals, and that "tea on the terrace" is what most women liked. The less important Ministers' wives were emphatically in favour of some common place for meeting; and urged that a determined effort to see Labour Members' wives should be made, *at times which suited these women*; and that they should not merely be sent cards for "at homes" at big houses. The only business done was to ask each woman present to let Miss MacDonald know what they and their husbands would be prepared to contribute towards a common-room for the Parliamentary Party, close to the House of Commons, with some adjacent room for the wives and other friends. . . . Throughout the proceeding, I myself was of two minds. I should like to keep clear of the whole business and get back to my book; but I do not want the Parliamentary Labour Party to become the plaything of London Society and the despised of the more serious element in the Labour Movement. It would mean ghastly disillusionment on the part of the active workers and the uprise of futile groups of exasperated revolutionaries. The personal conduct of the Labour Members and their wives will be just as important as the political policy of the Labour Cabinet, perhaps even more so, as political policy must be qualified by the fact that the Party is in a minority: personal conduct can be settled with a single eye to what is desirable from the standpoint of the future of society.

And this brings me to one of the most hotly disputed questions within the Labour Party, the question of the Ministers' salaries. Directly it became apparent that Labour was about to take office *Forward* opened hot fire on the "extravagant salaries paid to Ministers", and the I.L.P. Labour Members passed a resolution asking the Labour Cabinet to reduce all Ministers' salaries to £1,000 a year. To the simple-minded Labour man or woman the five thousand a year of the superior grade of Cabinet Ministers (not to mention the far larger remuneration of the legal officers) seems preposterous. He forgets that this £5,000 is reduced to £3,500 by income tax and supertax; that in the case of the occupants of the official houses this latter sum does not pay for necessary outgoings unless there is rigid economy and far less than the customary "entertaining". Ramsay MacDonald and Clynes will not make both ends meet on their £3,500, even if they stay in for the full year. What is even less considered is that in all professions what should equitably be measured is not occasional gains, mistaken for a continuous rate of pay over a long period, but the sum total during the whole career, and that a few years of office at what seems a large salary does not make up for long periods of underpayment as a Member of Parliament and for loss of connection in journalism, in business or in academic life, due to graduating on to the Treasury Bench. H. A. L. Fisher, for instance, finds himself penniless after a ministerial career of a few years without any likelihood of another spell of office; having lost his foothold in the academic career for which he had been trained. And who can grudge a windfall of fifteen hundred a year to a man like William Graham whose existence as a Labour M.P. for the last few years has been a disabling grind to make up £400 a year (or, more correctly, what remains of it after paying necessary expenses) to a bare livelihood for himself and his children?

There are of course other cases—men who are made immensely richer by the Minister's salary, far richer than *they* could have become by any career actually open to them, the Trade Union officials who are merely "seconded" from their T.U. offices and who do not as a matter of fact lose anything by this break in their daily avocation but, on the contrary, gain enormously in prestige and security—men like the stupider officials who get office because they are T.U. officials.

6

Assuming they do not entertain as Clynes *must* at 11 Downing Street or Thomas *will* as Colonial Secretary, and that they do not employ additional private secretaries paid by themselves, the extra thousands a year are saved, and if they keep in office for some years they become what they would never have otherwise hoped to be, small *rentiers* for the rest of their lives. Another class of persons who are unexpectedly benefited by official salaries are persons who already live on unearned income, Trevelyan, Buxton, and, to a lesser extent, ourselves, men who will not spend substantially more than they were doing as unpaid public servants. *We* may spend, owing to Sidney taking office, say £500 on extra entertaining and secretarial expenses—but unless we deliberately give it away, the remaining £3,000 is pure gain. (Do we not mean to pay for the new addition to the cottage out of this salary —if it lasts!) It is true that we have spent our lives in the public service without direct remuneration, but then we could hardly, as Socialists, have justified accepting the thousand a year unearned income if we had not done so. This same is true of Buxton and Trevelyan; they also could have afforded to do the work without any payment at all.

The truth is that this question of Ministers' salaries is complicated: because of the range and diversity in the circumstances of the recipients, alike in the way in which they have hitherto earned their income and in the character of the expenditure required of them as Ministers. What is as clear as noon-day is that: (1) if you regard the whole lifetime of the Parliamentary representative, or even of the prospective Minister, the vocation of politics is underpaid, not only relatively to the higher bourgeois professions like the law or business, but also relatively to other quite humble brainworking pursuits like minor Civil Servants and journalists and medical practitioners in poor districts. Secondly, that certain officials like the P.M., the Foreign Secretary and the occupant of 11 Downing Street (whoever he may be) are not only underpaid during their term of office but they are scarcely paid at all; all they get, even if they get that, is bare maintenance during their term of office, they cannot provide for sickness or unemployment, still less for old age. Nine out of ten of the occupants of 10 and 11 Downing Street have lost money and must lose money if they do the desirable amount of entertaining. Other recipients, who have to break away from well-paid work, may easily find themselves a good deal worse off after a term of office than they would otherwise have been—for instance, H. A. L. Fisher.

However, I doubt whether the amount of the Ministerial salaries will trouble us personally: no question of conscience will arise because I believe that we shall have a short run and I doubt whether the few weeks' or months' salary will cover the expenses of the coming election;

7

whether this time next year we may not be actually out of pocket by Sidney's career on the Treasury Bench, if you take into consideration the expense of being a Labour Member from the first days of his candidature in Seaham. There may be a few hundreds to the good; but I doubt it. Politics for the Labour man who is not a Trade Union official is a losing game from a pecuniary point of view.

February 11th. Passfield Corner.—Came down here with Sidney and Jessie for two quiet week-ends for him, and nine days for myself; Jessie took to her bed with influenza, so on Sunday I stumbled through household work, and this morning was up at six o'clock to get Sidney his coffee and a fire before he left by the 8 o'clock train. Now having secured an excellent neighbour to do my work, I am sitting alone by the fire writing in my diary after an afternoon nap and a cup of tea. Cold dank weather, but absolute quiet; just a far-off hint that birds sing in the coldest and wettest February! How I should enjoy retiring here and getting on with my book! How I look forward to the time when I shall be able to do so—when Sidney is once again out of office or when the routine of a Cabinet Minister's wife is sufficiently fixed to permit me to spend half the year here. Clothes, curtseys, parties, dances and dramatic circles, all the detail of cultivating social intercourse within the Labour Party, rebels versus Front Benchers, salaries and contributions out of salaries for collective purposes, are all absurd matters to trouble about when whole districts of Europe and some of the noblest individuals and promising races are dying of starvation and others are distorted with lust of power and greed of gain. How lacking in perspective seem most of my activities! But on looking back over a fairly intimate knowledge of the two great political parties who have hitherto ruled our national destiny—one remembers the careers of Joseph Chamberlain and Lloyd George, of Balfour and Asquith—not to mention the minor rôles of my brothers-in-law—the root of their inefficiency as rulers was more often than not due to their absorption in a too aristocratic and pleasure-loving social intercourse. . . .

Unless we can maintain within the Labour Party a far higher standard of manners—unless we can resist the scramble up the ladder —our terms of office and our wielding of power will leave the world no better than we found it. So I must go on taking my part in the social intercourse of the Labour Party until it has passed through the temptation of a Party in office, with the prospect of becoming a Party in power—I must do all that an old woman can do to keep its manners simple and unassuming and free from that ridiculous malady of social climbing. And the book must just wait, even if I risk being too old and tired to write it. . . .

February 15th. Passfield Corner.—Left Jessie with Miss Piercy, my new secretary, and ran up to London yesterday morning to attend the first of the Ministers' Thursday afternoon "at homes" to Labour M.P.s, friendly journalists and the leading officials of the Department concerned.

As we had started the idea of these weekly gatherings at Government offices, the first of them took place at the Board of Trade. About 40 of the M.P.s with half a dozen of their wives and some 30 other people turned up—there would have been more M.P.s if the critical debate on the P.M.'s Statement had not been going on. All in excellent spirits. There is certainly arising, whether it will last is not yet certain, an unusual comradeship between the Labour Ministers and the Civil Servants. "Every professional man likes his vocation to be appreciated by the layman," I suggested to the various officials I talked to, "and after all, the Socialists—at any rate the type represented by the present Government—idealise the salaried public servant: they look to him to save the world!" One or two of the Civil Servants looked doubtful—suspecting me of propaganda. But they are a polished set of men and they are making themselves extraordinarily agreeable to their present Parliamentary Chiefs. "The Foreign Office is far too pleased with MacDonald" complained Mr. George Young[1] to me (George Young left the Diplomatic Service during the war and has been refused reinstatement, mainly because of his Labour and somewhat cranky views), "they say they have got rid of a Cad in Curzon and found a gentleman in MacDonald". And of course that is the danger. J.R.M. is a born aristocrat and he will tend to surround himself with "well-bred men", in spite of their reactionary attitude towards affairs—another Balfour! but with the revolutionary tradition.

The excitement of the first week has been Asquith's pompous indictment of Wheatley's sweeping away of the derelict "Poplar Order"[2]—practically threatening the Government with dismissal if

[1] Sir George Young (1872-1952). Diplomat, afterwards author, journalist and professor. Three times Labour Parliamentary candidate.

[2] This action of Wheatley's in effect put an end to the "Poplar dispute", which had been running since 1921, when the Poplar Borough Council, headed by the mayor, George Lansbury, in protest against the inequality of the burden which unemployment placed upon the rich and the poor boroughs of London, refused to levy the precepts of the London County Council and the Metropolitan Asylums Board, and went to gaol for contempt of court. Their protest was effective; they were released, and an Equalisation Act passed as a result of which Poplar's rate fell by 6s. 6d. in the pound. In the following spring, however, Sir Alfred Mond, then Minister of Health, sent a Mr. Cooper, Clerk to the Bolton Board of Guardians, to investigate the expenditure of the Poplar Poor Law Authority. His one-man report accused the Poplar Guardians of extravagance and "coddling" of paupers, and the Minister then issued an Order commanding the Guardians to pay relief according to a scale drawn up by his officials. The Guardians took no notice; the District Auditor surcharged them without result; and after the fall of the Lloyd George coalition at the end of the year the

they do not reverse this somewhat hasty, though I think justified, proceeding. Considering the flagrant neglect by the Asquith Administration, extending to the whole period before the war, of the chaos of the Poor Law, it was a gross impertinence on the part of the Liberal Leader to attempt "to throw" the Government he had made, on this issue. Taken with Masterman's mean depreciation of the Labour Ministry in *The Nation* over the signature of M.P. (last spring he wanted to join the Labour Party!) it is an ugly opening of the striving of the Liberals to regain their lost position of an alternative government. Baldwin, on the other hand, comes out in opposition as an English gentleman. Indeed, his speech to the Conservative Party, though he reasserted his Conservative opinions, including protection as a cure for unemployment, was so genuinely admiring of the organisation of the Labour Party as the work of devoted enthusiasts day by day, that it looks as if Tom Jones had half convinced him that Socialism, as one of the dominant forces, has come to stay! In the lobby I ran up against Maxton[1] and Nichol and we began discussing this question of social intercourse. Maxton maintained that "the rebels of the Clyde" had better draw off the lightning so that we, the constructivists, might bring in socialism by administrative action and little uncontroversial bills. He defended their abstaining from all the social intercourse planned for the Party. "I am no good at this business." But it was clear that they lump together all social functions, whether of the great and wealthy belonging to the other political parties, or of Labour Party receptions given by the better-off members of the Party, like the Buxtons. They may come to the Ministers' "at homes" in the offices, but I very much doubt whether they will patronise the Downing Street gatherings. And so long as they are tolerant of the doings of other members of the Party there are some advantages in maintaining a "kernel" of socialist puritanism. What, of course, we need is a democratically managed club house—a meeting ground for *all* elements in the Party. Maxton expressed his suspicion of the Cabinet's attitude towards the Poplar principle of work or maintenance—"I except Wheatley and your husband," he said; "I am not saying this to please you but because I believe it," he added. It is curious how those Clyde men are reconsidering their attitude towards Sidney: his unpretentious ways and genuine concern to get things

---

Conservative Government left Poplar alone. Wheatley rescinded the Mond Order; it may be noted that, though the Poplar Council and the Poplar Guardians were strongly criticised at the time by the Webbs and the leaders of the Labour Party, twenty years later the rate equalisation provisions in effect extended "Poplarism" to the country as a whole.

[1] James Maxton (1885–1946). School teacher and pacifist. M.P. for Bridgeton, Glasgow. Chairman and pillar of the Independent Labour Party in its latter days.

done, impress them. Also I think Wheatley finds him to be a thoroughly "good comrade".

February 29th.—Went for the first time to House of Commons since Sidney took his seat on the Treasury Bench to listen to the debate on the Poplar order. The event of the sitting was Wheatley's brilliant speech in defence of his action, a new star in House of Commons dialectics, logical and humorous, with first-rate delivery. Whether his administrative action was wise or not, certainly he has scored as a Parliamentary artist, and he takes his place as a front-ranker in the game, a rival to Thomas for the leadership if J.R.M. breaks down. The Liberals showed up badly, willing to wound but afraid to strike; the Government scored a "subsidised victory": and all victories must be subsidised by one of the other Parties! The adjournment to-night on Henderson's electioneering speech about revision of Versailles Treaty—"an old speech from the last election but one, written by Tracey", remarked Jim Middleton, shows that the Government is going to be harried every day and all day, and I doubt whether it will survive this session. The situation may become intolerable unless the Liberals join in the Closure so as to permit necessary business to be done, which they will presently refuse to do. Meanwhile I live a harassed life, trying to start club premises for the Party and being up against suspicion, pennilessness, and apathy. Why I take so much trouble I do not know, except a desire to be helpful and to create a strong and united Party and prevent the futility of chaos, upon the brink of which we are always trembling, owing to the perpetual conflict between the stability due to mere stupid inertia and the movement due to the impulse to smash things up for the sheer delight in smashing. However, this episode in our lives will end presently like others have ended, in part success, part failure: a residue of success I think. And Sidney and I will retire to our cottage and the writing of books. What I fail to get in this distracted life is either time to think or opportunities for real intellectual comradeship. We see bevies of new Members every Wednesday and they seem to enjoy coming here, but there is no friendship, no continuous companionship with anyone of them. We and they are all too busy to do more than meet each other and pass a kindly good-day.

March 3rd.—Definitely refused to go to Buckingham Palace to an afternoon party which I imagine is to consist of Ministers' wives. The longer I watch the newspaper paragraphs about the Labour Ministers and their wives going to great houses to meet Royalties—the Londonderrys' for instance!—the greater seems to me the mistake that is being made from the standpoint of the morale of the Party. It is right that Ministers should pay their respect to the King as the Head of the Government, whether at formal levies or in private audience. But there is not the remotest reason why the *wives* and *daughters* should be dragged into smart society, with the inevitable "dressing up" and extravagant expenditure in returning hospitality. And once the wife has allowed herself to be presented and has made her curtsey she becomes part of the Court Circle and there is no way out of accepting invitations to meet Royalties at the houses of the Leaders of London Society. So I cut the knot by refusing—in the curiously ungracious formula, "Mrs. Sidney Webb is unavoidably prevented from obeying Their Majesties' command to, etc. etc.",—to take the first step into the charmed circle, and I shall not be troubled again! . . .

March 6th.—One of the kindest of our old friends is Arthur Acland[1]—now an old man and confined to his house but always anxious to be helpful. The other day I went for my periodical chat and told him the difficulty we had in raising the money for Club premises. The next morning came a note offering to put down the rent of a flat in St. Stephen's House for three years—£1,800 in all. So the last fortnight has been spent in getting the payment approved by the P.M., Henderson, Spoor and Lindsay[2] and the H.C.C., and in beginning to raise the necessary money for furnishing and for members. The subscriptions of existing members will not suffice. All went smoothly until I tried to persuade the newly formed Executive of the Parliamentary Labour Party, presided over by Smillie, to appoint representatives on the Management Committee! "A school of snobbery", sneered Smillie, emphasised by a denunciation from Johnston, Editor of *Forward*. The dour Scot objects to any social intercourse: we are to meet only at public meetings and committees and in the lobbies of the House of Commons. The private houses of the rich members of the Party are anathema, and any club to which these members and their wives belong is almost equally objectionable. It is all very pitiful, but it is the inevitable reaction of the Social Climbing of a minority of the members of the Party. But it is useless to be discouraged: we had just as many checkmates when we started the School of Economics, and yet it grew steadily until, thank the Lord of Destiny, it outgrew us. To be *outgrown* by the organisation you create is the ultimate test of victory.

[1] Sir Arthur Henry Dyke Acland, the Liberal politician, who, as Vice-President of the Privy Council Committee on Education, did so much to forward Sidney Webb's organisation of higher education in London. See *Our Partnership*.

[2] Hugh Scott Lindsay (b. 1879). Secretary of the Parliamentary Labour Party 1918-44.

March 15th.—The Parliamentary Labour Party is drifting badly in the House of Commons. Clynes is proving an incompetent and careless leader—curiously so. Is it the magnificence of 11 Downing Street that is overwhelming his energies? Ben Spoor, never a forceful personality, is weakened by recurrent malaria and has been absent most of the session; the dull-headed miners (the senior Fred Hall, a notorious old slacker[1]) who are subordinate to him, receive, but do not earn, over £1,000 a year as Household Officers. . . . The relations between the leading Ministers on the Treasury Bench either do not exist or are far from cordial. The P.M. is unapproachable by Henderson, who is responsible for the Labour Party organisation in the country; and apparently by Clynes, the Leader of the House. "No. 10 and No. 11 see no more of each other", said Henderson to me, "than if they slept and ate a hundred miles apart." Sidney was asked to go to tea with the P.M. the other day in his House of Commons room; but the call came, not from any desire to consult with him but merely a reluctant courtesy which Ponsonby told us was being extended to all members of the Party in twos and threes. This annoyed S. because he found the P.M. transacting business with a private secretary whilst other M.P.s were sent for to make up the party! "Half an hour which I ought to have spent at the Cabinet Committee on Unemployment", he complained. MacDonald asked him no questions and barely addressed him personally; but kept up an artificial conversation with the one or two present. Lord Thomson told me that he sees something of the P.M.—has stayed with him at Chequers—lunched with him at the U.S. Club—and that he gathers that his special associates are J. H. Thomas and Patrick Hastings, and that he consults Haldane. How long the I.L.P.-ers and Clyde men will stand the strain of this aloofness of one whom they have created Prime Minister, we wait to see. Oddly enough, even Henderson and Sidney are more loyal to their Chief than those who created him. "The best leader available; that's enough for me," says Sidney.

What interests me as a student of the British Constitution is the unlimited autocracy of the British P.M.—if he chooses to be autocratic or slips into it through inertia or dislike of discussion. It was MacDonald who alone determined who should be in his Cabinet; it is MacDonald who alone is determining what the Parliamentary Labour Party shall stand for in the country. So far as I gather from S. and other members of the Cabinet, they are not consulted about what shall be the attitude towards France: certainly no documents are circulated prior to despatch. So far as Henderson, Clynes and Sidney are concerned, the P.M. alone determines what line he takes toward

---

[1] Fred Hall (1855–1933). Yorkshire miner, elected M.P. for Normanton in 1906; Junior Labour Whip 1919. Treasurer, Yorkshire Miners' Association.

other countries. And it is clear that the P.M. is playing-up—without any kind of consultation with the majority of his colleagues or scruple or squeamishness about first pronouncements—towards the formation of a Centre Party—far less definitely Socialist in home affairs, far less distinctly pacifist in foreign affairs, say than Sidney would be if he were Prime Minister. MacDonald wants 8 million voters behind him and means to get them even if this entails shedding the I.L.P., the idealistically revolutionary section who pushed him into power. That ladder will be kicked down! MacDonald is in fact returning to his policy of 1910–14, as we always foresaw he would; but with a different facet. In those years he was willing to merge the Labour Party in the Liberal Party: to-day he realises that the Liberal Party is dead; so he is attracting, by his newly-won prestige and personal magnetism, the Conservative Collectivist element—but he insists that his collectivists shall dub themselves "Labour" and accept him as their Leader. I do not accuse him of treachery: for he was never a Socialist, either revolutionary like Lansbury or administrative like the Webbs; he was always a believer in individualist political democracy tempered in its expression by Utopian Socialism. Where he has lacked integrity is in *posing* as a Socialist, and occasionally using revolutionary jargon. If he succeeds in getting a majority of the electors into this revised version of reformist conservatism embodied in the Labour Party machine, things will move forward; the underlying assumptions will be changed by the rank and file workers, and the structure will necessarily adapt itself to the new outlook. It is another form of the famous policy of permeation, far more Machiavellian than that of the Webbs. But it will mean a new group rising up on the left to fight the Labour Party on the ground that it has denied the out-and-out Socialism the I.L.P. pretended to stand for. Already Smillie and Lansbury are at work disintegrating the Parliamentary Labour Party and undermining Mac-Donald's leadership with the Left. How that little knot of mild-mannered desperadoes—Arnot, Newbold[1] and Palme Dutt—must be chuckling at the disconsolate condition of the guileless I.L.P.! But it hurts my pride to see the Fabian policy of permeation "guyed" by MacDonald. Yet as a political performer he is showing himself a consummate artist. We had never realised that he had genius in this direction.

Meanwhile I gather that the P.M. is intending—or is it threatening?—a speedy general election. If Westminster looks promising, he may have the necessary defeat very soon—perhaps before Easter. This perhaps accounts for his carelessness of the way in which the

---

[1] J. T. Walton Newbold (1888–1943). Left-wing lecturer and historian. Elected as Communist M.P. for Motherwell, 1924; resigned from Communist Party in the same year.

Parliamentary Labour Party drifts on the rocks under the handling of Clynes and the Whips' Office. If he came back triumphant from the polls there would be some clearing out of all those not devotedly attached as well as those obviously incompetent, and if Sidney were cleared out as belonging to the first category I should not altogether regret it. For after all, *we are and have always been* Socialists and I doubt whether Sidney would take a salary to be anything else. One of the unpleasant features of this Government has been the willingness of convinced and even fanatical pacifists to go back on their words when once they are on the Treasury Bench as Under-Secretaries for the War Services. Hot-air propaganda in mean streets and industrial slums combined with chill moderation on the Treasury Bench and courtly phrases at Society functions may be the last word in political efficiency; but it is unsavoury, and leads, among the rank and file, to deep discouragement. Even Sidney is depressed. "So like Mac-Donald", says the always cheery and always cynical Galton.

March 17th. Parliamentary Labour Room.—Shall I pull off this new job that I have undertaken for the Labour Party? For some years there has been a grandiose project of a Labour Club nursed at Eccleston Square; and some hundreds a year have been spent in promoting it, with no success. The project was far too big—great club, both house and central offices, halls for meetings, and bedrooms—a project for which it would be necessary to raise a quarter of a million to provide the necessary premises sufficiently near Westminster. Meanwhile the Half Circle Club came along, and as it grew in membership there arose from time to time a demand for club premises to be used by the members and their menfolk. The rapid growth of the Parliamentary Labour Party and the absence of convenient rooms and cheap food in the House of Commons; the impracticability of wives and daughters being there in any comfortable way, led to a new call for a club house close to Westminster. We discovered a commodious ground-floor flat in St. Stephen's House; exactly opposite to the House of Commons. But it was £600 a year, a sum, for a membership of say 500, which put it out of bounds of a subscription of £1 1s. od. a year. By chance I mentioned it to my dear old friend Arthur Acland, with whom I have made a friend in his old age: he volunteered to pay the rent for three years. The offer was accepted by Ben Spoor and Henderson, and approved by the P.M.; Patrick Hastings and others said they would contribute handsomely to the furnishing. No sooner is the lease on the point of being signed and the project launched, than there begins a process of crabbing (crabs are just now to the front; the Parliamentary Labour Party side-tracking every possible suggestion), and promises of support are withdrawn. However, I think I shall pull off the scheme, and the financial liability is comparatively small. We have always taken risks in the service of the Cause and as yet we have never lost heart in the game we have played. Now, in my old age I have ceased to be nervous—there is not enough of one's life left to care to be cautious. But I have also ceased to be so keen to win. One has just got to go forward with the job—that is all. But I think it will be the last job I shall do for the Labour Party. Hence it is worth doing well. But I *shall* be glad when I can get quit of the whole business. It is unpleasant to be working in this atmosphere of hostility and suspicion, first from one group, then from another. How far pleasanter is the life of the student and the writer: no friction, no responsibility, just clear-cut work on our own, without any need to consider the vanities and ambitions of other human beings. What I should prefer is to get the necessary sum for furnishing and upkeep; and then clear out of the whole business and leave it to the younger persons to manage.

March 19*th*.—The flat first selected was disapproved of by a new committee and Henderson, and two commodious ones a little further off proposed to be taken. An agonising afternoon about the difficulty of getting out of the unsigned agreement with St. Stephen's House—my brain in a state of whirling exhaustion from morbid anxiety that we had given premature instructions! which shows me how unfit I am for this sort of job. This morning we seem to be in smooth water. If the Club gets into these premises which have practically been settled on by Henderson and the younger women, I can shunt the whole business on to the new committee, giving a handsome donation towards the expense of upkeep—£200 down and another £300 if we remain in office for the whole year. If all goes well, as it now seems likely to go, I shall be able to return to the Book directly I have recovered my nervous strength from this friction and responsibility to all sorts of separate persons and organisations—which will be delightful.

March 24*th*.—A really useful and happy week-end with Lion Phillimore who left me to select and invite the party—the result being that the Alexanders, Greenwoods, Col. Williams[1] and ourselves went down to Kendals on Saturday; Patrick Hastings and his wife motored down for lunch and tea on Sunday, the Bernard Shaws came over in the afternoon, and the Oswald Mosleys motored down to lunch and stayed the night on Sunday, taking Sidney and me up with them early Monday morning. . . .
The Georgian house, with its large and well-proportioned rooms and family portraits, situated in an old-world park garden, with the

[1] Thomas Samuel Beauchamp Williams (1877–1927), Colonel in the Indian Medical Service. Labour M.P. for Kennington.

brilliant Irishwoman as hostess, gave an admirable setting to these "select" of the Labour and Socialist Movement, and there was charm as well as interest in this gathering. The conversation was exclusively political—I doubt whether during these 40 hours there was a single allusion to women, wine, horses, sport, scandal or money-making: I admit that literary and scientific lore was, if not absent, at any rate, rare. Undiluted public affairs, and the philosophy upon which these are based, was the order of the day. It is significant that we hardly mentioned the P.M.—except to deplore his aloofness from the other leaders. MacDonald is accepted by us all but he is not *liked* by any member of the inner circle of the Labour Movement: he is far more popular with the imported persons—Chelmsford, Haldane, Thomson, and the non-political Lord Advocate.[1]

Meanwhile two series of events trouble the political world. The Westminster by-election[2] has killed the Liberal Party—Winston's defeat by a few votes is important to no one but himself. But his splitting of the Tory and Liberal vote, together with the Liberal's derisive poll, and Fenner Brockway's 6,000 for Socialism brings a new party into politics—the Liberal Unionists—and destroys all chance of a revival of Liberalism as the alternative creed to Conservatism. All this is favourable to the Labour Party. On the other hand, there is the outbreak of the London bus and tram strike following close on the transport and railway strikes—which may easily lead to a battle royal between the Labour Government and the sympathetic strikers if the Tubes come out. The Cabinet has decided that it cannot allow the paralysis of the Metropolitan services, and we may find ourselves on Saturday running trains on the Underground and electric power stations by blackleg labour. Whether or not the presence of a Labour Government has encouraged the outbreak of this industrial terrorism no one knows—our enemies say it has. But while putting down the terrorism of the men, the Parliamentary Labour Party will have to put down the autonomy of the employers, and they may introduce emergency legislation, and be refused it by Parliament—a defeat which the Government could not ignore and which would be followed by a general election—either immediate or directly business was wound up.

March 31st. Easton Lodge.—Sidney and I came down here late on Friday night completely exhausted; the last days of Emergency Cabinets with the routine Departmental and Parliamentary work, on the top of a mild attack of influenza, had strained Sidney's usual health

---

[1] Hugh Pattison, Lord Macmillan of Aberfeldy (1873–1952). Lawyer and chairman of many Government Committees.

[2] This by-election was fought on 19th March. The result was:
O. W. Nicholson (Unionist), 8187; W. S. Churchill (Independent), 8144; A. Fenner Brockway (Labour), 6156; J. S. Duckers (Liberal), 291.

and good spirits. The last day—the most strenuous of the week—was retrieved by a marked success in his speech winding up the debate on the Transport Bill, and resulting in a victory for the Government on both counts—the second reading and the reference of the Bill, not to a Committee of the whole House, as Baldwin had suggested, but to the Standing Committee. I, also, had had a succession of committees to attend to, and innumerable letters to dictate. We ended the working day with a most successful reception at the Board of Trade of 200 of the staff and some of their wives—a new departure. All the Heads of Departments turned up and representatives of all the various grades and sports associations, right down to girl typists. "We have never yet seen a President of the Board of Trade—leave alone his wife," said one delighted guest to the Head of his Department. I insisted on treating them all as "my husband's colleagues", and they seemed to thoroughly enjoy themselves. The Heads and the members of the Advisory Committee of the Board of Trade declared that the new departure was thoroughly justified. Sidney is certainly most popular in his Department. The Labour Ministers are liked by the Civil Service: hardworking and unpretentious in manner, they bring with them an atmosphere of comradeship in public service.

This morning Sidney returned to his work and I remain here with the Countess and a distinguished German professor—Kantorowicz of Freiburg[1]—who is our guest. With a private sitting-room in a palatial residence and lovely scenery, I am in a most restful environment. And now back to a spell of work on the Book after these distracting months of odd jobs for the Labour Party.

April 3rd.—Sidney reports Henderson as saying "that the epidemic of labour revolts reminds him [from police information] of what was happening in Russia in 1917 against the Kerensky Government". Those little bands of wrecking Communists are undoubtedly at work. The unthinking "leftism" of some of the minor Trade Union leaders makes them tools of these mostly middle-class mischief-makers. Also unfortunately MacDonald's present pose as an aristocratic charmer and courtly society man exasperates many of his honest and fervent disciples. "MacDonald is no Labour man, he is one of us," said Milly Duchess of Sutherland to her sister Lady Warwick; "he is the illegitimate son of the old Duke of Argyll," she added. "No," said another *grande dame*, "he is the son of the Duke of Richmond." According to the Countess, all the other Labour men and their wives who accept invitations to great houses are flattered to their faces but sneered at when they have left the room. There are certainly unpleasant resemblances between Kerensky and MacDonald; the same charm and elo-

[1] Hermann Kantorowicz (b. 1877). Eminent German jurist.

quence, the same combination of Utopian visions and negative policy for to-day. The saving fact is that the *circumstances* are quite different. If the Labour Party fails to keep order and allows wrecking tactics, there will be a rapid reaction into progressive conservatism and the sterner enforcement of the law against the revolting trade unionists. That is the situation for which Winston is preparing; and if the Communists succeeded in making the task of the Labour Government impossible he might get his chance of figuring as a constitutional and modified Mussolini. But already there are signs that the rank and file are getting tired of the game.

April 7th. Easton Lodge.—Ran up to London for one night to attend Management Committee of Parliamentary Labour Club and the Phillimore dinner and Clynes's reception. Found Sidney and Henderson much perturbed at Rent Restriction Bill fiasco.[1] Another example of Wheatley getting the Government into a deep hole, climbing out of it himself in a brilliantly successful speech, leaving the Government still deeper down in the hole which he had made! The trouble came from a clause which the Clyde men had insisted should be put in the Bill—viz., that no unemployed man who failed to pay his rent should be distrained or evicted by his landlord *unless the hardship* to the landlord was greater than to the unemployed man! How this clause passed the Home Office Committee (with Haldane as Chairman—S. is not on it) of the Cabinet—leave alone the Cabinet itself—passes my comprehension. It is clearly an administrative folly of the worst type, and would, if enacted, not only be abominably unfair to particular landlords but would lead to future discrimination against all persons likely to become unemployed (a point which, by the way, was not made in the debate). Attacked by Liberals and Conservatives, Clynes, as Leader of the House, floundered badly—first putting the onus of compensating the landlord on the Poor Law, and then undertaking that the State should recoup the local authorities. "Fifteen hundred a week to-day in Poplar: if the Treasury recoups, it will be £3,000 in a month's time," whispered Susan Lawrence to Jimmy Thomas. "Can't stand this sort of leadership—I am fed up with it," said Jimmy to Susan. The next morning all the newspapers were sneering at poor mild-mannered Clynes for his fumbling. Meanwhile the P.M. was (it was said) *deliberately* absent alike on Wednesday, Thursday and Friday. His secretary told S. that he

[1] The Labour Government made considerable efforts, with only partial success, to deal with the problem of rents. Besides the Bill mentioned in the text, a general amending Bill had to be abandoned at the Committee stage owing to obstruction, and only one very small Bill got through. Wheatley's Housing Act, however, which gave local authorities power and assistance to build houses for letting at controlled rents, did a good deal to help the situation.

thought the P.M. would not be sorry to be thrown out on this issue in order to let the Clyde men see the result of their folly. Is he beginning to be jealous of Wheatley's amazing *réclame* in the Press as the greatest Parliamentarian on the Treasury Bench? It would be unlike J.R.M., if he were not getting tired of the Clyde men and jealous of their brilliant protagonist in the Cabinet. Wheatley, vehemently asserting, in a week-end speech at Glasgow, his loyalty to J.R.M., looks like a belated attempt to appease his Chief. But MacDonald remains "the mystery man" to all his colleagues—who know little or nothing of his thinkings or doings. Certainly neither Henderson, Clynes, Sidney nor any other member of his Cabinet (possibly Thomas) are in his confidence either with regard to Foreign Affairs or Parliamentary or electoral tactics—one and all might just as well be Under-Secretaries!

Lion Phillimore's dinner at the Carlton restaurant to members of the Government attending the Clynes's reception was not a tactful undertaking though it was extremely pleasant, and from her point of view quite successful. The Clynes's reception at 11 Downing Street to the Half Circle Club and the Parliamentary Labour Party would have been most useful and agreeable—a homely gathering of friends— if it had not been for poor Clynes's dismal face—he had failed, and was obviously acutely aware of his failure. He is getting no help from the P.M., and the latter was conspicuous by his absence, so was his daughter. Altogether, personal relations within the Cabinet are not happy. Cabinet meetings are quite harmonious—but at these meetings only routine daily business is transacted—very few big questions of policy are discussed. The P.M. carries on his foreign policy without discussion. Meanwhile each of his Ministers goes his own way in his own Department without consulting his Chief. I could not have imagined a body which has less *corporate* responsibility than Mac-Donald's Cabinet. Are all Cabinets congeries of little autocrats with a super-autocrat presiding over them?

We came down here (Easton Lodge) for a fortnight, partly because I wanted some days' quiet in the country but mainly in order to observe this establishment so as to be able to give counsel about it, if I am asked. The Labour Party, under the influence of Henderson, has come to an arrangement with Lady Warwick[1] for a year. The Party is to pay £300—the rates on Easton Lodge and a little more—and, in return, they are to have the "full and free" use of the house and grounds

---

[1] Frances Maynard, Countess of Warwick (1861–1938). Friend of Edward VII, Joseph Arch, George Lansbury, H. G. Wells, etc. In her youth a brilliant Society beauty of the Lily Langtry era, she protested against a vehement attack on one of her balls which appeared in Robert Blatchford's *Clarion*, met the editor and was immediately converted to whole-hearted Socialism, and for the rest of her life devoted a great deal of time and energy to Socialist and philanthropic enterprises. Easton Lodge continued to be used for many years for Labour conferences, week-ends, and summer schools; it has since been pulled down.

with a low tariff for food—£2 2s. od. for a week—£1 1s. od. from
Friday to Monday week-end. The Countess continues to live here in
her own apartments; a picturesque, floridly ornamented and lavishly
equipped great barn adjoining the main structure of the house; and
when she is in residence, she acts as hostess. After ten days' observation I *doubt* the feasibility or desirability of the arrangement. The
house is far too gorgeous in its grandiose reception rooms and large
extravagantly furnished bedrooms. Owing to the devastation (by
fire) of 28 bedrooms during the War, there is an absurd disproportion
between the *number* of the bedrooms (there can only be 30 guests and
this entails a proportion of married couples occupying one room) and
the plenitude and magnificence of the reception rooms. Then there is
a grave disadvantage in having the Countess on the premises. She
remains virtually in command of all the arrangements and has always to
be considered and deferred to. I *like* the woman. She is human and
handsome, vital and genuinely good-hearted. In spite of an abominable
upbringing, she has lived *out* of her somewhat dissolute past, into a
dignified, open-minded, and public-spirited old woman. And her
Socialist faith, uninformed and emotional, has proved to be deep-
rooted and persistent. But at times she is a wayward child—in her
autocratic decisions—to which she gives immediate expression in words
and acts without consideration for other people's standards of personal
freedom and comfort. Every now and then a guest has the uncomfortable feeling that he or she is being watched and criticised; and that
any little divergences from the hostess's particular view of conduct or
talk are objected to. The Labour Party is *supposed* to be in "full and
free" possession; but each individual is frequently made to feel that he
or she is here "on sufferance"—which, in spite of the comfort, even
luxury, of the house, garden and grounds, makes the more sensitive or
individual guest ill at ease. I have even been tacitly reproved for
opening my "north window"!

Above all, there is exactly the same objection to this place as there
was to Lion Phillimore's luxurious dinner in a private room at the
Carlton Hotel: all this magnificence is altogether out of keeping with
the peculiar position of the Labour Party; a party which is apt, and,
in a sense, compelled to promise much and perform little. "The
inevitability of gradualness" in abolishing poverty should not be combined with living in luxury or the *appearance* of luxury. The experiment must go on for this year, but I am tempted to hope that it will
fail financially by the overhead charges being altogether unwarranted by
the use of it, and be terminated without soreness on either side before
Xmas 1924. If the Countess does not part with the place, the grounds
might continue to be used for galas and picnics. . . .

April 9th. Easton Lodge.—Sister Kate[1] has been here for three days and I was interested to see that the effect the place made on her was almost identical with that made on me and of greater value because she was wholly disinterested. She said in effect: "The Labour Party could not very well have refused to try the experiment because after all it is what you al' say ought to be done with these places. Lady Warwick was right to offer it—her proposal is the only way she can do what she thinks, or ought to think as a Socialist, about the collective use of such charm and comfort. All the same, this strange combination of an almost degenerate luxury in furniture and equipment—this appearance of lavish expenditure on senseless abundance in the machinery of life, is out of keeping with the Labour Party and must be either repugnant or demoralising to the simpler and more unsophisticated members!" Strangely enough, she and the Countess are far more sympathetic than the Countess and I—a common sentimentality binding them together. I am, of course, disqualified for the ordinary communal life by my need for privacy as an intellectual worker. For me, a private sitting-room is not a luxury but a necessity, without it I cannot carry on my special work; and I cannot afford the time for a visit to the country without a daily task. During these few days I have got through some work on the book: and getting through work was a condition of coming. But that purely personal and exceptional requirement may not come within the scheme of management of this establishment. "I think you are quite right *not* to go on with the plan of having a private sitting-room for particular guests," I said to the Countess this morning. And all was peace between us! In her innermost heart she resented my withdrawal during the greater part of the day from the rest of the company; though her hospitable nature compelled her to beg me to come again and occupy the flat and enjoy the privacy in my own way. "*Your* flat, Mrs. Webb," she said, with a slightly ironical stress on the *your*.

April 12th. Grosvenor Road.—The Clynes lunched with us on Sunday alone, in depressed spirits. The "bad press" that Clynes has had over the Rent Restriction Act fiasco and his management of it, was rendered all the more painful by the consciousness that Mac-Donald had deserted him and J. H. Thomas had virtually "engineered" the disparagement of his leadership with the P.M., the back-benchers, and the capitalist press. It appears that Clynes had received in writing strict orders from Mac. as to his line of retreat from the objectionable clause, orders which did not meet the House of Commons situation but which he did not like to disobey. He had not been informed about

---

[1] Kate Courtney (1847–1929). Widow of Leonard Courtney, and the second of the Potter sisters.

the Bill; the Law Officers had not seen it; and all concerned with its production disavow special responsibility for the silly notion of making the landlord forfeit the rent of such unemployed persons who chose not to pay it. But Clynes was left to bear the whole brunt of the muddle. Evidently the P.M. neither consults nor encourages him—sends his orders in writing or by his secretary and never sees him. . . .

Clynes, of course, under these disheartening circumstances, is not making an efficient Leader of the House. He himself is over-reticent and retiring, and lacks physical vitality and mental alertness. He is always gentle and kindly, his English is excellent, and his voice penetrating and musical. In a closely knit team in friendly consultation he *might* be equal to the task of leadership. But with a Chief who dislikes him and a colleague like J. H. Thomas who is always trying to trip him up in order to take his place, he droops, like a snowdrop in an icy wind, beneath the rank grass of the Labour benches. The Labour Government had better go out this summer. Three or four years' government by a Conservative Party reinforced by Churchill's liberalism would give the Labour Party time to organise itself under the leadership of the new generation of Labour M.P.s—the Frank Wise[1]-Wheatley-Greenwood-Shinwell-Alexander-Mosley generation —free alike from the cold timidities of the old Trade Unionist and hot-air conditions of the I.L.P. leaders. There would be only one advantage in Labour remaining in, and that would be the more complete disillusionment of the left wing about the sincerity of J.R.M.'s Socialism and proletarian sympathies. MacDonald has been useful to placate the ordinary man; I doubt his usefulness in the future. But the younger men will have a tussle to remove him—he will drop the I.L.P. and rely on the ordinary citizen who seeks an alternative to a Conservative Government, just a shade more hardworking, public-spirited and progressive, and professing a more philanthropic and democratic creed than the old Liberal Party. And Sidney and I will watch with a smile this policy of inverted permeation, the permeation of the Socialist party by the philosophy of the philistine citizen, instead of the permeation of the philistine citizen by the Socialist creed. . . .

Easter Week. 32 Maureen Terrance, Seaham.—Five days here with Susan Lawrence: she and S. speaking twice a day, and I only twice during the time. I came here, weak from influenza, on the top of the distracted and noisy existence of London. I simply long to get out of it all, to lead again the life of "learned leisure"—resting and

---

[1] Edward Frank Wise (1885–1933). Civil Servant who in 1923 became economic adviser to the All-Russian Central Union of Co-operative Societies, M.P. for East Leicester, 1929–31. A strong Socialist, one of the founders of the short-lived Socialist League in 1932. Wise, had he lived, would have certainly played a considerable part in politics.

writing according to my strength. I watch Susan with her wonderful
health (she is only 52 I remember) reading, writing and speaking, and
I admire.

Susan Lawrence is a remarkable woman. More than "well-to-do",
with a forceful intelligence, presence and voice, more forceful than
attractive, she is one of the best of souls. Brought up a Conservative
and a churchwoman, she championed these creeds with capacity and
courage for twelve years, first on the dying School Board, and then on
the County Council. "Trying to carry social reforms by a moderate
party is like running temperance reform by a company of licensed
victuallers," said she. Susan and Sidney have always liked and respected
each other. For so able a woman she is strangely emotional about
persons and causes; but the way she expresses her love, pity or indignation is oddly irritating. She has read enormously, and gets up a case
exactly like a lawyer, but her remarks are not original, and she lacks
intellectual perspective. Above all, she is free from all the pettiness
of personal vanity or jealousy. Is she lovable? I have never heard of
anyone being in love with her—I am inclined to think this lack of the
quality of lovableness accounts for a certain restlessness and reckless-
ness, a certain dare-devil attitude towards life—as if she cared not
whether she lived or died. She is an enraged secularist and would be a
revolutionary Socialist if she had not a too carefully trained intellect
to ignore facts, and far too courageous and honest a character to hide or
disguise her knowledge. As a speaker she interests women more than
men; her very masculinity and clearness of mind attracts women.
Clever men appreciate her serviceable talent and lack of egotism, but
she tires of them. What I most envy is her capacity to digest any kind
of food at any time of day, and to sleep for ten hours whenever she
needs it, not to mention smoking all day long and strenuous exercise
when she has a mind to it. Of her John Morley would certainly have
said, as he did of me: "Charming, no: able but not charming." All the
same, she is heroic: as a woman chieftain she would have led her people
into battle and died fighting.

Susan took away a melancholy impression of the state of mind and
the state of things in Seaham, the lack of civilisation in homes, streets
and surroundings. "A town on a beautiful coast," she said in effect,
"and all defiled with soot in the air, old boots, dirty paper and broken
tins on the ground; romantic ravines looking like newly-made railway
cuttings, no music, no public library, no hospital; the large unkempt
picture palace in a back street, and suspicious smells pervading back
courts and closed-up corners—railway lines and coal trucks everywhere. The only civilised buildings are the schools—Hail to the
Education Act—the Saviour of the industrial districts."

On Easter Monday we three went in state to the annual performance of the Seaham Operatic Society—the one and only attempt made by the citizens of Seaham to entertain or instruct themselves and each other—a performance repeated every night for a week and representing a very considerable effort and expenditure. *Dorothy* is a vulgar and futile comic opera, lacking all merit, artistic or intellectual, making out that human nature is many degrees lower in character and intelligence than "the man in the street" or the ordinary woman in the home. Most depressing of all are those little groups of spindle-legged and pale-faced boys with vacant expression, loitering round public-houses and at street corners at all times, day and night. No wonder that the miners do not throw up leaders capable of leading, and that their association is a monument, not to organising capacity but to the herd spirit. All the same, the very dreariness of these pit villages, the absence of any vitalising ferments, makes our task as representatives easier to fulfil and richer in result than it would be in a more civilised constituency.

Throughout the Easter recess MacDonald has continued his remarkably successful "word-spinning" (to use Lansbury's term of abuse). His speeches in Wales are exactly suited to his present pose as a political charmer of no particular party and as a capable citizen anxious to carry on the business of the country with the consent of all parties—with special compliments, by the way, to the Conservative Party and their leader. His constant insistence that there is no need for an election, that no one wants it, and that the Labour Government is quite prepared to carry on for two or three years, puzzles us. We are so completely outside his confidence that we do not know whether these sayings are said in order to get a longer term or merely in order to throw on to other parties the odium of all the insecurity and upset of the general election which he believes is imminent. We are inclined to think that he consciously and subconsciously desires continuance in office—from what his friends say, he is enjoying himself vastly, whether he is week-ending at Windsor Castle or receiving the homages, always paid to attractive persons in great positions, by the bulk of the inhabitants of Great Britain. It is amazing the guileless, the stupid *worship of Power* by the British people of all classes and all parties. Look at the relative position of Lloyd George and MacDonald to-day to what it was in 1918! It is a woeful ordeal to those subjected to it; equally demoralising and disconcerting, whether it be the Up or the Down.

May 2nd.—"Snowden has had a great triumph," Sidney reported to me on the Budget night. The Budget itself is extremely skilful, and the explanation of it was Snowden's masterpiece. Altogether, the Dark Horse has turned out a winner. We were wrong about Snowden.

25

In so far as a minority government is concerned, compelled to follow Liberal free trade lines, he has turned out to be the best available Chancellor. Thomas, too, is scoring success after success as a political "performer"; he is disliked and distrusted as a "bad colleague", but his cleverness as "an old Parliamentary hand" and as an after-dinner speaker is incontestable. C. P. Trevelyan is wonderfully well "self-advertised" as a go-ahead administrator—and he *is* quite fond of his job—far more determined and industrious than any of his recent predecessors. Clynes remains under eclipse and will not again be Leader of the House after this spell is finished. There are a number of able younger men eager to win their spurs as Under-Secretaries, and to become members of the Cabinet, whilst another group of clever men—Wise, Dalton, etc.—await their destiny on the threshold of Parliament. Of course the unsavoury element in Parliamentary life is the intense competition for the limelight, alike among Cabinet Ministers and private members: "the stock" of individual members going up and down with dramatic, undeserved and incalculable suddenness. The itch for recognition becomes, in fact, rather a horrid symptom, manifested in all sorts of ways, by different persons—conscious and unconscious. Sidney is free from it to a quite unusual degree; he is too proud and too modest to resist or even resent being thrust into the background whenever it suits MacDonald or Thomas, or even an Under-Secretary. This instinctive dislike of any form of competition for place or power, this preference for working in the background of a movement and doing any job that needs to be done, irrespective of prestige, would, I think, have always disqualified him for any notable success in parliamentary life, even if he had taken to it earlier in his career. I am glad that he has had a spell of Parliament, capped by becoming a Cabinet Minister, but I am not certain that I want that spell to last too long. Perhaps I am biassed by my own dislike for the daily life of a Cabinet Minister's wife; but it seems to me that after this spell of office is over, his special gifts will be wasted in Parliament —he will be doing work which other men can do equally well and many men yearn to do; instead of doing work which few men want to do and which no man *can* do with anything like the same real success. However, *he* must decide, not I.

May 17th.—Four months of continuous and distracting toil in London since S. took office (with only one interval of five days, and that at Seaham) ends today with the opening of the Parliamentary Labour Club by the P.M. with a surging crowd of Half Circle Club and Parliamentary Labour Party in and out of the premises. The Club owes its existence to my initiative and Arthur Acland's generosity. But to Mrs. Noel Buxton belongs the credit of finding fit premises and furnishing them with distinction and charm. These delightfully quiet rooms, within five minutes' walk of the House of Commons, are certainly a testimony to the worthwhileness of the H.C.C.: what we have got to do within the next three years is to collect a permanent endowment fund of some thirty thousand pounds. The venture is not nearly so wild as seemed to be the London School of Economics when we started in 1895 to build up the organisation on a few hundred pounds[1]—there is far more wealth and far more talent, not to mention the prestige of a great political party with its leaders in office, from which to draw the money and brains to create a live centre of social life for the Labour Party, than was afforded by our poor little group of Fabian intellectuals out of which arose the London School of Economics: the biggest, most vital centre in the world of research and instruction in the science of sociology. As a set-off to this success, I am left deadly tired with an ever-increasing longing for the peace and quiet of an author's life in a lovely countryside, alone with my thoughts and absorbed in the effort of expressing these thoughts—past and present—in an attractive literary form. I sometimes dream of making my tale sufficiently attractive to provide part of the endowment of the future Club! . . .

During these last days of London life I have had two miners' wives from the Seaham Division staying with me for the Women's Conference (1,000 delegates from all parts of Great Britain). What interested me was the moral refinement and perfect manners of these two women who had never seen London before and never stayed in a house with servants. One of them was a delicate, excitable and intellectual woman—a bundle of nerves—the other a phlegmatic Scot—they were attractively clothed and their talk was mostly about public affairs—the one emotionally stirred by the Socialist faith and familiar with all its shibboleths; the other shrewd, cautious and matter-of-fact in her political expectations. They were completely at their ease, and their attitude to their host and hostess was more that towards a class teacher and a minister of religion than to social superiors. I don't think they had any trace of feeling that they belonged to a different class though they realised that we had greater knowledge and a wider experience of life. The conference was a real success: education, mothers' endowment, and birth control were the questions which really interested the assembly. And there was a certain impatience at having to listen to Ministers or even to women officials; they wanted to talk themselves and hear from fellow-delegates from the Sections. At

[1] For the story of the Hutchinson Trust, out of which the London School of Economics was founded, see *Our Partnership*, pp. 84 ff. The initial capital was £5,000, not "a few hundreds"; nevertheless the achievement was sufficiently remarkable.

the Albert Hall meeting they were of course enthusiastic about the P.M. and Margaret Bondfield and the other Ministerial speakers— and with the singing of part religious and part revolutionary hymns, the great gathering likened a religious festival more than a political demonstration. What a strange blend of ancient tradition and modern outlook is the British Labour Party! . . .

May 25th. Bryan's Ground.—Sidney came down here for 48 hours but had to return this (Sunday) afternoon by a slow train in order to be at the P.M. Monday lunch* at which the inner circle (Henderson, Clynes, Thomas, Snowden, MacDonald, Sidney and usually Ben Spoor) discuss the forthcoming week's business. For to-morrow the P.M. issued a note saying that the adjourned debate on reduction of the Labour Minister's salary (censure on failure to find work for the unemployed) would involve, if reduction were carried, the resignation of the Government, and he wanted to consider whether such an inti- mation should not be issued to the Press so that Liberals and Conser- vatives might know what exactly they were doing. In view of the West Toxteth victory and the disappearance of the Liberal poll in the Glasgow Division,[1] we doubt whether either of the Oppositions— specially not the Liberals—will dare to run us out. It looks as if an election now would just about finish up the Liberals as a separate party. Sidney sees many advantages in such an election and has always favoured going to the country in June. Sidney has had a strenuous week in and out of Parliament. He is still enjoying his work, and so far as his own department is concerned he succeeds in and out of Parliament. In *general* debate on a *general* question he is not so good—he does not always seize the operative points or wind up triumphantly. But he has the satisfaction of feeling that Fabianism is justified—that slowly attained, incomplete and mixed communal control is all that is either practicable or desirable, and that the rival policies of revolutionary action or "workers' control", anti-socialism or fiscal "protection", are all on the down grade and cannot be put in force. Unemployment is certainly the crux—and up to to-day the Labour Party has not succeeded in putting forward a practicable policy—probably because such a policy could only be developed slowly through a long course of years and with great deliberation and con-

---

* These Monday lunches, which continue (June 23), were started by the P.M. after Easter. The company consists of what might be termed the Fathers of the Labour Movement. [B. W.]

[1] In West Toxteth, Liverpool, on the retirement of R. P. Houston, Labour won the seat. Polling: J. Gibbins (Labour), 15,505; T. White (Unionist), 13,304. In Kelvingrove, Glasgow, on the death of W. Hutchinson (Unionist), Captain Walter Elliot held the seat for the Unionists, increasing the majority from 1,000 to 4,000 over A. Ferguson, who was in effect a Communist. The Liberal poll dropped from 4,662 to 1,372.

tinuity of action. Where I think the Labour leaders have been at fault—and we among them—is in implying, if not asserting, that the prevention of unemployment was an easy and rapid task instead of being a difficult and slow business involving many complicated transactions and far more control of capitalist enterprise than anyone has yet worked out.

June 2nd. Bryan's Ground.—Ten days alone in this enchanting countryside: living comfortably according to my own habits in the gardener's cottage, working quietly at the book in the mornings, long lonely rambles—5 to 8 miles—in the evenings, and little visits to the nieces in between. . . . So far as I am concerned, I have thoroughly enjoyed the time—the peace and beauty, the only breaks in the silence being the songs of the birds: robin, finch, blackbird and thrush and the wilder calls of peewit, curlew and the owl. Especially sweet is it to listen to the last song of the thrush or blackbird or the first hooting of the owl in the gloaming just before I go to bed; and to hear the distant lark of the hills in the morning and then the sudden outburst of an uncounted orchestra of birds—far and near, of every sort and kind, as if a conductor, invisible to mortal men, had raised his wand and opened the overture for the day.

Meanwhile the Labour Government has once again been saved by Liberal votes after a silly and undignified manoeuvre by the Liberals to put it in the wrong without putting it out. Probably not a deliberate policy but the result of cross-purposes and compromises between the competing leaders of the Liberal Party—one section thinking that delay is fatal to Liberalism, the other that an immediate election means extinction!—the truth being, that whatever they do, the Liberals are doomed. The electors have now realised that the Labour leaders can govern, that they do not, when called upon to act, act differently from what [*sic*] the Liberals and more progressive Conservatives would act if they had equal sincerity and industry—and that they are bringing to politics a wider international outlook and more fervent industry in domestic administration than either of the other parties. Of course we shall not get a majority at the next election; that would be impossible without a better Press and without ampler funds; but we shall gain seats and increase our vote if we go to the country within a year of taking office. The accusation that we have not fulfilled our wilder promises, nor carried out our more reckless pledges, does not injure us with the voters who did not vote for us last time: on the contrary, it stands to our credit! What the ordinary citizen feared was that we should do these things! Now he thinks that we *can't do them and don't want to do them*; a comforting and encouraging discovery to all but our own Left. But then, who *is* the Left to vote for other than the Labour candidate? It will mean a few Communist candidates queering the pitch as at Glasgow last week,[1] but no British political party is killed by its left—it is killed by the desertion of the average sensual man who sees in some other party a better chance of getting what he wants —orderly progress at home and peace with other nations abroad. "All the same," I warn Sidney when he looks particularly complacent, "this Labour Government is a fluke, and a fluke which will not be repeated during your political life-time."

June 16th. 41, Grosvenor Road.—Back again in London, the month at Bryan's Ground having slipped away like one blessed day of peace and happiness—the physical comfort of silence from man and his ugly works—for instance, the rush of motor traffic in front, and the builders' yard below—perfect ease of body and mind combined with creative work; and, for the last twelve days, companionship with "my boy", now, in age, an old man, but singularly boyish in his happiness. The impression of the Cabinet he leaves on my mind is of the pre-eminence of the P.M. over his colleagues; the absence of any friction within the Cabinet; the blundering of Tom Shaw, the brilliancy of Wheatley and the sound position held by Snowden and Graham—of the others I get no impression from Sidney. But he tells me very little about the Cabinet—he is not, I think, intentionally reserved, but he is so occupied with the details of his own department that I doubt whether he notices what happens. Also both of us feel this Cabinet is an abnormal episode—probably a quickly-ending one. "I don't look upon you as a 'pukka' Cabinet Minister"—and he laughs and agrees. What troubles me is a fear that he may miss the work when it comes to an end; whether he will find the going back to the writing of books is a lifeless task after the more varied activities of the Treasury Bench. What would suit *him* best would be for the Labour Government to stay in for a year; and then to be in opposition three or four years. In another four years he would not care to be in office even if the Labour Party secured a majority, and he would have become bored with the House of Commons and be ready to return and hand over a safe seat to a younger man. For the Party itself, we both feel that a General Election *before the end of the year* is by far the best—and perhaps Lloyd George will give it us. What I have to do meanwhile is to divide up my time and energy between two jobs— helping Sidney at Seaham and the Labour Party's social life in London, on the one hand, and, on the other, making a pleasant students' home at Passfield, and getting on with my book while I am doing this home-making. If I keep my health I shall do it. The two lives will fit in well with one another—they are complementary. This particular

[1] Aitken Ferguson, see *ante*.

book is so concerned with myself that I might easily become egotistical
and self-conscious—a prey to morbid vanity: helping Sidney at Seaham
and the P.L.P. in London is a tiresome and disinterested job; one in
which I do not think about myself—rather aridly impersonal and
uninteresting—and therefore rather depressing to the poor little self
and its dreams, and hence I go back to the book with enjoyment and
zest in the intervals of freedom.

June 23rd.—Yesterday morning, being Sunday, as I was returning
home from the usual walk round St. James's Palace, I thought I
would look up Haldane whom I had not seen for many weeks. He
was in his dignified study—surrounded by the portraits of philosophers
and statesmen—two flights up, and welcomed me warmly. "Are you
more satisfied with the Cabinet than you were when I last saw you?"
I asked. "Yes," said the beneficent one, who always reminds me more
of a French 17th century *abbé* than of an English politician. "They
are becoming more intelligent." And then in his pleasant but somewhat self-centred manner, he told me how *he* had at last got the Production Committee, of which Snowden was Chairman and Sidney a
member, to interview Merz[1] and others and get an electricity scheme
on foot (S. had already told me about it), and how at last he had interested the P.M. in the "Thinking department" we had suggested on
the Machinery of Government Committee four years ago. C. P.
Trevelyan was doing well at the Board of Education, he added;
Wheatley was a brilliant Parliamentarian, but his administrative capacity remained to be tested. Haldane's one complaint was of the T.U.
element in the Cabinet; Henderson, Clynes and Shaw were frightened
of their "own people" and might refuse to make such terms with the
capitalist as would mean a move on with productivity—more especially
with regard to electricity. Eventually I promised to arrange with S.
that he, Haldane, should meet Herbert Morrison—now obstructing
electricity proposals as non-democratic. Haldane was, as usual, busy
manipulating civil servants and ministers to his way of thinking—the
only person he said, somewhat sarcastically, he did *not* see was the
P.M. But then that is a common complaint among MacDonald's
colleagues! Who knows what the P.M. is arranging with Herriot?
Not one of his colleagues was with him at Chequers—and I very much
doubt whether he has talked with any one of them about it. There is
to be no Cabinet this week. Anyway, in a Cabinet of twenty members,
all of whom attend a gathering absorbed in all the routine and more
pressing work, it is obvious there can be no consultation about foreign

[1] Charles Hesterman Merz (1874–1940). Leading consultant engineer, senior
partner of Merz & McLellan, and son of the Webbs' old friend J. T. Merz, the
scientist and engineer.

affairs. Meanwhile each Minister is absorbed by his own department and thinks and talks of little else. There are, of course, advantages in this one-man-government—it works with little or no friction (if there is no consultation there cannot be divided counsels). And there is always the attack of the enemy to herd them together, when necessary for self-preservation. But democratic control *there is not*: not even the control by an inner circle—leave alone an Executive Committee depending on the support of a representative assembly. It is one-man-government, undiluted in so far as the P.M.'s work is concerned; and one-man-government in each department until the department gets into a mess. If the mess is sufficiently serious, all the separate individuals combine, whether they agree or not, to save the group's life as a group, whether the attack is from within the Party or from the acknowledged enemy, and the Minister concerned has to obey orders in return for his safety. But if all goes well, the individual Ministers are left uncontrolled. It may be that the activities of a modern state, as mighty and multifarious as Great Britain, can only be governed in this way—that committee government is impracticable. The question arises whether our plan of having two separate organs for municipal and external affairs respectively[1] will not, sooner or later, have to be adopted if we are to have even a semblance of democratic control—other than the control by turning out the Government, a meaningless sort of control, because it is purely negative, and after the event. What puzzles me—Is MacDonald an able statesman as well as a clever parliamentarian and attractive popular preacher? My mind is literally a blank on this subject: I have not the remotest idea whether the P.M. is a genius, a mere spinner of words, or a sufficiently able man to make a good job of the country's business, on more or less Labour lines? This year, I assume, will show his calibre. He has certainly had good luck, up to now; and persistent good luck usually means a strain of unusual talent, if not genius. But I know no more of J.R.M. than I do of Baldwin: he and I are complete strangers.

June 28th. Passfield Corner.—One week of getting more furniture in, superintending builders' and finishing operations, making provision for a drive to the house, seeing the Lady of the Manor about bridging the ditch, and our neighbour Anketell about an exchange of land; and at last I am again at work on the book, Sidney having departed yesterday after a happy week-end together. The cottage with its comfortable study and delightful loggia, its woods and views and walks, is almost too good to be true! To make a new home when one is nearing seventy seems, in some moods, a melancholy task: one is

---

[1] Set out in *A Constitution for the Socialist Commonwealth of Great Britain*, by S. and B. Webb (1920).

haunted by a vision of the funeral procession wending its way down the new drive, a few years hence, perhaps a few months hence, of one of us, leaving the other one desolate and alone. For, barely a mile away, there is another little house—more dignified than this, with the Wey running through the meadow in which it stands: the first and last time I saw that house, sister Georgie[1] was standing in the hall looking after the last workman and planning her garden, much as I am doing to-day. A few months after she died in a London nursing home. And she was just a year younger than I am. That vision adds a note of melancholy. Also there is present in my mind that this new home must mean a certain separation from Sidney—at any rate while he remains in Parliament. I comfort myself by remembering that for some years I always lived in the country during the spring and summer months whilst he was mostly in London on County Council business. But we were at work on the same book: he came back to me as a work-mate; we toiled together all the days he spared from administration; we talked about what we were both keen about. Now when he returns, we love each other; but he has interests about which I know little and I am absorbed in creative writing in which he has no part, but that of a kindly and helpful critic of style. Still it would be purposeless for me to waste my strength, and such wits as I have, in doing odd jobs which are not needed; or fussing about matters in which I cannot help. He is happy and contented in his new task, and so am I in mine; and we have a Sabbath rest together when the week's work is done. If only I could do more work: I am so deplorably slow, so easily tired—not ill, but just too much of a weakling to do more than a few hours' work —and any other task, like the monthly letter to Seaham or entertaining Labour men, just cuts the thread of my thoughts so I have to start all over again.

July 8th.—Ran up to London for one night, to complete furnishing; to dictate the answers to a pile of letters that had accumulated, to give a dinner at the P.L.C. and take the guests on to the Gerald Goulds'[2] reception at the Hotel Victoria, to spend an hour or so talking to Labour Ministers and Labour journalists in a heated room; to walk back with S. and drop in at the House of Commons and await his arrival for a chat before bed. Then, the next morning, to begin shopping again, to see Miss Dawson[3] about the P.L.C., and Galton about the Fabian Society between lunch and catching the 4.50 from Water-

---

[1] Georgina Meinertzhagen (1850-1914). The fourth of the Potter sisters.

[2] Gerald Gould (1885-1936). Author and journalist, associate-editor of the *Daily Herald*, 1919-22; his wife was Barbara Ayrton Gould (d. 1950), M.P. for North Hendon from 1945-50, and for twenty years on the Labour Party's Executive Committee.

[3] Lilian Dawson, for many years secretary of the Fabian Women's Group.

loo—and I am back, in the cool of the evening, sitting in the loggia and rejoicing in my new home! Five more days here, preparing a lecture for the Edinburgh Fabians when I receive my LL.D. at Edinburgh next week, thinking about the garden, and then back again in the fray of a Minister's wife, journey to Edinburgh and three days, functions, and twelve days in London entertaining Seaham folk and seeing something of the P.L. Party, and then at last, in the first days of August, settling down here for nine weeks' steady work at the book, varied by planning the drive and the garden, and entertaining Kate Courtney and others as guests. Always in the background the consciousness of amazing good fortune and a certain uneasiness of conscience as to whether one is justified in making oneself so comfortable in one's old age? Also a less personally responsible questioning about the soul of the Labour Cabinet. Each Minister is hard at work—there is certainly no slacking—but there is a good deal of self-complacency and a certain atmosphere of drift. And of course the fervent ones in the Parliamentary Labour Party are disappointed—bitterly disappointed; they would be disappointed even if all that was conceivably practicable had been done—they had worked themselves up to believe that all social evils could be swept away by a sweep of the hand of a Labour Cabinet; they had no inkling of the resisting power of the big machine. . . .

July 10th.—Assuredly some of the younger authors can write. Aldous Huxley is a brilliant *littérateur*; but at present a shallow-hearted thinker. E. M. Forster—a much older man, but one who has written fewer books, because he has thought and felt as well as searched after "le mot juste"—appears to me in his latest novel *A Passage to India* as a genius, and not merely a man with an exquisite gift for words. Here, for instance, is a passage about old age (Mrs. Moore) which my own experience tells me has a significance and is admirably expressed:

"She had come to that state when the horror of the universe and its smallness are both visible at the same time—the twilight of the double vision in which so many elderly people are involved. If this world is not to our taste, well, at all events there is Heaven, Hell, Annihilation —one or other of those large things, that huge scenic background of stars, fires, blue or black air. All heroic endeavour, and all that is known as art, assumes that there is such a background, just as all practical endeavour, when the world is to our taste, assumes that the world is all. But in the twilight of the double vision, a spiritual muddledom is set up for which no high-sounding words can be found; we can neither act nor refrain from action, we can neither ignore nor respect Infinity. Mrs. Moore had always inclined to resignation! as soon as she landed in India it seemed to her good, and when she saw the water flowing through the mosque-tank, or the Ganges, or the moon, caught in the shawl of night with all the other stars, it seemed a beautiful goal and an easy one. To be one with the universe! So dignified and simple. But there was always some little duty to be performed first, some new card to be turned up from the diminishing pack and placed, and while she was pottering about, the Marabar struck its gong." (Pp. 208–9.)

And there follows an analysis of the poor old woman's thoughts: "The abyss also may be petty, the serpent of eternity made of maggots; her constant thought was: 'Less attention should be paid to my future daughter-in-law and more to me, there is no sorrow like my sorrow,' although when attention was paid she rejected it irritably." (P. 209.)

In this description of an old woman's mind, what appeals to me are the phrases "the twilight of the double vision", "a spiritual muddledom is set up". Certainly with me there is the strange consciousness of standing on a bare and bleak watershed of thought and feeling—in itself a place without thoughts or feelings, but with countless thoughts and feelings streaming out of the past and into the future in directions so various and manifold that I can no longer estimate their relative value. And the concrete questions which I have investigated—trade unionism, local government, co-operation, political organisation, no longer interest me: I dislike reading about them, thinking about them, talking about or writing about them.

In my present state of mind they seem stale and unprofitable. It is states of mind that interest me. It amuses me to discover the assumptions and instincts on which any particular series of theoretical or practical conclusions have been built up. Even more exciting are the thoughts of the younger intellectuals, regarded as hints of what is to become of the human race in the near future. All the existing issues—the ones with which Sidney and I have been concerned, into which we have thrown the prime of our energies—will be, probably in a few years, dead and gone, settled by, or buried beneath, the work of the rising generation. And yet I do not know what the nature of that work will be! Hence the aptness of the phrases "double vision" and "spiritual muddledom". I am conscious of the past and I am conscious of the future: I am wholly indifferent to the present. It is my *duty* to be interested in the Labour Party and the Labour Government, and I honestly try to show the symptoms of being interested. But I am not really interested except in so far as Sidney's activity and happiness are concerned. Not that I think what happens to the Labour Movement unimportant: all I feel is that I am personally no longer concerned with it. During the last few weeks I have been pressed to serve on two Royal Commissions and one Government Committee—

London University, Lunacy and the Export Trade. The very sound of these words bored and irritated me. I should have loathed having to turn my mind on to all the maze of technical detail, and I am glad enough to plead "old age" and to suggest some younger woman who would be proud to undertake the task. What rouses thought is: How can the human mind acclimatise itself to the insecurity and uncertainty of this terrible doctrine of relativity, latent in all modern science—long before Einstein applied it to the astronomical universe? It is a most disconcerting conclusion, that there is no absolute truth; and that the thoughts of the man are no more and no less valid than the analogous brain activities of the dog or the bee! What becomes of the existing standards of morality or capacity? They are obviously temporary; belonging to just the present state of things, here and now. Sooner or later they have got to be scrapped in order to invent standards more suited to another order of things? But *who* is to settle *when* these codes and tests are to be superseded, and *what* are to be the substitutes? Is morality a question of taste, and truth a question of relative standpoints? And are all tasks and all standpoints equally valid? What, in fact, is my own standpoint from which I survey the world of the past and the future? For it is exactly these questions which I shall have to answer in the last chapter of my book! And it is this point in space and time—the exact point at which I stand—that seems to me so singularly bleak and bare—so featureless.

July 21st.—An exhausting 48 hours in Edinburgh receiving the LL.D. from the University. On the evening of arrival, a ceremonious dinner with speeches lasting four hours in the great hall of the University; the next day, lengthy process in the crowded McEwen Hall of being "capped" with sixteen other honorary graduates, followed by the endless procession of hundreds of ordinary graduates, culminating in the scenic crowning of the Olympic victor—Liddell—with wild olives amid the enthusiasm of the whole congregation of students, dons and friends; the walk through the town in cap and gown to the Cathedral: listening to an inaudible and dully-read sermon by the Moderator; then another ceremonial meal, the lunch given by the Students' Union—at which I was one of the speakers—lasting another three hours; a reception at the Principal's—after that I struck work and refused to attend the evening function. On the following evening I lectured for 1½ [hours] to the Fabians, and then left by 10.50 night express for London. The consequence was that I had a most unpleasant experience on the night journey back—a warning against such overstrained nerves. I was cold and very hungry when I entered the sleeping compartment but I dozed off almost immediately. I seemed to wake up; the train had stopped with a jerk: I heard vaguely cries of "fire, fire", and jumped up in the dark; tried to open the door, but though I did unbolt it I could not open it. I seemed to hear footsteps hurrying past the door, and a panic took possession of me. I called out again and again "open the door"; the only answer I seemed to get was "the carriage is on fire, come out of your berths", which intensified my panic and heightened my cries. Presently I heard the voice of the attendant calmly telling me that I was trying to open the door of the next compartment—occupied by a gentleman!—which of course was bolted on the other side; and that we were stopping at Berwick in the ordinary way. Horribly ashamed of myself, I apologised humbly, saying that I had been dreaming.

Now the interesting fact is that only *part* of my brain was awake— I had not the control of my reason—or I should have looked out at the lighted station and recovered my sanity. Which made me think of the not infrequent cases of travellers who wake up and walk out on to the line, or get out by the window as the French President[1] did (he had been suffering from nervous exhaustion). Perhaps if I had been alone in a first-class compartment I might have done the same!

The Macmillans, with whom I stayed, were well-bred pleasant people. "Our Lord Advocate" is an attractive man, accomplished leader of the Scottish Bar, conservative in temperament and opinion but a great admirer of J.R.M. We did not talk politics. He is a devoted lawyer—lucid and methodical, even meticulous, in his knowledge, but with no trace of the prig; unassuming in manner and outstandingly public-spirited—a great addition to the Labour Government. From him I gathered, and also from others, that Liberalism is practically dead in Scotland. Leslie Mackenzie[2] fears that if the rent and rates question on the Clyde is not grappled with by this or a future Government, there will be bloodshed and revolutionary strikes. Maxton is reported to have said in answer to James Barr's[3] question as to what was going to happen in the near future, "Ramsay will become leader of the Conservative Party and he will be in for twenty years." Yesterday morning, having recovered from my nervous exhaustion, I had a chat with Haldane. He is much discontented with the T.U. element in the Cabinet: "They are unintelligent and timid, and never grapple with anything that needs thought." Snowden, Sidney and Wheatley he considered the most useful members, with Arnold in the Lords. "Sidney is self-effacing; but he always knows his subject and has control of his officials." "Those Trade Unionists simply accept everything their officials tell them. Fortunately we have a first-rate and

---

[1] Paul Eugène Deschanel (1865–1922). Elected French President in 1920; but resigned shortly after falling out of a train.
[2] Sir Leslie Mackenzie (1862–1935), doctor, M.O.H., medical inspector and civil servant; authority on medical inspection and health of school-children.
[3] Rev. James Barr (1862–1949), pacifist and I.L.P.; M.P. for Motherwell.

progressive Civil Service." Thinks that J.R.M. spends far too much time at casual entertainments: no one can get at him to discuss business—only Thomson sees him, and *he* avoids "shop". Dufour Ferrond (German Embassy), whom I met at lunch yesterday, said that this Labour Government was the most secretive in its foreign policy of any that he had experienced, and that J.R.M. was the most inaccessible Foreign Minister he had ever known! All depends on whether the P.M. pulls off a satisfactory settlement with France. If he does, the Labour Government is in for another nine months—until the next Budget—if he does not, and neither Russian loan nor Irish boundary business "comes off", we may be turned out in November.

At the "inner circle" lunch yesterday at 10 Downing Street the P.M. reported favourably of the Conference (I wish I shared his optimism!) but was anxious to discuss future plans in view of the possible prolongation of the Labour Government. He remarked that it was fortunate the Cabinet had had no casualties, because he did not know how he could fill up any of the leading parts. There was only William Graham who was due for promotion and he could not be spared from the all-important post of Financial Secretary. If Patrick Hastings claimed the next high judgeship, who was there to succeed him as Attorney-General? He was discontented with Shaw and also, in another sphere, with Chelmsford. Then what was to be their policy, supposing they survived for another Budget? There were difficulties in going out on the Budget—because of the time-table for Budgets—which would make it almost impossible to get a Budget through if they had to take office after an election in June. He thought it not improbable that a Labour Government would be in, off and on, for many years—neither the Conservatives nor Labour Party having a clear majority in future Parliaments, and the decreasing body of Liberals throwing their force first on one side, then on the other! So after the Conference is over there are to be a succession of inner circle meetings—I suppose with some additional members—to discuss the future. This curiously constituted group—Thomas, Henderson, Clynes, Snowden and Sidney—six in all, is more the inner circle of the *Party Caucus* than the inner circle of the Cabinet. It is almost inconceivable that none of the other ministers know of its existence and I wonder when one or other of them will protest? Ben Spoor usually attends as Whip (he is ill again, and absent) so he must know, and Wheatley came one Monday when Housing was urgent, and Tom Shaw when unemployment was discussed. Meanwhile the growling of the fervent ones of the back-benchers grows louder, and what exactly will happen if a Labour Government remains in, on an extremely moderate programme, I fail to foresee. The Liberals, we are told, are determined to run a candidate against every Labour man, in order that the Conservatives may get a majority or nearly a majority. Then the Liberals hope that, if they co-operate with Labour as an opposition formulating together an advanced programme, they will be admitted into a future Labour Cabinet on dignified terms! A curious calculation: Defeat Labour at the polls in order to work with it as an opposition!

At Lord Arnold's dinner at the H. of C. on Thursday to the Government and their wives to meet the P.M. I sat between Henderson and Wheatley—just where I should have placed myself. H. was deploring the absence of brains at Eccleston Square[1] now he could no longer be there. "I sometimes wonder whether I should not have done better in the interests of the Party to have refused office and stuck to my job of Party organisation. . . ." With Wheatley I had a good deal of talk—I like him and he interests me as a possible successor to J.R.M.—the most unexpected and outstanding success of the Front Bench. "The Clyde think J.R.M. has betrayed them. They believed he, unlike Webb, was a revolutionary, willing to run risks for principles. We always believed that the Webbs were disinterested and self-devoted, and full of facts and plans, but the Clyde Socialists thought the Webbs' scheme would take half a century to get into shape, and that, in the end, it would turn out to be a soulless bureaucracy! But 'Mac' made them feel that he had vision and fervour, and that once he was leader they would be in sight of the promised land. To-day, Maxton declares that it is the capitalists who have put him in power, and that they are quite right, because such a Labour Government in office means Socialism thwarted and capitalism kept in being, *with the consent of the workers*."

The bitterness about the Court and other social functions is extreme and is causing a lot of heart-burning—I gather from other M.P.s.

Another Cabinet function took place last night—a conducted tour of Wembley Exhibition, a luxurious dinner and the spectacle of the Pageant afterwards. All the Cabinet self-complacent, the workmen members enjoying the outing with their wives, the bureaucratics, like ourselves, walking through it in the spirit of camaraderie; slightly bored, but also self-complacent. The P.M. when recognised by the crowd of sightseers was "gaped at" with a sort of wondering and good-natured curiosity—"these Labour Ministers are not a bad sort" was the expression on the upturned faces—but there were no cheers. With the third of my M.P. lunches at the Parliamentary Labour Club, and the Henderson wedding, the "Labour Season" comes to the end; and, God be praised, we settle down in the cottage for ten whole weeks.

[1] The Labour Party set up its headquarters at 33, Eccleston Square in 1919, and removed to Transport House in 1928.

The last of the lunches was the pleasantest because the most varied in composition. Haldane, Macmillan, Rhys Davies,[1] the Hodges,[2] Alastair MacDonald, Oswald Mosley and the First Secretary of the German Embassy and his wife—the Dufours.[3] Haldane reported a serious Cabinet; it is meeting again tonight: Allied Conference hopeful, but the Irish situation and Russian conference in somewhat desperate straits—a report confirmed afterwards by Sidney. H. thoroughly dissatisfied with P.M.—evidently feels that he is not sufficiently consulted: had not been invited to Chequers (Lady Londonderry had stayed there); disapproved of Wembley expedition; Foreign Secretary inaccessible and neglected Parliament and his work for social functions. What riles H. is that the P.M., Snowden, Thomas, run the show so far as Allied Conference, Russia and Ireland are concerned, without consulting anyone else. Sidney does not take the same view: Thomas represents the Dominions, Snowden national finance. He still reports that J.R.M. is head and shoulders above the rest of the Cabinet. But then S. is a modest man; and looks at the matter objectively. Haldane signified that when this Government is brought to an end by a general election he will dissociate himself from the Labour Party, an preturn to a detached position in the House of Lords—as an Elder Statesman ready to work with any Party. "I certainly shall not act as Leader of the Opposition; MacDonald must find someone else." So that's that.

August 30th. Passfield Corner.—Already one month of the recess past. . . . Outwardly, the session ended with a blaze of glory for the P.M. and his London Pact[4] between Allies and Germans; with a more ambiguous success for Ponsonby and the Committee of the rank and file in making, at least, a nominal peace with the Bolsheviks in the Russian Government; a popular *réclame* for J. H. Thomas in showing up the guilt of Lloyd George in deceiving alike Free State and Ulster over boundary clauses of the Irish treaty, and thereby necessitating a new Boundary Commission Act, and possibly, if it is rejected by the House of Lords, a general election in October on the issue—"Is there to be civil war in Ireland?" The Labour Cabinet

[1] Rhys John Davies (1877–1954). Miner, Co-operative employee, Socialist and pacifist. M.P. for Westhoughton (Lancashire), 1921–51; Under-Secretary to the Home Office in 1924 Government.

[2] Frank Hodges (1884–1947), Secretary of the Miners' Federation of Great Britain and Civil Lord of the Admiralty in 1924 Government. See *Diaries, 1912–24.* Alastair MacDonald was the elder son of the Prime Minister.

[3] Albert Dufour-Feronce (b. 1868), represented Germany in Great Britain from 1919 to 1926, first as Counsellor and then as Minister. From 1926–32 he was Under-Secretary-General to the League of Nations.

[4] The "Dawes Plan" for the settlement of post-war reparations. The Anglo-Soviet Treaty mentioned here was a draft and was never ratified; it perished when the Government fell.

has shown its will and its power to pacify the world, and *if* it remains true to itself and united, some say, it could carry on for another year!

But within the charmed circle of the Cabinet there is disintegration going on; within the Party disaffection is spreading. Haldane had his revenge for the P.M.'s neglect to call him into counsel in Foreign Affairs and invite him to Chequers as one of his intimates. The now famous Dent case[1] nearly lost Parmoor to the Government and infuriated many of the faithful. Whether or not this unpleasant type of sanctimonious and acrimonious J.P., who insists on defying the law, and refuses to pay his education rate, should be summarily dismissed from the local bench by the Lord Chancellor, was brought before the Cabinet, in the very last days of July. Sidney says that there was much objection to the threat of dismissal. Haldane said little beyond explaining the impossible position of a J.P. who defies the law deliberately and continuously. But the general impression left by the discussion was that sleeping dogs were to be left alone, and any action deferred. A few days afterwards, the man was defiantly dis-benched by Haldane, without further consultation or explanation. Parmoor wrote to Sidney —thought he ought to resign from the Cabinet and from the Bench— Sidney soothed him down, and he holds on. Then came Snowden's deliberately published criticism of the London Pact and his insinuation that British trade interests had been betrayed in the accepted French interpretation of the Dawes Plan of reparations plus their freedom to remain in the Ruhr for another year—a criticism apparently designed to take the gilt off the gingerbread of J.R.M.'s reputation as a European Peace-maker. Also Snowden has let it be understood that he is against the Russian loan, and therefore the Russian Agreement. The Snowdens lunched here the day after the interview and it is clear that the P.M. has no friend in the Chancellor of the Exchequer. All of which shows that the P.M. has not shown as much tact in the management of his Cabinet as he has in the European negotiations. I am inclined to think that one of his best friends is Sidney, who goes placidly on with his own departmental work and tries to smooth down the hurt susceptibilities of other members, being still firmly of opinion

[1] This case caused a good deal of excitement at the time. Mr. Dent objected to the expenditure of public money on denominational schools under the Education Act of 1902, as did Dr. Clifford, the Nonconformist leader, and others, and like them had refused thereafter to pay his local education rate; they were known as Passive Resisters. He had been appointed to the Bench in Yorkshire; and in May 1924 received a letter from Haldane, the Lord Chancellor, inviting his resignation. He refused to resign and shortly afterwards was dismissed. There was correspondence in *The Times* and elsewhere, and an angry resolution from the Free Church Council: questions were asked in the Commons, and in October Isaac Foot, the Liberal M.P., endeavoured to raise the case on the adjournment, but was prevented by the Speaker from discussing the Lord Chancellor's action. This was six days before the Campbell debate, and one week before the resignation of the Government.

that J.R.M. is the very best available leader for the Labour Party, and quite irreplaceable either in Parliament or in the country.

Meanwhile we do not know what is happening to the Party in the country. The I.L.P. at its much-advertised Summer School has been skilfully engineered by Clifford Allen,[1] who is acting as J.R.M.'s hidden hand, in keeping the Left loyal to their former Idol. Much depends on what happens at the Labour Party Conference in October. The little band of Communists headed by the impossible Tom Mann are very active and much-advertised: Maxton and the Clyde brethren are restive; and the Trade Union world chaotic. We are not seeing any of them and are more ignorant of the internal currents than we should be if Sidney were outside the Cabinet or even out of Parliament. What with the stress and strain of Parliament and the Cabinet for a man of his age, and his rooted antipathy to leadership, Sidney is only too glad to spend the recess in blissful leisure tempered by reading political biographies with a view to a book on the Cabinet as an institution when he retires. So the days roll on in our regular routine of early hours, and reading, walking, talking about the cottage and the garden, seeing one or two Labour friends, discussing the past and the future, or some problem of politics, with no particular care whether the Labour Government remains in or goes out (Sidney mildly in favour of a dissolution, if not in November, then in February) and even indifferent as to when exactly we retire from public life and under what circumstances. Sidney does his level best for his country and his party; he works up to the limit of his strength during the working months. But in his heart of hearts he remains essentially a detached observer without any keenness for one way over another, or [as] to his own continued participation in the exercise of power. . . .

September 2nd.—J.R.M.—perhaps arising from his successful negotiation—seems latterly to have become even more aloof and autocratic towards his Ministers. For instance, Sidney saw announced the other day the appointment by MacDonald of a Committee to advise the F.O. as to the effect of the Dawes Scheme of reparations *on British trade*—without a word of consultation with the President of the Board of Trade! When Sir Arthur Chapman[2] enquired about it at the F.O. they told him that the P.M. had not consulted the F.O. officials, they knew nothing about it! It appears that MacDonald just fired off letters to certain representatives of the "interests" through Miss Rosenberg[3] asking them to serve. Sidney, however,

[1] Lord Allen of Hurtwood, the pacifist leader. See *Diaries, 1912–1924.*

[2] Sir Arthur Wakefield Chapman (1849–1926), Liberal, brother of Cecil Chapman, the Metropolitan Police Magistrate. Active in local government; chairman of Surrey County Council, 1911–17.

[3] Rose Rosenberg (d. 1955), long private secretary to MacDonald.

regards the whole matter of the Labour Administration as so short-lived and exceptional that he is not concerned to criticise except that he hopes it *will* be shortlived, or he fears trouble. Also he is studying the Cabinet as an institution—with a view to writing a book—and any new feature, especially a new defect, interests him—it is like a new case to a surgeon. He is quite uncannily detached and personally unaffected—refuses to be ruffled at anything. "Taking everything into consideration, MacDonald has done better than could be expected: all the same, the sooner we are out, the better for the Party and also for MacDonald." "Meanwhile I suggest you ought to think out how the autocracy of the P.M. can be prevented, whatever party is in power," say I. It's bad for the country and hopelessly demoralising for the P.M. Lloyd George lost his head, MacDonald is going the same way—even Baldwin "plunged" into a general election without consulting his friends. MacDonald said the other day that responsible office was "an inspiration": but the irresponsible power of the P.M. leads, not to inspiration, but to [the] intoxication so often mistaken for inspiration! And the less accustomed the holder is to the exercise of power, the more he succumbs to the "headiness" of the position. "All the same, I shall not raise the question of that Committee," says Sidney, and he sits down and writes a pleasant letter to the P.M. on another matter—the preparation of a Bill for the nationalisation of the mines and his proposed consultation with Shinwell. . . .

September 24th.—First Cabinet harmonious discussion exclusively about India, going through word by word the instructions sent to Reading with regard to demand for special powers. When they had finished and were about to break up, the P.M. said he wanted a general discussion about [the] state of affairs, and would they come back at 3 o'clock. When they re-assembled, they talked at large about prospects; agreeing generally that there would not be an election over Russia, as no one wanted it except Lloyd George and Winston Churchill. But that they would play for an election on King's Speech. J.R.M. talked gloomily about his "being sick of it"; the Party had behaved so badly, the Parliamentary Executive regarding themselves as a court-martial and the *Daily Herald* queering his pitch perpetually. "Supposing we did come back in a majority, would you welcome it?" he asked. And when most of them replied "Yes," he said that he thought it would be a grave misfortune, as the Party (not the Cabinet!) was not "fit to govern". All thought that they had improved their position in the country and would gain seats, tho' nowhere near a majority. . . .

October 1st.—General Election decided on by the Liberals in spite of grave warnings of *Manchester Guardian*—it remains with the Liberals and the Labour Cabinet to decide whether they will have it on the silly little issue of the Campbell prosecution[1]—or rather, the withdrawal of it—or on the Russian treaty. Anyway, that ends the episode of a Labour Government, and by Xmas, at any rate, we shall be out of office. Meanwhile in the near future we personally will have to shift our home from London to the country, as we cannot keep up both establishments for long without outrunning our ordinary income. The Cabinet Minister's salary has led us into expenditure for ourselves and for the Party, and now we shall have to pull up sharp, and Grosvenor Road (directly I can find comfortable diggings for Sidney) will have to go. If he is still in office or likely to be soon again in office—which is almost inconceivable—we shall hold on; but if it looks like a Conservative Government for three or four years—leave alone a débâcle of the Labour Party—quiet rooms where he could stay for the Parliamentary week during the session would be amply sufficient. I should prefer to live permanently down here and go up only occasionally—perhaps for a couple of months in the last weeks of autumn and the first weeks of winter.

October 10th.—The end of the tale of the Parliament of 1923–4 and of its Cabinet is soon told. The two Oppositions decided to kill the Government on the Campbell issue. Some say they drifted into their decision; others that the Russian treaty proved [un] expectedly popular and that the Liberals, in particular, would have lost, not fourteen, but fifty, in the division lobbies if they had stuck to damning the Treaty. Anyhow, the Conservatives ran away from their direct censure, and beat the Government by the meaner Liberal way of the Court of Enquiry into the conduct of the Attorney-General—an enquiry which the Cabinet could not accept without lowering its prestige a few weeks before it was to be sent to the country on the Russian issue.

No one can accuse the Labour Party of any lack of swiftness in its call to battle. Before twelve hours had passed away, the P.M. met his colleagues with the King's consent for a dissolution *that very afternoon*! "The King's Speech must be written and ready for him to see at one o'clock," said he, looking round the table. "Webb, you had better

---

[1] The Campbell case, which brought about the dissolution and the subsequent fall of the Government, started with an article in the Communist *Workers' Weekly*, edited by an ex-service man named J. R. Campbell. The Law Officers began a prosecution for sedition, but abandoned it in face of left-wing protest. Although they asserted that the withdrawal had no political implications, they were not believed; the Liberals called for a Select Committee, which MacDonald said he would regard as a vote of censure. The Conservatives thereupon joined hands with the Liberals, and the Government fell.

go and do it." So Sidney and Tom Jones summoned the heads of the different departments; and a dozen men sat down at tables and drafted paragraphs, while Sidney strung them together and polished up the whole. At three o'clock the Council was held: and the Dissolution proclaimed.

Thus the Parliament of 1923–4 has followed, in its untimely end, the Parliament of 1922–3.

The following day Sidney was kept hard at it, drafting the manifesto for the Party; in the intervals between the MS., typewritten and printed form, he struggled to get his own Seaham election campaign started. Yesterday he went off to Seaham, and I follow on Wednesday.

Meanwhile the Labour Party Conference had given a most appropriate *mise-en-scène* for the fall of the Labour Cabinet—with its enthusiasm for the P.M. and its decisive rejection of the Communists' application for membership. So far as the Party itself is concerned, no issue could have been better—the Russian treaty and the withdrawal of the prosecution of Johnson[1] have made the Party solid and enthusiastic; all the querulous criticism or serious misgivings having vanished in a quite amazing way. Even the Attorney-General stands out as a hero of social democracy; and as for the P.M., he has again become the idol of the Left and the respected leader of the Right of the Labour Movement respectively. But this unity and enthusiasm is confined to our own Party—Heaven knows what is happening to the ordinary man who might, or might not, vote Labour, and on whom the result of the election depends. One fact is clear. There has been a rapid drawing together, in the constituencies, of Liberals and Conservatives against Labour, and many minority Labour seats are doomed. On the other hand, fourteen Liberal Members—including the ablest lawyer of the Party (Jowitt of Hartlepool)[2] and the estimable Mrs. Wintringham,[3] voted with the Labour Government in the crucial divisions and it looks as if they might join the Labour Party after the election. This defection—a defiant defection in face of the enemy—must mean a good deal of discontent among the troops behind the Parliamentary line. Our forecast is roughly 3, 2, 1—Conservatives 300, Labour 200, and Liberals 100. The Conservatives may get back a working majority— they may even sweep the country. Sidney says he would prefer that they should have a small majority, *so long as Labour improves its position* and keeps its record of being a growing force. . . .

[1] Clearly a mistake for "Campbell".

[2] William Allen Jowitt, first Baron (b. 1885). Elected to Parliament as a Liberal; became Attorney-General in second Labour Government, and remained with MacDonald for a year after its fall. Lord Chancellor in the 1945 Labour Government.

[3] Margaret Wintringham, Independent Liberal, became M.P. for Louth in 1921 on the death of her husband, but lost her seat in the election of 1924.

The General Election, October 1924.

October 29th. 32, *Maureen Terrace, Seaham Harbour.*—All over except the shouting! Sidney has been here about twenty days and has had about thirty meetings. I have been here thirteen days and taken fifteen meetings; ending up last night with two crowded meetings at our strongholds—Horden and Easington. For us, in this remote corner of England, far away from reporters and other candidates, it has been the pleasantest of electoral ordeals—devoted workers in their hundreds together with the sense of "belonging" to the miners' community, as leaders and representatives in the sphere of public affairs. Especially gratifying to us has been the growing affection of these men and women for the Webbs: they and we are co-religionists, we have the same faith, but we hold the faith in a different and complementary way—through intellectual conviction with us, and through personal experience of the manual workers' life with them. From all appearance Sidney's majority will not be less than it was last year and may be more.

But in the country at large the Labour Party has had a bombshell thrown into its ranks in the Zinoviev Letter,[1] whether authentic or forged, and the inept Foreign Office reply—all due to MacDonald's shifty and bungling management—magnified by the loud shouters of the press and the platform on the eve of the election.

The P.M. has shown signs, throughout the contest, of neurosis— he has lost his balance and floundered about badly. His task, be it said, has been intolerable, and made worse by wounded personal vanity and his prevarications about the Campbell prosecution. In this latest business of the Russian letter he has let his Party, his Cabinet and the Foreign Office down, through carelessness or incapacity—total inability to take counsel. He ought to have had by his side some colleague, Lord Thomson or Parmoor. MacDonald is, in fact, a melancholy example of the demoralisation which sets in when a man becomes pre-eminent in his own sphere, uncontrolled in the exercise of power—especially a man who is wholly unaccustomed to and untrained for these giddy heights of personal decisions on great issues.

---

[1] The "Zinoviev Letter", a copy of which reached the Foreign Office on October 10th, was a document purporting to be signed by Zinoviev and Kuusinen, the President and Secretary respectively of the Comintern, and by Arthur Macmanus, a British member of its Presidium, giving instructions for military insurrection in working-class areas of Great Britain, for subverting the allegiance of the armed forces, and for "paralysing the military preparations of the *bourgeoisie*". MacDonald received his copy on October 16th, in the middle of the election campaign, and corresponded with his officials over a draft reply. But on the 24th the Foreign Office, alleging that the *Daily Mail* was about to publish the letter, sent both it and the draft reply (which MacDonald had not yet released) to the Press, four days before the polling. Whether the letter was authentic or a forgery (both of which explanations are possible) its production, when the draft Russian treaty was a subject of electoral controversy, was fatal to the Party, the more so because MacDonald himself never issued any explanation or said whether he believed it or not.

What effect the explosion will have on today's polling, in doubtful constituencies, we shall see tomorrow. Here I think it will prove to be a very damp squib. It may mean the loss of seats, on balance, for the Labour Party. On the other hand, working-class voters may remain unaffected—they may even react against the virulence of the Russian stunt and its irrelevance to all the questions in which they are interested.

Three days ago before the Zinoviev Letter episode, Sidney went through the constituences one by one—consequent calculation, Conservatives 355, Labour 195, Liberal 65. Probably our bias makes us put Liberals too low. The bomb may bring Labour down to 185—even less—and raise the Liberals to 90 or 100. I doubt whether the Conservatives will have less than 330 or more than 360. The swing, however, on all counts, accelerates in their direction.

The next three weeks will be exciting: then there will be the calm of being in opposition for three or four years. Whether Sidney fights another election depends on whether he feels he is of use to the Party. Also whether he could hand on his safe seat to an intellectual who would be of use to the Party—we have already too much of the dead stuff of miners as M.P.s—no one—not even the miner M.P.s themselves—wants one more of this brand! Whatever happens at the General Election, the course of events will be worth observing and recording from the inner circle of His Majesty's Opposition. And there are going to be ructions in Downing Street during the next ten days before the meeting of Parliament which will be amusing to watch—Wedgwood and Lansbury from their different standpoints will be on the war path against MacDonald, and all the members of the I.L.P. will be more or less disgruntled with their old favourite. Sidney having no career before him to be injured by MacDonald's errors will remain benign and philosophical. He will certainly not enter into any intrigue against MacDonald. And all the trouble over Russia may ultimately turn out to the advantage of the Labour Party. The "larger expediency" is that the Communist gang should be once more discredited—the blister pricked—even at the cost of risking loss of blood.

The Fall of the Labour Government.

Which of course was foreseen; but even we did not forecast the catastrophic character of the rout, so far as the Parliamentary representation of Labour is concerned, nor did we anticipate a two thousand drop in our own majority. Poor Eccleston Square, obsessed by the unbroken enthusiasm of meetings and demonstrations, was in the depths of depression on the day of the declaration of the sweeping defeat, of the vast majority of 514 candidates—with a loss, on balance, of forty seats.

A more careful consideration of the response of the huge electorate to the virulent anti-communist propaganda carried on by Liberals and Conservatives alike makes us almost content with the verdict. Sidney in a speech a week before the day, one of the few of his speeches which was reported in the *Times* and *Manchester Guardian*, prophesied that, whatever else happened, this General Election would be noted by future historians as "the funeral of a great political party" —the last act of the story of Liberalism. And so has it proved to be. The Liberals come out of this battle of creeds a mere group—and a group divided among themselves—at least half of them supported by Tories and in effect adherents of the Baldwin Government; whilst the other score are mostly moderates with a few energetic and progressive persons—Kenworthy,[1] Wedgwood Benn,[2] Harris,[3] etc. who will probably join the Labour Party in the course of this Parliament. The assassin of the Liberal Party is Lloyd George:—as unwilling assistant his poor dupe, Asquith—who, to save his own seat, sounded the fatal battle cry of "Labour the common foe of Liberalism as well as Conservatism." Incidentally, I note that it was to this much advertised call to all Liberals to vote Conservative that we owe the drop of two thousand in Sidney's majority—the three thousand Liberals (the remnant of Hayward's Liberal majority over Labour of 1918 election) who abstained last year, in the absence of a Liberal candidate, having, this time, voted solidly for Ronald Ross.

Still a majority of 10700 is not contemptible!

The big joke of the General Election is that the grave of anti-communism, which the Liberal leaders dug so energetically for us, swallowed them up instead, whilst the Labour Party was left with a million increase on their total poll; denuded it is true of forty members, but with the hostile force on their flank completely demolished. Now that the smoke of the battle has cleared away, all the Conservative leaders in the country are talking dolefully of the five and a half million "avowed Socialists". "Who are these new Socialist voters?" asks a correspondent of the Conservative press. "They are the new voters—the young men who have got on to the register," whispers back the more experienced of the Conservative wirepullers. "Who were the extra two millions who voted Conservative?" "The old women," retorts the observant Labour election agent, who watched

[1] Joseph Montague Kenworthy, Lord Strabolgi (1886–1953). Retired Royal Navy, Liberal and then Labour M.P. for Central Hull; Opposition Chief Whip in House of Lords, 1938–1942.
[2] William Wedgwood Benn, Lord Stansgate (b. 1877), son of Sir John Williams Benn, the L.C.C. Progressive leader, Liberal M.P. for Leith, became Labour M.P. in 1928: Secretary for India, 1929–31, and for Air, 1945–6.
[3] Sir Percy Alfred Harris (1876–1952), Liberal and Progressive. Liberal M.P. for South-West Bethnal Green, 1922–45, and L.C.C. member for the same division, 1907–34 and 1946–52; the last Progressive member to sit on the L.C.C.

elderly wives, widows and spinsters trooping into the polling booths, clutching the Conservative polling card as a talisman of safety against the nationalisation of women and the confiscation of all property from millionaires' millions to Post Office savings.

All the same the débâcle of the Parliamentary Labour Party has left sore hearts and angry minds among the rank and file. Exactly as the European prestige of MacDonald in the first months of the Labour Government was the big achievement of Labour in office, so the motor-car-cum-Communist[1] fiascos of the Prime Minister in the last few months has been the cause of the heaviness of the electoral defeat of the Parliamentary Labour Party. Defeated, Labour would have been anyhow, owing to the pact of Conservative and Liberals in the constituencies held by Labour minority representatives. Indeed in face of this mixture of blunders and prevarications garbed in the righteous indignation of a would-be-saint, it is astounding that the ranks of Labour remain so splendidly solid. But given reasonably sensible and straightforward conduct on the part of our leader, we should have maintained our number of M.P.s whilst increasing our vote by another half million.

Sidney reports that the last Cabinet held yesterday afternoon (only J. H. Thomas absent) discussed the meaningless report of [the] Committee appointed to go into the evidence about the Zinoviev letter. This *copy* of a letter came from the most trusted agent of the F.O. in Moscow on October 10th. It was communicated to the Secret Service departments of the War Office, Admiralty, Air Ministry and Scotland Yard for their observation: all these departments regarded it as a fake and merely added it to the pile of suchlike documents. The Foreign Office, however, after examination, came to the conclusion that it was genuine and sent it on to the P.M. on the 16th. They did not show it to Ponsonby though he was at the Office when it came, nor even to MacDonald himself, when he was there on the 13th, apparently because it is not the Foreign Office habit to consider the Under-Secretary of any importance, and they wished to verify the letter before troubling MacDonald with it. From first to last they did not regard the letter of any electoral significance. They sent with the letter a draft reply. Subsequent proceedings on the part of the P.M. and the Foreign Office are public property.

At this last meeting of the Labour Cabinet, all the members were

[1] In March, 1924, MacDonald received from Alexander Grant, an old friend of his who was also the senior partner in MacVitie & Price's biscuit factory, a gift of £30,000 ordinary shares in the firm for the purpose of buying and keeping up a Daimler car; in the following May, Grant was made a baronet. These facts, disclosed in September, created a nine-days' buzz but little more; most people agreeing in the end that Grant's philanthropic services merited the honour, and that MacDonald had been guilty of no more than ineptitude. He gave up the car and the shares, however.

sympathetic with the P.M. Haldane made a pretty little speech and announced his retirement from politics and return to judicial work. MacDonald asked for opportunities for consultation among the leaders of the Opposition. The Labour Cabinet dispersed for the last time amid kindly words from one to the other. "No Committee to which I have belonged has been more harmonious in its proceedings than the Cabinet," sums up Sidney. And yet there has been little or no friendship or intimacy among the members except that J. H. Thomas has compelled the P.M. to talk over matters with him. In Lord Thomson the P.M. has found his pleasantest colleague because Thomson never talks shop for the good reason that he knows none! According to Henderson an immediate election on the withdrawal of the prosecution issue was decided on by the P.M. and Thomas, before the matter was brought before the Cabinet.

Here ends the episode of a Labour Government and also of a Minority Government—an episode which Sidney thinks, on the whole, good for the education of the Party—and as far as he is concerned, a good joke which like most good jokes ought not to be repeated. J. R. MacDonald remains an enigma: *we* certainly did not expect and cannot now explain either the brilliant success of his handling of the Franco-German situation or the shocking fiasco of the last phase of his Premiership—culminating in the complete collapse of any Cabinet leadership during the General Election.

November 6th.—This morning Sidney said goodbye to his department. The Board of Trade is perhaps the least arduous and significant of any of the older and larger Cabinet departments: it has been hollowed out by handing over all that relates to Customs, etc., to the Treasury; all that relates to employment of labour in industry to the Ministry of Labour; all that relates to mines to the nominal subordinate but really independent Department of Mines which the pushing Shinwell erected into a "*Ministry of Mines*"; all that relates to railways to the "*Ministry of Transport*". There is little left but Bankruptcy and mercantile shipping, patents and other odds and ends— all matters of administrative routine. The President is kept occupied with interviews and deputations—a sort of buffer between pressure of outside interests on the Cabinet or the Prime Minister. The post has suited Sidney; but it would have been better for the Party to have given it to Henderson so that he could have devoted himself to Eccleston Square; while Sidney, I think, would have been a more discreet administrator than Henderson at the Home Office. However, it was a pleasant office for Sidney; and he was certainly popular with everyone concerned. I doubt whether he will be again in office unless he is compelled sooner or later to go to the Lords in default of other peers—which I trust is not likely as it would diminish our income and raise awkward questions.

November 21*st*.—Three weeks in London has wearied and sickened me more than the fortnight's meetings in Seaham. The perpetual noise—night and day—and the seeing of persons I feel I must see, together with an unsuccessful attempt to do some reading for the book, has reduced me to a state of dizziness by day and sleeplessness by night which is almost intolerable. All I have accomplished is the monthly letter to my Seaham women; and various lunches and dinners to Labour men preparatory to retiring to Passfield. Great bitterness among the Left—especially among the Clyde men and among the defeated candidates. Henderson and Clynes and, I think, all the older and saner members of the Party are determined to keep J.R.M. as leader, feeling that once the Party acquires the habit of casting out leaders when they displease the Left, rot has set in. These two men are really public-spirited—for they both have cause to be bitter against the ex-P.M.—Clynes especially so. Wheatley is the "runner-up"— but I think he does not mean to be too previous in being "run" for the leadership. However, I should not be surprised if before Baldwin appeals to the electorate again, MacDonald will be out of the leadership of His Majesty's Opposition. If he is saved it will be by the loyalty of Henderson, Clynes, and Sidney and other members of the right wing.

The anguished discussions of the Liberals over their catastrophic defeat fill the columns of the *Manchester Guardian*, the *Daily News* and the *Westminster [Gazette]*. What is supremely interesting is thaᴛ all the correspondents who desire the survival of the Liberal Party as a possible Government or at any rate as an independent Opposition, talk almost hysterically about "Liberal principles" or "Liberalism", but when they come to describe their own faith or policy, they scatter in every conceivable direction—*always excepting protection*. Anti-socialism, anti-Trade Unions, super-tax, prohibition, mild Socialism, combination with the Labour Party, coalition with the Tories, all these varieties of political policies are there, either isolated or mixed. There is no *document* to which this extraordinary crowd can refer, as containing the creed of the Party; no leader to whom they turn for guidance; they are simply a crowd without being a herd—a crowd drawn together because they happen to dislike the two other political Parties. It seems inconceivable that they should succeed in becoming a Party—in spite of the pressure of many wealthy and some able men obstinately determined to keep Liberalism alive as a separate organised force. My own impression is that the present agitation will slowly simmer down and that before three years are up, the Liberal

Party will have practically disappeared. If the Labour Party is not let down by its leaders or wagged out of life by its tail, it must come into office the election after next. But it will have been permeated by the best brains of the younger generation of Liberals, and its policy will be decidedly mixed alike in means and ends.

MacDonald, Henderson, Clynes and Sidney lunched together after the Morel[1] Memorial Service (Thomas and Snowden being unavoidably absent) and the six are to meet again next week to discuss the internal affairs of the Party.

From what MacDonald said he is feeling a very cold current from the Clyde and from the disaffected I.L.P. members, and is even doubtful whether an attempt to run Wheatley for the leadership may not be made. Anyway he thinks that there will be trouble and that the Clyde will resolutely refuse to be led and will resort to obstruction and violent language on all sorts of questions, great and small. Also there being no Standing Orders no one knows on what plan the Party Executive will be elected. There may be an attempt to exclude ex-Cabinet Ministers on the part of the rank and file with the result that these will fall back on the shadow Cabinet—so that there will be two bodies. All of which is the reaction from an autocratic Prime Minister standing above and aloof from his Party. It is however curiously characteristic of the Labour Party that we none of us know *what is happening in the Labour Party*. The leaders so seldom see each other and are so reticent when they do meet. The I.L.P. has a life of its own; the Clyde is self-contained, the T.U. officials are dispersed in their homes all over the country and live within their own occupational circles—or at least within the Trade Union official world. Always friendly and polite, they are never intimate, and they seldom consult: except on immediate questions that must be settled one way or another. Otherwise any casual change might happen in the leadership or the constitution of the Party without the majority intending it. It is annoying to be at the very centre and yet to know so little about the life of this circle! Which tempts me to close my eyes to the present and concentrate on the past—and get on with my book.

December 2nd. Passfield.—At last in our dear new home and at the beginning of the last lap of life together—short or long. Surrounded at present with wage-slaves digging, planting, building and path-making —some dozen of them in all. Shocking sight—the aged Webbs adding acre to acre—the original eight has now grown to near twelve![2] laying out these acres in park-like avenues, cutting down trees to make

---

[1] Edmund Dene Morel (1873–1924), the great anti-slavery and anti-imperial propagandist, who wore himself out fighting exploitation in the Congo and elsewhere.

[2] Mrs. Webb's estimate of the size of Passfield Corner varied from time to time.

vistas, discussing with the expert from Kew (or rather bred at Kew) what trees and shrubs to plant—good to look at. We salve our conscience by assuring each other that we are preparing a country residence for the staff and students of the London School of Economics, but in our heart of hearts we see pictures of two old folk living in comfort, and amid some charm, writing endless works, and receiving the respectful attention of an ever larger public. But my greatest satisfaction is to get back to my particular work and to see before me a good year's work with few distractions. The chapter on *Observation and Experiment* I hope to finish well before Easter: the *Ways of Discovery* will provide me with a text for the spring and summer: and *if* I keep my health next winter may see me thinking out the final chapter with the prospect of publication in October 1926. "Then," say I to the Other One, "we will go for a holiday."

December 12*th.*—A fortnight ago J.R.M. wrote to ask me to entertain the ex-Cabinet to dinner before the meeting of Parliament to discuss the King's Speech—21 in all! Sidney answered for me that we could only dine twelve and suggested that the ex-Cabinet should all dine at the P.L. Club. MacDonald decided to break up the party for dinner between Trevelyan, Haldane and ourselves—all meeting at Haldane's to discuss the King's Speech. So we entertained J.R.M., Snowden, Buxton, Wedgwood and Thomas—two others allotted to us not being able to come.

The ex-Prime Minister is badly shaken in courage and self-confidence and I doubt whether he will recover his status in the Party. He is bitter against the Left—still more against the Communists—he feels he has enemies in Snowden and Wedgwood inside the Parliamentary Executive; a "runner-up" in Wheatley; friends in Henderson, Clynes and Sidney—not for love of him but from realisation that anyone else as leader would be worse. What exactly is the I.L.P. attitude I do not know; there is a bodyguard of devotees; on the other hand there is the growing hostility of the Clyde—there is Brailsford who is at heart contemptuous and shows it in his writing. How far men like Trevelyan are loyal to Mac I am not sure. C.P. is playing an astute hand which I do not understand—it is conceivable that he also is a "runner-up" for the Premiership. I am inclined to think that Mac's successor as Labour P.M. is not yet in sight. But whoever he is he will have a hard run for it!

The Parliamentary Executive is going to be the dominating force in the life of the Labour Party during its term of Opposition and though it is not predominantly Left in composition, it is not pro-MacDonald—the three last on the list given below being his greatest friends—possibly also W. Graham?

The Executive was selected by sending out to every member the whole list of M.P.s so that votes must have been considerably scattered if the result is scanned. Sidney did not fare well with only 23 votes, the smallness of his vote I attribute to the I.L.P. caucus. Henderson also, considering his high status in the Party and his magnificent service, is remarkably low down. Wheatley and Trevelyan were selected to move the official amendment to the Address—which is again significant—and Thomas and Wedgwood to wind up.

Mr. G. Lansbury	67
Mr. R. Smillie	65
Rt. Hon. P. Snowden	62
Rt. Hon. J. H. Thomas	53
Rt. Hon. J. Wheatley	52
Mr. J. Maxton	51
Rt. Hon. C. P. Trevelyan	45
Rt. Hon. W. Graham	43
Rt. Hon J. C. Wedgwood	40
Rt. Hon. A. Henderson	38
Mr. H. B. Lees Smith	38
Rt. Hon. F. O. Roberts	34

Ex-officio

Chairman and Leader	J. R. MacDonald
Deputy Chairman	J. R. Clynes
Chief Whip	Ben Spoor

PART II

1925

FEBRUARY 1925—DECEMBER 1925

February 12th.— . . . Work accomplished: a complete chapter on *The Field of Enquiry* (30,000 words at least) finished—an elaborate piece of work, showing the stimulating social environment in which I began to practise the craft of a social investigator—leaving for another chapter, on Observation and Experiment, my own experiences. Also a long letter to the Seaham women (2,900 words) mainly about Russian Communism—not a bad output for ten weeks. Now I have to break off to clear out of that part of Grosvenor Road that we have let to Susan Lawrence and to write the February letter to the Seaham women. Today after a rackety three days in London I am feeling desperately the worse for wear, and I shall not get back to the Book until the first week in March. But it is a comfort to have a real home to come to! And Sidney has been very happy here getting on with the Poor Law book and picking out extracts from political biographies for his study on Cabinet Government.

We have had little political news. A visit from Lord Arnold brought us some gossip; so did a dinner alone with Haldane, who by the way has joined the Fabian Society! Arnold told us that he was actually touring with J.R.M. when the latter received the Zinoviev Letter, but he —Lord Arnold—was not given any inkling of it though the P.M. said to Arnold's brother, with whom they were staying, that he had received "very serious news" from the F.O. Secretiveness seems almost an obsession with J.R.M. Ponsonby, who was lunching here, told us that from first to last he was not consulted; though he had had complete charge, with no opportunities of consulting with P.M., of the Russian negotiations. MacDonald shows no signs of making it up with the Left, and at the reception of the P.L.C. at Mortimer Hall the night before the re-assembling of Parliament, at which J.R.M. spoke, though there were twelve members of the ex-Government, not a single prominent I.L.P. member put in an appearance. The I.L.P. and Clyde members are not abusive but they are very cold and go straight forward with their "pure Socialism" policy, without paying the remotest attention to anything J.R.M. or other front-benchers say. Arnold told us that at the meeting of the ex-Cabinet at Haldane's house the night before the opening of Parliament in December he stayed behind with Snowden and Thomas and that they were discussing the probability of the split in the Labour Party—they and other members of the Right joining the Liberals to form a new party! So perturbed were they about the doings of the I.L.P.! Personally I sympathise with the I.L.P.—we of the Right are too damned comfortable, and we are sinking into a senile complacency with things as they are. The world as it is is far too agreeable for all the members of the Labour Party who belong, in effect, to the governing class. What the Left propose is frequently neither practicable nor desirable; but the Right is not leading the Party forward; it is merely hanging back in the attitude of the "Thoroughly Comfortable". How difficult it is for the well-to-do to lead the very poor towards the promised land!

Two political events have taken place outside the Parliamentary Labour Party, which will influence its development: the gathering of the Liberals and the T.U. Delegation to Russia and their report.

The gathering of the Liberals on the much-advertised proposal for raising the one million fund was a fiasco from what one hears and sees in the press. The assumption, without re-election, of the leadership by Asquith after he had accepted a peerage was resented, and the prospect of Lloyd George as second in command did not improve matters. No one believes that the Liberal Party will raise even £100,000 unless some wealthy members put down large sums—and even this seems unlikely as there is nothing to buy with the money. The Liberals have no policy: one third of the party is individualist, another third are labour-collectivist—another third are protectionist or imperialist. "Stragglers" will join the Conservatives at the next election.

When I looked down from the Ladies' Gallery last Tuesday it was a shock to see no Liberal on the front opposition bench; and to watch Lloyd George ("Trimblerigg")[1] almost a comic figure gesticulating from under the Gallery. Whatever else has happened the Liberal Party as a force in the country is dead and gone. The only chance for the remnant is the possibility of a split in the Labour Party and the formation of an entirely new party by some of the Labour leaders. If the T.U. levy were to disappear and the Trade Unions themselves develop serious rifts this might happen; but the British working-class is conservative in its ways, and now that it has taken to a Labour Party it is not likely to turn back or break up into two hostile forces. The spirit of the Lord is predominant in the English people, especially in the working-class, owing to the pressure for a hundred years of the "Great Industry".

---

[1] *Trimblerigg*, a satirical political novel by Laurence Housman, published in 1924. Its chief character was generally assumed to be a study of Lloyd George.

February 20th.—Ran up to London for two or three days to attend Labour Party Reception and make arrangements with Susan Lawrence to take over two floors of Grosvenor Road, drawing-room with study and two second-floor bedrooms, leaving us with dining-room, two attic bedrooms and box-room—for £200 a year unfurnished—a sum which will cover all our out-goings except service, lighting and heating. Now that we have the cottage with 9 acres of grounds, a gardener and his wife, I am making it into my permanent home, and Sidney's too, except for H. of C. days during the 6–9 months session. It seems wasteful to have Grosvenor Road on our hands even it were wise for us to afford it. But I felt that Sidney had a right to a comfortable abode close to the H. of C. even if owing to the noises and distraction I could not live there. Also he hates moving away from surroundings to which he is accustomed—the dining-room, with all his books and papers and Emily to look after him, is all that he requires. And we both like Susan Lawrence. When I have to be in London for a few days I would rather have someone else in the house to talk to—I can't work so I like to gossip! It seems an ideal arrangement especially after the solitude of this place. On both sides—may it turn out to be as good as it looks! . . .

February 20th.—The brilliant and venomous attack on J.R.M.— *The Diplomacy of Mr. Ramsay MacDonald*—just published in the *Labour Monthly* and now spread broadcast over the whole world—is the most damaging incident since the Zinoviev Letter. The internal evidence points to George Young* as the author, prompted and helped by Josiah Wedgwood. The worst of it is that whether or not the details of the indictment of his foreign policy is true the characterisation of J.R.M. is what we should have thought accurate twenty years ago! I have not followed the foreign policy—I have not the requisite knowledge—but all the moral and intellectual defects laid bare in this pamphlet one knows to be MacDonald's in other episodes of his life. The feeling of the I.L.P. seems to get bitterer every day, and if J.R.M. fails to go to the I.L.P. Conference at Easter there will be wholesale disaffection and he will fall from the leadership of the Party next year—to be replaced by? It is conceivable that they might put back Clynes—the I.L.P. could not carry Wheatley nor could the Right carry Thomas, and Snowden is held back by the hatred of his wife. There is no first-rate man as yet in the Parliamentary Labour Party—for that matter in the Labour movement very few who are equal to the front bench. . . .

* George Young denies authorship: there is some suggestion that it is partly C.P.T. [Trevelyan]. [B.W.].

March 2nd.—Four days moving out of the drawing-room, two second floor bedrooms and study of Grosvenor Road to let in Susan Lawrence . . . Oddly enough having got rid of the money drain and any obligation to entertain I think I shall be more ready to stay in London than if I had the whole house! There will be no responsibility nor worry, and freedom to go to picture-galleries or concerts or the theatre when one is up there! Also I like Susan Lawrence and shall enjoy occasional chats and gossip with her. And I have no sentimental regrets in giving up the drawing-room where I have sat with Sidney and entertained all sorts and conditions of men and the bedrooms we have jointly occupied for thirty-two years. Never to see them again in the form we knew them, seeing that Susan is redecorating according to barbaric or modern (?) taste. I am really tired of London life. All the same I shall like to return now and again to the old dining-room where we have written large portions of our books. And as far as Sidney is concerned so long as he can come down every morning to his coffee and his newspapers in the old room with all his books and papers about him he is quite satisfied except that I am absent!

March 19th.—Spent three days, one with Lion [Phillimore] at Radlett, two with the B. Shaws. G.B.S. in excellent spirits: back from Madeira, feeling very successful and fully appreciated. His prestige since the publication of *St. Joan* has bounded upwards, everywhere he is treated as a "great man", and his income must be nearer thirty than twenty thousand a year! Charlotte purring audibly; these two are very happy together and both are full of kindness towards old friends and new.

The Booths were delighted with my account of Charlie and his work and very complimentary about the chapter generally. At Charlotte's request I am sending them the four chapters: I don't think G.B.S. will find the time to read it all. I suppose I am tired, but I have become rather morbid about the book—far too anxious for its success and counting too much *on its being a success*. I don't think Sidney quite likes it: he does his best to approve, still more to help me; but there is something about it that he—not exactly resents—but which is unsympathetic. In his heart he fears I am over-valuing it, especially the extracts from the diaries—the whole thing is far too subjective, and all that part which deals with "my creed" as distinguished from "my craft" seems to him the sentimental scribblings of a woman, only interesting just because they are feminine. However I have enjoyed writing it and the book as a whole will have *some* value as a description of "*Victorianism*". But I must try and not get self-conscious about it like Graham Wallas is about that book they have been so long incubating. Old people ought to be *less* anxious for applause. Poor dears, I am afraid they are more affected by personal vanity than the young. It is now or never with them! . . .

May 1st.—Three successive weeks spent, in eight days at Seaham, a week at Freshwater with Kate Courtney recovering from the strain of public speaking, and five days in London having thirteen teeth out, on the likelihood that pyorrhea was responsible for my depression of spirits and general malaise of the last months. Now I have six months to complete the book and if possible to get it printed. It is time I did so because the dragging on of this task and the uncertainty as to whether I have been right to undertake it is becoming nerve-racking. G.B.S.'s letter is encouraging though he is evidently puzzled as to what will be its fate—whether it will be a success or a failure on publication. Charlotte does not like it (I gather from her letter) in the main because her uncle, Brian Hodgson, is not sufficiently appreciated! Which balances the Booths' admiration because *their* great man *is* hero-ized. And then Charlotte does not really like me any more than I really like her: our continued friendly and mutually respectful relations and quite genuine loyalty and friendliness towards each other are a testimony to good manners in the widest sense—to tolerance and kindliness on both sides.

Assuming that I get back my normal health I shall have done with the book and all its problems of discretion, frankness, and freedom from self-consciousness in six months' time. Meanwhile as the Parliamentary session advances I am more than ever glad that we have retired to the country and back to our books: life in London would have been a dreary business. The Parliamentary Labour Party, with all its struggling personalities, young members and old, its little cliques, I.L.P., Clyde, Trade Union, pro-MacDonald, anti-MacDonald, is not an altogether agreeable milieu for Sidney to work in. The next few years will see him more and more inclined to retire from the fray and spend the few years left to us in finishing up the researches we have begun. We must not allow ourselves to become depressed because our careers are behind us: when you are nearing seventy that is inevitable. The bitter fate is to feel baulked when you are young or in the prime of life: we have had our cake and we have thoroughly enjoyed eating it. Now we must be content to help others to do likewise.

Sidney dined alone with the Parmoors last night, I being too exhausted by teeth extraction to go. He reports that Alfred dislikes working with Haldane in the House of Lords and distrusts him and all his works. Says he is hand-in-glove with Baldwin and Birkenhead and very busy with the Imperial Defence Committee—all of which we knew. Haldane has one overpowering impulse: he likes to be and to feel himself to be behind the scenes at the seat of power. That is one reason he came over to Labour; that is why he has always been anxious to collaborate with any Government—Tory, Coalition, as well as Liberal. Being himself in office was only a slightly superior form of being in power. It remains to be said he is personally loyal to old friends even when they are not in power. With Alfred he has never been friends and for him he has a kindly contempt; regards him as an amateur in politics and without political capacity. Alfred is a deeply religious man and his political opinions and activities are merely the extension of orthodox Christian ethics to public affairs. What puzzles me is why did J.R.M. go so far out of his way to secure Haldane as his Lord Chancellor? He must have known that Haldane stood for all that he, MacDonald, had denounced; he knew him to be an imperialist in foreign affairs and national defence, and somewhat cynical on all home issues. Was it a common hatred of Liberalism—of Asquithian Liberalism—that drew them together? Or was it simply to form an impressive Cabinet?

May 23rd.—Five days in London finishing up the dental operation successfully and gossiping with friends in intervals. Susan Lawrence in great state of delight over C. P. Trevelyan's attack on MacDonald in Committee of Foreign Affairs about his complaisance to Foreign Office officials and his handling of Zinoviev Letter, and, demanding, on behalf of the Party, a definite assurance that the next Labour Foreign Secretary would insist on (1) having his own *private secretary* with his own opinions and (2) put the Under-Secretary definitely above the permanent head of the office. Told J.R.M. that if he had consulted Arthur Ponsonby or any of his colleagues in the Cabinet he would never have drafted the letter to Rakovsky.[1] From Colonel Williams, who was also present, I heard the same story told in criticism of C.P. and in praise of J.R.M.: how C.P. was tense with passion and refused to consider the evidence about the attitude of the Foreign Office officials, always asserting the opinion of the Foreign Office officials held by the Parliamentary Labour Party, as if that were the decisive fact whether or not that opinion was justified. "Trevelyan is playing for the leadership of the I.L.P. and through that for the Chairmanship of the P.L.P.," remarked the cynical Galton. Then the General Council of the T.U.C. are apparently deciding to break up their present connection with the Labour Party, and there are rumours that they are taking over the Labour Research Department as their

[1] Christian Georgievich Rakovsky, born 1873 in Bulgaria, became Bolshevik leader in the Ukraine in 1917. Soviet representative in London, 1923-5, and Ambassador to France, 1925-7. Exiled 1928.

organ of information and are looking out for offices away from those of the Labour Party. It looks as if they are going the way of the C.G.T.[1] in France before the War, though I doubt whether the rank and file of the T.U. movement or even the T.U. officials in the provinces will let this happen. "There are the many T.U. officials who are looking forward to a political career," observes Sidney. The simple truth is, that owing to MacDonald's loss of prestige—to the universal distrust and disillusionment of the active workers—the inner circles of the Labour Movement are more at cross-purposes than I have ever known them before. What MacDonald is counting on is that this feeling is confined to the few thousands of active workers and that the mass of the Labour voters are still under the spell of his distinction and charm as the first Labour Prime Minister.

And now when I have got through my June letter to Seaham with a long pull and a strong pull I will finish the book and have done with it!

June 9th. 2 a.m.—Indigestion and sleeplessness. The book drags on and I sometimes wonder whether I shall end it, or whether it will end me! Perhaps I and the book will end together. Not that I think I shall die; but I doubt whether I shall write another book—which means my end as a publicist. It is clear to me from Sidney's and Shaw's criticisms that I must shorten the extracts from the diaries—which as the M.S. is getting far too long will be all to the good. Also with my growing disillusionment—and I *am* disillusioned—the notion of another volume of *Our Partnership* is evaporating. What I *might* do would be to prepare my diaries without thought of publication. The other plan would be to go on with research. But I very much doubt whether I shall have the strength for that seeing that it would mean running up and down to London. I may have simply to vegetate here with garden, wireless and quiet reading and a few friends coming in and out and every now and again helping Sidney. For it seems to me that I may be sinking into the dim twilight of old age. Have I any longer any convictions? Am I becoming a mere shadow of an intellect? However I have felt the unreality of my intellectual life before and recovered.

What has upset me is growing uncertainty about the book; largely because the persons whose judgment I most value do not think much of it. G.B.S. and Charlotte for instance have been staying here for two or three days; he asked me somewhat perfunctorily how it was

---

[1] The *Confédération Générale du Travail* from its foundation in 1902 held strongly syndicalist and anti-Parliamentary views. "M. Renard of the Textile Federation," wrote G. D. H. Cole in *The World of Labour* (1913), "regularly proposes reaffiliation with the Socialist Party, and is as often overwhelmingly defeated."

getting on but showed not the remotest desire to see any more of it; Charlotte has not even mentioned it, though she has been unusually affectionate and appreciative of the comfort and attraction of our new home. Laski, to whom I gave it, was interested in the first two chapters —was cold about the others—and left the impression of non-approval —certainly no special admiration. What I have to be constantly dinning into my mind is that one's work is never so good and never so bad as one thinks it in days of inflation and days of depression. Anyway, it is clear, I have got to finish the book and publish it, if only to rid myself of this morbid anxiety about this child of my old age. I have to make it as good as it can be made as a help to other students— the "finish" has to be perfect, for upon the perfection of the finish will depend its usefulness to future generations. Courage, old lady, courage!

G.B.S. has been thirty days ill with a nasty attack of influenza. In spite of his amazing success in *St. Joan* he is dispirited for he, too, has become involved in a book which he cannot end—a book on Socialism, designed to explain matters to a stupid woman. It will be a marvel if it is not a bad book and I think he knows it is, and yet will not let go. He has spent too much time over it. We have had some talks together; it is clear he does not believe in the scientific method of observation, reasoning and verification. To him it is "Magic" used to bemuse others. "What we need is more thought—more new thought, *thoughts that will wake people up.*" By this he means exciting assertions, paradoxical arguments, new and strange meanings to common terms. For instance in the debate with Belloc last night he accused the R.C. church of being *ulra-rationalist—it had failed because it was rationalist*! Whilst Voltaire had succeeded in influencing mankind because he was an ingrained protestant. What he meant by rationalist was the *logical carrying out of the love of power*, his illustration or proof being "burning heretics"; whilst Voltaire was a spiritualist because he asserted the *right to that thought*. Of course there is a grain of truth in what he says; but he says it in the least convincing way. Then what he means by new thought is some hypothesis which will startle people, because it is wildly at variance with their own experience. To him it is irrelevant, whether it turns out to be in accordance with fact; so long as the idea has "troubled the waters", that is sufficient justification. He is the only able man I have ever known who denies not only the supremacy of the scientific method over other parts of human nature but its validity in any one of its innumerable operations: he might make an exception perhaps—though I am not sure—in the making of machinery, though even here he would say that it consisted in "trial and error", without any reasoning. To him the use of the intellect is limited to dialectical logic for the purpose of making men discard one idea for another so as at anyrate to get the direction of man's activities *changed*. What is terrible is to be bored by reiteration.

One change in G.B.S.'s mentality I note. He has lost his old habit of self-advertisement, of telling people that he is a great genius, that he is infallible. And this change is coincident with, even if it is not caused by, his late-won prestige. His self-esteem is fully satisfied. If he speaks of himself, which he seldom does, he suggests that he has lost his capacity, that he is "finished". And this is not by way of extracting a denial: it is unmistakeably genuine. "It is time we old people blew ourselves up," he muttered in an undertone. Charlotte is intent on his starting another play instead of meandering on with this work on Socialism. And I think she is right. He is a magnificent critic of life and a consummate literary craftsman: he is absolutely futile as a constructive thinker—he has no sort or kind of intellectual or moral consistency—all his solutions of problems, whether the problem be theoretical or practical, fall to pieces directly you examine or try them. . . .

June 21st.— . . . This amazingly indiscreet letter of J.R.M.[1] reveals a state of mind and manner inconsistent with the leadership of the Parliamentary Labour Party. Sidney says that MacDonald talks of nothing but his new house and the arrangement of his books; appears absorbed in pleasure of cultivated and elegant social intercourse. "It may be," Sidney adds, "that one day he will resign the Chairmanship." It almost looks as if Lansbury's saying to Susan Lawrence that J.R.M. and J.H.T. were arranging some sort of concordat with Lloyd George by which a new party uniting the right of the Labour Party with the Liberals would take office after the next general election [? was correct]. Otherwise why should MacDonald flout the Left? Is it only a childish giving way to bad temper?

Foreign affairs are becoming exciting; not the endless controversies centring at Geneva (I have long ceased to follow the difference between the Pact and the Protocol or to attempt to unravel what is

[1] This refers to a resolution of protest sent up by the Partick (Glasgow) branch of the I.L.P., when MacDonald had stated in a letter to a Bulgarian Socialist that three British Labour men who had recently toured that country were not an official delegation and represented nobody. The Partick resolution provoked MacDonald to the following outburst:

"What does the Partick branch mean by passing such a resolution? Perhaps it would mind its own business and regard Socialism, not as the creed of a lot of blithering easie-oosie asses, who are prepared to pass any resolution without knowing its meaning, and on any subject without understanding it, but as something which requires rectitude of thought and consideration of action. . . . I really would advise your branch not to interfere in matters that it knows nothing about, and to refrain from passing resolutions which show not only their inability to state the facts, but their equally great inability to come to any conclusions about them."

This use of a sledge-hammer to crack a very small local nut gave great pleasure to the opposition press.

happening to the French policy of keeping Germany permanently disabled) but two events: the coalition between Catholics and Socialists to form a Belgian Cabinet[1] on the one hand, and, on the other, events in China. The first marks the final disappearance of the old embittered feud between secularist-socialist and Christian or Catholic political democracy—a feud which never worked in Great Britain but which devastated the Continent. But far more significant is the anti-foreign movement in China organised or helped on by Russian Communism.[2] For I am inclined to forecast a certain sympathetic understanding between the materialistic creed-autocracy of Soviet Russia with its superficial but strenuous centralised authority and the integration of China with its determination to assert a definitely Chinese civilisation against the Western world and its realisation that there must be a strong autocratic government based on rigidly exclusive caste but leaving the immemorial peasant life to go on unhindered, as it does in Russia to-day. China has neither the religious impetus nor cohesive public spirit; yet without some sort of concentrated purpose she cannot confront Western civilisation on terms of equality. A thousand years ago Mohammedanism might have done it if she could have believed in a God. The Gospel of Karl Marx with its complete materialism translated by the Russians into an autocratic Government may yield a basis for orderly life among the millions of China.

June 22nd.— . . . Sidney reports that the joint meeting of the G.C. of T.U.C. and the L.P. Executive was most disheartening. Robert Smillie with his little bodyguard of pseudo-Communists is trying his level best to damage the P.L.P. and cut off Trade Union support from MacDonald, and the General Council, which has always been restive, is now openly and defiantly so. For the first time for some years they have summoned a T.U. Congress on Unemployment without any kind of consultation with or participation of the Labour Party leaders. J.R.M. actually suggested to Sidney that there should be a meeting of "the old gang" to consult together about this growing disunity; but

[1] In the general election of April, the *Parti Ouvrier Belge* increased its vote by 100,000 and became the largest single party. After some discussion, a joint ministry of Socialists and Christian Democrats—the Poulet-Vandervelde Ministry—was formed, in which the Socialist Vandervelde was Foreign Secretary; it fell, however, in the following year.

[2] This allusion is to the anti-foreign, and particularly anti-British, riots in China, which began in May when the police of the International Settlement in Shanghai opened fire upon a demonstration of students. This demonstration had possibly been inspired by the publication of the testament of Sun-Yat-Sen (who had died in March) which demanded *inter alia* the abolition of the special rights held by aliens in China. A boycott of British goods in South China followed, and in 1926 the revived Kuomintang, then enjoying Communist advice and help, began the march which eventually reached Nanking.

both Sidney and Henderson thought that would not be desirable. If it got out that there was such a meeting the Parliamentary Labour Executive, instigated by Smillie and Lansbury, would be on their hind-legs. The plain truth is that J.R.M. has lost all his morale with the P.L.P. as well as with the inner councils of the T.U. movement, and his growing alienation from the I.L.P. is only symbolic of a general "rotting" of his influence. He is also suffering from professed arthritis and looks very ill. He still commands big audiences, but he has no body of ardent friends and is getting more and more isolated. But no one is coming to the front: at present it is chaos. According to J.R.M. the recent by-election[1] showed a current against Labour, owing to the flirtation with communism, tariffs and birth control; and he declares that by this chaotic extremism the Labour Movement is recreating the Liberal party. Certainly the Liberals must be smiling in very broad smiles over the revolutionary speeches of Smillie, Maxton, Lansbury and Cook,[2] on the one hand, and, on the other, the vision of J. H. Thomas in frock coat and top hat at Ascot and J.R.M. taking tea with their Majesties at the Air Force pageant! Poor old Labour Movement: you will get the power your leaders deserve and I fear it will be a minus quantity. Mussolini is far more probable than Lenin; but Mussolini will not be needed; the Capitalist ascendancy can do without the autocrat; it is broad based on the solid sense of the British People, so long as there is no practicable alternative Government—and at present the Labour Party is *not fit to govern* and shows no signs of becoming so.

Meanwhile the position for Socialism is not hopeless—quite the contrary. Fabian Socialism is being more and more accepted. But to-day it does not look like being carried out by a Labour-Socialist party based on the Trade Unions. If J.R.M. had been a man of fine character and a convinced Socialist he might have guided a powerful Socialist party; he had the necessary artistic gifts, the personal charm, the sonorous voice, the untiring energy and the sympathetic manner with those he liked. But he is an egotist, a poseur, and snob, and worst of all, he does not believe in the creed we have always preached—he is not a Socialist and has not been one for twenty years; he is a mild radical with individualist leanings and aristocratic tastes. And yet he has pretended to be in sympathy with the simple-minded and ignorant enthusiasts of the I.L.P. and the Clyde.

[1] Either the Ayr District of Burghs (June 12th), whose result was:—Colonel Moore (C.), 11,601; P. J. Dollan (Lab.), 8,813; W. M. R. Pringle (L.), 4,656: or Eastbourne (June 17th) whose result was: Admiral Hall (C.), 12,741; Harcourt Johnstone (L.), 5,386; Colonel Williams (Lab.), 3,696.
Both showed a drop in the Labour poll.
[2] Arthur James Cook (1884-1931), the fiery left-wing miners' leader from South Wales, became general secretary of the Miners' Federation of Great Britain in 1924.

What puzzles me is the gross discrepancy between the alarmist views, held not only by left-wing Labour men but also by competent Conservatives and Liberals, about the industrial decadence of Great Britain—confronted by the absence of all *signs* of extreme poverty among the people at large. Compared with the eighties, even with the early years of the 20th century, *there is no outward manifestation of extreme destitution*: no beggars, few vagrants, no great and spontaneous demonstration of the unemployed, no "bitter outcries" or sensational description of sweaters' dens and poverty-stricken homes; no Lord Mayor's Fund or Soup Kitchens. Also even in one of the "stricken trades"—cotton—there is a bigger holiday exodus from Oldham this year than there has ever been, and £300,000 is being spent by Oldham folk on this year's wakes. In the mining areas— again one of the black spots—there is no appearance of the poverty which we have been led to expect. The Communists are dwindling; Socialism is certainly not making headway, and the more revolutionary the utterance of Labour men the less inclined are the people of England to listen to them. Are the mass of the people of Great Britain getting poorer or not? That is a question which I cannot get answered. Certainly our own class is getting no poorer: in spite of the enormously increased taxation and high prices we "rentiers" are just as well off as before the war—for the simple reason that we are getting 5-6 per cent as against 3-4 per cent for our money. Are the people of England spending their income *more wisely than before and therefore getting better value for the same income*—is the relatively *large* amount spent on common services an enormous advantage? What is the explanation of this curious combination of the permanent unemployment of 11 per cent of the population with a general sense of comparative prosperity on the part of the bulk of the population—a prosperity which is reflected in the diminished death-rate and the general appearance of the children at school—the common people in the trams and the streets, and also in the absence of spontaneous revolutionary feeling? Or are we living in a fool's paradise fostered by the Press—are we living in some abstruse way on credit—running up debts which some day we shall have to pay?

July 4th—What we old people have to be continually recalling to our minds is that however desirable it may be to go on working, we have to resign ourselves to becoming nobodies, we have to take our lives lightly as if one's continued existence was of little consequence to ourselves or to anyone else. It is silly to worry because one can't work as one used to: obviously it is only a question of a few years before one will be tumbling out of life, in one way or another, and the only thing to be done is to tumble out of it as gracefully as possible, without making oneself a nuisance to younger folk. Now that I have recovered my sanity I feel ashamed of myself for worrying over the book I am writing or troubling myself over Sidney's comparative inactivity in the House of Commons. He may be quite right to leave the field clear for the younger men and remain a silent member. If the majority of M.P.'s were not silent, Parliamentary Government would become impracticable. So long as the old do not obstruct the young, so long as they take back seats and don't worry, they serve as part of the necessary audience for the actors: they can even offer a useful suggestion, if not a criticism, now and again! . . .

August 8th.—Hendersons came down for the week-end. He is full of the decline of MacDonald's influence owing to his recent lapses of good sense—refusing to speak or even write a letter for Purcell in the Forest of Dean election,[1] and his extraordinary speech after the débâcle of the Government before the combined obstinacy of the miners and mine-owners, denouncing the subsidy[2] on the grounds that Baldwin had given way to communistic direct action! What Hendersons says is that these incompetencies are the result of MacDonald's exclusive association with a "smart set"; the only members of the Labour Party he consorts with are the De La Warrs, Thomson and Mosley and J. H. Thomas and one or two smart ladies, whilst he is constantly in the company of the great who emphatically don't belong to the Labour Party. There are about thirty Labour Members, the Clyde, Lansbury, Wedgwood, and, Henderson adds, Trevelyan, who have made up their minds to turn MacDonald out of the leadership, and Henderson prophecies that they will succeed. Henderson favours Snowden and says the I.L.P. and the Clyde will support him.

Sidney came down for good last week with a heavy cold and considerably exhausted. He has quite made up his mind not to stand at the next election and has told Henderson so. It is clear he can be of

---

[1] Forest of Dean election result: A. A. Purcell (Lab.), 11,629; M. W. Beaumont (U.), 8,607; H. West (L.), 3,744.

Albert Arthur Purcell (1872–1935), by trade a french polisher, became an organiser for the Furnishing Trades Association and a member of the General Council of the T.U.C. He sat for Coventry from 1923–4, and was a strong supporter of alliance with Russia.

[2] At the end of July, negotiations between the miners and the coal-owners, who were trying to force a reduction in wages, had reached an *impasse*; lock-out notices had been issued, and Baldwin had stated that it was necessary for workers in all industries to accept lower wages. A national conference of Trade Union Executives, convened by the General Council, ordered an embargo on the movement of coal, and empowered the General Council to call a strike on any scale that seemed necessary. The Government, which had refused to intervene, thereupon gave way, offered the industry a subsidy for a period of nine months, and set up a new Commission (the Samuel Commission) to investigate the industry. Meantime it set about making preparations for the struggle foreseen when the subsidy should run out. See pp. 89 ff.

little further use to the Labour Party; the turmoil within the Party is too great; only the young and vigorous man can swim in those troubled waters and it is a waste of his remaining energies to walk through the lobbies and at best lead at Standing Committees—the younger men can do that—he is more use finishing up our books. We have got to settle into our last home before we cease to be able to adapt ourselves to new conditions.

August 17th.—I have pasted in this page of to-day's *Daily Herald* because it expresses the "headiness" of the leaders of the left wing brought about by Baldwin's surrender to direct action.[1] The direct action was inevitable owing to the cynical arrogance of the coal-owners and non-redress of grievances by Parliament; the surrender of the Government was plausible as a way of gaining time to meet an unforeseen exhibition of strength by the Trade Union movement, a war which would have reacted, in a calamitous way, on national prosperity. All the same the turn of events means a tremendous accession of popularity and apparent power to the left wing of the Labour Party. The I.L.P. and their middle-class friends, fearing to be superseded, *as the left wing*, by the communistic T.U. leaders (Cook, Purcell and Co.) are plunging head over ears into grandiose schemes of immediate and revolutionary changes, in the interests of the workers. Most of their proposals—Mosley's state organisation of credit, for instance—are as impracticable as they would be mischievous if carried out; whilst Maxton's notion that if it came to a stand-up fight by *direct action*, against the continuance of capitalist enterprise *as an institution*, the workers would win is pathetically absurd. Of course all this talk may fizzle out. Red Friday may be succeeded by another Black Friday[2] next year, the miners being left to fight alone. But if the General Council of the T.U.C. were really to put into execution their threat of a general strike there would be a repetition of 1848 on a far more imposing scale. If I had to prophesy I should forecast some such catastrophe to the Labour Movement as the price of a return ticket to sanity. Who will emerge as the leaders of this saner movement I do not know—not J.R.M. or Thomas, not Clynes or Henderson, though these two trusty men will be in the leading group; not Snowden, he is hampered by his wife and has not sufficient elasticity. Of men

[1] The page pasted in contains two columns of fiery attack by Arthur Cook, speaking in South Wales, and James Maxton addressing the I.L.P. Summer School—both on the theme that "the master class would fight every inch of the way and would use every weapon", but that the workers "by the use of well-organised and industrial power could bring Capitalism to its knees".

[2] April 15th, 1921—the day on which two of the partners in the Triple Alliance, the N.U.R. and the Transport Workers, went back on their promise to strike in support of the Miners; regarded in the Labour Movement as the first great post-war betrayal, the second being MacDonald's action in 1931.

now in the front rank, Snowden and Henderson are the most likely to lead or be among the leaders. But I doubt whether, after the almost inevitable class conflict of the next twelve months, any of the "old gang" will dominate the party. It might end in the break-up of the Labour Party. If the conflict were sufficiently bitter, and the defeat of the manual workers sufficiently disastrous, it *would* do so; and we might see a new party spring up out of the remnants of the Parliamentary Labour Party and dwindling liberalism. That is what Lloyd George and Thomas are busy engineering. But they won't succeed —no one trusts them—"Taffy was a Welshman, Taffy was a thief". Anyway *we* shan't be in it! though we might be writing about it. . . .

August 18*th*.—With Miss Piercy away for a fortnight's holiday; with Beveridge, the Mairs,[1] Laskis and Smellie[2] (in the bungalow) round about us, driving, walking and picnicing, and above all with the proofs of my six chapters rolling in, I am in a thoroughly idle mood and inclined to be lazy at any rate for ten days—before beginning my last chapter. When once I start on it, I don't think it will take me more than six weeks—at most two months—that will mean September or October, including a week at Seaham, leaving November and December for proof corrections and the appendices etc, so as to get quit of it in time to go to Sicily some time in January. We both of us want a change before we settle down permanently in the country, to the old life of reading and writing tempered with a due amount of neighbourliness—it looks as if we should find the associates of our old age more in the School of Economics than in the political world. If we have a sufficient income I should like to be helpful to the abler but poorer students and to the younger and less important lecturers. Our usefulness to the Labour Party is exhausted; all that remains to be done is to retire gracefully and graciously without taking sides in the coming struggle between the discredited Right and inflated Left. On balance, *my* sympathies are with the Left—their leaders are sounder in character and more honest in their convictions; they won't have the opportunity to carry out their wild and chaotic schemes—but they will put fear into the hearts of Conservatives (and Liberals) who will think out applications of alleviation and pass them into law and administration. Permeation of the upper and middle class will still be the main method of advance—fear taking the place of persuasion. But there will be a good deal of spluttering on both sides, and some nasty scraps between Reds and Blacks. . . .

[1] David Mair and his wife Janet, now Lady Beveridge and then secretary of the London School of Economics.

[2] K. B. Smellie, now Professor of Political Economy in the London School of Economics.

August 22nd.—The Philip Snowdens spent a long afternoon with us —he in the best of forms and she looking exceedingly attractive in black. Every time we meet they seem to be more "moderate" in opinion, more satisfied with the *status quo*, more hostile to the I.L.P. and left-wing Trade Unionists: Snowden said that he had tried to "convert" Wheatley—had chaffed him about his stunt that the capitalist system was falling to pieces and that there would be a Socialist revolution in 8 years. "Not in eighty years" said Snowden, "but we are going on very nicely to a modified capitalist system." Mrs. Snowden was full of anger against the "ca' canny" of the manual worker and wanted to preach "harder work" and more sense of obligation. In opinion, Snowden is now a collectivist liberal; Mrs. Snowden a liberal conservative; neither are Socialists and they are far more intolerant of revolutionary Socialists than we are.

Meanwhile the *expression* of the revolutionary Socialism becomes every day more conspicuous among the communistic Trade Unionists on the one hand and the I.L.P. on the other—the two rival left wings try to outdo each other. Maxton, Wheatley, Lansbury and Cook are the four leaders of this revolutionary Socialism, and judged by their public utterances they have really convinced themselves that the capitalist citadel is falling. In our opinion capitalism may be "in decay", but it is only by the slow erosion of private enterprise and increment of collective control that it is changing into the Socialist state. Any attempt to upset it suddenly and violently would mean its entrenchment against crumbling away—and possibly a fascist re-action, hampering Trade Union action, and the re-establishing the authority of the House of Lords. If it comes to anything like a fight—by which I mean an upheaval which would upset the comfort of the citizen— the capitalists will win hands down. The analogous outbursts in 1848 and 1889 were followed by the quiescence of 1850–70 and 1890– 1910 respectively. Any upheaval today will be followed by yet another period of quiescence which will last until 1940 or thereabouts. But by that time the controversy between capitalism and public administration will be a dead one; we shall have discovered the middle way! Manual workers and brain workers alike will be under the harrow of a "costing system" applied to all forms of production, distribution and exchange.

September 16th.——Sidney and I in our long walks in this delightful country constantly discuss the disturbed state of the Labour world and the swing to the left by that old stager the T.U.C. My own feeling is that we are too far removed from working-class life—too "thoroughly comfortable" in our way to be able to estimate the force of the new movement. A. J. Cook on behalf of the T.U. Left, and

Maxton and Wheatley on account of the Clyde, talk about immediate revolution—whilst George Lansbury thunders threats of the immediate dissolution of "capitalist civilisation". Sidney persists in his optimism: trade will get better, the Conservative Government will carry out virtual nationalisation of the mines and we shall slither along towards an equalitarian state as we have done towards a political democracy. The revolutionary talk may *delay* this evolution exactly as the French Revolution delayed the coming of political democracy—but it will not prevent it happening. And there will be no catastrophe. I don't feel so happy about it. It seems to me there *might* be a burst-up ending in collapse and a period of panic repression, similar to that of 1815–24. There is no leadership within the Labour Movement, and there is growing discontent; those who have courage have no intellect and those who have intellect have no courage. *We* are too old and too tired to be of use. My sympathies incline towards the Left; but I know too little about what is going on to have any opinion worth having. What comforts me is the thought that the birthrate goes down and the productive capacity of the nation goes up—*that* surely must lead to a bigger production of commodities and services per head *if we can only get the necessary adjustment between demand and supply.* That problem cannot be insoluble? . . .

September 19th.—"A depressing party" said I to Sidney as we travelled back from London late last evening from J.R.M.'s "house-warming" at Hampstead.

The surroundings were charming; an old Georgian twenty-roomed house stowed away in a romantic corner of old Hampstead, perched over a wide view of London. Inside all was dignified and attractive—books everywhere—the home of a scholar and a gentleman. The company was sparse and heterogeneous; a few Hampstead friends, four of the late Cabinet—Henderson, Thomson, Thomas and Sidney, five of the Under-Secretaries, Lord Arnold, Margaret Bondfield, Ammon, Greenwood and Alexander, one or two Labour M.P.s, a few Society dames and the Maurice Hankeys, who had strayed in out of curiosity. Our host looked very ill and was evidently depressed. . . . Thomas had less bounce than when I last saw him and no one was in good spirits. "I see nothing to boast of in the Stockport victory,"[1] said Henderson gloomily—"Labour wins the seat but it is the Liberals who are winning votes—*we* are not reaping the result of the unpopularity of the Government! What we've got to do is to ignore the T.U.C. and dominate our own conference." "If J.R.M. can't do that it's a bad look-out. Instead of going abroad he ought to settle

[1] Stockport election result: A. E. Townsend (Lab.), 20,219; T. Eastham (U.), 17,892; H. Fildes (L.), 17,296. Labour gained the seat.

down and win back his own party to his leadership. He's had his holiday at Lossiemouth not to mention Balmoral!" said I.

Lord Arnold came to lunch the day before for a walk and a talk. He is a singularly pleasant unaffected and useful member of the Party, a great success in the Lords and a devoted friend of MacDonald's: it is he who is taking him abroad. Arnold is cheery, thinks the T.U.C. is "all talk", that J.R.M. holds his own in the country, that Labour will settle down when they have sputtered a bit, that trade will improve and Liberals continue to come over to Labour. Of course he, also, is "thoroughly comfortable" and enjoys his present position as a successful representative in the House of Lords.

To sum up, being wise after the event, I think it was a mistake to have taken office as a Minority Government. MacDonald has too poor a character and was too casual and inexperienced. And the rest of the Cabinet were a scratch lot—*they looked better than they were*—they had too little faith—they were too accommodating to the manners and customs of a "Society" they had always denounced. And it was MacDonald who led them astray. . . .

September 19th.—Baron Palmstierna (Swedish Minister) motored down to lunch—he is an attractive and extremely intelligent man and likes us. We gather from him that the circle in which he moves—foreign diplomats and the British ruling class—political leaders of all parties and great industrialists and financiers—are *certain* Great Britain is going down in trade and wealth and that presently her credit will be severely imperilled. The brain-workers are inferior in training, the manual workers are ca' canny, and all have too high a standard of leisure and pleasure; the nation as a whole is slipping down the slope of casual and sloppy thinking into a period of great hardship and poverty, possibly revolution. One heard it all before—just before the Great War; I remember our friend Kato (Japanese Ambassador) saying almost exactly the same thing as Palmstierna said yesterday; but the cloud then was not bad trade—our trade was booming—but a rebel Ireland and our *incapacity for War*. Our Empire and trade were going to be destroyed by force of arms! because we could not or would not fight!

It does not, however, follow that our foreign and home critics are wrong today because they were wrong in 1914. Sidney still scoffs at the notion and refuses to agree to my selling our War Loan! He says the pessimism of the British ruling class is "calculated", whilst that of foreigners is the customary detraction of a powerful country by less favoured peoples. I simply have no opinion about it except that I think it is probable that Europe and the white race are declining from their high estate of dominance. About that I am not particularly distressed. With regard to wealth and especially the wealth of the upper and middle classes we should probably be a better people if we had less riches. And I can't believe [that] with the steadily increasing productivity due to science *the world as a whole* is going to get poorer. What I fear is that the working class may not have the capacity and the patience to go steadily and peacefully forwards towards the equalitarian state. They may sputter and ca'canny and get the worst of it. However that is their affair, they'll get the government they deserve. Oddly enough what is bad for our creed is good for our purse! If Lansbury and Cook succeed in upsetting the constitutional Labour Party, there will be no *capital levy* and there is just a possibility that a conservative re-action might carry anti-trade-union legislation and a tightening of all collective expenditure. The poor might again become poorer and the rich richer, as happened after the collapse of the revolutionary trade unionism of 1834. Again Sidney is optimistic in believing that the Conservative Government will go forward in our direction; that, exactly as the Labour Government failed to go rapidly forward, so the Conservative Government will find itself prevented from going backward. Public opinion in both cases will insist on the *middle way* —but it will be a collectivist middle way. In his heart of hearts I think he still believes in Fabian permeation of other parties as a more rapid way than the advent of a distinctly Socialist Government. A strong Socialist H.M.O., *very seldom in office*, he thinks would be the likeliest instrument of progress. Possibly Lansbury and Cook have after all their uses in keeping the Labour Party out of office.

September 27th.—Graham and Audrey Wallas here for two or three days. A "grand old man" in the art of lecturing, more especially for U.S.A. audiences. Much beloved, also, at the London School of Economics, of which he may be said to be one of the Fathers if not Founders. He is a dear old friend and I find him interesting to listen to. If one is too tired to talk oneself one just sets him off—and he flows on continuously into reminiscences and reflections. Sidney, who does not appreciate "unnecessary communications" even from me, is apt to get bored or impatient. But this visit they and we had something to talk about together; we three spent the time we were not working in our separate sitting-rooms, in reading each other's MS. books and criticising what we read! Graham brought twelve chapters down, Sidney submitted his great description of the eighteenth-century Poor Law, whilst I contributed my proofs. Graham's psychological treatise[1] is pleasant to read and full of suggestiveness, but it leaves no positive impression except that of general distrust of democracy and of governmental action. I asked him why he launched off into psychology when

[1] *The Art of Thought*, published 1926.

we stuck to the study of social institutions. He answered that, in 1898, he began to doubt his old faith in democracy; *did he or did he not believe in the psychological basis of democracy* as set out by the Utilitarians? He found he did *not* believe in the democratic theory of life and his books are the result. "But what is your alternative," I asked, "is there any better form of Government for Great Britain or for U.S.A.? I admit political democracy is no use for China and Russia, difficult for Italy—but for us?" "No reason to believe in a particular institution because there seems to be no better alternative institution," he replied. Which is logic but not common sense! . . .

October 2nd. 2 a.m.—"*The election of the Executive of the Labour Party.* The great surprise in the election of the Labour Party Executive is the defeat of Mr. Sidney Webb," was announced, in a clear tone of pleasant satisfaction, over the wireless last night.[1]

It was no surprise to me, though I confess to a slight shock when I heard it broadcast to millions of listeners! We both of us expected that he would be defeated and I had suggested last spring that he should not seek re-election. "I prefer to be compulsorily retired," he answered, "then I shall feel quite free to devote myself to our books."

Otherwise the Conference, from newspaper accounts and S.'s letters, has gone unexpectedly well for the Parliamentary leaders— more especially for J.R.M. who has done brilliantly—re-asserted his dominance. The Liverpool Conference of 1925, in fact, reminds me of the Dundee T.U. Congress of 1889 when the Socialists were completely routed by Broadhurst and Co. just because, like the Communists have done, they over-reached themselves in personal abuse of the Front Bench. The dramatic change from the neo-Russian Communism of the Trades Union Congress of a few weeks ago to the silent voting down, by a two million majority, of the successive Communist resolutions at the Labour Party Conference, is certainly baffling to the student of British democracy—for practically the two Conferences represent the same membership. It is all a question of platform leadership: in both cases the thousand delegates trooped after the man who sat on the platform and managed the business!

Today the question arising what will be the relation between the Executive that sits at 33 and the Executive that sits at 32 Eccleston Square? Henderson and Bramley[2] are hardly on speaking terms;

---

[1] The five elected to the Local Constituency Section of the Labour Party Executive (voted upon at that time by the whole membership of the Conference, including Trade Unions) were: Herbert Morrison 2,724,000, George Lansbury 1,967,000, Rhys Davies 1,550,000, Morgan Jones 909,000, Will Lawther 880,000.
[2] Fred Bramley (1874–1925), the Organising Secretary of the Furnishing Trades Association, and a strong partisan of alliance with Russia, became General Secretary of the T.U.C. in 1923.

Citrine,[1] the assistant secretary, who owing to Bramley's bad health, counts considerably, is communistic in sympathy, and Pugh,[2] who is anti-P.L.P., is Chairman of the General Council. On the other hand, Margaret Bondfield and J. H. Thomas are again on the General Council and they are forceful people. We shall look on, with interest, and if we live, we shall probably describe it, in the next edition of the *History*. One advantage of Sidney's defeat is that it will confirm his intention to retire from Parliament at the next general election. Some days ago he wrote to Herron[3] offering him the seat in so far as he has any influence in deciding who shall succeed him. Last session, partly on Henderson's suggestion, he offered the reversion to J.R.M.; but the latter felt himself pledged to Aberavon and safe there.

So ends Sidney's ten years' connection with the guidance of the Labour Party. Looking back on it I am quite satisfied; so, I think, is Sidney. He helped Henderson to build up the Party in those difficult years 1915–20, and now he can leave it in the hands of younger men with a clear conscience that *he* has not shirked the task; he has been relieved of his duties. *I* had already retired. After the fall of the Labour Government, I knew the day of the older statesmen was over! All that remains to be done is to settle Herron or some other young man in Seaham, whither we go on Sunday. If they like the prospect of Parliament perhaps the Herrons may join us there.

Should there be an industrial upheaval next spring, which I am beginning to doubt, there may be a general election this time next year on the issue of "Is the Community to be master in its own home—if so give us power to put down general strikes." . . .

October 29th. 5 a.m.—*Done it*: and never before have I been so relived to see the last words of a book; for never before have I been so utterly and painfully uncertain as to its value. In all the former books, from *Trade Unionism* down to *Statutory Authorities*, there has been no great expectation on the one hand, and no fear of ridicule on the other. Our books have a restricted but certain sale; the subjects are not popular but our work has a monopoly value; every book is always one of the best, if not the best work on the subject. But autobiographies and reminiscences are almost as thick on the ground as novels; they are judged by good critics as works of art, not as works of information. Whether they interest the multitude depends on the

---

[1] Walter McLennan Citrine, Lord Citrine (b. 1887), originally an electrician from Merseyside, became Assistant Secretary to the T.U.C. in 1924, and General Secretary after Bramley's death.

[2] Arthur (Sir Arthur) Pugh (1870–1955), steel smelter and General Secretary of the Iron, Steel, and Kindred Trades Association. Long a leading Trade Unionist, and though distrustful of the Parliamentarians, certainly not Communist in sympathy.

[3] The Rev. J. D. Herron, Sidney's agent at Seaham.

vogue of the person who happens to be the author. Idiotic stuff by the Prince of Wales would sell better than the greatest autobiography in the world by an unknown "Smith". Added to this uncertainty is the unpleasantness of selling your personality as well as your professional skill, you are displaying yourself like an actress or an opera singer—you lose your privacy. But to-day the book is done and in spite of all opinion to the contrary, I believe it is well done! The relief is enormous. By the time it is published I shall be absorbed in another work. It is certainly odd how completely detached one becomes from a piece of work. Once it is published one barely thinks of it and never looks at it—unless one wants to refer to it in the book one is writing!

. . . What troubles me is that before I die I should like to work out more completely than I have done in *My Apprenticeship* my conception of the place of religion in the life of man. All that is happening in the word to-day whether it be the absence of any definite rule of conduct, as we have it here in England, or the positive preaching of violence, oppression, and intolerance in Italy and Russia, or the cynicism of capitalist dictatorship in the U.S.A., confirms my faith in religion, as I understand it—that is the communion of the soul of man with the spirit that makes for righteousness, in order to raise human values and ennoble behaviour. But can you get the habit of prayer without a church and a rite? Is there not a technique of religion as there is of science and of art? And can you get good conduct without an agreed *rule* of conduct accepted by the faithful? Human nature in its weaker moments is so dependent on habits, so lost without companionship in thought and feeling. In my own life I have so often felt the lack of a church and a rite—that is why at times I have regretted giving up the national church. And yet to belong to any of the Christian churches would be professing what I do not believe to be true—that the half-mythical figure of Jesus of Nazareth is somehow or other an object of admiration, worship and prayer. The day is past for associating particular human beings, or anthropomorphic conceptions, with this straining after union with an all-pervading beneficence. And yet what can we put in the place of the incarnation of God in a particular man as the lover and lawgiver of mankind? Christ and Buddha have dominated the two greatest religions of the world; and even the Jew and the Moslem have had their divinely inspired Moses and Mahomet. We have authority *without infallibility* in science; why not leadership without infallibility in religion and morality? My real trouble is that I do not admire, still less reverence, human personality. All my religious feeling streams *away from it* to something higher.

November 10th.—Maurice Hankey, the Permanent Secretary of the Cabinet, and his wife spent a week-end with us. An attractive personality, trusted and liked by all Cabinets in succession for the good reason that he likes them and is absolutely loyal and amazingly appreciative of the different statesmen he serves. A simple-minded soldier of the conventional type, devout Christian, a puritan in habits, a perfect gentleman in manners. He *assumes* that the men he serves are public-spirited however they may differ in opinion and in capacity. He has plenty of shrewd intelligence, but no intellect; abundance of good temper but no wit; irony or sarcasm would, I think, be inconceivable on his own part and somewhat unintelligible from others. "Who would you pick out among all the distinguished men you have worked with as the most *intellectually* distinguished?" I asked. "Lloyd George and Balfour," he answered—which hardly showed discrimination, for whatever else Lloyd George may be he is not a distinguished *intellect*, still less a distinguished character! Which is only another way of saying that Hankey, like other simple-minded persons, mistakes *power* over other people for real distinction of thought and feeling. But this absence of censoriousness—this slightness of critical faculty, combined with absolute integrity, kindliness and loyalty and quick-wittedness, make him an ideal secretary to Cabinets. If ever a man was perfectly suited to his job it is Maurice Hankey. And his wife is a fit mate—not so experienced but better cultivated and more open-minded. What with political gossip and exchange of experiences we four talked incessantly and thoroughly enjoyed ourselves. The Secretary of the Cabinet was chiefly anxious to bring about better relations between his masters and ex-masters; held that all governments had to toe the line of public opinion and that any *grave* divergence of policy was impracticable for English statesmen, whatever policy their party favoured. Which, in a sense, is true. Permeation of one British class or party, by another, still holds the field. *The middle man governs,* however *extreme* may seem to be the men who sit on the Front Bench, in their reactionary or revolutionary opinions.

After the Hankeys came the Parmoors, Alfred rapidly aging but soothed and comforted by the devoted and admirable Marian. In his old age he becomes more and more "Utopian"—he denounces "Capitalism" with more fervour than we do!—not on economic but on ethical grounds. The Parmoors and we have become warm friends. Before the Labour Government came in they were distinctly hostile, though always courteous and friendly in manner. Why Alfred was estranged from us between 1912 and 1924 still puzzles me! . . .

November 22nd.—The Shaws have been here for three days; Charlotte has taken a fancy to this cottage, or rather she now dislikes

Ayot and is glad to get away for visits. They are both at the top of their form. And they are good enough to be complimentary about the two last chapters of the book, quite unexpectedly so—especially G.B.S., who declares that my style has become like his and that he finds nothing to alter! Certainly he had made no corrections. Meanwhile he is putting in a great deal of work on *The Intelligent Woman's Guide to Socialism*: trying to reduce each thought to its simplest and most lucid expression "so that any fool can understand it". He is also meditating another play—on revolution or the coming of Socialism. I suggested to him the dilemma of a man of science turned politician —how far is he to say what he knows not to be true in order to get the majority to accept measures and administrations which he believes to be right?

What has always been disconcerting to me in G.B.S. are the sudden revolutions in his ideas. For instance two years ago he gave out that a child's thought should be left completely untrammelled by the authority or even by the influence of elders. To-day he is praising the Soviet practice of teaching a rigid Communist gospel to all children in all schools—compelling them to accept the "true word"—in this case the world of a militant minority. Of course he would be the first person to denounce such a policy (if it actually happened); it is merely the outcome of his impatience with contemporary influences—all the more absurd because what he wants is some chance for *the minority against the majority* and that could hardly be brought about by state autocracy in education: unless the minority seized power as they have done in Russia. G.B.S. never tests or finishes his processes of reasoning —it is all brilliantly expressed improvisations to meet new emergencies or to carry out sudden impulses, usually dislikes and indignations. Bertrand Russell has the same characteristics.

December 5th.—In another month we shall be leaving for our five weeks' holiday—a sort of watershed in our career. During the last three years Sidney and I have both been living a new kind of life—he in Parliament and I in literature—in a sense a separate life—though I have been helping him in his politics and he me with my book. Also we have changed our home from London to the country, I completely, he partially.

These three years have been nerve-racking and unless I had retired to the country I should have broken down and I doubt whether even he would have weathered it.

I have not exactly enjoyed my association with the Parliamentary Labour Party; I have done my level best, but there remains the fact that I dislike MacDonald and do not really respect him, and it is disagreeable to try to help a person you neither find agreeable nor think admirable. Sidney's other colleagues are, some of them—Henderson and Clynes for instance—men one admires and is interested in—but their companionship is not exciting! Perhaps I am too old to become acclimatised to a new social surrounding. Also I do not and have never liked political life—there is too big an element of intrigue—too continuous a conflict of personality—too little essential comradeship. That is not peculiar to the Labour Party. Look at the relations of the ex-Liberal Cabinet Ministers—men who worked together for twenty years or more—what has happened to all their friendships?—Haldane and Asquith, Lloyd George and Runciman?

My relations with the miners and miners' wives in Seaham, in so far as friendly feeling is concerned, has been the best part of the business.

The work on the book has exhausted health and strength and upset my state of mind. I have learnt a good deal from it—I have ruminated over my experience of life and the reflections have sometimes been pessimistic. Somewhere in my diary—1890?—I wrote *"I have staked all on the essential goodness of human nature"*—I thought of putting the entry into the book—I did not do so because it was too near the truth! Looking back I realise how permanent are the evil impulses and instincts in man—how little you can count on changing some of these—for instance the greed of wealth and power—by any change in machinery. We must be continually asking for better things from our own and other persons' human nature—but shall we get sufficient response? And without this how can we shift social institutions from off the basis of brutal struggle for existence and power on to that of fellowship? No amount of knowledge or science will be of any avail unless we can curb the bad impulse and set free the good. Can this be done, without the authoritative ethics associated with faith, in a spirit of love at work in the universe?

One reason for my happiness with Sidney is that *he* does not seem to have any evil impulses; he does not want to get the best of every bargain; he has an instinctive liking for equality and a definite impulse towards inconspicuous and unrewarded service. But then as he is always saying he has got my love and what does he want more?

Our life together is, in fact, ideal. In the dark days of winter I miss him for the four days a week. But the new home besides giving me health and beauty and a growing pleasure in birds and plants, has introduced me to music! With the wireless I am gradually being taught to listen to music and I am beginning to go to concerts at Haslemere and in London. Indeed I am fearing this new taste may become a too expensive pastime and, in my old age, I may take to music like some take to a drug. It soothes the restlessness of old age—restless because the time grows short and the strength less to get through the task one has set oneself.

Besides music I have more time for miscellaneous reading than in London—about a volume a week—mostly light reading—the best-written novels. What interests and disturbs in the output of writers like Aldous Huxley and L. S. Myers, D. H. Lawrence and hosts of others is the utter absence of any kind of ethical code and of any fixed scale of values. Judging by the types of character they choose to portray there is a preference for men and women who combine a clever intellect with unrestrained animal impulses (e.g. *Antic Hay* and *Barren Leaves, Clio*). Analytic descriptions of these lascivious and greedy creatures, with their wit and clever dialectics—creatures who are too low-toned for passionate vice (leave alone heroic virtue) abound in the modern novel. Reduce all human activities, whether of head or heart, the emergence and intellectualisation of the instincts of self-preservation or sex and the love of power seems to be the recipe for novel-writers, carried out with astonishing dexterity. There is no tragedy in this human nature—it is all low comedy, fastidiously and artistically expressed. Perhaps the most striking of these desecrating studies is Laurence Housman's savage caricature of Lloyd George in *Trimblerigg*, which is also incidentally a caricature of nonconformist Christianity.

The other uncomfortable thought is the spectacle of Russian Communism and Italian Fascism—two sides of the worship of force and the practice of cruel intolerance—with the still more penetrating idea that this spirit is spreading to the U.S.A. and even creeping into Great Britain! Great Britain changed from feudalism to capitalism without a physical force revolution; France did not do so; and it was the nationalist wars which swept the continent that masked the violence of the change over to capitalism in Central Europe and Italy. Will Great Britain escape again? in the transformation of capitalist to collectivist civilisation? The spirit of liberalism seems dead, and it was the faith and belief in political democracy that eased the transition from the feudal to the capitalist dictatorship. . . .

December 23rd.—This year ends on a note of happiness and encouragement. Sidney has been re-elected on to the Parliamentary Executive, and I have my book and all arrangements for publication in the U.K. and U.S.A. finished and done with. When we come back from our holiday eight weeks hence the book will be on the editors' desks! We are well established in our new home and like it "better and better" every day!

The Labour Party itself is in a wholesomer condition than it has been since the Labour Government went out of office. The General Council has been rescued by Thomas and Margaret Bondfield from out of the hands of the little knot of silly folk who led it into the

Sidney Webb in Downing Street

Beatrice Webb in 1926

Beatrice Webb in the early 'twenties

Scarborough morass of pseudo-communism. Two of the Left-wing leaders—Wedgwood and Wheatley—were left off the P.L.P. Executive, and Lansbury is below Sidney on the list of those elected! J.R.M. has recovered his position to a certain extent—sufficient for his leadership in the country; and the saner members of the front bench—Henderson, Clynes, Graham—are distinctly in the ascendant. Against this is the mess being made of the miners' case by A. J. Cook and the hardening of the Tory capitalist determination to put Labour in its "right place". We are going to have an infernal row next summer *unless* Labour is willing to take the attack on hours and wages—first among the miners—lying down. But living out of the way I hear little or nothing of what is happening in the country.

To my mind by far the most significant event of the last two years is the spread of wireless and the admirable way in which the B.B.C. is using this stupendous influence over the lives of the people—in some ways greater than the written word because it is so amazingly selective and under deliberate control—and on the whole an eminently right control. This new power must necessarily be a monopoly and cannot be left to Gresham's Law of the bad coin driving out the good. Such control as is exercised by the consumers of the service, is not, as with the Press, exercised by a multitude of individual buyers and individual advertisers; it can only be by individuals deliberately intervening by writing letters of complaint or suggestion, and the common, illiterate or apathetic person cannot write letters or make effective protests. Moreover there is at present no pecuniary self-interest involved—no one is the richer or the poorer because one programme is adopted rather than another. And the result is certainly remarkable. Every item in the day's programme is not to one's taste; but the ensemble is admirable if one considers the tastes of the millions of listeners as valid. The B.B.C. is always on the side of the angels—there is nothing that is low or bad broadcasted —there is much that is fine and inspiring and plenty of what is informative and encouraging. And music—with a surprising amount of good music—is becoming the daily delight of millions of men, women and children. One characteristic is especially praiseworthy—the tolerance, religious and political, of all schools of thought. Even Soviet Russia has been described and praised and the Roman Catholic Church and the cultured agnostic seem to have an equally fair field with the conventional Protestant preacher, whether Anglican or Nonconformist. But what a terrible engine of compulsory conformity, in opinion and culture, wireless *might* become?

To our little household it has been a source of delight. The curious result to me personally is that I have attended as many concerts these last six months as I have in the last twenty years! Music has become my main recreation; and, if I can afford it, I shall make my future visits to London chiefly for the purpose of hearing more and more music. I am already contemplating a course of reading on music and musicians.

Gradually we are making ourselves a neighbourhood round our home. There are a few members of the Labour Party within easy motoring distance—the Snowdens, Ponsonbys and Lord Russell— there is an ex-Colonial Bishop and his wife—Crossley[1] by name— who being "Labour" called on us and offered to introduce us to the notables in the district, which I refused—decisively—as the vision of conventional and conservative retired officers and other *rentiers* appearing from time to time, involving the hire of a motor-car for return visits, was not an enticing prospect. One lady living within half-a-mile—the good-looking and energetic wife of a Scottish engineer who has settled down here but is mostly away on the Clyde— insisted on "calling", and she and I are now getting up some sort of club for the women of Passfield to meet from time to time. Then there are various school teachers, a district nurse, a dissenting minister —friends of my gardener and his wife—more or less Labour in sympathy, and with a good deal more to talk about than the ordinary *rentier*. I do not wish to live an isolated life; I accept the obligation of near neighbourhood especially towards the intellectual proletariat— the minor professionals—who are hard-worked and denied the pleasures of life while rendering fine service to the community, very scantily rewarded. But I see no reason for knowing the gentry of the neighbourhood even if they cared to know us—they would not know us because we and they had a common interest—they would only know us out of curiosity and because we were "personages". With elementary teachers and nurses and members of the Labour Party I feel I have a common interest and that we can be mutually helpful and therefore should be neighbourly. We are planning a Labour demonstration in the summer for J.R.M., Snowden, Ponsonby and others to address—just to "liven up" this countryside. . . .

December 31st.—This is my last entry before our holiday. Perhaps Christmas would have been gloomy if it had not been for the coming holiday under happy circumstances; though with the R. H. Tawneys for the week-end before Christmas, the Anderson Fenns for three days after, we had plenty of talk. Mrs. Anderson Fenn—the Labour organiser for the N.E. counties—is a delightful little person of great talent as organiser and speaker—and charming—delicate and pretty to look at with a curious virility in her slight figure. Her husband is

---

[1] Owen Thomas Lloyd Crossley (1860–1926), Bishop of Auckland, New Zealand, 1911–13; and Assistant Bishop to Bishop of Llandaff, 1914–20.

tall and good-looking—a scientific worker and cultured man. They are distinguished people—intellectually and morally, but possessing no social status. No one realises it and they go on their way unnoticed by the leaders of the Labour Party. We took them to see the Snowdens and also the Ponsonbys—both Snowden and Ponsonby being among Mrs. Fenn's forty M.P.s for whose Women's Sections she is responsible. But by the Snowdens she was treated just as a salaried subordinate to whom they were distantly civil. Arthur Ponsonby was more oncoming—but in neither case was there the remotest recognition that this man and woman were among the élite!

She was, by the way, against the circulation of my book among the miners' wives. After reading the proofs rapidly she thought it would simply bewilder them and not add to their understanding of us and our lives. Our world was too varied and complicated and its issues too remote from their lives—it would separate them from us; it would not bring us closer to them.

A good deal depends on the pecuniary results of the book; its cost of production has been considerable; if I include a proportion of the secretary's salary, the total cost will be at least £1,000. To replace that means the sale of 2,000 copies leaving only a few hundred over for profit, and to add to the £200 down from U.S.A. Quickly following will be the volumes on Poor Law which will cost £800 merely to print and bind. So unless we can sell another 1,000 or so of *My Apprenticeship* during the next years, we shall hardly swing clear of positive loss on these publications. Of course the capital expenditure comes back to us in the following years—as even the *History of the Poor Law* will sell itself out *in the end*—but it means a squeeze at the time. The only book that has paid us is the *History of Trade Unionism and Industrial Democracy*—these two bring in a steady £300 a year and seem likely to continue to do so. I should imagine that our books up to to-day have just about paid for themselves, including in the cost, all out-of-pocket expenses, on secretary etc, but not our own maintenance. Which is about what we hoped to do. We have used our income from property as a fellowship for research and unpaid administration. And we have had a jolly good time of it, always doing exactly what we had a mind to!

PART III
1926

FEBRUARY 1926—DECEMBER 1926

February 18*th*.—Back at Passfield again: refreshed in mind but exhausted in body by our Sicilian tour. Also I shall feel better when I get through the outcoming of the book on February 25th—assuming its appearance is not a dismal failure—in which case I shall go through a worse period before I recover a philosophical outlook! . . .

March 15*th*. 2 *a.m.*—It is during sleepless hours in the night that I get things down in my diary; during the day I am either at work or reading newspapers, and interesting books, or listening to wireless or wandering about the country or merely chatting or brooding—I have no inclination to write. But in the loneliness and silence of the night impressions and thoughts fly through my brain and if I refuse to express them I begin to worry. Also to begin to write is an excuse for a cup of tea!

From that master-negotiator House to that bungler Austen Chamberlain! Why is it that the great majority of those who have watched Austen at one and the same time respect and despise him? It is not that they respect his character and despise his intellect—they *despise his character* and they are not without a certain respect for his intelligence. The answer is, I think, that he is undoubtedly a man experienced in affairs, with certain gifts and accomplishments, and he is personally disinterested. But he is dull and closed-minded and in his outlook on public as distinguished from private affairs he is morally as well as intellectually dense and equally unaware of the subtler nuances of right and wrong and of truth and untruth. I recollect an instance of this coarseness of fibre. He was dining with us in the early nineteen-hundreds when I was studying local authorities, and we were discussing possible improvements in municipal government. I suggested that what seemed to be most wanted was an independent and expert audit of the City accounts—instead of the amateur citizen auditors—and the presentation to all ratepayers of the expert auditors' report. His reply was instantaneously rapped out "I should object to that"—and then he paused as if trying to discover his reason: "any such expert audit would tend to make municipal enterprise more efficient—too efficient in fact—*it might supersede private enterprise.*" Now that was not only an unintelligent reaction—because if there is a danger of that supersession, it is not likely to be stopped by the absence of such an obvious reform—but it shows moral denseness as well as stupidity. To try to save one social institution by degrading another is rather like encouraging your wife to be unfaithful in order to enable you to marry someone else! Chamberlain's behaviour to the Germans, in his intrigue with Briand to "do" them out of the results of Locarno, showed a like moral denseness, and his conduct gives the impression of meanness in public affairs as well as stupidity. The same moral denseness is seen in his attempt to dodge British public opinion, and even apparently the instructions of the Cabinet. There is even a suspicion that Brazil's veto—which he professes to deplore—has somehow or other been arranged for by Briand, with a view to delaying Germany's entry until a commission is appointed to narrow down the constitution of the League in the interests of France. Whether Austen has been a dupe or a fellow-conspirator in the final fiasco no one feels certain. Personal vanity and personal prejudice probably accounts for a good deal of Austen's moral and intellectual denseness—he is proud of talking French with Briand and has kept the "war mentality" towards the Germans. Also he thinks he is a "diplomatist"—he is not content to be the plain business man with all his cards on the table—the only part he could play well. "Behind that imposing monocle there is a white-washed but empty chamber," said a sharp newspaper man. . . .

March 30th. 5 a.m.—Haldane's imposing review of my book, accorded the pride of place in the *Observer* of the 28th by the friendly Garvin, symbolises by its friendly critical attitude our long-standing and close association with this remarkable personality.

For more reasons than one the book has roused some antagonism in his mind. Perhaps he had a right to expect more recognition of his spontaneous and useful friendship to Sidney and me during our engagement and on our marriage. But I doubt whether this slight subconscious grievance did more than release what is and has been a genuine and permanent judgment about us—the sort of judgment which he would give in conversation with an intimate friend. "The Webbs are very able, whether as writers or organisers, they are honest and public-spirited; they are remarkably hard-working and purposeful. But alike in intellectual gifts, personal culture and social standing they are restricted in range—they are in fact 'little people' who have accomplished a useful but not out-standingly important work."

And of course in one sense he is right; we have, in fact, never claimed to be otherwise than useful citizens, how useful depends on the rightness of our particular scale of values.

Haldane's reaction is due, in the main, to a radical difference of opinion on three important questions. First we have no personal respect or liking for certain centres of power—social circles or institutions which Haldane has not merely appreciated as a man of affairs but which he has approved and admired. "The City", by which he means the dominant financial groups, used to be one of his idols—an idol, by the way, which has latterly been somewhat cast into the background—I know not why. The second idol has been "Good Society"—the tip-top circle which includes the Court (more especially the entourage of Edward VII), and the greater and more distinguished aristocrats, plutocrats and social charmers. His adoration of and subordination to Rosebery in the days of that hero's glory shocked us. Haldane delights in the glamour of the great ones of the world; or did: in their exquisite material surroundings; he loves to be "in the know" of all influential personages and to be mixed up in all public affairs. He is, in short, a *power* worshipper. The second point of difference is our total inability to sympathise with or even to understand his peculiar brand of metaphysics—Hegelianism. In his opinion this philosophy alone is the "pathway to reality", and to him it has united science and religion—the good, the beautiful and the true.

Closely connected with what he would call our deficiency in culture is our prejudice against what he calls "University education", the sort of diffuse and general culture, about men and affairs, literature and philosophy, which were characteristics of John Morley and the little set of politico-literary-philosophic personages who were in the last decades of the 19th century always breakfasting and dining with each other. These two latter criticisms give point to his objection to my denunciation of "London Society". "Have you a right to criticise a social institution which you have not known and which you are incapable of appreciating?" he asks. My answer is that we have been able to realise the net social effect of London Society better than he because we have looked at it from below and watched its effect, not on the few who have dominated it, but on the multitude who have accepted its scale of values in the conduct of their own lives. And here I come to the root difference between his scale of values and ours—the difference between the aristocrat caring for the free development of the select few and the democrat eager to raise the standard of the mass of men. In many ways these two aims can be pursued together, in others they can be harmonised by wise compromise. Whenever and wherever this has been the case Haldane and we have worked together without enquiring too curiously about each other's instinctive aims. But now and again our diverse scales of values have obviously clashed and then we have become for a time antagonistic or indifferent to each other. There has even been not a little mutual contempt.

To finish this entry about Haldane, how does he rank among the other distinguished men I have known?

He has not the intellectual gifts of Bernard Shaw, Mandel Creighton, Francis Galton or even of Arthur Balfour. To realise this one has only to read the books he has written and ask the experts about them. By common consent Haldane's writings are amateurish and undistinguished in substance and form; if they had not been the writings of a great public personage they would not be read. Whether he is a great *lawyer* I do not know; but I doubt whether his most distinguished colleagues think so. Perhaps his greatest mental achievement has been his reorganisation of the War Office, 1905–13. He is by no means a saint though not a sinner. But in spite of this absence of genius whether of intellect or character he has *personality* in a remarkable degree. When you think of him relatively to other men of talent he stands out in a singular way. And this personality has attractive as well as salient factors: a genuine beneficence to his fellow men and amazing loyalty and kindness to old friends especially when they are aged or unfortunate; an untiring public spirit and desire to serve the community; humour and wit, a massive power of mental work, and an unceasing curiosity about men and affairs. All these qualities taken together make him a big man—a bigger man than Arthur Balfour for instance. Even his little weaknesses are attractive, his over-enjoyment of high living, his naïve vanity about being at the centre of things and his gay malice when and where his self-esteem has been wounded—for instance about the Liberal leaders who threw his official career to the die-hard patriots during the War! In a word Haldane, especially in his later years, is a charmer as well as a man of power. He is also a lovable man, an unusual characteristic in the politician. And there I will leave it. . . .

April 16th.—This is my answer to Brailsford's request for my criticism of *The I.L.P. Policy of the Living Wage*. This policy advertised by the I.L.P. Easter Conference and the break with J.R.M. will, if persisted in, end the I.L.P.'s influence with the T.U. Movement, whilst damaging MacDonald's position among left-wingers. It might lead eventually to the I.L.P. leaving the Labour Party or merging itself in a new outside group like the Communist Party of to-day. I doubt this latter development—the left-wingers are always hankering after active work on local bodies or in Parliament and that is denied to persons outside the recognised political parties. The alternative career of the T.U. official is the monopoly of active Trade Unionists, and the I.L.P. does not attract, as leaders, active workers in the T.U. Movement; they prefer working within their own Movement. Hence if there is to be a distinct left wing of the P.L.P., it will tend to be made up of T.U. officials who are secure in their industrial leadership and can afford to defy the political leaders and political machine of the Labour Movement. What seems to me probable is that the resources in money and brains of the I.L.P. will dry up. Most of the larger subscriptions and the keenest interest have come from genuine admirers of, or persons wishing to ingratiate themselves with, MacDonald. Trevelyan, Dalton, Wise, Mosley, etc., will now cool off and turn their attention to local Labour parties, and Henderson may yet see his desire fulfilled of having only one local organisation affiliated to the Labour Party, carrying on propaganda. For some of the present leaders of the I.L.P.—for Brailsford, Fenner Brockway, Maxton—I have a warm regard; they are simple-minded enthusiasts. But they suffer from an intolerable conceit as to their own capacity for settling all questions alike on ethical and scientific grounds—they are "The Elect" whose task is to lead the rank and file to the promised land of the co-operative commonwealth by their own straight and narrow way. The Report I have criticised is a monument of this combination of conceit and ignorance and is quite unworthy of J. A. Hobson who signs but cannot have written it. Brailsford is probably the author[1] with Wise's help, and Creech Jones[2]—T.U. official—has contributed what knowledge there is of the T.U. Movement. If any such document were published it would be riddled through with criticism. It is possible that my criticism reinforcing J.R.M.'s and Ellen Wilkinson's[3] will stop the publication of anything so definite as the policy laid down in the Report and that the policy of a living wage will evaporate in Utopian talk. . . .

May 3rd. 4 a.m.—On the night of the great strike.

"The Decay of the Capitalist System" has certainly begun in the biggest and most characteristic of British industries and unless the Government ends the reign of the profit-maker it will end the Government—may indeed break up the country. Why the capitalists of the coal-fields are so dreary and incompetent a lot is a curious question: but the verdict that they have been and are wholly unable to run their business with decent efficiency has been given over and over again by all parties in the state. There is not a Conservative politician or journalist of repute that dare advise that the colliery-owners be left to go on as they are doing at present. Each successive court of enquiry, whatever its composition, has declared against them. But alas! this conversion of those in power has been more apparent than real. They

[1] The pamphlet on The Living Wage was written by H. N. Brailsford. J. A. Hobson was in close collaboration, and Brailsford was also assisted, particularly as regards proposals for State purchase in bulk, by the civil servant E. M. H. Lloyd.

[2] Arthur Creech Jones (b. 1891), National Secretary, Administrative Group of Transport and General Workers' Union, 1921–29; Colonial Secretary, 1946–50.

[3] Ellen Cicely Wilkinson (d. 1947), Trade Union organiser, National Union of Distributive and Allied Workers; M.P. for Jarrow and East Middlesbrough; Minister of Education in 1945 Labour Government.

have not any honest determination to do the job; they want to *seem* to do it but to leave it undone. It is that mean wriggling of the Baldwin Cabinet, to some extent justified by the wriggles of the Liberal Commission of Herbert Samuel and Beveridge[1]—typical Liberals—that has brought about the General Strike of to-night. The General Strike will fail; the General Council may funk it and may withdraw their instructions on some apparent concession by the Government, or the men may slink back to work in a few days. We have always been against a General Strike. But the problem of the collapse of capitalism in the coal industry will remain, and woe to the governing class that refuses to solve it by taking control, in one form or another, of the organisation of the industry.

Away here in the country I have not been able to watch the march of events. The General Council of the T.U.C. has certainly succeeded in giving an epic quality to their slow and reserved but decisive attitude towards the miners' dispute. There has been no tall talk and hot air during the negotiations; and the egregious A. J. Cook has been ignored. In fact when the announcement came on Friday evening that the railway workers and other key men would cease work to-night —it crept over the wireless—it did not appear in the newspapers until twenty-four hours later. The phrasing of the Labour communication was quiet, careful and dignified, always offering to continue negotiation, always asserting that a settlement could be arranged on the basis of a definite plan of reorganisation first and reduction of wages afterwards. The one note of hysteria came on Saturday night from Baldwin, again over the wireless and again not appearing in the newspapers. "Before giving the weather forecast and news bulletin," said the announcer in a hurried voice, "there is a message from the Prime Minister." Then in a stentorian voice some other person gave this message, two or three times, each time with louder and more pompous emphasis: "Be steady, Be steady"—pause—"Remember that peace on earth comes to men of good will." Perhaps if Baldwin himself, in his kindly and commonsense accent, had spoken his own words the effect would have been different. But in the emissary's melodramatic shout it sounded not a little absurd. What is wanted is to face the facts with knowledge

---

[1] The Report of the Samuel Commission (see *ante* p. 67 n.) recommended the nationalisation of mining royalties, as had the Sankey Commission of 1919, but rejected the proposal for public ownership of the industry itself in favour of a plan for voluntary amalgamation with compulsion in reserve. It further recommended cutting the cost of production either by an immediate heavy wage reduction or by a lesser reduction coupled with a lengthening of hours. Both sides rejected the Report, the miners refusing any change in hours or wages, and the owners proposing drastic wage-cuts and district instead of national negotiations. On May 1st a special conference of Trade Union executives voted full strike support to the miners, and on the following evening, after the Government had broken off discussions, the General Strike was ordered.

and determination. *Goodness*—i.e. diffused sympathy—is beside the mark. In a great crisis these sloppy emotions rouse irritation or contempt in the listeners to wireless—even to a far greater extent than to readers—there is no contagious enthusiasm at the end of the 'phone; you listen coldly and critically to all that comes, and bathos is easily detected in the silence of your own sitting-room.

May 4th.—When all is said and done we personally are against the use of the General Strike in order to compel the employers of a particular industry to yield to the men's demands, however well justified these claims may be. Such methods cannot be tolerated by any Government—even a Labour Government would have to take up the challenge. A General Strike aims at coercing the whole community and is only successful *if it does so* and in so far as it does so. Further, if it succeeded in coercing the community it would mean that a militant minority were starving the majority into submission to their will, and would be the end of democracy, industrial as well as political. Sooner or later—in Great Britain sooner rather than later—the community as a whole would organise to prevent such coercion by penal legislation. But there arise emergencies when it is better to fight even if you cannot win than to take oppression lying down. And this is especially so when the struggle is within a good-natured community which will recognise that men who fight and lose must be generously treated by the victorious party; that a willingness to fight, with the certainty that you will lose, implies a big grievance. Whether these considerations hold good on this occasion I do not know. To us it was as clear as noonday that with the T.U. Movement in its present state of mind this weapon of a final strike *would be used*. When it has been tried and failed, as fail it will, the workers will be in a better frame of mind for steady and sensible political action. Moreover, the governing class will have had a nasty shock and being English, they will learn from it and compel the coal-owners to reorganise or clear out. It is another nail in the coffin of *uncontrolled* capitalist enterprise—a corpse which has not yet been buried in spite of the general acceptance of the policy of the National Minimum of civilised life; and a century of Factory and Mines Acts.

The sensation of a General Strike which stops the press, as witnessed from a cottage in the country, centres round the headphones of the wireless set. Five instalments of news at 10, 1, 4, 7 and 9.30 break up the day. At the first of these, the announcer prefaces the bulletin of news by a carefully worded declaration of impartiality and fairness and an earnest appeal not to oscillate, at any rate deliberately, to prevent the reception of news. But directly the news began it was clear that the B.B.C. had been commandeered by the Government and that the main purpose was to recruit blacklegs for the closed services. Granted this the evidently harassed announcer (we could hear the agonised whispers!) did his level best to seem detached and disinterested. They treated the G.C. of the T.U.C. as if they were of almost equal importance to the Cabinet and they gave out their communiqués exactly as they gave out the messages from Downing Street. There was not a word of condemnation in B.B.C. announcements, not even the citation of condemnatory criticism from the foreign press. Also there was a clear distinction made between business announcements from the Civil Commissioners, and their own news through press agencies. "We can't help being used by the Government—it is right we should be so used with the newspapers shut down; but when we are on our own we stand above the battle and view the Strike as we should a cricket match," was their tone. The net impression left on *my* mind is that the General Strike will turn out not to be a revolution of any sort or kind but a batch of compulsory Bank Holidays without any opportunities for recreation and a lot of dreary walking to and fro. When the million or so strikers have spent their money they will drift back to work and no one will be any the better and many will be a great deal poorer and everybody will be cross. It is a monstrous irrelevance in the sphere of social reform. If it be prolonged a week or ten days it may lead to reactionary legislation against Trade Unionism and possibly to a General Election. But I doubt it. If the Government keeps its head and goes persistently and skilfully to work in reconstructing services the General Strike will peter out; and the noxious futility of this mild edition of the dictatorship of the "proletariat" will be apparent to everyone, not least to Trade Unionists who find their funds exhausted and many of their most able members victimised by being permanently displaced by patriotic blacklegs! There will be not only an excuse for but a justification of victimisation on a considerable scale. One reiterated communication over the wireless is a solemn undertaking by the Cabinet that all who return to work or accept work in these days of the community's peril will be permanently "protected and secured" in their employment—which implies "at the expense of the strikers".

For the British Trade Union Movement I see a day of terrible disillusionment. The failure of the General Strike of 1926 will be one of the most significant landmarks in the history of the British working class. Future historians will, I think, regard it as the death gasp of that pernicious doctrine of "workers' control" of public affairs through the Trade Unions, and by the method of direct action. This absurd doctrine was introduced into British working class life by Tom Mann and the Guild Socialists and preached insistently, before the War, by the *Daily Herald* under George Lansbury. In Russia it was quickly repudiated by Lenin and the Soviets, and the Trade Unions were reduced to complete subordination to the creed-autocracy of the Communist Party. In Italy the attempt to put this doctrine into practice by seizing the factories led to the Fascist revolution. In Great Britain this belated and emasculated edition of the doctrine of workers' control will probably lead to a mild attempt to hamper Trade Union activities. Popular disgust with the loss and inconvenience of a General Strike will considerably check the growth of the Labour Party in the country, but will lead to a rehabilitation of political methods and strengthen J.R.M.'s leadership within the Party itself.

On the whole, I think, it was a proletarian distemper which had to run its course and like other distempers it is well to have it over and done with at the cost of a lengthy convalescence. Above all, as the Italian Fascist Government has discovered, the subordination of the Trade Union entails an almost equal state control for the capitalist employer. In a word the Workers' Control Movement has led throughout the world to the extension and strengthening of state bureaucracy—a form of government which the Syndicalists and the Guild Socialists were intent on superseding by the vocational organisation of the workers. The Webbs may end their joint work as they began it by pleading the validity of vocational organisation within the modern community however organised!

May 7th. 2 a.m.—Russell[1] brought Sidney down in his car, and came in for a pipe and a talk. They were both of them—particularly Russell—far more apprehensive of a long strike and of bloodshed in the streets before it ended than I had been. Sidney says that the 40 miners' Members are obdurate about any reduction of wages or lengthening of hours and were furious with J. H. Thomas for suggesting that if the coal-owners' notices were withdrawn the miners would consider the question of a temporary reduction of wages during the immediate re-organisation of the industry. Also reports show that the working-class generally is far more anxious to strike than the G.C. of the T.U.C. and that in certain industrial areas—Newcastle and Glasgow—there is a very ugly spirit which, if the stoppage continued and there were hunger, might mean outbursts of violence between the workers and the police. Sidney was impressed with the powerlessness of the P.L.P. and the self-will of the Trade Unionists. He does not think that the Cabinet will have a General Election after the strike is over or propose any drastic anti-Trade Union legislation; he thinks that the governing class is considerably scared—and cer-

[1] Probably John Francis Stanley, Earl Russell (1865–1931), elder brother of Bertrand Russell, who was a Fabian, a neighbour, and Parliamentary Secretary in 1929 to the Ministry of Transport.

tainly Jix's[1] sensational appeal for fifty thousand special constables over the wireless last night looks as if he, at any rate, is in a funk! If there were to be a General Election after the strike is over Sidney says he would not stand for re-election. "I feel I cannot help in Parliament, especially if the mood of the P.L.P. is to become embittered—I am no good at that sort of fighting—and so long as I am in Parliament I can't get on with our work." He reports Henderson as angry with the miners, and J.R.M. and J.H.T. as depressed at their powerlessness to bring about a settlement. Philip Snowden, being dead against the Trade Unions, is philosophical. The inner circle hates the General Strike and sees no good coming out of it. Josiah Wedgwood is said to be denouncing the P.L.P. and to have practically retired from taking part in Labour politics. Labour M.P.s are being sent in motor-cars by Eccleston Square this week-end to address meetings in the provinces. The House of Commons is in a state of tense feeling and Conservative and Labour members are exercising self-control. "When we crowd round the tape to see the news," members are silent lest offence be given!

May 14*th. General Strike*, 1926.—Little more than a nine days' wonder, costing Great Britain tens of millions and leaving other nations asking whether it was a baulked revolution or play-acting on a stupendous scale. In the first two or three days there was complete stoppage and paralysis of trade; but hosts of volunteers started skeleton services, and Hyde Park and Regent's Park became great camps of soldiers living in tents, with improvised shelters for the store of milk and other commodities. Not a shot has been fired; not a life is lost. In one town the police and strikers played cricket [*sic*; but see p. 97]; and the victory of the strikers is published to ten million listeners by the Government-controlled wireless! Slowly buses and trams begin to appear; the London taxi-cab drivers decide to "come out", but the next morning the buses are seen in the London streets obviously driven by professionals!

On Monday, the seventh day of the Strike, Sidney and I travel up by the milk train to London—it is crowded but not a single remark did we hear about the Strike; the third-class passengers at any rate were unusually silent—even for English passengers—more bored than alarmed—and the same silence is in the streets—more like a Sunday with the shops open but with no one shopping. Just a very slight reminiscence of the first days of the Great War, the parking of innumerable motors in the squares and by-streets and here and there officers in khaki, even one or two armoured cars in attendance on

[1] William Cecil Joynson-Hicks (1865–1932), afterwards Lord Brentford. Home Secretary, 1924–9.

strings of motor buses piled up with food. It is characteristic that Government lorries sometimes driven by army engineers are labelled "food only", as if to appeal to the strikers not to interfere with them. No strain or fear on the faces of the citizens, male or female—only a sort of amused boredom. Universal condemnation of the General Strike but widespread sympathy with the miners.

Susan Lawrence, however, was in a state of emotional excitement— I might almost say exaltation. She had taken six meetings on Saturday and another half-dozen on Sunday in the East End: "A glorious spirit"; "the world would never be the same again"; "we poor politicians are out of the picture"; "the General Council had taken command"; and "never again would the workers be trodden under foot as they are now". "We are living in *momentous times*, on the eve of great things"—all of which I receive rather coldly—suggesting that we might be on the eve of a very commonplace and continuous reaction? "A revolutionary reaction—a terrible time—perhaps— many of us in prison," she replied. "No, the same old thing—the strike will peter out and all that will be left in the Labour Movement will be an empty purse and universal disillusionment and a still more divided Party," I answer. "There is no earthly use in it all except to get rid of a proletarian distemper; the last gasp of the workers' control day-dream. There will not even be a revolutionary reaction. Thomas and Baldwin will see to that—they will broadcast messages of Peace and Goodwill every few hours until we are all hypnotised into loving one another!" I mocked. A few hours later I met Mrs. Trevelyan in Dean's Yard. "Charles is having marvellous meetings— (at Newcastle)—a new spirit of revolutionary fervour." "A tragic disillusionment," I retorted. "Perhaps *this* time but *next time*," she said and rushed on.

Two other impressions left over from these critical days—in both cases of the varying moods of the strikers. On Tuesday morning I passed through the Fabian bookshop to see Galton. The hall was occupied by a score or so of men—the strike committee of the London branch of the Railway Clerks' Association (so I was afterwards told)— and one of them was speaking through the 'phone.—I caught the words "I recommend that we go in." "What's up?" I asked Galton. "The usual thing," he said in his cheery cynical voice, "they've got cold feet. A week ago that man, who is the secretary of the Committee, told me that in three days' time the Cabinet would be on their knees, that the soldiers and police were on their side and a lot of other bunkum. Yesterday afternoon he came with tears in his eyes 'Twenty of our men went in this morning. I saw my boss this morning,' he added, 'and he says my place is still open but will be filled to-morrow. I can't afford to stay out—I am going in and I am going to advise the others to do so too.' " In the afternoon of the same day, Galton told me, at a meeting of about 50 the majority determined to stay out but 15 including the Chairman and Secretary left the room for their respective offices.

The second episode filled me with dreary forebodings of terrible disillusionment. On Thursday morning—the very day of the "call-off" of the Strike—I motored with Susan into her constituency. Just before we started Laski had phoned up and told me confidentially that the G.C. was going to Downing Street at 11 o'clock and that the Strike would be settled. So I warned Susan to be careful what she said. All was quiet along those wide streets of the Poplar and East and West Ham constituencies. Our first meeting was 1,000 railwaymen at Ilford, then we visited the Council of Action, and an open air meeting in Susan's constituency from where we went to the Poplar Council of Action. In all these gatherings the men seemed determined but depressed and I gathered from Susan's manner that she also was disappointed—possibly my cold scepticism depressed her. But she worked herself up into a fine spirit of demagogic optimism—"the enemy was weakening—they (the G.C.) were winning hands down —John Simon[1] was the first rat to leave the sinking ship—they—the strikers—have all been heroes—ready to become martyrs—but to-morrow they would be in command of the nation's resources"— and so on. The men were silent—but they listened to her intently— and gradually their strained expressions relaxed. "It is the first good news we have had," one of the committee whispered to me. "Are you not too optimistic?" said I to her as we motored from one meeting to another. "What I wanted to do was to hearten them up—we must always do that in a strike. The men are splendid; we *must* and *shall* win." A little before 2 o'clock we drove into Palace Yard and she jumped out. "The strike is settled," said the constable in a non-committal and respectful tone. She hurried in and I walked off to lunch through a grinning crowd of sightseers and special constables, thinking mostly of the amazing change in Susan Lawrence's mentality —from the hard-sensed lawyer-like mind and conventional manner of the "Moderate" member of the School Board whose acquaintance I had made five and twenty years ago to the somewhat wild woman of demagogic speech, addressing her constituents as "comrades" and abasing herself and her class before the *real* wealth-producers. To-day Susan is a victim to spasms of emotional excitement which drive her from one weird suggestion to another. She lives in an unreal world. In order to keep in touch with what she imagines to be the proletarian mind she has lost touch with facts as they are. And yet she is a real good soul, devoted and public-spirited. It is a bad case of the occu-

[1] The late Viscount Simon.

pational disease so common among high-strung men and women who come out of a conservative environment into proletarian politics. By continuously *talking to another class in the language they think that class speaks instead of in their own vernacular* they deceive themselves and create distrust in their audience. What will those East End workers think who listened to Susan yesterday, coming straight from the centre of things, to tell them they were winning hands down, when they heard the news a few hours later, "General Strike called off unconditionally"? What is the good of having professional brain-workers to represent you, if they refuse to give you the honest message of intelligence but treat you to a florid expression of the emotion which *they* think the working class are feeling or ought to be feeling? The next step is that the brain-workers deceive themselves and think that they *have* the emotion they are expressing. Which subtle insincerity destroys their usefulness. They are neither brain-workers using their intellects, nor exponents of the intuitive decision of the unthinking multitude who if left alone to feel their way for themselves are by no means such fools as some people think. If it had not been for a few ambitious spirits like Bevin, egged on by middle-class theorists, there would never have been a General Council endowed with power to call out the whole movement—powers which they have sooner or later to use or make themselves a laughing stock like the Triple Alliance on Black Friday. If you create an instrument sooner or later you will use it. "The General Council have not as much sense or courage as the typists in my office," said Susan as I met her on the stairs and greeted her affectionately. "One good reason against the method of a General Strike," thought I but did not say it.

May 18th. Churchill's announcement in the House to-day that the General Strike will have cost the Government no more than three-quarters of a million—a sum which the death of a couple of million-aires will pay—puts the cap of ridicule on the heroics of the General Strike. The three million strikers will have spent some three million pounds of Trade Union money and lost another four or five in wages; they will have "gone in", owing to Baldwin's wisdom, on the old conditions in wages and hours, but considerably shackled with regard to future strikes of a lightning character. If anti-Trade Union legislation does not follow it will be due to the utter failure of their movement to carry out its bombastic threat of paralysing the country's life. The Government has gained immense prestige in the world and the British Labour Movement has made itself ridiculous. A strike which opens with a football match between the police and the strikers and ends in unconditional surrender after nine days with densely-packed reconciliation services at all the chapels and churches of Great

Britain attended by the strikers and their families, will make the continental Socialists blaspheme. Without a shot fired or a life lost—the most sensational episode being Winston's silly suppression of the Archbishop of Canterbury's letter[1] and the placarding of this letter by the General Council—the General Strike of 1926 has by its absurdity made the Black Friday of 1921 seem to be a red-letter day of common sense. Let me add that the failure of the General Strike shows what a *sane* people the British are. If only our revolutionaries would realise the hopelessness of their attempt to turn the British workman into a Russian Red and the British business man and country gentleman into an Italian Fascist! The British are hopelessly good-natured and common-sensical—to which the British workman adds pigheadedness, jealousy and stupidity. What oppresses me is the fear that these elements of crass stupidity and pigheaded obstinacy may prevent the revival of British trade and that Trade Unionism may diminish and not increase efficiency. The miners in particular are plunging about without any idea in their heads except resistance to cuts in wages or lengthening of hours—they don't care a damn about the reorganisation of their industry and they are even hostile to nationalisation of royalties because of their obsession about no compensation to royalty owners. In their conduct towards the General Council they have been impossible—demanding a General Strike but refusing to consult about the settlement they would accept. The General Council has been equally impossible in their treatment of the Parliamentary Labour Party; they drifted into the General Strike, and suddenly closed it down, in both cases swayed by the impulse of the moment without any consideration for the necessities and interests of those with whom they were co-operating. And yet they mean so well! They are so genuinely kindly in their outlook; they would gladly shake hands with anyone at any time, whether it be a Tory Prime Minister, a Russian emissary or their own employers. They play at revolution and they run away from the consequences with equal alacrity. The General Strike of 1926 is a grotesque tragedy. The Labour leaders and their immediate followers, whether political or individual, live in the atmosphere of alternating day-dreams and nightmares—day-dreams about social transformation brought about in the twinkling of an eye—and visions of treachery in their own ranks and malignancy on the other side—all equally fantastic and without foundation. We are all of us just good-natured stupid folk. The worst of it is that the governing class are as good-natured and stupid as the Labour Movement! Are we decadent or is this growing alarm about the future only a reflection of my own old age? I have lost my

---

[1] The Archbishop of Canterbury (Randall Davidson) wrote an appeal for mediation to which the Government refused circulation.

day-dreams, I have only the nightmare left—the same sort of nightmare I had during the Great War—that European civilisation is in the course of dissolution. Sidney scoffs at my fears, "And even if Europe fails," says he, "there is always the U.S.A.—a self-confident and overwhelmingly prosperous race. The U.S.A. may not be to one's liking but it is clear she is not going to develop *our* social disease—her will to wealth and power is not going to be paralysed by social conflict and social disorder. Anyway," he adds, "there is nothing *we* can do—all that remains for us is to finish up all our books."

May 22nd.—W. Gillies came down to lunch yesterday afternoon: he had been watching events at 33 from 32 Eccleston Square and he had been at the Conference of Executives on the Saturday at which it was decided to send out the notices for the General Strike. Cramp[1] was in the Chair; there was no discussion; before the vote was taken a document reciting the result of the negotiation with Baldwin and his refusal to insist on the notices being withdrawn by the mine-owners had been circulated to the Executives at 12 o'clock on Friday night and at 10 o'clock the following morning they were asked whether or not they agreed to the G.C. proposal to call out the first line of defence —Railways, Transport, etc. The roll of the Unions was called and one by one their representatives gave their decision—the vast majority and all the great Unions answering "Yes": one or two of the little Unions said they had not any authority to vote one way or the other. "Pure fatalism," whispered Cramp to Gillies, "we can't win." But neither he nor anyone else said this to the meeting. Gillies told me that he had never felt before, at any meeting, that the persons concerned were being carried away by the feeling *that they had to do it, that the rank and file would expect it,* that another Black Friday would be intolerable. The calling off the Strike was equally without discussion —all the members of the G.C. were in favour of it—largely because they were indignant with the miners for not accepting the Samuel Memorandum.[2] Here again was a fatal misunderstanding through lack of discussion and agreed decision. The G.C. had imagined that when the miners asked them to call a General Strike it was agreed to put the G.C. in command of the negotiations with the Government and the mine-owners. The miners declared that they had throughout said that they *would not accept any reduction of wages.* No records had

---

[1] Concemore Thomas Cramp (1876–1933), became Industrial General Secretary of the N.U.R. in 1920.

[2] Sir Herbert Samuel, Chairman of the Coal Commission which had just reported, had kept in touch with both sides during the dispute; and drew up a Memorandum of suggestions for settlement which he showed to the General Council, who in the belief that it implied a "firm offer" from the Government (which it did not) urged the miners to accept it and on their refusal called off the strike.

been kept as the two secretaries—Cook and Citrine—had been sent out of the room when the G.C. and the Miners' Executive were in session! Gillies thinks that it was this revelation that the miners intended the G.C. to go on until the Government and the mine-owners had accepted the *status quo ante* that induced the G.C. to call off the strike at once. They thought that Baldwin had accepted the Samuel proposals; but, as Gillies observed, the miners' stubborn refusal to accept the compromise relieved the P.M. from his private under-taking even if he gave one, which seems very uncertain. "It is not a question of bad leadership," summed up Gillies, "there was no leadership at all—the G.C., including Thomas, seemed to drift back-ward and forward as if moved by some external force which had no relation to their own minds." As for the Miners' Executive, they knew their districts would not accept a reduction without a fight how-ever hopeless and disastrous the fight was. When the joint research department brought before them a table of figures showing that the *status quo ante* meant closing so many mines and another 300,000 unemployed, "Let them be unemployed," said Herbert Smith.[1]

All the intellectuals who watched the G.C. and Miners' Executive during these days—Gillies, Laski, Tawney—made one observation: those fifty or sixty men who were directing the G.C. were living a thoroughly unwholesome life—smoking, drinking, eating wrong meals at wrong times, rushing about in motor-cars, getting little or no sleep and talking aimlessly one with another. During the day before they called off the Strike the assembled executives were sitting in groups singing songs and telling stories, soothed and enlivened by a plentiful supply of tobacco and alcohol. At crucial meetings at which important decisions were taken there was no real discussion; the Secretaries were usually sent out of the room and nothing was re-corded. There were perpetual misunderstandings between the General Council and the miners; they were silent or "rowed" each other according to their moods. After a Council meeting some of the members would adjourn to a neighbouring public house and discuss matters at the bar with reporters present. It is characteristic of Smillie that he left London for Scotland on the outbreak of war, the other miner representative on the G.C. being absent on account of illness. So, as A. J. Cook complains, the miners were unrepresented on the General Council throughout the "nine days". Citrine, the able secretary of the G.C., was treated as a shorthand typist and was seldom allowed to attend the meetings, leave alone offer advice.

Croft,[2] the Labour organiser for these parts, who came down here

---

[1] Herbert Smith (1863–1938), Yorkshire miner; became President of the Miners' Federation of Great Britain in 1921.

[2] Harold Croft (b. 1882), National Union of Clerks and I.L.P.; became Labour Party Organiser for the Home and Southern Counties in 1924.

from Eccleston Square to advise me about our gathering in July, told me that "next door" are being swamped with abusive telegrams and letters since the calling off of the Strike and are quarrelling among themselves as to who is to blame. If the General Strike has done nothing else it has destroyed once for all the absurdity of a G.H.Q. for the Labour Movement made up of the representatives of the big Trade Unions. It was one of the many silly notions of the Guild Socialists.

May 31st.—Meanwhile the political movement has had an immense lift-up. The remnant of the Liberal Party has been smashed to smithereens by Asquith's intemperate letter to Lloyd George, practically dismissing him from the leadership in the House of Commons and almost from membership of the Liberal Party. Lord Grey's priggish and empty speech at the National Liberal Club on Friday, "standing behind Lord Oxford" and wondering why the letter was "so long delayed"—a clear intimation of a long-standing determination to break with Lloyd George—has made matters worse. The occasion of the split is admirably suited to Lloyd George's claim to be a democratic leader; Asquith and Grey pronounced in favour of the Government; he argued in favour of the men. Supposing Lloyd George were to go on the stump advocating the policy of a living wage obtained by state control of capitalist enterprise, and supposing he were incidentally to come over to the Labour Party, what would happen then? Philip Snowden would certainly welcome him and he might get a following not only among Liberal and non-political electors, sick of the Government, but also within the Labour Movement itself. And he could not be excluded if he chose to start a local Labour party in his own constituency and appear at the Labour Party Conference as its representative. Some time in 1919 Sidney wrote an article for the *New Republic* suggesting such a possible development of Lloyd George's career, a suggestion which caused its author to be denounced by ardent Labour men and even to be frowned on by the Front Bench men. It may still come true and it will not be the left wing Trade Unionists who will object—to them Lloyd George may seem preferable to MacDonald, Thomas, or even Henderson, as the exponent of a forward, perhaps of a demagogic policy. He has also a money chest: he might bring over brains.

The other event is the amazing victory on Friday at Hammersmith;[1] the Labour man beating the Tory by 3,600 and leaving the Liberal with 1,900 votes and the loss of his deposit. This is a by-election which will influence events. The Tories were intoxicated

[1] North Hammersmith election result (in a seat previously Conservative): J. P. Gardner (Lab.), 13,095; S. Gluckstein (C.), 9,484; G. P. Murfitt (L.), 1,774.

by the unconditional surrender of the G.C. and have been dreaming of a General Election which would resemble that of 1900 only more so. Now Baldwin has only to threaten them with a dissolution and they will come to heel like spaniels. It will certainly stop all anti-Trade Union legislation. Personally I think it was the robbing of the Insurance funds[1] which lay at the bottom of the turnover.

But the calling off of the General Strike allayed fears whilst the stoppage of the coal supply and sympathy with the miners have caused a reaction in favour of Labour. "Why not give to Labour men the chance of settling their own industrial disputes—they did it while they were in office without giving subsidies. Anyway get this Government out: they have muddled the whole business," is being said in third-class railway carriages and buses. And the victory will react on the Liberal split and widen it. It may lead the collectivist section to come over to Labour. Further it will give a sharp point to the arguments in favour of political action versus industrial war. The Parliamentary Labour Party will again dominate the situation. After the unconditional surrender there was despair of industrial action; to this has been added renewed hopes in salvation through the ballot box.

There remains over from this sensational episode of the General Strike, the miners' lock-out—a far bigger challenge to capitalist enterprise. The million miners are obdurate and no one can take their place; they have a stranglehold on British industry and can paralyse it as effectually though not as suddenly as the railwaymen.

There are only two ways of beating them: sheer starvation, or a sufficient importation of coal to make them feel that the struggle is useless. But dare the Government let them and the wives and children starve? At least the women and children are getting food at the rate-payers' expense, and the men must get some of that food, and the huge public subscription must eke out the rest. If there were to be any sensational stoppage of food in the pit villages or if coal were to be freely imported a drastic sympathetic strike would burst out again. It may end in the collieries which can pay the old wages opening at these rates, whilst the others will remain shut down until their employees accept lower rates—at which the miners could not complain seeing that no one can compel employers to work at a loss. In that case would the miners who refused to work at lower wages in the profitless pits get the dole or not? It would be a pretty tangle for the Government to sort out. Meanwhile the unemployment figures are

[1] The allusion is to the Economy Act, sponsored by Winston Churchill and passed in June. This Act provided for the reduction of Government expenditure under several heads, notably health insurance, where the State contribution for men was reduced from 2/9 to 1/7 per week. The Bill was hotly, but vainly contested by the Labour Party.

rushing up and everyone connected with the dependent industries is getting more and more alarmed and depressed.

Here is my *Letter to the Women of Seaham*.[1] All the replies are cheerful in tone and the women quite confident that they will win. There is clearly no question of extensive distress at present; some Seaham miners have come up to London on a holiday, leaving their wives and children on out-relief—at least two were going to the Derby! The children are getting better food at school than they had at home, and the women, in some ways, get more out-relief than they were taking [from] wages before the lock-out. But there are already signs that this relief is being cut down and the *Daily Herald* is sending out agonising messages from some areas. I don't believe that the modern humanitarian state can tolerate the anarchy and irresponsibility of capitalist enterprise; to be successful the capitalist entrepreneur must be ruthless and autocratic as he is in U.S.A., and the Government of the country must be vested in the capitalist class as it is in the U.S.A. in practice if not in theory. That is Mussolini's philosophy. Political and economic power must be in the same hands; otherwise there will be chaos. Are we approaching this chaos in Great Britain? . . .

June 12th.—At the back of my mind is a certain personal discomfort about the miners' lock-out: ought we or ought we not to give and ask others to give to the fund for the miners' wives and children? Neither Sidney nor I would have given a penny to it if no one would have been the wiser. I gave my name to the Committee and sent a cheque for £10 simply because I conformed to the loudly expressed opinion of the world of Labour—with which I secretly disagreed. "Not a cent off the wages, not a second on the day" was *not* the best way to get the reorganisation of the industry. Whether the miners could have got it by any other way—whether given all the circumstances the Government would have consented to go beyond the Samuel Report and get the reorganisation *done* and not talked about I am not so sure. I think the miners and the General Council could have got it if they had been skilful, if J.R.M., Henderson and Thomas had been allowed to negotiate. Assuming the Government refuse to do it, is there the remotest chance of the miners compelling reorganisation by holding out indefinitely for conditions which cannot be given without reorganisation? Sidney thinks that by holding out they are *diminishing* the amount of reorganisation which will be actually accomplished; that they are making it easier for the mine-owners to slither on without improvements, and that the probable outcome of a prolonged struggle will be to break down the dyke of the national wage, and generally to worsen conditions of employment throughout the industry. Hence

[1] Not preserved in MS.

that ten pounds was misgiven; the truth being that it was easier to give than to explain why we were against the fund. Also we were not *certain* that we were right: so we sent our ten pounds; but refrained from asking anyone else to subscribe. A weak, perhaps cowardly, compromise! Perhaps we ought to have *not* given; but remained silent about our reasons; not feeling sufficiently confident of their rightness in opposition to the current public opinion of the Movement. Moral pedantry? What does it matter? Disgruntled old folk we are.

June 18th.—The letters from the Seaham women reveal no distress and some light-hearted enjoyment of the excitement of the strike; the children, one mother tells me, regard the school feeding "as a picnic that happens every day", the food being better than they got at home—the relief provided by the Guardians is nicknamed "Kind Joe", and some women, at any rate, are better off than they were before the lock-out. Miss Purves, the Federation secretary, an able and experienced woman—the daughter of a local tradesman—is puzzled to know what to do if the Central Women's Committee send down any funds—"the families are amply provided for". What I fear is a horrible time of disillusion and suffering when the men are back at work with some of them out-of-work and all the conditions worsened; with credit exhausted and outstanding debts. Here again I may be foolishly alarmed; but one wonders whether the easy-goingness of the Government and the owners, of the miners and the Labour Movement, in face of the stoppage, is warranted? Everyone concerned can't be going to win! And for the country as a whole it may turn out to be a Rake's Progress! . . .

June 23rd.—G.B.S. and Charlotte here for the inside of a week. Since we were with them in April he has been seriously ill with kidney trouble and continuous temperatures—threatenings of organic disease. Now Almroth Wright[1] tell him that he has apparently cured himself. It has been a depressing time; Charlotte says he has lost interest in everything, though he went on working at his book. This book on Socialism is turning out to be a nuisance—a veritable bog of dialectics— also he is obsessed with his correspondence—Charlotte says he is jealous of his right to write letters! But ill or not ill he is just the same dear friend and somewhat sobered but still brilliant sprite that used to stay with us at The Argoed over thirty years ago. He never changes; he never grows old; he has the same delightful personality; he is less vain than he used to be—indeed he is not vain at all; he has lost all the old bitterness and with it the capacity for invective—but that is

[1] Sir Almroth Edward Wright (1861–1947), the distinguished physician and pathologist, famous also for his violently anti-feminist views.

perhaps due to his outstanding success. The wonder is, not that he has
lost the spirit of revolt, but that he has retained the demand for
equality and his consideration for the under-dog. He is brooding over
a new play—a political play. The King abdicated in order to contest
the Royal Borough of Windsor[1] and gain freedom to tell the
people what he thinks of the long line of incompetent ministers; he
is in fact, to lead H.M. Opposition! Intellectually G.B.S. is as
active as ever—indeed he seems rather febrile—too restlessly assiduous—as if he feared he would not be able to finish his job. Let us
hope he will die in harness! Charlotte is anxious about him and
clings to us as her oldest friends; but they are both still enjoying life,
and particularly his immense prestige in all parts of the intellectual
world. G.B.S. and Sidney have both retained their power of work
whilst I seem to have lost mine—I am sauntering through the days—
doing little—except sketch out work for Sidney to do! However I
keep him well and happy. Which used to be considered the whole
duty of woman. Charlotte is as good a wife to G.B.S. as I am to
Sidney. We have a great respect for each other as wives; and a long
standing good comradeship which has stood the test of years. We four,
each one of us, will be saddened by the death of either one of the other
pair, and will stand by the survivor. . . .

June 30th.— . . . Meanwhile the chasm between the Cabinet (who
have now become parliamentary agents to the coal-owners) and the
miners, who, maintained by the rates and public subscription, herd after
Cook and Herbert Smith, is widening past repair. I see no reason why
the stoppage in Great Britain's basic industry should not continue
almost indefinitely in a stalemate until one or other party goes under
in disastrous collapse with the other side almost as badly damaged by
the process.

There is one outstanding new fact—never seen before in our
country. The two political parties, one of which *must* be in power, are
to-day definitely and permanently pledged to carry out, in the political
sphere, the demands of one or other of the combatants in the industrial
world. And it is exactly this drastic drawing of the lines of conflict
that has finally smashed the Liberal Party. Asquith, Grey and Simon
found themselves fighting with the capitalists: Lloyd George and some
others deliberately ranged themselves with the Trade Unionists. The
report of the Liberal Royal Commission has proved to be a rotten
bridge. Why? Because whilst its diagnosis bore out the miners' contention that longer hours and lower wages could not save the industry
from decline, its recommendations were rooted in permissive legislation which left the colliery owners free to go on as before. "He

[1] Presumably an early draft for *The Applecart* (1929).

who is not wholeheartedly with us is against us", is the to-day's cry
on both sides. For the present, at any rate, "the inevitability of gradualness" and the desirability of compromise are at a discount. The die-
hards are in possession. Sidney, though he sits for a mining constituency, and was a member of the Sankey Commission, and might therefore be said to combine the representative and the expert, remains
silent. He helped the miners' members to draft amendments to the
Government Bills; but the Miners' Federation demanded unqualified
opposition at every stage to the Hours Bill and the Front Opposition
Bench have felt compelled to carry out this decision. It is not unfair to
say that the Parliamentary Labour Party has become the parliamentary agent of the Miners' Federation exactly as the Government has
undertaken the owners' case. Thus neither H.M. Government nor
H.M. Opposition are free to consider the welfare of the community.
The House of Commons today is in fact a tied house; but tied not as a
body but in two mutually hostile groups, each pledged to fight out, in
the government of the country, the struggle which is being carried on,
openly or covertly, throughout industry at a fearful cost to the country.
The question is how soon will the struggle of endurance in the coal-
fields be transformed into a destructive war; will the miners call out
the safety men? Will the Government call off the out-relief? Either
of these measures, certainly the two together, would mean riot and
repression and might lead to a general election on the crucial issues.
Ought the *capitalist* or the *organised workman* to govern the country?
Alas! for the plain citizen and the long-suffering consumer! Or it
might lead to bloodshed. Out of this turmoil might emerge Lloyd
George as arbiter; or Winston as Mussolini. It is clear that in their
own imagination, each of these two active politicians sees himself as
The Man of Destiny! Of the two I back the Welsh Wizard—a
stronger and bigger fighter.

But I think the British will prefer cricket to melodrama. One side
or the other will be beaten according to "the rules of the game" and
will accept the decision of an undistinguished umpire—probably a
Civil Servant or legal luminary. Some sort of order will have to be
evolved or Great Britain will go into rapid decline.

Lloyd George announces his intention of going to Russia in the
recess and will come back as a qualified admirer of the Soviet Republic.
Austen Chamberlain, to whose lifeless voice and pompous intonation
we listened over the wireless the other night, is booming Mussolini as
the saviour of Italy and the originator of a "great and successful
experiment" in social reorganisation. *We* regard Soviet Russia and
Fascist Italy as belonging to one and the same species of Government;
the creed-autocracy insisting on the supremacy of one social philosophy bringing unity to the people over all conflicting creeds and

sectional interests. Russian Communism and Italian Fascism are both alike a reaction from caste or syndicalist anarchy. The British people have a mild attack of this epidemic of self-will and the identification of one political party with militant capitalism and the other with militant proletarianism is the form this epidemic takes. It will be interesting to observe which type of reaction will set in in our country, or whether we shall revert to a brand-new form of social democracy incorporating our tradition of liberty with an accepted social order? Are we declining? Or are we inventing a new rule of life? . . .

July 24th. 2 a.m.—On the twenty-third of July thirty-four years ago we were married and yesterday we celebrated it by spending the whole day together like two young lovers, driving in the morning to Petersfield to redeem the land tax on this plot of land and going for a long walk in the afternoon—finishing up by listening to a symphony concert over the wireless in the evening. The Other One is extraordinarily well and happy; perhaps getting a wee bit restive at dissipating so much time at Westminster and thus not getting on with the book. But we credit on the other side of the ledger the variety of four days in London and the week-end here. This session he has been leading (brilliantly according to the "Commercial Supplement" of the *Manchester Guardian*) the Labour Party on the Merchandise Marks Act—a job that has satisfied him that he is useful to the P.L.P. And he is getting off the first four chapters of the book to the printers in the next few weeks—we shall undoubtedly get the whole of the first volume done by Christmas. For my own part, except for my chronic melancholy—perhaps *indifference to life* is the better phrase—due to declining vitality, I am content with this last year. The labour and worry spent on *My Apprenticeship* has been justified, so far as public appreciation is concerned. "Original and distinguished" has been the general verdict. It is clear that the book will influence thought and be read by students and thinkers and quoted by future historians. From a pecuniary point of view the outcome is less flattering. Four months' sale in U.K. and U.S.A. (1,200 in U.K. and 500 in U.S.A.) has paid our printers' bill for nearly four thousand copies (U.K.) and yielded two or three hundred pounds' profit. We calculate that the remaining 2,500 will bring in £1,500 in the course of five or ten years. If we get £2,000 out of the book, in five years, we shall be fortunate. When one reckons the cost of the private secretary and two years of writing, the profit cannot be more than £1,500 and that sum will take many years to dribble in! That is to say that I have been earning during the last three years £400 a year and saving it. That is all. Not a "best-seller" most assuredly but a useful contribution to our capital! My panic that the book would fall dead on the one hand, or, on the other, my delusion that I was going to make a little fortune out of it—seem to-day about equally ridiculous. My literary reputation has gone up considerably but our past income of £500 a year from books will not be *increased*. This masterpiece of my old age may just about keep this modest reward of all our labours, past and present, intact for another ten years. Which means when Sidney retires from Parliament we shall have about £1,500 a year to spend; assuming of course that Great Britain retains its present production and goes on distributing the national income in the same way as heretofore. Fifteen hundred a year would enable us to live here comfortably, but we should have to cut down some of our social activities—like this Labour gathering on Saturday. Meantime it would be wise to give up a *resident* secretary, which would save £100 assuming I could find a local substitute. But if our works ceased to sell it would be a tight fit—and if added to that shrinkage, the programme of the Labour Party of direct taxation were carried out, I doubt whether we could do it, without somewhat limiting economies. Think of the temptation to moderate one's views according to one's pocket! What weakens the Labour Party is the ignorance and folly of the proletarian leaders, like Cook, and the almost inevitable apathy of those leaders, like Snowden, MacDonald, Thomas, Clynes and ourselves—men and women who have always had or have acquired a high standard of comfort and a taste for all the refinements of life. If you are "thoroughly comfortable", especially if you have no margin of disposable income and you are also old and therefore incapable of re-adjusting your daily life, it is not human nature to be keen about the re-distribution of wealth according to the ascertained objective needs of the whole population.

July 28th.—Here is the best report of G.B.S.'s birthday speech to the leaders of the Parliamentary Labour Party and over a hundred prominent Fabians and Labour M.P.'s.* His acceptance of Mac-Donald's invitation was quite unexpected; for he loathes public dinners and always refuses to be fêted. But this occasion he warmly welcomed and evidently regarded it as an important event, for his speech was unusually serious and carefully thought out. He had wished it to be broadcast and he began by scoffing at and scolding the Government for its intolerant ban. The gist of his message was twofold: no amount of good-will, florid rhetoric or rigid generalisation, would enable the Labour Party, when it came into power, to bring about the greatest practical measure of social equality and collective control. For the Labour Government's task was infinitely more difficult than the task

* *Manchester Guardian*, July 27th, 1926 [B.W.]. There is no record of this speech in the MS.

of a capitalist ruling class. Enterprise had, as Keynes pointed out, a high yield in apparent efficiency, so far as the production of commodities was concerned. All that was required of the Government was to let things alone unless life and property were at stake. But capitalism was bankrupt in the larger sense of the term: it did not produce social welfare. The evil motives which underlay its activities led to wars between races and classes, to a scandalous inequality of conditions between man and man and to the hideousness of an industrialised country. But the Labour Party had not yet discovered *the technique of Socialist administration*, and their first duty was to work it out. During their first term of office they had shewn they could do the daily job of government, under capitalism, as well as if not better than the Conservative Party. Their foreign policy in particular was more successful just because they were disinterested in their vision of international amity; their leaders as a matter of fact knew more about the people of other countries than the Conservative leaders. Even in home affairs they had shewn themselves more skilful in avoiding disastrous industrial war and in easing the conditions of the workers. All the same there was no sign, so he hinted, that leaders or followers really *had* any well-thought-out scheme for controlling, still less superseding, the capitalist methods of international trade and finance or of directing the nation's income into the right hands and the most needed services. The second proposition, more familiar to the audience, was that the Socialist Party must concentrate on the *distribution* of the national dividend and that if they controlled this wisely and in the common interests, productivity would take care of itself. His final words about his life-long participation in the Labour and Socialist Movement were spoken with a depth of feeling—with a wistfulness—which is uncommon in G.B.S. Indeed he gave the impression of a seer dictating his last testament to his disciples and friends. When I looked round this remarkable gathering—J.R.M. in the Chair—Henderson and his two sons, Clynes, J. H. Thomas, Tom Shaw, Margaret Bondfield, Susan Lawrence, Ponsonby, Trevelyan, the Buxton brothers, Olivier, Pease and ourselves—even Belfort Bax[1] and John Burns (amongst other familiar faces) I wondered whether G.B.S.'s 70th birthday would not prove to be the last assemblage of the men and women who had been mainly responsible for the birth and education of the Labour and Socialist Movement of Great Britain. Only two of the pioneers were dead: Keir Hardie and Hyndman. The greatest of all, whether among the dead or the living, was the guest of the evening—wit and mystic, preacher and dramatist.

[1] Ernest Belfort Bax (1854–1926), Socialist author and philosopher, founder with H. M. Hyndman of the Social-Democratic Federation, and of the Socialist League with William Morris.

July 31st. 2 a.m.—The miners' delegate meeting has endorsed the Miners' Executive resolution that they accept the memorandum of the Bishops, signed by Herbert Smith and A. J. Cook—immediate resumption of work on April terms with subsidy to inferior mines awaiting the interpretation by the Royal Commission of their own Report, and arbitration on all questions arising out of it, including wages, except hours. If they had agreed to this six months ago there would have been no General Strike and no miners' strike. To-day the Government and the owners think they are on the eve of victory and will refuse to negotiate on these lines; the employers, clearly, want a fight to the finish. But the miners are still in a strong position; a far stronger position than any considerable body of strikers have ever been. There is no possible substitute for their labours; if they don't hew coal no one else can; and if British coal is not worked British industry can hardly survive as a going concern. Hitherto the miners could be starved into submission: to-day humanitarian sentiment and working-class control of local authorities makes that impossible with regard to the miners' families and difficult in the case of the men themselves. But obviously the mining areas cannot be indefinitely taxed: they are piling up debt which must sooner or later be liquidated by the state. Already some Boards of Guardians are trying to deny the right to subsistence; will they succeed? How far is the deliberate refusal of maintenance to persons who will not work on the capitalists' terms practicable? That is one issue which will be decided in the next two months. And if it is not possible to starve the miners into submission and the deadlock continues—which would be disastrous to the capitalists—will there be a General Election on the *Right to Maintenance of the Striker and his Dependants*? If so we shall come very near the advocacy by the Tories of compulsory labour under threat of starvation with the inevitable reaction on the part of the working-class electorate in favour of the confiscation of unearned income so as to bring all men under the same dispensation. I am inclined to think that this miners' strike is going to be by far the most momentous industrial struggle in my life-time and among other things it may settle whether Great Britain is going to solve the problem of democratic government or not. The last chapter of the second volume of our *History of English Poor Law* may give the answer to this vital question!

August 2nd.—Our gathering of near on 2,000 members of the L.P.s of Hants, Surrey and Sussex, arriving in 80 charabancs, to listen to J.R.M. and Margaret Bondfield, with Ponsonby, Russell and De la Warr and ourselves as minor performers, went off brilliantly, to the great satisfaction of Croft, the headquarters organiser, and to the amused astonishment of the neighbourhood. We did what we intended to do; we showed Headquarters how to wake up these tracts of commons and residential parks, of small towns and seaside resorts, unprovided with halls for big meetings, at a low cost or at no cost at all. For if we had had a little more experience we could have made the occasion pay its way. The secret is that with charabancs and the increasing habit of jaunts of town workers into the country, combined with the difficulty experienced by ardent Party workers of seeing their leaders in a homely sort of way, these garden parties are bound to attract large numbers and are also an advertisement of the existence of the Labour Party in an effective form. There is the risk of bad weather; but even here it can be almost overcome if you provide, as we did, a monster marquee. Our luck was a delightful warm grey day ending in a burst of sunshine when J.R.M. was giving his second speech and final farewell. All the same the arrangements have cost me thought and anxiety and expense and I shall not do it again in a hurry.

The leader of the Labour Party was in his best form. He is an attractive creature; he has a certain beauty in colouring, figure and face, a delightful voice and an easy unpretentious manner, a youthful enjoyment of his prestige as a Prime Minister, all of which is amusing to watch. But his conversation is not entertaining or stimulating—it consists of pleasant anecdotes about political and society personages—occasionally some episode in his own career—told with calculated discretion. When he and I walked round the garden together he talked exclusively about his weekly visits to Christie's and the pieces of old furniture he was picking up. Directly you turn the conversation off trivial personalities on to subjects, whether it be general questions or the domestic problems of the Labour Party, J.R.M. dries up and looks bored. Not once did we *discuss* anything whatsoever and even the anecdotes led nowhere. Does he ever exchange ideas? Certainly not with us. At the gathering he looked cheery and he spoke well and at the farewell message his words were lit up by affectionate intimacy and homely wit which delighted his audience. My general impression is that J.R.M. feels himself to be *the* indispensable leader of a new political party which is bound to come into office within his life-time—a correct forecast, I think. He is no longer *intent* on social reform—any indignation he ever had at the present distribution of wealth he has lost; his real and intimate life is associating with non-political aristocratic society, surrounded with the beauty and dignity which wealth can buy and social experience can direct. Ramsay MacDonald is not distinguished either in intellect or character, and he has some very mean traits in his nature. But he has great gifts as a political leader, he has personal charm, he has vitality, he is assiduous, self-controlled and skilful. In all these respects he is unique in the inner circle of the

Labour Party made up, as it is, of fanatics, faddists, refined and self-effacing intellectuals and the dull mediocrities of the Trade Union Movement. The Labour Movement has not yet thrown up any leader who is equal in intellect and personal character to the greatest men of the older parties—to Gladstone, Disraeli, Chamberlain and Balfour and even Lloyd George. Where we excel is in our non-commissioned officers—women as well as men. I doubt whether there has ever been a mass movement which has combined in its rank and file so much moral refinement and intellectual enlightenment. But it has not yet found an adequate leader. Ramsay MacDonald is a magnificent substitute for a leader. He has the ideal appearance. ("Every day he grows more distinguished looking," writes the *Nation*.) But he is shoddy in character and intellect. Our great one has yet to come. Shall I live to see him? Or will it be *she* who must be obeyed? . . .

August 9th.—There must be a scarcity of politically constructive minds if J. M. Keynes seems such a treasure! Hitherto he has not attracted me—brilliant, supercilious, and not sufficiently patient for sociological discovery even if he had the heart for it—I should have said. But then I had barely seen him; also I think his love marriage with the fascinating little Russian dancer has awakened his emotional sympathies with poverty and suffering. For when I look around I see no other man who might discover how to control the wealth of nations in the public interest. He is not merely brilliant in expression and provocative in thought; he is a realist; he faces facts and he has persistency and courage in thought and action. By taste an administrator, by talent a man of science, with a remarkable literary gift, he has not the make-up of a political leader. Not that he lacks "personality"; he is impressive and attractive—he could impose himself on an audience and gather round him a group of followers and disciples; if he could tolerate a political party as God makes it, he could lead it. But he is contemptuous of common men especially when gathered together in herds—he dislikes the human herd and has no desire to enlist the herd instinct on his side. Hence his antipathy to Trade Unions, to proletarian culture, to nationalism and patriotism as distinguished from public spirit. The common interests and vulgar prejudices of aristocracies and plutocracies are equally displeasing to him—in fact he dislikes all the common or garden thoughts and emotions that bind men together in bundles. He would make a useful member of a Cabinet; but would he ever get there? Certainly not as a member of one of the present Front Benches. I do not know which one—Conservative or Labour—he would despise most. As for the rank and file! Heaven help them. What Keynes might achieve is a big scheme of social engineering; he might even be called in to carry it out, but as an expert and not as a representative. As an ardent lover of the bewitching Lydia Lopokova this eminent thinker and political pamphleteer is charming to contemplate. . . .

August 21st.—The agony of the miners' resistance to the owners' terms has begun; how long and how fierce it may be no one can say; I am inclined to think the end will come before the Trade Union Congress the first week in September; Sidney says "the end of September". The calling of the Delegate Conference to give the leaders power to negotiate, the barely successful struggle to get their freedom, the request for a "conference with the mine-owners", the insolent behaviour and insulting words of Evan Williams, the colliery owners' chairman, and his final refusal to have any further dealings with the Miners' Federation—the departure of Baldwin for Aix-les-Bains, are all definite steps in the débâcle. Taken with the failure of the General Strike it is a big catastrophe; it is the biggest defeat Trade Unionism has ever experienced—somewhat akin to the collapse of 1834. But, as in the Great War, it is very doubtful whether the victors will not lose as much as the vanquished. The capitalist owners have proved themselves as malicious as they are stupid; the Government has shown itself as incompetent to end as to avert the most costly industrial dispute that has ever occurred; it has proved so partisan that it has turned many Conservative workmen into good Labour supporters. So far as I can see the only organisation that comes out the stronger for this disaster is the Parliamentary Labour Party—for the simple reason that the prestige of the General Council of the Trade Union Congress has been destroyed and the strike as a weapon has been discredited. Indeed the agony of the Miners' Federation *might* mean a Labour Government after the General Election of 1928. . . .

September 1st.—Sidney came back from two days and one night in London exhausted and unusually depressed. He had spent six hours or more looking up references for the book, at B.M. and H. of C. During the rest of the working time listening to the dreary debates on E.R.[1] and the miners' strike or at Parliamentary meetings of one sort or another. "The Miners' Executive," he said, "had given out to the press that they were going to meet us in order to settle a joint policy; when they came at 8 o'clock on Monday night, they had nothing to say but that they could say nothing before the Delegate Meeting on Thursday!" J.R.M. tried to persuade them to make up their minds to ask the Government for a meeting with the mine-owners with an

[1] i.e., Emergency Regulations, put into force (under the Emergency Powers Act of 1920) during the General Strike, and renewed in a special Parliamentary session at the end of August. They were again renewed in the four following months.

"open agenda"; A. J. Cook was frankly in favour, but Herbert Smith was obdurate. It is like watching a man committing suicide—it is worse because the leaders are killing not themselves, but the men's organisation. Six months ago they could have kept the 7 hour day and the National Agreements; today they have lost both and are at the employers' mercy about wages. Meanwhile the Parliamentary Labour Party is left without a policy; they are tied to the tail of the miners without being consulted as to which way the tail should wag. A. J. Cook goes to tea with Lloyd George and is reported to have been much impressed—no doubt his present conciliatory policy is due to Lloyd George's tact. He does not come and consult—nor do any of the other members of the Miners' Executive—with *any* members of the Labour Front Bench or even with the miners' M.P.s. These pitifully inarticulate Trade Union officials dare not consult or confer with anyone who counts, on terms of give and take. All they are willing to do is to state their terms, in a muddled way, and then leave the room—they run away from discussion. I very much doubt whether they really *discuss* the situation with each other. They repeat, repeat, repeat the old slogans and then take a vote—and the vote tends in favour of some other body making the decision! The miners' leaders are suffering from general paralysis of the will and have been for some time. Robert Smillie, in spite of his impressive personality and sombre eloquence, never had a policy, industrial or political. All he has are dogmas like "no compensation for royalty owners"— the sort of dogma that actually prevents things getting done. "And what do you think is the next step for the British Labour Party?" I asked him as we sat over the fire in the Roker Hotel in the autumn of 1921. "Communism, I imagine," he answered with a solemn intonation of the word Communism. "Russian Communism?" I enquired, laying stress on Russian. "I suppose so," he answered rather more vaguely and turned the conversation into a tale about his first meeting with Keir Hardie. When the General Council last April (on which he represents the Miners' Federation) were deciding whether or not they should call a General Strike, Robert Smillie left London for Scotland, on the plea that, in such a crisis, he must be among his own people, and he remained there throughout the nine days and was therefore absent when the General Council called off the General Strike, though he knew that the other representative of the Miners' Federation, Richards,[1] was away ill and that the Miners' Federation would be unrepresented. A deplorable lack of moral in this heroic figure—who by the way was the last idol of H. W. Massingham. . . .

[1] Thomas Richards (1859–1931), Secretary of South Wales Miners' Federation and Vice-President of M.F.G.B.

BOURNEMOUTH T.U.C.

September 10th.—Two days at the Bournemouth Trade Union Congress—the same old crowd—mostly grey-headed—not bald-headed—the British Labour Party keeps its hair on actually, as well as metaphorically!—of heavy solid men meeting punctually at 9.30 in the morning and adjourning five minutes before the time in the afternoon—a habit which amazes our continental comrades. The same sensible procedure, strictly enforced; the same orderliness and unfailing good nature, and, in spite of unemployment and empty Trade Union chests, the same jokes and laughter. Behind these persistent traits there was a difference; the feeling of elation and bursting self-confidence of Bevin, Bromley[1] and Bramley, the self-assertion of the General Council as the centre of the British working-class power—which we were told was the note of Scarborough, 1925, have swept over and passed away. There is almost a note of panic in the talk of the delegates among themselves—there is bitterness about the General Strike; there is anger against the miners among the boilermakers and shipwrights and the cotton workers; anger against the G.C. among the miners—determination in the heart of each of the larger sections, N.U.R., Cotton, General Workers, that *never again* will they lose control of their own actions. Of course there are individual delegates and smaller unions who still want to create a G.H.Q. which shall dominate affairs—these all still refer to "workers' control" (but all such resolutions were defeated by large majorities). The unexpected vote against Easton Lodge[2] and the development of a grandiose scheme of working-class education was significant of the turning of the tide against "proletarianism". "Capitalism is not dead—it is not weakening", was the burden of the speeches. The miners sat silent and depressed, except for the outburst of anger against Bromley when he rose to second the G.C. appeal for contributions towards their fund. They were not treated well by the G.C., and if some of the delegates gave Cook an enthusiastic reception—there was a marked coldness on the part of others. Apathy tempered by pessimism was the atmosphere of the Bournemouth Congress.

We were chatting with Ammon and Lansbury in our hotel on

---

[1] John Bromley (1876–1945), General Secretary of the Associated Society of Locomotive Engineers and Firemen, and a strong "left-wing" Trade Unionist.

[2] At the T.U.C. Congress of 1925 proposals were accepted in principle for the taking over by the General Council of Ruskin College and the London Labour College, and consultations were to be arranged between the General Council and the Education Committee of the Co-operative Union.

Later in the same year Lady Warwick offered Easton Lodge as the home for a residential college; and the General Council, receiving the offer favourably, sent a circular to its constituent bodies recommending (a) a levy on the Unions, (b) that it should be empowered to raise a loan to meet capital charges, and (c) that the Unions should establish scholarships. When the proposal came before the 1926 Congress, however, it was criticised as "too vague", and the reference back was carried by 2,441,000 to 1,481,000. Thereafter the scheme was dropped.

Monday when A. J. Cook came up; and rather to our surprise he stayed on to talk to us, which I encouraged as I wanted to look at and listen to "Billy Sunday" of the Labour Movement as he is nicknamed. The son of a soldier, born and brought up in the barracks, a boy on a farm, migrating when a young man from the Somerset to the South Wales mining area, passing through a fervent religious stage, coming under the influence of the Central Labour College and Noah Ablett[1] (whom he helped to write *The Miners' Next Step*), graduating into Trade Union politics as a conscientious objector and avowed admirer of Lenin's, and finally engineered into the high position of the General Secretaryship of the Miners' Federation by Communist nuclei—[this] summarises his past career. He is a loosely built, ugly-featured man—looks low-caste—not at all the skilled artisan type, more the agricultural labourer. He is oddly remarkable in appearance because of excitability of gesture, mobility of expression in his large-lipped mouth, glittering china-blue eyes, set close together in a narrow head with lanky yellow hair—altogether a man you watch with a certain admiring curiosity. Sidney had represented him to me (he was on the L.P. Executive with him) as rude and unpleasing in manner. But with us that afternoon he was friendly—even confidential—and poured out an incoherent stream of words—vivid descriptions of Winston Churchill, J.R.M. and recent negotiations—at least his narrative would have been vivid if it had been coherent. He is obviously over-wrought—almost to breaking-point—but even allowing for this it is clear that he has no intellect and not much intelligence—he is a quivering mass of emotions—a mediumistic magnetic sort of creature—not without personal attractiveness—an inspired idiot, drunk with his own words, dominated by his own slogans. I doubt whether he even knows what he is going to say or what he has just said. To-day he is in a funk: he sees that the miners are beaten and that all his promises of speedy and complete victory will rise up against him. "I shall tell them that we must have our Mons; a well-led army must retreat before a stronger army; *we shall win* like the British army did—perhaps four years hence." If it were not for the mule-like obstinacy of Herbert Smith, A. J. Cook would settle on *any* terms. He has led his army of a million miners into a situation where they must surrender—at discretion on any terms Winston can impose on the mine-owners. It is tragic to think that this inspired idiot, coupled with poor old Herbert Smith, with his senile obstinacy, are the dominant figures in so great and powerful an organisation as the Miners' Federation. Neither one nor the other is intellectually articulate; they can neither comprehend nor express complicated facts and argu-

[1] Noah Ablett (1883–1935), miners' agent, syndicalist, and Marxist economist. Chairman of the Central Labour College the Marxist residential college in Kensington.

ments. Relatively to the difficulty and magnitude of their job, A. J. Cook and Herbert Smith are mental defectives. An honest mule and an inspired goose, makes bad leadership for any herd. To think that these two men have controlled the industry and trade of Great Britain for six months! It is a caricature of Trade Unionism. No wonder the Trade Union Congress is depressed and the older and saner leaders full of foreboding. A catastrophic ending to the absurd idol of "Workers' Control"—the mines for the miners and damn the consequences. The consequences have certainly proved to be damnable ! . . . .

As a dramatic contrast to A. J. Cook, the proletarian leader, there was J. R. MacDonald, also staying at our hotel. He has been a useful consultant during these last days, and it was he who suggested to the miners' leaders the formula which Winston accepted as a basis of Government intervention. Naturally enough the ex-Prime Minister has been telling all whom it may concern that it was *he* and not the "would-be Tory premier" who had brought the beginnings of peace to the world. But what interested me was J.R.M.'s conversation. He was particularly gracious to us; came to our table and took us into his private sitting-room. But he was evidently absorbed in the social prestige of his ex-premiership enhanced by a romantic personality. Immaculately groomed and perfectly tailored—too deliberately so for artistic effect—it made him look commonplace—he went out of his way to tell me that he was going on to stay with Mrs. Biddulph near Cirencester[1]—"The Hon. Mrs. Biddulph," he added, and then described her as a patron of good English craftsmanship in furniture. Once again he spoke about the difficulty of getting old pieces of furniture—"the Americans are buying it up"—and described his adventures with this dealer or that. "Then I am going to stay at"—I forget the place—"with the Princess Hartsfelt (?). She was a Cunningham you know. Do you know her? A remarkable woman." After that visit, I gathered, he was going on a motor trip in North Africa with Noel and Charles Buxton and then to London for the session, with the Labour Party Conference intervening. I was always trying to bring him back to politics—but without result except an outburst of suspicion of Tom Jones who had been advising Winston and trying to keep him (MacDonald) out of the picture. Of course so long as he does his duty in public speaking and in attendance in Parliament, his social relations are his own concern; and his very detachment from all Labour questions, coupled with his long experience of public life, may make him a wiser counsellor than A. J. Cook or even G. D. H. Cole.

[1] Presumably the wife of Claud William Biddulph, of Rodmarton, Cirencester, second son of the first Lord Biddulph. Mrs. Biddulph was a Howard, grand-daughter of the sixth Earl of Carlisle.

But MacDonald is not working at his job; he is not thinking about it; he is not associating with those whom he has and would have to guide and from whom he could get enlightenment. His thoughts and his emotions are concentrated on his agreeable relations with the men and women—especially the women—of the enemy's camp—his mentality is approximating to that of Dean Inge—he is becoming impatient with the troublesomeness of the working class. He did not attend the Trades Union Congress gatherings at Bournemouth; he was not associated with any of the delegates except ourselves—he was motoring with members of the Rotary Club. Nor did he want to talk to us about politics—he wanted to talk about old furniture and "Society" personalities. As I know little or nothing about either of these topics our conversation was always on the point of petering out. And yet, though he has lost his influence with the inner circle of the devout, J.R.M. is the inevitable leader of the P.L.P.—there is no one else in the Party who has anything like his prestige in the country at large, and it is the outer circle of the electorate that counts in gaining a Labour majority—the devout we have always with us. It remains to be added that with J. H. Thomas in Canada and Arthur Henderson in Australia and the absence of any striking personality among the T.U. officials (Bevin was distinctly in abeyance as a leader) the dominant impression left on my mind by the T.U.C. of 1926 was chaos along the rank and file—disheartened chaos and the absence of leadership. We ourselves felt like ghosts—"Ancients" coming back from the backwoods of historical research to our old haunts—there to discover other ghosts wandering among a gathering of bewildered and frightened children.

What interested me in this Congress more than the state of mind of British Trade Unionists, was the presence of two foreign influences. The Russians were there in spirit though not in person. It was the Russian Trade Unions, virtually the Soviet Government, who were the financial backers of the miners, contributing about two-fifths of the total relief funds—£600,000 out of the million raised in Great Britain and abroad. And Tomsky's[1] sensational indictment of the G.C. and the Trade Union leadership generally, though it was a magnificent futility, advertised the participation of Russian Communism in the direction of Great Britain's Labour Movement. Then silent and slightly contemptuous, barely noticed by the Congress, were the two delegates from the American Federation of Labour—one of them was appointed *while present at the Congress* to a post of £5,000 a year in a capitalist undertaking and did not trouble to stay out the first two days—the other made a perfunctory speech of good will. These men

---

[1] Michael Pavlovich Tomsky. One of the old Bolshevik leaders; Chairman from 1917–29 of the All-Union Central Council of Trade Unions. A member of the "Right Opposition" of 1928–29; committed suicide in the purges of 1936.

represented the new departure in U.S.A.—a Tied Trade Unionism, working in close accord with Trustified Capitalism—exactly the organisation which has become the avowed aim of British employers. The British Labour Movement seemed passive and indeterminate— a no-man's-land between the more virile cultures of Russia and the U.S.A. respectively—between two militant autocracies each claiming to dominate the world—according to the dictates of rival economic creeds—one the creed of the Have Nots and the other the creed of the Haves. Shall we escape being devastated by a clash of creeds? Shall we come to rest as we did in the 16th century during the continental fight between the Pope and Protestant—in a sort of Anglican com-promise—that will bring rest to our soul?

But to return to the personalities of the Congress. G. D. H. Cole, A. J. Cook, J. R. MacDonald, the intellectual fanatic, the inspired idiot and the accomplished substitute for a leader, are singularly anta-gonistic to each other. These three men, taken either apart or together, yield no workable policy for the Labour Movement. The silent refined little man, J. R. Clynes, who came for a week-end with his wife, has more wisdom than any or all of them. But he lacks vitality—and like Sidney, he has no desire to control his fellow men. He has throughout been against the Guild Socialist inflation of the objects of the Trade Union Movement; against the General Strike, against boasting and bolstering of direct action by A. J. Cook. Unlike J.R.M. he has been solidly in favour of every advance of democratic control and social equality, whether by collective bargaining or by legislation or by increased taxation or public administration; he is still a convinced Socialist; he always says what he thinks and no more than he thinks, and he knows exactly what he does think. He and his wife are devoted mates, refined in their enjoyment of good literature and good music, assiduous and single-minded in their service of the Labour Movement. But alas! though he is an admirable counsellor he is not a leader of men—he is too modest and silent to be a force, whether on platform or in committee; he is what he looks, a small man. J.R.M. has little or no regard for him and he obviously does not like Mac-Donald though I have never known him say a word against him. His only resemblance to the other three is that like Cole, Cook and MacDonald he is not a "good mixer". Could one pick out four men who were so fundamentally dissimilar and antagonistic to each other? In outlook and in standpoint they are mutually exclusive and yet how typical of the Labour Movement. Arthur Henderson's great super-iority is the fact that he *can* work with and make use of all four of them; he is, in fact, a first-rate manager of men—the only one in the front rank of the Labour Movement. Without Arthur Henderson, Heaven help the Labour Party! But *he* also is no leader of men—he has no personal magnetism. So we shall have to put up with our Magnificent Substitute—J.R.M. As I write these words I see him purring in the home of a high-placed woman friend—the Honourable or the Princess—enjoying his social prestige as ex-Premier; and at odd intervals concocting new phrases of sympathy with the miners or denunciation of the Government.

However, regarded as Labour leaders, we all suffer deterioration, by being too damned comfortable. That is the tragic dilemma of democratic leadership—in a society made up of the rich and the poor those who are in the position to know cannot feel; those who are in the position to feel do not know! . . .

September 24th.—Baldwin has squashed Winston's attempt to bring the coal-owners to heel now that the miners' leaders are at last willing to accept not only the Samuel Report but something much less advantageous than the report. For practical purposes the Conservative Cabinet falls into line with the owners and sends a derisory offer to the Miners' Executive; the men are to be ordered back to work on the district owners' terms; and if *when hours have been lengthened* they object to the rates of pay this wage question is to be submitted to an Arbitration Board (constitution not explained) with an "independent chairman". It is open to question whether the miners would not do better to surrender without conditions so that they would be free to fight when circumstances were more favourable. What they will probably do will be to drag on for another two months and slink back to work, like beaten dogs to their kennels, some time before Christmas, leaving their national organisation in ruins and the T.U. Movement utterly discredited. It is the biggest defeat of industrial democracy, moral as well as material, in our life-time. . . .

Margate Labour Party Conference.

October 12th.—The swing to the right, especially among the Trade Unions, is even more emphatic at the L.P.C. than at the Bournemouth Trades Union Congress. The Communists were snowed under on the first day; on the second day the ragged remnant of the Miners' Federation (Cook and Smith did not appear) put up a fight for the embargo and the levy. But as this was virtually an appeal on purely industrial issues, from the T.U.C. to the L.P.C., it was easy for J.R.M. and J.H.T. to carry the Congress overwhelmingly against them. They kicked back by voting against the Executive on the reference back of the birth control passage in the Report; afterwards they were silent and subdued, voting against most of the existing Executive Committee. The I.L.P. contingent made themselves ridiculous by putting up Mosley to support the miners in a passionate speech in favour of "forcing a dissolution" and voting a levy; they are in open revolt against J.R.M. and J.R.M. is contemptuous of them. But what was more significant of the changed mentality of the T.U. was Bob Williams's[1] public recantation, as Chairman, not only of revolutionary but of *militant* Trade Unionism and the despairing private talks of other T.U. officials—Shinwell, Tillett, etc. about the decline in membership in their own Unions. "This talk about the decline of capitalism is all nonsense," was the refrain. Rumours of the new departures in trusts and syndicates in Germany and U.S.A., of the penetration of Russia and the control of Europe by American financiers, are rife among T.U.—and are spreading a sort of defeatism and desire to come quickly to terms with the Mammon of Unrighteousness. On the other hand there is a certain optimism among the politicals and among Parliamentary candidates—they *think* they are doing well in the constituencies—that there is a swing of the pendulum which will bring the Labour Party into office at the next General Election—an optimism which is not shared by J.R.M. and the Front-Benchers. J.R.M. is, despite the I.L.P., completely in control of the rank and file of the political movement and I think of the Trade Unions. J. H. Thomas is under a cloud, Clynes is ignored and Arthur Henderson's absence is *felt*. There is no sign of any new leadership, either by individuals or groups. The predominant tone is chaotic—no one knows what to be at—intellectually the Movement is drifting—the only direction apparent on the surface being away from direct action and workers' control—in favour of all forms of communal control and especially of expert and bureaucratic control. There is today no reason why Keynes, E. D. Simon[2] and Herbert Samuel should not be among the leaders of the Labour Party—they are certainly more advanced than J.R.M. and J.H.T. in their constructive proposals and would probably carry more weight with the Labour Party Front Bench than the I.L.P. group do—Brailsford, Wise, Fenner Brockway. J. R.M. would rejoice in having these Liberal intellectuals as possible Cabinet members. For the rest, the company at the Queen's Hotel was distinguished by its elegance and its aristocratic flavour—the Mosleys, De la Warrs and other lithe and beauteous forms—leaders of fashion or ladies of the stage attended by 6 ft. tall and well-groomed men— J.R.M. easily the most distinguished looking of the lot. "What a transformation," said I to William Sanders, "from the Labour Party Conferences we used to attend before the Great War!" It was all very pleasant. But . . . "J.R.M. is *not* a snob," said that charming

---

[1] Robert Williams (1881–1936). Coal-trimmer and journalist; General Secretary of Transport Workers' Federation, 1912–23; considered to be very revolutionary until Black Friday, 1921.

[2] Lord Simon of Wythenshawe; subsequently joined the Labour Party.

boy De la Warr to me, "but he genuinely prefers the aristocrat to the proletarian as every-day associates."

On Monday the ex-Prime Minister is off for a motoring tour to Algiers with the two Buxtons and will not be back till the end of November, a fortnight after the opening of Parliament. However, he deserves his holiday—he has been speaking continuously since Parliament rose "at his top form, *as an idealist*, about the *future of society*," observed that super-organiser Egerton Wake[1] with marked approval, and with sardonic emphasis on *idealist* and *future of society*.

October 15th.— Sidney was not elected to Labour Party Executive. I suggested that he should not stand but he said that he wished to offer his services once more and would prefer to be dismissed—a queer little spark of pride. This emphasises the rightness of his decision not to stand for Seaham again. Hugh Dalton is coming to the front— the most cautiously skilful of the younger men. . . .

October 19th.—The Miners' Federation has taken the last desperate step and declared war on the coal-owners and on the community: they revert to the slogan "not a cent off the pay, not a minute on the day"; they call on the safety men to come out, they demand an embargo on coal and a levy on all trade unionists in work; and they openly base their last chance of success on withdrawing power and heat from the whole body of consumers at a time of year when all will feel it. Apparently they build on the decline of coal imports, owing to the approach of winter, and on the possibility of stopping the drift back to work by another promise of speedy victory, if the men stay out and heating becomes impossible. The coal-owners, who have plenty of coal for their own use, whether as companies or individuals, are equally cold-blooded, and the Government is hoping that by withdrawing relief to the women and children in one area after another they can starve the mining population of food before the miners deprive the rest of the community of heat and light. This immense industrial conflict is the last word of sectional egotism and class stupidity leading, one might almost say, to the suicide of each and all of the three parties to the dispute—the nationalisation of a ruined industry—the worst of both worlds! And owing to the fact that the two great political parties —H.M.G. and H.M.O.—have become agents of two exasperated and exasperating combatants, no one in the front rank dare say one word of common sense to either party, because in the last stages of a pitched battle it would be used to defeat his clients. The victory of the coal-owners or of the miners would be deplorable—one hardly dare say which of the two would be most destructive to the commonwealth.

[1] National Agent to the Labour Party from 1919.

October 24th.—Back from autumn visit to Seaham. In the six days we had twelve meetings—crowded-out meetings—and we saw many of our leading supporters. The surface facts show no exceptional distress: indeed the pit villages look clean and prosperous and the inhabitants healthy (death rate unusually low). Various people told us that the men and boys had benefited by the rest, sun, and open air and abstinence from alcohol and tobacco (the M.O.H. added from "over-heating"). And the women freed from coal dust and enjoying regular hours; whilst the school-children, through the ample supply of first-class food (eleven meals each week at a cost of 3/6 per child at wholesale prices) were certainly improved in health and happiness. The one want was clothing and boots, and our gift of £100 to the Repair Fund was much appreciated. From the early hours of the morning until late at night there was a continual rumbling of hand-barrows past our hotel at Roker; and on the roads there were always long lines of push cycles going to and fro with bulging bags of slack and coal to the miners' homes, or peddling the stuff to other workers.

The state of mind of the miners and their wives was less easy to discover than the state of their health. I had a lunch of the thirty chairwomen and secretaries of the Women's Sections and a delegate conference of about 400 representative members. They all seemed in good spirits, hard at work running relief funds, and collecting money by whist drives, football matches (women players), dances and socials; they had raised, in the last two months, £1,700 for the central relief fund for pregnant and lying-in women and infants. Some of the lodges were paying a few shillings a week to the unmarried men; the Guardians were paying 12/- a week to the wives and 4/- a week (3/6 deducted for school meals) to each child. But to return to the state of mind of the women. There was certainly no sign of strain. As I looked at the gathering of 400 miners' wives and daughters, in their best dresses, and the prettily decorated tea tables, with piles of cake and bread-and-butter, it might have been a gathering of prosperous lower middle-class women—in appearance these women looked as comfortably off as Mrs. Anderson Fenn and myself—their clothes certainly were quite as respectable and attractive. Neither were they gloomy—they were in a jolly talkative state of mind; they were enjoying their lives.

The men and boys were more silent and sullen; some of the elder men were anxious and wistful. Sidney's speeches were not encouraging about the future, and though the audiences were respectful, even affectionate, in their attitude towards him and his wife it was clear that they were disappointed with his guarded and deprecatory attitude towards the strike and some of them said so.

The Shotton branch passed a resolution complaining of his lack of sympathy and understanding of the miners' case shown in his address on the General Strike.

At the Conference on the General Strike there was an outburst of anger—a rhetorical speech from one of the ablest of the younger men —Wm. Parker, a T.U. leader—showing bitterness; if the miners could not get what they wanted by the strike they would resort to armed revolt. There were hostile but futile questions from Communists, and the chairman of the meetings at Wheatley Hill burst out in defence of the constitution of Soviet Russia. A. J. Cook was everywhere acclaimed a hero. That inspired fool is like the gangrenous gas of a badly wounded body. But for the most part there was silence— a moody silence—and in private conversation the responsible men were anxious for an immediate district settlement. Debts are piling up. There was an uncomfortable feeling that the worst is yet to come. We think there will be a universal and bitter disillusionment when the working life is resumed on lower earnings and for longer hours, and with all the savings gone. At present the majority of the miners and their families believe that they will win—they think they can starve the country of coal before they are starved by lack of food. So far as Durham is concerned, given the present expenditure of the Poor Law Guardians and subscriptions from the public, it looks as if this optimistic calculation were correct. G. D. H. Cole said, when he was with us after a visit to Durham, "I don't see why the Durham miners should *ever* go back."

The mining population seem to take it for granted that it would be a public scandal—an infamous proceeding—if they were to be "driven back into the pits by starvation", i.e. by withholding of full maintenance for themselves and their families during their refusal to work on the coal-owners' terms. It never seems to occur to them that *they* are withdrawing maintenance from the families of shipbuilders and ironworkers by remaining idle. The employers' terms are none too good—and the industry if *properly conducted* could afford even better terms. Which seems a justification of the miners' obstinacy and egotism. Unfortunately this blind resistance is not the way by which reorganisation of the coal-mining industry will or can be attained. The Great Strike, like the Great War, will bring more anger and more misery. It will not bring reconstruction. We came back gloomy about the future, but we can do little or nothing to help to make it better. We gave our £100 not because it would help—but out of gratitude to the miners for their generosity towards us—we were paying back some of our election expenses—that was all! . . .

Sidney reports that at the meetings yesterday of the Party Executive with the miners' leaders the poor men were glum and made no suggestions as to what line the Party should take in the debate; whilst at the full Party meeting a resolution proposed by David Kirkwood[1] was passed congratulating the miners on their "courageous leaders"; not one in five of the M.P.s present really agreed. But the alteration made in D.K.'s draft from *sterling* leadership to *courageous* leadership was a refinement which enabled even the right-wing members to vote for it with their tongue in their cheek. "For it is possible for a fool to have courage," said one of them. "Foolhardy" would have expressed their meaning; if they had expressed it with honesty—but no one dared move the rejection of a resolution which will seem to the public an endorsement by the Labour Party of Cook's and Smith's policy during the last six months. The weak side of the Labour Party's constitution—its organic dependence on the big Trade Unions—has been discovered by the events of this year. The sooner the remnant of the Liberals throw themselves into the political Labour Movement and transform it into a constituency party, the better for the country, assuming that this could be done without the Trade Unions forming another party of their own. What I think more probable is that the Trade Union Movement will itself break up—the larger portion adhering to the P.L.P. with a minority movement becoming definitely Communist. One result will be that the miners will become intensely pro-Russian and a war with Russia will become difficult if not impossible. . . .

November 8th.—Last night Susan and I entertained the P.L.P., and today Sidney and I lunch with the Oswald Mosleys to meet Mackenzie King. So ends my week's dissipation and I go back to the cottage to work—rather a wreck. Like Haldane I do not intend to give way to old age—the only question is how to distribute one's waning energies—whether in study or social intercourse. A week in London means talk—endless talk and unaccustomed food and hours—small doses of alcohol and too many cigarettes—consequent unhealthiness. In the country one works too hard. Don't fuss over the last years of life, a voice tells me. Take yourself lightly for the world will do so! Self-importance and self-pity in ancients, and too careful husbanding of strength is absurd. The ancient should fade away from the sight of fellow-mortals noiselessly—leaving, like the Cheshire Cat, a smile, and then the memory of a smile. There is comedy in the way we old people—Shaws, Haldane, Graham Wallases, etc. etc.—gaze and listen to each other—watching for the signs of senility and wondering whether the symptoms are as apparent in ourselves as they are in all the others! While the younger folk class us all in the herd that

[1] David Kirkwood (1872–1955), later Lord Kirkwood, Clydeside engineer and leader of the war-time shop steward movement there; chief of the "Clyde deportees" of 1916.

are "getting old" and must just be tolerated and humoured and sometimes "honoured". G.B.S. has indeed ascended above the herd of the "getting old" and has become in his life time an Idol, enthroned in an international Temple, all by himself. The wonder is that with all this idolisation G.B.S. has gained the grace of humility and unselfconsciousness. . . .

The Rout of the Miners

November 15th.—The Miners' Federation delegate meeting surrendered yesterday to the Government terms—the worst possible terms—barely better than unconditional district surrender to the employers—and they surrendered in the worst possible way. They refuse responsibility but refer the terms to the districts with a *recommendation* that they be accepted—which means that some districts will accept and others will not.[1] Hence the Government will be able to repudiate its own proposals—whilst the miners will stream back to work imagining that peace has been declared! A. J. Cook has characteristically taken to his bed so as to be out of the fray whilst the army he has misled crumples up and, in cold literalness, disappears underground! No critic or enemy of the Trade Union Movement could have planned or even imagined so catastrophic a defeat. All the circumstances of this great industrial war—the General Strike, the bleeding white of the Trade Unions, the Russian million subsidy, the five million outdoor relief, the enormous loss to the community—are all facts that provoke reprisals on the part of a reactionary Government, and lead to revolutionary discontent or hopeless apathy among whole sections of the working class. The shock may disintegrate the present industrial order; but I cannot see how it can lay the foundation for a better one. No class, no party and no individuals come well out of it, either in their fortunes or in their reputations. The only group who may score are the most incompetent of the colliery owners; and the only person who may feel himself to be a victor is the ineffable Evan Williams! *He*, certainly, ought to be grateful for A. J. Cook! The two worst losers are the Miners' Federation and Baldwin's Government. And just because these two are the worst losers, the political Labour Party gains—but gains in an evil way—not by its own merit, but because its leading rival within the Labour Movement and its principal opponent without have shown themselves equally shifty, incompetent and ruthless in their class egoism. . . .

[1] The district negotiations went very much as Beatrice had predicted; in most of them the employers' terms of settlement were very severe. The strike was formally terminated by the Federation on November 26th.

December 1st.—Tawney, who has watched the Miners' Executive throughout the dispute, says that the Federation is an impossible body, and wants the national organisation built up on the N.U.R. principle; but is hopeless because the miners' leaders seem to him incapable of learning. The Executive, made up of "Ambassadors" from different local associations, do not discuss and refuse to take any responsibility for policy. The local miners' agent who sits on the Federation Executive is always thinking "What shall I say to my men?" If they don't like the policy of the President and General Secretary they sit dumb but vote for it being "referred to the local associations" and then go and grouse with their particular pals in a neighbouring "bar". He "likes" A. J. Cook, thinks him self-devoted and honest. But he takes the colour of anyone with whom he is associating, he has not the remotest sense of responsibility, he seems, Tawney says, to be enjoying the débâcle. He is another Tom Mann, but far more hysterical in temperament. He is bound to become the tool of the Communist Party—he is now off to Russia and will probably come back a full-blooded Communist propagandist—may go to S. Africa to reorganise the S. African Labour Party. Meanwhile the Federation is a half-submerged wreck, dangerous to all other traffic. Tawney, in spite of his definitely "proletarian" sympathies, does not differ from us in his present gloom about the Trade Union Movement. *He* argues that the Trade Union leaders became inflated with a vision of power altogether out of proportion to their ability and that the Movement is now undergoing a precipitate deflation which may lead to temporary disintegration.

Keynes and Henderson[1] (of the *Nation*), with whom we lunched in London, are full of the "industrial revolution" which is paralysing the northern districts and rapidly developing the new southern industrial centres in Essex, Kent and Herts. Altogether a disquieting outlook. No wonder J.R.M. dreads a Labour majority: a year of office would disrupt the Party or, at any rate, the inner circle of the faithful. . . .

[1] Sir Hubert Douglas Henderson (1890–1952), political economist. Editor of *The Nation and Athenaeum*, 1923–30; later professor of political economy at Oxford.

PART IV
1927

JANUARY 1927—NOVEMBER 1927

January 8th.—Mr. Justice Sankey, another massive man mentally and physically—but in appearance as simple-minded as Haldane is sophisticated—a singularly charming person—formerly Conservative and a Churchman, he has become, like Parmoor, a good Labour man and would have been Labour Lord Chancellor if Haldane had not refused to join the Labour Cabinet except in that capacity. Sankey, like Haldane, is beneficent and generous—he spends himself on others!—but in a more personal way. He is not, I think, quite so simple as he looks and he does not altogether lack the love of power. He would like to stand for Deptford when he retires two years hence. From nine o'clock yesterday morning to 12 o'clock at night we talked incessantly—Lord Russell intervening for lunch—on public affairs and the conduct of life—whether law, politics, economics, ethics or religion—the conversation often taking the form of a cross-examination by him and an exposition by us—the lawyer *v.* the class-lecturer—varied by legal episodes—trials of spies during the war and the Irish rebels afterwards—told most agreeably. Coming immediately after 48 hours of the Laskis I am left a wreck! However, it is good to exchange thoughts—and when one has retired to the country it must be in spells. And now back to work to complete the four chapters before I go to London. . . .

January 22nd.—Enter my 70th year: I am well and happy and hard at work on the second volume of the *Poor Law*. This book will be our last big piece of research: (we shall perhaps publish a volume of materials on Regulation and Police already written)—after that, Manuals and Handbooks, and possibly, but not likely,—*Our Partnership*.

January 29th.—Four busy days in London. Three long mornings at the B.M. rushing through piles of volumes with Miss Piercy at my side copying out extracts. Sidney, on the other side, at his own researches; three "dining-outs"—Haldane, Parmoor, and a staff dinner at the S. of E.; one lunch to discuss new political quarterly—Tawney, Robson,[1] Lloyd,[2] Kingsley Martin, Delisle Burns,[3] Leonard Woolf;

[1] William Alexander Robson (b. 1895). Now Professor of Public Administration, London School of Economics.

[2] Charles Mostyn Lloyd (1878-1946). An old friend and colleague of the Webbs from Poor Law days; head of the Ratan Tata Foundation, London School of Economics, and assistant editor of the *New Statesman*.

[3] Cecil Delisle Burns (1879-1942), civil servant, lecturer and historian; from 1927-1936 Stevenson lecturer in Economics, University of Glasgow.

and, the last afternoon, taking the chair at a Housing Conference of the Labour Party. Result considerable exhaustion!

Haldane looks old and ill; but he is hard at work on his Privy Council Judgments—they are short of Judges, and those they've got are aged—some over 80 and most over 70! Elizabeth [Haldane] looked anxiously at him. He was beneficent—but had little to say. I asked how he, an old Liberal, accounted for the collapse of Liberalism—"The Liberal leaders lacked 'the Spirit'—they had ceased to desire change, they were obsessed by old formulas." "And enveloped in luxurious and leisured London Society," I added. "Perhaps so," he answered doubtfully.

The group of School of Economics lecturers who want an organ were full of concern at the low standard of knowledge and thought in the Labour Movement and the chaos of revolutionary tosh and reactionary platitudes typified by A. J. Cook on the one hand and Philip Snowden on the other. So they want to express themselves in substantial articles. But the quarterly would mean a capital of £4,000 to run it for three years and no one has got the money—G.B.S. refuses to give a penny to Labour—and active members of the party who are also well off, like Noel Buxton, are full up with claims and commitments. So that scheme will come to nothing.[1] I think these eminently superior persons including ourselves underrate the quantity and quality of the quiet self-education of the Labour Movement—the Herbert Morrisons and the Alexanders and the Greenwoods—the I.L.P. is so vociferous, they take the limelight by their theatrical manifestoes. Meanwhile the bitter abuse by the miners' leaders of the General Council culminates in the *Miner* of this week in the enclosed cartoon,[2] which is highly discreditable. According to Will Henderson, *Citrine* made the speech of the afternoon at the National Conference. He is the first really able Secretary the T.U.C. has *ever* had.

February 5th.—The Leonard Woolfs spent the week-end here—we had lost sight of them and were glad to renew relations with this exceptionally gifted pair. A dozen years ago when we first saw them they were living under a cloud—she on the borderline of lunacy, he struggling desperately to keep her out of a mental home—for some years it seemed doubtful whether he would succeed. Now the cloud has passed away; her appearance has altered; instead of a beautiful but loosely-knit young woman, constantly flushing and with a queer uncertain—almost hysterical manner—she is—though still beautiful—a spare, self-contained ascetic-looking creature—startlingly like her father—Leslie Stephen; the same tall, stooping figure, exquisite pro-

---

[1] It did not, however; it resulted in the *Political Quarterly*, which still continues.
[2] Not preserved in MS.

file; refined—almost narrow and hard intellectuality of expression.
Woolf also is matured and has lost his nervous shyness. Wholly unconventional in their outlook on life and manners, belonging rather to
a decadent set (Clive Bell is her brother-in-law) but themselves puri-
tanical—they are singularly attractive to talk to. In one matter they
are not up-to-date—for they are rigid secularists, regarding theology
or even mysticism as *L'infâme*. Here his Jewish blood comes in—he
quite clearly is revolted by the Christian Myth—the anger of a Jew
at an apostate from the Judaic faith—(considering the persecution of
the Jews right up to the XIXth century by the Christian Church, I
wonder why they are not more obsessed by hatred of the author of
Christianity). He is an anti-imperialist fanatic but otherwise a
moderate in Labour politics—always an opponent of "workers'
control" and "proletarianism". She is uninterested in politics—
wholly literary—an accomplished critic of style and a clever artist in
personal psychology—disliking the "environmental" novel of late
Victorian times—especially its latest exponent—Arnold Bennett.
Like other work of the new school of novelists—I do not find her
work interesting outside its craftsmanship which is excellent but
précieuse. Her men and women do not interest me—they don't seem
worth describing in such detail—the mental climate in which they live
seems strangely lacking in light, heat, visibility and variety—it is a
dank mist of insignificant and monotonous thoughts and feelings—no
predominant aims, no powerful reactions from their mental environment—a curious impression of automatic existence when one state of
mind follows another without any particular reason. To the aged
Victorian this soullessness is depressing—doubtless our insistence on a
Purpose, whether for the individual or the Universe, appears to them
a delusion and a pernicious delusion. The last hours with them were
spent in a raging argument about denominational education and the
validity of religious mysticism—they were against toleration—what
was "manifestly false" was *not* to be taught at the public expense and
not to be thought by persons above a certain level of intelligence who
claimed to be honest with themselves and other people. I pleaded for
"the endowment of error", and threatened them with fundamental-
ism—or Roman Catholicism—if they insisted on universal and
compulsory sectarianism.[1]

[1] Leonard Woolf, in giving permission to publish this passage, has allowed me to
append the following extract from a paper which he read recently to his Memoir
Club, and which adds a vivid footnote to the scene:
"One Sunday when we were staying for a week-end with them at Passfield
Corner, the conversation at lunch got on the subject of the teaching of religion in
schools. When I said that I did not think it desirable that religion should be taught
at all in schools, she was vehemently against me and carried the conversation from
the luncheon table to the library. It was the first time that I realised to the full the
strength of her passions and mysticism. She seemed to get angry that I mildly main-

February 7th.—Ellen Wilkinson reached here on Friday for lunch, in a state of collapse from over-speaking at great mass meetings mainly about China. I have known her slightly for 10 or 12 years; she was one of the Guild Socialist and University Federation group of 1913–19. The daughter of a Lancashire cotton spinner of rebellious temper and religious outlook, she passed from the elementary school to the pupil-teacher centre, from thence on a scholarship into Manchester University, where she took a good degree. After a year as a suffrage agitator, she became an organiser of the rapidly growing Co-operative Employees' Union under Hallsworth[1] and finally landed herself in the House of Commons in 1924 as M.P. for Middlesbrough. "The mighty atom" she was immediately nick-named. For the first session she was the darling of the House; in the next session she became a for-midable debater, and now as "Miss Perky" she is somewhat under a cloud of disparagement, suffering the penalty of immediate popularity and premature success. She is amazingly vital and a first-rate debater. She is not vain or self-conscious; with her tiny lithe figure, delicate pale face, and brilliant red-brown hair and red brown eyes, she is per-sonally attractive, at times extremely pretty. But *feminine* she is not; I suppose it would be said that she was "under-sexed". Her manner with men is straightforward and off-hand—even a trifle hard. If she had been a man she would have been a excellent common-law pleader —of the Patrick Hastings type. She has not a distinguished intellect —neither as a reasoner nor an observer is she subtle or artistic—perhaps her life, from a poor scholar in Manchester to a hard-worked organiser —has been too continuous a grind, too shrill a cry of revolt to result in the finer mental processes. But she is a real good sort—direct, de-voted and public-spirited—free from malice—and for so notorious a person peculiarly lacking in personal vanity. Her opinions do not strike old people like ourselves as wise or particularly relevant; she is a left-winger who has altered her views to suit the fashion of the hour; she was in 1913 syndicalist, in 1917 communist, and now "agin MacDonald" and enthusiastic for "Socialism in our day". "Ellen Wilkinson, regarded as a practical politician, is a fool," says Sidney. But the H. of C., and the amenities of social life it brings

tained my opinion, and marched up and down the room arguing almost violently. Indeed, up and down she marched faster and faster, and as she whisked herself round at each turn faster and faster, talking all the time, suddenly at one of the whisks or turns something in her skirt gave way and it fell on the floor entangling her feet. She stopped, picked it up, and holding it against her waist, continued her march up and down, never for a moment interrupting her passionate argument in favour of the teaching of religion in schools. Sidney and Virginia sat silent all through the discussion."

[1] Sir Joseph Hallsworth (1884–1949). Originally shorthand-writer and teacher; General Secretary of the National Association of Distributive and Allied Workers, 1916–47; wrote much on factory and shop conditions.

with it, is taming her spirit and she is becoming, unknown to herself, moulded for the Front Bench and eventually for office—I should imagine she would make a good departmental Minister—far more efficient and more popular than either Susan or Margaret. Altogether Ellen Wilkinson, if she does not work herself out by rattling over the country addressing mass meetings or get embittered by mere anti-MacDonaldism—has a big political career before her. But she will not *alter the policy* of the Labour Party by hard thinking, or new observation, or spiritual insight—she will be an interpreter of other people's thoughts and intentions—a marvellously alert and vivid one. I like and admire her and find her easy to talk to—distinctly entertaining in her political gossip. (She would like Wheatley as Party Leader by the way.) She believes the present trend of Trade Unionism is towards *One Big Union*! She believes it because it is the catchword of to-day—just as "workers' control" was the catchword of yesterday. Certainly the One Big Union is inconsistent with workers' control; but that does not trouble her.

Unfortunately the life of the popular Labour M.P. leaves neither time nor energy for anything more than a series of catchwords as the refrain of constantly recurring week-end speeches. The Labour leader needs periods of solitary confinement with leisure to think and read books, in the midst of silent beauty, if she or he is ever to develop the necessary genius for social reconstruction.

If the Labour Movement fails to provide the right environment for the development of statesmanship, the government of the country will remain, during long periods, in the hands of the present governing class who have both brains and leisure; with short intervals of futile Labour Cabinets, tossed in and out of power by conflicting waves of rebellious doctrine, each successive term of office ending in apathy of disillusionment and party disintegration. However, beneath this choppy surface of Parliamentary life there may be a strong undercurrent of good will and good sense which will carry reconstruction by common consent. That has happened in the past and may happen in the future.

Our other guests for the week-end were Kingsley Martin and his attractive young wife. K.M. was a Cambridge Fabian of the War period and has already written rather brilliant and thoughtful books—he has certainly literary talent and a quick and appreciative mind; he is to-day assistant lecturer at the School of Economics—one of the Tawney-Laski group. Unkempt and with the appearance of being unwashed, with jerky ugly manners, but tall and dark—with a certain picturesque impressiveness of the Maxton type, he is a fluent and striking conversationalist—intellectually ambitious—with a certain religious fervour for social reconstruction. Just at present he is in revolt against the Beveridge-Mair dictatorship and in the black books of those high and mighty personages because of his booklet on the General Strike. He was a brilliant Cambridge graduate, the son of a singlehearted nonconformist minister—an old and respected member of the F.S. and he was offered a fellowship at his college. One of the promising younger members of the F.S. Thoroughly Fabian in his methods, he differs from Sidney in thinking that the Communist propaganda is likely to disintegrate the Labour Party and lead to revolutions and strikes and a Fascist Government in Great Britain, though of course less pronounced than in Italy. We five talked incessantly all our waking hours from 4.30 on Saturday afternoon when the K.M.'s arrived to 9 o'clock on Monday morning when the whole party, minus I, left for London. Whether in pairs or triplets or all together—the two aged Webbs were, I think, as provocative and emphatic as the three young Socialists. Our relation with the younger folk is all that can be desired.

February 14th.—I am working well at the Poor Law book; having finished the chapter on the Royal Commission of 1834 I am now beginning the chapter on the Royal Commission 1905-9—rushing through the 35 volumes of evidence and reports, refreshing my memory of those troublous days. From my diary and the correspondence with Lord George Hamilton[1] about my enquiries—I think I shall be able to make a lively chapter which will "excite interest". But we are getting nervous about the length of the book; each of us is inclined to over-elaborate—and the vice of one accentuates that of the other. With our over-punctuality, Sidney and I alone are always ten minutes early for a train or an appointment; when we go together we are 20 minutes early! We have become too comprehensive and meticulous in the writing of a book. These bad habits increase with old age. Otherwise I am very happy in my country life varied by occasional visits from friends. Sidney also, is singularly content. Whether, when he retires from Parliament, eighteen months hence, he will be equally content with a country home all through the year, remains to be seen—at present 8 months House of Commons for three or four days a week is a big break in the monotony. But old age *must be* monotonous: with declining energies we may hope to adjust ourselves to this "inevitable". What one has to aim at is a state of placid beneficence: ceasing to worry over trifling mishaps in one's little household—and in this Sidney helps me—his state of mind is one of continual gratitude for his good luck in life—and rightly so, because we have been fortunate in our freedom to do the work we believed in,

---

[1] Chairman of the Royal Commission on the Poor Law, 1905-9. See *Our Partnership*, Chapter VII and *Webb Diaries*, 1912-24, pp. 98-9.

blessed with a loving comradeship and endowed with sufficient means to do it without financial strain. This Poor Law book is our last work of research. After that two or three "Short Histories" and a manual of sociological research—possibly some use of my diaries or at any rate their preparation for publication by our literary executor—and then—our passage through the twilight into the Unknown reservoir of life—let us hope with not too long an interval of loneliness for one of us.

What troubles me about this volume is—what exactly will be our recommendations? How can we devise some treatment of the Unemployed which will be "less eligible" than wage labour without being blatantly *inequitable* to the men and their families who are out of work through no fault of their own? There is little or no difficulty about the non-able-bodied; that is a mere question of how much the nation can afford to spend—there is no psychological problem—for the more you spend on the infant and child within any conceivable practical limits the better for the race. And that is also the case with nearly all sickness and the segregation of mental defectives, whilst expenditure on the aged and impotent is a harmless luxury. But the maintenance of the able-bodied in idleness is an ultra-dangerous business. And yet confronted with the idle rich man how can you justify to a political democracy harsh treatment in the interests of the community?

Can we in Great Britain escape the compulsion of Communism or Fascism? The answer, I think, is that, as usual, we shall just muddle through about the middle course of the stream of tendency without wrecking ourselves on either set of rocks. But it won't be a pretty or a pleasant business, and we may lose some of our liberties and much of our wealth in the process. I wonder how long we shall tolerate our savings going out of the country with our industries calling for more capital per man employed? When will the thinker or group of thinkers arise who can devise some way of controlling the amount of savings and distribution of the national income among workers and services in the interest of the whole nation? The pecuniary self-interest of each individual will not do it. . . .

February 28th.—Another two days and nights in London lunching and dining out, back home to entertain Beveridge and the senior officers of the Army Class to lunch and tea and then the Wedgwood Benns for the week-end—talking, talking, talking—by Monday morning totally unfit for work—then at least five days off work. Resolve not to go to London again before we leave here at Easter.

Wedgwood Benn (son of Sidney's old L.C.C. colleague, Sir John Benn, and brother of Ernest Benn, the publisher and noted individualist) is an acquisition for the P.L.P. He is a neat little man, neat in person and precise in intellect and a good fellow in every sense of the word. Considering his excessive "moderation" in opinion he is very popular even with the left wing of the Labour M.P.s. From the time he entered the House of Commons in 1906 he was devoted body and soul to mastering the technique of Parliamentary procedure and has become a real expert "in Opposition". He knows every rope and keeps himself up to date in all the questions of the hour in so far as these crop up in the House of Commons. Apparently he spends three hours a day in reading *The Times* and *Hansard*, and aided by secretaries he has a wonderful plan of filing the information so that he is able to turn up what Ministers have *said*, or what has appeared in the newspapers and Parliamentary papers. He has even a file for jokes and smart sayings; the result is that his questions, interjections and speeches are apt and amusing and he can put spokes into the wheels of the Front Bench. For the rest he is unpretentious, and most agreeable, with no malice and a good streak of kindly wit. He is in fact a man of alertness, assiduity and good nature. But he has no awareness or understanding of the problems underlying political events and his coming over will not add to the constructive capacity of any future Labour Government. Formerly a convinced economic individualist, he is now a Fabian Socialist. What has converted him? (1) Distrust and disapproval of Lloyd George; (2) a conviction that there should be two parties and only two—representing progress and the *status quo* respectively; (3) a rather vague objection to trusts and the doings of financiers and bankers—of uncontrolled and syndicated capitalism. Alfred Mond is his political *bête noir*. He came over to Labour in the best possible style—resigning his seat and leaving the Labour candidate to contest it at a by-election—a seat which he would certainly have won if he had chosen to re-contest it as a Labour candidate. He is fifty years of age and has a pleasant little woman as wife twenty years younger than himself, and two little boys. He is the last word of respectability and has a peculiarly pleasant manner and agreeable disposition and will be an excellent party man always playing a straight game. . . .

April 5th.—Henderson and his wife staying here. Was there ever a more sterling character than his? conduct more uniformly guided by public spirit and personal devotion and good comradeship? He is thick-headed—intellectually he is a clumsy instrument—but there is shrewdness in his judgment; the sort of realisation of the facts which arises from long experience of men and affairs and an absence of self-deception. Further, he is never elated and never gloomy—he just plods on along the chosen way towards some dimly perceived social betterment.

We agreed that though the Liberals are absurdly elated by the Leith and Southwark elections[1]—partly-assumed elation in order to hearten up their movement—the prospects of the Labour Party have darkened during the last year. The T.U. Movement is far more crippled by the General Strike than we anticipated; it is nearly bankrupt and its members are diminished and disheartened—and leaderless. The political movement is also leaderless. With regard to the crucial issues of the General Strike, Poor Law administration and China, the Front Bench held different views from the most active propagandists and *dared not say so.* The I.L.P. and the Clyde have practically repudiated J.R.M.'s leadership—the I.L.P. leaving him out of their delegates to Conference and therefore depriving him of a nomination for Treasurer or to the Executive. The *Daily Herald* does not pay its way, and it is our only organ; Eccleston Square is running on borrowed money and there is no sign of the Miners' £10,000. Meanwhile the Liberals are secured in the Lloyd George £2½ million fund, and have a capable leader in Herbert Samuel. Henderson says they will return 80 to 120 members and that the Labour Party with 250–280 members will be back in the position of the 1923 election. Over and over again we discussed what the Labour Party ought to do and would do under the circumstances. He of course inclines to a concordat with the Liberals on policy—would be personally ready to admit them to office but realises *that* would be impossible. He startled us by saying that one of the Liberal conditions would be the deposition of J.R.M. in favour of Philip Snowden as Premier. We exclaimed that if the Liberals made that condition, even the I.L.P. and the Clyde would swing back to J.R.M. Liberal insistence would damn Snowden in the eyes of the P.L.P. With the present state of mind of the Labour Party, Sidney and I feel singularly indifferent to their coming into power—so does Henderson—the Labour Party as at present constituted is not fit to govern. J.R.M. is a fine façade, a platform performance; Snowden is no longer a Socialist; Thomas has never been one and is a social climber, more blatantly so than Snowden's wife—see the wedding of Peggy Thomas, with Baldwin and Lloyd George signing the register and a host of Tory and Liberal notables exactly at the time of the T.U. Bill! Henderson is a first-rate general manager, but he is not a first-class statesman with a policy of his own to carry out. Wheatley and Maxton—in many ways the most attractive figures in the Labour Party—and their I.L.P. fol-

[1] Leith by-election result: Ernest Brown (L.), 12,461; R. F. Wilson (Lab.), 12,350; A. Beaton (C.), 4,607. (This was Wedgwood Benn's seat.)

North Southwark by-election result: E. H. Strauss (L.), 7,334; G. A. Isaacs (Lab.), 6,167; L. Haden Guest (Ind. Constitutionalist), 3,215.

Dr. Haden Guest had held the Southwark seat as Labour, but resigned after a quarrel.

lowers, are Utopians and pseudo-revolutionaries—peddling phrases without understanding what is involved and without constructive capacity—Johnston, the editor of *Forward*,[1] is the best of the Clyde lot and a good party man; but he is slight in mental make-up.

Hugh Dalton is probably the ablest of the younger men, but he is obviously playing the political game; some of the Old Hands discount his capacity whilst his contemporaries distrust his sincerity; Mosley, brilliant but without weight, deemed to be a political adventurer by many Left as well as Right-wingers; C.P.T. worthy but dull; W. Graham weighty as well as worthy but if anything duller; Noel Buxton a charming gentleman, but mediocre in intellectual calibre and physical strength. As for Sidney, he has retired from any attempt to lead; he tries to be helpful but he is an aloof and slightly bored spectator with the historians; a subordination of current events to a past and a future. The rest of the Front Benchers, and the rank and file of the back-benchers, are just nowhere. Deficient in brains and starved in money, it is a miracle that the Labour Party steadily grows in voting power. The impression left on the observer's mind is of a slow underground social upheaval, moving independently of leaders or organisation—propelling a lower strata [*sic*] of society into a more dominant position. This soulless momentum gives a certain colour to the materialist conception of history. But will this mass momentum continue if leadership fails? In the U.S.A. the brain-working profit-makers have gained control, disintegrated political democracy and recast the machinery of government into a sort of industrial feudalism based on pecuniary self-interest.

The Conservative Government Class War.

April 12th.—The Trade Union Bill is the governing class reprisal for the General Strike and the miners' refusal to accept the employers' terms, coupled with A. J. Cook's propaganda of Russian Communism. The big property-owners are suffering from the fear-complex exactly as their ancestors did at the time of the French Revolution, and the outcome is an anti-working-class combination; a muddle-headed attempt to nullify both the industrial and the political organisations of the wage-earners. If the Bill had dealt solely with the general and national strike, as attempts to coerce the rest of the community, there would have been some sense in it; though most of us think that, from the Conservative Party point of view, it would have been better to let the Trade Union Movement stew in its bitter not to say burning juice of the aftermath of the reckless venture in direct action. But the clause against the political levy shows class malice and meanness in a virulent form. A levy is the only way in which a working-class party

[1] Thomas Johnston (b. 1882), Secretary of State for Scotland, 1941-45.

can raise funds and it is certainly more ethically fastidious than the "Sale of Honours" or subsidies from the great financial interests. It will not be the Labour Party that will suffer; on the contrary the T.U. Bill will give us a united platform and dish the Liberals in the constituencies. Sidney says the Bill makes him feel superannuated; he can make out an admirable case against it (see *Labour Magazine* for May), but he is not really indignant about it; he does not believe the political levy clause will be eventually detrimental to the political fund, even if it is not dropped or repealed—the party organisation is too firmly established and the class feeling stimulated by this attack will overcome the new obstacles. As for the anti-general and national strike clauses, in the interest of British Trade Unions, protecting them from their own folly, he would be glad to see them passed. It will save a future Labour Government no end of trouble by freeing them from intimidation. The worst clause, in our opinion, is that forbidding public bodies from insisting on T.U. membership, as a condition for employment. Membership of vocational organisations *ought to be* compulsory, so that T.U. and professional societies may take their proper place, as part of the normal machinery of self-expression in the government of the country.

P.S. When the T.U. Bill was circulated Sidney revised his opinion— it is drafted with malice and if carried and enforced would make any strike by a large body of men impracticable. But then he does not believe it would be enforced. . . .

April 23rd. 41, *Grosvenor Road.*—Back from Seaham: the miners and their wives are deep down in gloomy bewilderment—the responsible ones deploring the mess made by their leaders, despairing about the condition of the industry and furiously angry about the T.U. Bill. The irresponsible ones talk vaguely about another strike. Long talk with Ritson,[1] M.P. for Durham division. He is bitter and contemptuous about A. J. Cook and his association with Communism; declaring that it is known for certain that he was paid during the stoppage by the Russian Government. Gave a long-winded account of the way in which miners' M.P.s were deliberately excluded from all counsel with and even from all information from the Miners' Federation Executive and their officials. . . .

There are hundreds of datal men out of work—practically all who are pensioned or slightly incapacitated. But the Seaham division is fortunate, as all the mines are working, and the hewers are making good money—£5 or £6 a week in some cases.

We motored over to Manchester to see the Clerk of the Union— an able official. He is much concerned about the "full maintenance"

[1] Joshua Ritson (1874-1955). Miner, M.P. for Durham, 1922-31 and 1935-45.

of men who refuse to go to Doncaster where colliery-owners are advertising for men. He says that Poor Law administration has become waterlogged with voluntary abstainers from work and that the manufacture of able-bodied paupers is going on at a great rate. There is no machinery for ascertaining whether or not the men are seeking work—the Labour Exchange having broken down owing to the jamming of the machine by the Unemployment Insurance. Consequently he has become an anti-democrat. He is dead against the Chamberlain Bill, though he says it would make no difference to him personally as he is Clerk to all the local authorities. He puts all the demoralisation down to the War and the advent of the Labour men on Boards of Guardians and the relaxation of the control of the Ministry of Health. The Outdoor Relief Regulation Order[1] is a farce and the exceptions have become the rule and the scale of relief means complete maintenance. Clearly if he had been entirely frank with us he would have advised a return to the principles of 1834—but he sees that that is impracticable with the present state of the franchise. So he muddles on as best he can and has in fact kept his Board sufficiently straight not to be superseded, like Chester-le-Street, by Government Inspectors.

May 3rd.—Heard the opening of the T.U. Bill, Second Reading. Hogg[2] was nervous and made an obviously disingenuous speech: the Tories sat silent with the expression "it's dogged that does it"; and the two rank-and-filers I heard, repeated, apparently with conviction, the party slogans of personal freedom and emancipation from minority dictatorships. (A. J. Cook, by the way, chooses these days to shout that there must be "a fortnight's cessation of work to coerce the Government"—as if he desired to give points to the enemy during the second reading debates.) The Labour Party was a ragged mob, shrieking irrelevant and vulgar interruptions, continuously repressed by the Speaker. Clynes was "adequate" but not virile. I heard only the last part of Slessor's[3] oratorical effort which did well enough. But the P.L.P., with its usual bad manners, trooped out whilst Clynes was speaking and had not come back to listen to their one legal expert. We dined with Alfred and Lord Thomson in a private room near the House of Commons kitchen. Alfred was as benign as usual and an even more thorough-going supporter of the striker or would-be striker, and denouncer of any interference with the right to strike than we are! Thomson, of course, is a perfunctory supporter of the Labour policy. It was a depressing evening; there is unreality in the Parliamentary

---

[1] See p. 173.
[2] Douglas McGarrel Hogg, Lord Hailsham (1872–1950). Then Attorney-General.
[3] Henry Slessor, Lord Slessor (b. 1883). Solicitor-General in 1924 Labour Government.

debate—the Tories are determined to make hay of Trade Unions while the sun of their majority shines; the Labour Party is equally determined to use the T.U. Bill as an election bogey—there is no interchange of thought and no desire to compromise or gain the largest measure of consent. Each party appeals to its own mob. The Liberals have been submerged by the tempest.

Fanaticism is in the ascendant. Susan is in high spirits delighting in the H. of C. daily rag and spending her week-ends demagoging in the provinces.

Meanwhile all other social reconstruction is arrested, and all the other misdeeds of the Government sink out of sight. The next Labour Cabinet is provided with a clean-cut policy which will cause no "stops in the mind" of either the reactionary or the revolutionary in the ranks of Labour.

May 8th.—Tom Jones, whom I have not seen to talk to since the Reconstruction Committee time—except for the Sankey commission episode—spent a week-end here. He came down satisfied with the T.U. Bill and contemptuous of the Labour Party's obstruction; he left—I think—disillusioned as to the effect of the Bill on the Labour Movement and on the reputation of Baldwin. Apparently neither he nor Baldwin were capable of understanding its clauses and he declares categorically that the P.M. would not have agreed to it, *if* he had been aware that under its terms the miners' refusal to accept the employers' new terms, in May 1926, would fall within the definition of an illegal strike. From his account B. is stupider and weaker than we thought— he lives an isolated life, never reads or talks with experts and has a horror of clever brains "like Keynes and the Webbs!"

Tom Jones has had a remarkable career. When first we knew him he was a raw Glasgow graduate, destined by his family to become a methodist minister. Losing his faith he took to philosophy and social economics, came to London School of Economics as a Russell Fellow, became an assistant lecturer in Economics at Glasgow, then Professor in Belfast, was taken up by Lloyd George and made secretary of the Welsh National Insurance Commission; then when Lloyd George became P.M. transformed into an assistant secretary to the Cabinet, second to Maurice Hankey where he still is. He is undistinguished-looking, short and stumpy, with badly fitting clothes, homely manners and speech, the very antithesis of the model civil servant. It is typical of Jones that he has never been presented at Court and asked that his name should be taken off the Garden Party list. He is easy to talk with, has the gift of intimacy. When with us he assumes that he and we have the same views (he is still a subscribing Fabian); he is by way of being a professional brain-worker—has had academic ambitions and pretensions, and is genuinely interested in education and research. What amused me in talking to him was to note that his dozen years as a confidant of a succession of P.M.'s and Cabinet Ministers from Lloyd George to Baldwin (excluding J.R.M. who refused to have anything to do with him, disliking his dowdiness and familiar ways and suspecting him of being Baldwin's spy) has not given him any insight into public affairs, superior to that of the clever student or professor of public administration. Of course he can give you tit-bits of political gossip; but with regard to the *problems themselves* he knows less than many persons who are excluded from the inner circle. The Great Ones—those actually exercising power—have no time to solve the questions submitted to them; they have to depend on others who can concentrate on investigation. Their success or failure as governors of men will depend on whether they can acquire this knowledge second-hand—a knowledge which is often hid from them by the inaccessibility of high office and the absorption of Ministers in mere official routine and social ceremonial. Jones says that Lloyd George's great quality was his readiness to get this knowledge and to be intimate with anyone who could help him. Which I think is true. Winston has that gift of accessibility and eagerness to know. Haldane also, and, in a certain but much more limited fashion because of his indolence and fastidious aloofness, A. J. B. (Balfour), Jones says, devoted all his remaining energies to the Civil Research Committee of which T.J. is secretary. "He and Haldane are the only statesmen who really care for the advancement of science and learning," was Jones's opinion. We three agreed that the chasm between the two parties and the way in which even the experts are divided from each other by party ties, does not make for mutual comprehension or the scientific study of conflicting questions. The Class War is developing, and the way is being cleared for some sort of doctrinal despotism. He intimated that this Cabinet would like to make Great Britain "safe for capitalism" by a reconstruction of the Second Chamber. We suggested, half in fun, that if that happened it *might* lead to a revolution carried out by some future Socialist Cabinet having a huge majority in the House of Commons and resisted by the Second Chamber somewhat in the fashion of 1689. "The creation of peers by the King does not exhaust the resources of civilian revolution," we explained—the King and Commons, or the Commons without the King, might go on governing without the Second Chamber's assent. Of course the success of this coup d'état would depend on whether the House of Commons was supported by public opinion including the Police and the Army and Navy. However, in Great Britain as we know it, the matter would be compromised by the intervention of the King. Jones thought that the King would insist on a General Election before he gave his consent to the reconstruction of the House of Lords. Whatever else happened the majority of the electors would vote for candidates pledging themselves against it. If the reconstruction were carried without a General Election, we might have a General Strike and a refusal or hint of refusal on the part of the Army to take sides against the strikers. Probably the reactionaries would win, but it would be the end of political democracy and probably the beginning of social disintegration. Anything might happen. "And we shan't live to see it—what hard luck," said I, closing the subject in order to discuss the possibility of the Civil Research Committee undertaking an enquiry into "Money payments into the homes of Unemployed persons." . . .

May 24th.—G.B.S. and Charlotte staying here; Sidney and I reading proofs of *The Intelligent Woman's Guide to Socialism and Capitalism* and giving him our criticism. Sidney corrected innumerable small mistakes and argued with him all the morning about what he considers major fallacies and perverse mis-statements of financial problems. G.B.S.'s dogmatic conclusion is that Socialism consists of two ends; equalisation of incomes and compulsory labour—and he suggests as the proper slogan for the Labour Party, "*The Redistribution of the National Income.*" This morning while he was eating his breakfast I gave him the result of a midnight meditation on the book—not as criticism but merely as observations. "There are three objects in a propagandist work," said I, "the two first are perhaps incompatible with the last. (1) The book has to arrest the reader's attention and interest him from the beginning to the end. (2) By argument and illustration all the defences, intellectual and emotional, against the 'new truth' or new doctrine, have to be broken down. Unless this preliminary clearance is carried out it is likely that the mind will refuse even to entertain the new ideas. And (3) the new truth or new dogma has to be stated in such a way that it does not appear impracticable, inconceivable or undesirable. Now you have achieved the first two requirements with brilliancy and success—you arrest attention and interest to the end, and you have knocked down all the contrary dogmas, you have explained away all the facts that would prevent the reader from listening to your constructive conclusions. But in stating the two ends of Socialism, *equality of income*, and *compulsory labour*, you have insisted on hammering in the thick edge of the wedge; neither equality nor compulsion are made to appear conceivable, practicable or desirable. Indeed, you contradict yourself more than once in the book, and you give the impression that you are advancing your conclusions not because you really believe in them but because they are startling." (It is amusing to note that artists like himself are to be allowed to keep their individual gains, however unequal!)

He was, I think, rather impressed, especially as I insisted that I did not want him to alter anything he had written; it was *his* method of presentment, and it was useless to cavil at the defect of so distinguished a quality!

The Shaws are so happy here that they are returning for another week-end. But though I enjoy having them and it is always useful to discuss with them it means that I do not get on with the book! Friends coming down to lunch from London have added to the strain; it is clear I must limit the amount of my entertaining; we cannot afford to do it easily without regard to cost, and I am too frail for the extra effort of contriving comfort with economy and yet carrying on my daily task of work. . . .

June 20th.—Among the younger men—a member of the two Executives, National and Parliamentary—is an old acquaintance of ours, Hugh Dalton, who, with his wife, has been staying with us this week-end. Over six feet, large and loose-limbed, practically bald and somewhat pasty-faced, Dalton was meant to be athletic but has been sedentary; hence he is not, in early middle life, personally attractive. When we first knew him in 1907 he was a tall slim and graceful Cambridge undergraduate, straight from Eton and a home in the outer-Court-circle (his father being Canon of Windsor and Court Chaplain). At that time Dalton belonged to the remarkable group of Cambridge Fabians—Fred Keeling,[1] Rupert Brooke, Strachey,[2] etc. We saw little of him between 1909 and 1914. On his return in the autumn of 1918 he renewed our acquaintance and his membership of the Fabian Society; presently he became a lecturer at the L.S. of E. and then a Labour Party candidate at one or two elections, but did not win a seat until the General Election of 1924. He is not popular with his colleagues at the L.S. of E.; they say that he is a "careerist", considering all things by the light of his own security and promotion. He is inclined even to pose as such. In the Labour Party he *is* popular; the Right Wing trust his judgment and knowledge, the Left believes in his fervour for "Socialism in our time". He gives *us* the impression that he believes in the "inevitability of gradualness"; that he is "sound" in his conception of the way reconstruction will come—not from workers by "workers' control" or "proletarianism"! Dalton dislikes and distrusts J.R.M. and puts his faith in "Uncle Arthur". Henderson thinks him the most promising of the younger men; even suggests that when the old gang go off the stage, Dalton may be first favourite

---

[1] Frederic Hillersdon ("Ben") Keeling (1886–1916). One of the founders of the Cambridge Fabian Society, and later assistant editor of the *New Statesman*; killed in action.
[2] James B. Strachey, the psycho-analyst, brother of Lytton Strachey.

for the leadership of the Party. And certainly he has knowledge, a good voice and admirable manner; he is a lucid and impressive speaker, and would, I think, prove to be an energetic and sane administrator. But he has no personal magnetism and though an intellectual and moral man, he has neither intellectual nor moral uniqueness or distinction. And in his curiously deferential and ingratiating method of address with persons who are likely to be useful to him, there is just a hint of insincerity; in his colourless face there is a trace of cunning. Is his faith in Socialism genuine and likely to endure? I am inclined to agree with Henderson that if the Labour Government arrives during the next ten years Dalton will certainly attain Cabinet rank— just after William Graham and before Mosley. I neither like the man nor do I dislike him: but as stuff for the Front Bench he is far above the average of his fellows. He is undoubtedly an asset to the Parliamentary Labour Party. . . .

July 7th.—Up in London for three days starting various persons and agencies on an enquiry into the rapid growth of able-bodied pauperism between 1922–7. In many ways worse than 1830–4. Also at work preparing a lecture on the past and future of the Poor Law for Fabian Society and an Oxford Union lecture in the autumn —all with a view of making up our minds what conclusions we are coming out at according to our present knowledge, so as to test these by investigations into particular facts. Some days—the best part of a week were spent on the Seaham letter[1] which has made a certain sensation—the M.G. giving it three-quarters of a column and a leading article. What will be interesting is whether it will rouse any protest in Seaham, where Communistic feeling is distinctly prevalent. The outlook for the miners is gloomy—it will get worse before it is better. Henderson thinks that A. J. Cook and those who are running him will back up the Miners' Federation on the issue of the affiliation of the Communists to the Labour Party. The Labour Movement is in the melting pot and what will come out of the pot is unforeseeable. Certainly among other things a revivified Liberal Party. "Proletarianism" is being rapidly discredited among the rank and file of the manual workers—but the communistic cells multiply in the holes and corners of Trade Union organisation, causing discord and dissension. Trade Unionism among the miners, whilst becoming more virulent, is, on the whole, decaying, and I am not sure that this is not true of some other industries. The events of 1926—the General Strike and the Miners' lock-out—have proved that British Trade Unionism is wholly unfit to become the mainspring of a great political party— likely to be called upon to form a Government. The Trade Union

[1] Not preserved in MS.

leaders have little intellect, and taken as a whole they have shown neither caution nor courage.

Meanwhile the Conservative Government has committed suicide, so far as the next General Election is concerned, by its House of Lords reform proposals. Here again the Liberal Party gains. For the first time since the Great War there seems a possibility of a Labour-Liberal Coalition—made up of our *Right* Wing and the *Liberal* Left —an attempt which would mean a new Proletarian Party—probably calling itself Communist? If British industrial conditions worsened and misery were to prevail I doubt whether political democracy would survive—we should see one or other of the creed autocracies seizing the power—I fear it would not be representative of the desire for social equality!—though in a semi-constitutional way—House of Lords reform and compulsory arbitration with regard to the conditions of employment, and suppression of "seditious" opinions. But Sidney does not believe that British trade is declining and that the standard of life for the multitude will go down. He remains an optimist. He believes that other people are as reasonable and kindly as he is himself. He is too happy to be a pessimist. But our exceptional luck in having each other and a privileged position seem to me irrelevant. Of course if there continues to be a large margin of national income to play with Great Britain will muddle through all her present problems. But supposing the margin were to shrink and a sort of paralysis were to spread from one industry to another—more and more pauperisation of temporarily-unemployed persons—and gradually-reduced public services —supposing the Framework of Prevention were to shrink and the margin were to be absorbed in mere Relief of Destitution—we might find ourselves in the worst of both worlds—the worst type of capitalism and the lowest form of Communism. . . .

July 28th.—Walter Citrine, the General Secretary of the T.U.C., and his wife spent the week-end here.[1] An electrical engineer by

[1] Lord Citrine, in giving permission for the publication of this remarkable comment, writes:

"Although the picture is not exactly flattering to me in places and I really cannot recognise myself at times, I think it should be published. It was Mrs. Webb's candid opinion of me as she saw and judged me at the time, and while I think some of her judgments as to my state of mind are rather fallacious, I think it would be wrong for it to be deleted from her Diaries.

"I laughed heartily at the picture of myself lying on the window seat with my boots on her best shawl. I really don't recall it, but I suppose I must have done so perfectly unconsciously.

"She says nothing about meeting me when I was half-way down the stairs first thing on Sunday morning and arguing with me so insistently while we were at the table that I had literally no breakfast, not even the single egg with which she seemed to be satisfied."

He adds: "I most certainly cannot recall anything I ever said to give her the impression that I was contemptuous of the members of the General Council."

training, becoming in early manhood a national official of his Union and secretary of the Liverpool Engineering Federation, he arrived four years ago as the Assistant Secretary at 32 Eccleston Square, succeeding Fred Bramley as General Secretary last year. Under forty years of age, tall, broad-shouldered, with the manners and clothes and way of speaking of a superior bank clerk; black hair growing low on his forehead, large pointed ears, bright grey eyes set close together, big nose, long chin and tiny rather "pretty" mouth, it is difficult to say whether or not he is "good-looking". In profile he is; in full face he is not. When arguing his features twist themselves up and he becomes positively ugly. By temperament and habit of life Citrine is an intellectual of the scientific type. He is sedentary, takes too little exercise for his health; he is assiduous, always improving himself by reading and writing and working at his job unremittingly—he has no "silly pleasures"; he is a non-smoker, non-drinker, small slow eater, takes a daily cold bath, sleeps with his windows open—altogether a hygienic puritan in his daily life. . . . I think he is very ambitious— expects too much relatively to his faculties. He keeps a note-book and puts down the points made in conversations; he keeps a diary in short-hand describing events as they occur; and he likes to talk about all these mental processes. He has the integrity and loyalty characteristic of the better type of British mechanic. I think he is too public-spirited and too intent on real power to go the way of Frank Hodges and become a hanger-on of the directors of capitalist industry. His pitfall will be personal vanity and the sort of conceit which arises from continuous association with uneducated and unselfcontrolled official superiors. Citrine is contemptuous—and largely justifiably contemptuous—of the members of his General Council and the T.U. Congress, and like all the other brain-workers who were in the inner circle of the T.U.M. during 1926 he gives a picture of deplorable lack of grip— alike of intellect and character—among those who led the millions of Trade Unionists in and out of the General Strike—whilst the leaders of the Miners approach, according to his estimate, mental deficiency. And yet he believes in the future of T.U.s as a great controlling force *through the weapon of the national or sympathetic strike*, or rather the threat of it, and was indignant when we put forward the thesis that T.U. as an organ of revolt was obsolete and that it would become during the next two generations a subordinate part of the machinery of Government, and that this evolution would take place under British political democracy as well as under the creed-autocracies of Russia and Italy and the industrial feudalism of U.S.A. He may be right and we may be wrong; he is a young man within the Movement, we are old people outside the Movement. But once a tendency is started it tends to become ubiquitous. "Proletarianism" as a form of government was born dead. In the Russian Revolution, the Dictatorship of the Proletariat is certainly a Dictatorship, but it has nothing whatever to do with the Proletariat, if you mean by the Proletariat the bulk of the people who are governed.

Vocationalism seems to intensify the defects of working-class mentality; and working-class mentality seems to emphasise the shortcomings of vocational organisation. As an autonomous institution manual workers' Trade Unionism has passed its prime of life. This was the gist of our argument. Citrine listened and contradicted, and we three wrangled vigorously, hour after hour. Lying full-length on the window-seat in a free and easy way with his boots on my best Indian shawl he slightly annoyed me. But he has character, industry and intellect. He is the first "intellectual" to be at the centre of the T.U. Movement. Will he sicken of the job? He means to re-organise the T.U. Movement on some thought-out model and to give it a definite and consistent "economic" policy which will include political questions such as foreign affairs. (He has, by the way, no use for G. D. H. Cole; he delights in Laski.) He assumes the eventual separation of the political Party from the T. U. Movement, would, I think, welcome it; he does not like "paying for a policy he does not control—he is distinctly jealous and resentful of the Parliamentary Labour Party, still more of the I.L.P. He was perturbed when I casually observed that in the T.U. Movement he had "poor material to work with", and that he might find, in the course of years, that he was "ploughing the sands" and that all his plans, one after the other, would slip up owing to the personal rivalries and sectional interests of T.U. leaders and general will-less-ness of the rank and file. He asked us what we thought of the Trade Union Movement being the formal basis of the P.L.P.; whether we thought this combination strengthened the cause of the manual workers. Sidney explained that a Labour Party had to be erected when the Liberal Government refused to carry out the Fabian policy of the National Minimum, and that though the association was theoretically unsound and might not continue, there was at the time no other way of getting a workers' party started. It was clear that Citrine had a notion floating in his head that the advantage was all on one side—that if the Labour Party were dropped the T.U. Movement might have greater political power emancipated from the "politicians". "What in your opinion," he asked, "would be the result if the T.U. withdrew their affiliation?" Sidney looked discreet and non-committal; he was not inclined to discuss the suggestion. "The result would be," I ventured in an offhand tone, "that the Trade Union Movement would find itself broken up into three camps— some Unions would refuse to withdraw from the Labour Party— the N.U.R. for instance—others would become non-political, and others Communist. The Trades Union Congress would cease to count. On the other hand the remnants of the Labour Party and all its intellectuals would coalesce with the Left Wing Liberals into a new party probably with a new name and constitution." "That *might* happen," I added; "the Trade Unions have never had much political sense: it might be better for the cause of Labour that the anti-Conservative party should be dissociated from Trade Unionism." "We should have our own Members of Parliament," was Citrine's curt retort. In spite of his contempt for the leadership of the T.U. Movement he altogether over-estimates the solidarity and economic power of British Trade Unionism.

But when we come to write our book on Twentieth Century Trade Unions—if we ever get time—Citrine will be useful to us. And what he will make out of the Movement, during the next ten years, raises my curiosity.

August 2nd.—Two nights at the Fabian Summer School, Cirencester—some 80 persons—two-thirds women—decorous in the first degree—four hours on the Poor Law and the present-day problems. Out of this discussion it is clear to me that we must, in our cursory investigations this winter, concentrate on discovering all the reasons for a national authority for the able-bodied, amalgamating treatment for the unemployed with the prevention of unemployment. There is at present no technique either in treatment or prevention—this has to be invented and we shall not invent it. But it will not *be* invented until there is a specialised authority, with salaried officials and a concentrated function. That authority must be national because of the unequal incidence of the cost under local rating and the need for variety and mobility in the treatment. There is a good year's work on the book— but I am now keen on it, and so is Sidney. At any rate we shall clear the ground for younger and more scientifically-trained minds to build on—like Chadwick did for Public Health. We must avoid pretending to a technique which we have not got—analogous to his 2 inch pipe.[1] Insurance has not solved the problem—it is neither prevention

[1] This reference is to the fierce battle which Edwin Chadwick, as Secretary to the General Board of Health, fought between 1848 and 1854 with a host of opponents, both "vested interests" and technical men, over the mechanics of sewerage. In summary terms, the question at issue was between large brick sewers and small earthenware pipes. In course of time the pipes, which Chadwick endeavoured to force upon all areas, came to be the established method; but he certainly advocated them dogmatically and in advance of experimental knowledge. The famous *Times* leader, on the occasion of the winding-up of the Board of Health, summing-up Chadwick, declared that "when he falls at last a sanitary martyr to a choked two-inch pipe drain and is carried by policemen in one of Shillibear's patents to an extramural cemetery, he will want no monument. A thousand costly but now useless Union workhouses will attest his humanity and prescience." *The Times*, August 1st, 1854. See S. E. Finer, *The Life and Times of Sir Edwin Chadwick* (1952).

nor treatment—it is in fact a form of relief—perhaps the least de-moralising form.

August 17*th*.—In spite of horrid S.W. storm of rain and cold grey skies Sidney and I have been happy at work on the book—he gallop-ing on with the big central chapter—"Sixty Years of Administration" —and I crawling along with the "Framework of Prevention"— feeling distinctly old for so heavy a task, but still content to be doing it. In and out of our daily life, in an agreeable sort of way, come friends, mostly of Labour sympathies—Ellen Wilkinson and her sister settled for a fortnight in the bungalow—the Anderson Fenns—all alike gloomy about the present mingled apathy and "extremism" of the Labour movement. Ellen interests me with her hard-grained capa-city and absence of emotional temperament—undersized, with her brilliant gold red hair and vivid talk she is attractive to men, but not attracted *by* them and therefore not seductive. Her platform opinions are ceasing to correspond with her intimate thoughts. The social engagements of a good-looking and amusing woman M.P., with plea-sant voice and easy manners, are eating up the earlier fanaticisms. The question is whether the faith itself is not slipping away? She is aware of this danger. "But look at the Clyde group" she urges, "Maxton is just ruined as a leader by living, eating and talking with Wheatley, Campbell Stephen,[1] Buchanan,[2] and a few others—they think that when they have talked and talked and talked always in the same jargon and with the same malice and suspicions towards other members of the party that they have done the job."

Ellen Wilkinson is becoming every day more of a Labour *politician* and less of a Labour missionary—but I think she will remain an honest politician.

How eminently respectable are those three women labour M.P.s— Susan Lawrence, Margaret Bondfield and Ellen Wilkinson—you can barely think of any one of them having an "intrigue"—even a flirtation—they all lack the temperament of the lover—they are dis-tinctly celibates. Endless activities and continuous self-expression uses up all their energies—whether of body or mind; there is no energy left to go sour! But thought and feeling become superficial— there is not time to observe or to think or to brood over the meaning of things. Rush and push, push in the House of Commons, rush in the constituencies; is the order of their days. Margaret has her reli-gion as relaxation; Susan and Ellen have their travels, their gossips

---

[1] Campbell Stephen (1884–1947). Trained for the ministry, became left-wing Socialist; M.P. for Camlachie, 1922–31, and from 1935 onwards.

[2] George Buchanan (1890–1955). Pattern-maker; Clydewise shop stewards' leader in the First World War. Minister of Pensions, 1947–8, and thereafter Chairman of national Assistance Board.

and their smokes; not one of the three seems to need emotional companionship. They have many men friends; they may all have had offers of marriage; but I doubt whether any one of the three has had a lover.

August 22nd.—W. Mellor[1] and his wife for the week-end; a model couple but without children. Mellor has distinctly improved the *Daily Herald* during his first year in the Editor's Chair—it has more character and consistency, better news—the new "features" added from time to time are striking. He has certainly justified Estlin Carpenter's[2] good opinion of him when that benevolent and scholarly old man 15 years ago paid me £100 a year for two years to take Mellor on as secretary of the Fabian Research Department. Of course Mellor is still rough-minded, without wit or subtlety of expression; but he is honest and shrewd and a good judge of men and very hard-working. Also he is singularly discreet about persons, i.e. about J.R.M.! He is depressed about the state of the Labour Movement; the absence of leadership, the jealousies and backbiting, and the atmosphere of malicious mutual criticism; the absence of serious study or frank discussion with a view to reaching agreement. I took them over to see Snowden and the conversation was gloomy—Snowden said that he felt "in his bones" that we were not doing well in the country—that the Labour Movement—political as well as Trade Union—was disintegrating and that we should be fortunate if we kept our present number of M.P.s. He was especially indignant with the stream of purely political manifestoes from the General Council of T.U.C. What between the G.C. and the I.L.P. issuing pronouncements on all questions, from China to currency, there was no place left for the Parliamentary Labour Party or the National Labour Party—who alone were the political organs of the Movement. He prophesied that the T.U. basis in the Labour Party would disappear within ten years, especially if the Labour Party took office again. All this pessimism is, I think, partly due to Snowden's wish for a coalition with the Liberals. But that is not the case with Mellor; he is still proletarian in his sympathies—but he is ceasing to believe in the capacity of the manual working class to throw up an alternative Government and he is inclined to think that Great Britain will decline in wealth and productive power—a decline which, under a series of reactionary Governments, will mean a lowered standard of social welfare; discontent and disorder met by forcible suppression. Sidney resolutely

---

[1] William Mellor (1888–1942). One of the leaders of Guild Socialism; secretary of the Fabian Research Department, 1913–15; editor of the *Daily Herald*, 1926–31.

[2] J. Estlin Carpenter (1844–1927). Unitarian preacher, writer and philanthropist; Principal of Manchester College, Oxford, from 1906 to 1915.

refuses to join this wail of despair. Relatively to other times, even to other countries at the present time, the inhabitants of Great Britain are progressing in health and capacity: Human Society is a poor business but it is better not worse than in the past. As for the future of the Labour Party, whether it is or is becoming the predominant instrument of progress is after all unimportant except to its leading men. If the P.L.P. fails the task will be undertaken by some other organisation or group of men. Men may drop behind but measures will march forward. So says Sidney!

September 12th.—The T.U.C. of 1927 has come and gone. If Scarborough (1925) was the high-water mark, Edinburgh (1927) is the low-water mark of that tidal wave of revolutionary sentiment, which sweeps the British proletarian mind backwards and forwards decade after decade—without effecting any substantial achievement to compensate for the disturbance of the nation's life.

The Minority Movement[1] was denounced and all Trade Unions ordered to disaffiliate or be cast out of Congress; on the receipt of exceptionally bad language from Russia the Anglo-Russian Committee was dissolved; "organisation by industry" with a view to "workers' control" was declared impracticable; finally the quondam Left-leader—Hicks[2]—advocated, in his presidential address, a systematic attempt to secure industrial peace by opening up negotiations, on a big scale, with the employers' organisations. Like all tidal manifestations this forward and backward swing does not mean progress— no permanent advance is made. Relations with Russia have been worsened not bettered by the formation and break of the Anglo-Russian Committee. The method of negotiation would have saved the situation last year, to-day it looks like surrender. One must be grateful that A. J. Cook and his backers have been publicly dismissed from leadership; even Robert Smillie turning against the "Billy Sunday" of the Trade Union Movement. But Pollitt[3] and the Minority Movement were left gasping with hysterical rage. Soviet Russia, after her million-subsidy to the miners' dispute, finds herself cast out of court—even the miners refusing to vote for the continuance

---

[1] The Minority Movement began in 1923, as a by-product of the "bolshevisation" (i.e. disciplinary centralisation) of the Communist Party under instructions from Moscow. Its original purpose was to be an agency through which the Communists could capture the direction of the industrial and political activity of organised Labour; but it developed into an industrial wing of the C.P., stirring up unrest and distrust of official leadership. It was first banned by the General Council of the T.U.C. in February, 1927; but maintained existence into the 'thirties.

[2] Ernest George Hicks (1879–1954). Bricklayer; General Secretary of the Amalgamated Union of Building Trade Workers, 1921–40. M.P. for East Woolwich and Parliamentary Secretary to Ministry of Works, 1945–50.

[3] Harry Pollitt (b. 1890). Boilermaker; General Secretary of the Communist Party of Great Britain.

of the Anglo-Russian Committee. The Left, at home and abroad, is embittered by the completeness of the breach with the grandiose policy of class war trumpeted from Scarborough only two years ago.

Susan Lawrence, who was in May, 1926, enthusiastic about the General Strike and indignant at its unconditional calling-off, now writes from Edinburgh approving of the new tone of moderation:

"As to what you say with regard to the Trades Union Congress, I think the Congress was rather a remarkable one. There has clearly been a change of heart among the rank and file, and they are in a very sober and steady mood. It was very remarkable to see how completely they had made up their minds with regard to the Communist question. The Communists have made themselves, both locally and nationally, so much of a nuisance, that the Movement is frankly bored with them."

September 20th.—This time last year before leaving for our autumn tour we sent off the final chapter of Vol. I.; this year we despatched to the printer five chapters of Vol. II. of English Poor Law History amounting to three-quarters of the whole—some 400 pages. For the last eight weeks Sidney has been working continuously, from morning to night, whilst I have been putting in regular morning's work every day of the week. We have been very happy honeymooning in our walks and our talks together, gossiping and discussing with friends and relatives. As recreation when done Sidney has relapsed into miscellaneous reading and I have listened to music on the wireless or enjoyed the rare intervals of sunshine in this most gloomy of summers. The book is a monstrous performance—one of the most monstrous, in its bulk and weight and elaborate and meticulous detail, that the Webbs have perpetrated during their thirty-five years of partnership! Sidney has excelled himself in hunting up lost links in the narrative and in completing the argument on each count.

Meanwhile we have started an investigation into the present administration of outdoor relief to the able-bodied up and down the country. Whether my strength will hold out to take part in this work, or, at any rate, to effectually supervise it remains to be seen. Also I am not confident that either Sidney or I have the mental vigour and resilience to tackle new problems—we can still collect and marshal already known categories and facts—perhaps as skilfully as ever. But can we discover the *new* issues and gauge the new proportions of the problems involved, e.g. chronic unemployment? And is there any practicable solution, should this unemployment prove not only to be chronic but also progressive? If such a disaster is actually imminent will any change in administration, policy and procedure avail to alter the result? Might it not be a question of muddling through, curbing and checking the present Poor Law administration, until a lowered birthrate, emigration, and even a higher death-rate brought about a new equilibrium of population with national resources? These pessimistic doubts, are they themselves signs of senility? It seems ridiculous, with the immense strides in the technique of production and the opening out of the world's resources that there should be less work —fewer commodities and services to divide among an industrious and active-minded people! Any permanent increase in the poverty of the poor must be the result of wrong policy or bad administration. But have we or any other contemporary investigators and thinkers the capacity to discover how to prevent unemployment and how best to treat the unemployed?

The first task is clearly to prove that there *is* a problem to be tackled—akin to the problem of the health of towns in the forties and fifties, and that a new class of technicians specially trained to deal with the question of unemployment has to arise before the best can be made of the situation. Secondly, that the emergence of specialists depends on the creation of a national authority specialising in the subject. Where I think we went seriously wrong in the Minority Report was in suggesting that we knew *how to prevent unemployment*. We did not. All we knew was that it was high time to set about getting this knowledge and that this could and would not be done by six hundred local authorities whose one and only business was the relief of destitution. If in our last two chapters we manage to get this thesis over the footlights we shall have done well. . . .

October 21st.—Our days at Roker were filled in with Sidney's seven meetings, and my usual lunch to the 30 officials of the Women's Sections, and the Federation meeting in the afternoon—the mornings being taken up with Poor Law interviews and expeditions. Having settled that Sidney retires at the end of this Parliament our visit was spiritually perfunctory; our chief interest being who will be his successor. . . . Sidney intends to give notice early in the session, so if and when we next visit Seaham, it will be to chaperone the new candidate.

Meanwhile G.B.S. has created a sensation: he has gone out of his way to testify to the excellence of Mussolini's dictatorship—to its superiority over political democracy as experienced in Great Britain and other countries. Hence an interchange of letters, public and private, between him and Friedrich Adler[1] (the secretary of the Socialist International). This correspondence arose out of an episode last February—an interview with Shaw in the *Daily News*; a telegram from the Italian Socialists objecting to the same; a reply by Shaw to

[1] Friedrich Wolfgang Adler (b. 1879). Secretary, Austrian Social-Democratic Party, 1911–24; Secretary, Labour and Socialist International, 1923–40.

Adler which the International office refused to publish, on the ground that it would appear in the Italian press without any rejoinder. There the matter was allowed to rest. But G.B.S., fortified in his admiration of Mussolini by spending 8 weeks and £600 in a luxurious hotel at Stresa, in continuous and flattering interviews with Fascist officials of charming personality and considerable attainments, handed to the Italian press, in the middle of October, a deliberately provocative answer to Adler's February letter—this letter being broadcast, considerably garbled, throughout Italy. From the published correspondence in the English press and still more from a private correspondence with Adler, it appears that G.B.S. puts forward the Mussolini régime as the *New Model* which all other countries ought to follow! His argument seems to be that either the Haves or the Have-Nots must seize power and *compel* all to come under the Fascist or the Communist plough. It is a crude and flippant attempt at reconstruction, bred of conceit, impatience and ignorance. It will injure G.B.S.'s reputation far more than it will the democratic institutions in Great Britain. But it reinforces the Italian tyranny. It is only fair to add that this naïve faith in a Superman before whose energy and genius all must bow down is not a new feature in the Shaw mentality. What is new and deplorable is the absence of any kind of sympathetic appreciation of the agony that the best and wisest Italians are today going through; any appreciation of the mental degradation as implied in the suppression of all liberty of act, of thought and of speech.

He and Charlotte lunched with us the day we passed through London. He talked incessantly; first about the statue of himself that the Russian prince-sculptor[1] is executing—which public gallery it ought to grace; and then—without any challenge from us—about his politico-literary escapade. For the first time, I noticed that he "gabbled" as he told us, in a confused way, how the recent correspondence with Adler came about. He was very insistent that we should agree with him; and peculiarly exasperating in his dialectic. So we all got rather hot—but presently I turned away and talked with Charlotte about Jane Wells's[2] death and funeral; and Sidney tried to turn the conversation, with G.B.S., on to other subjects. G.B.S. alarmed us by saying that he had added three "constructive" chapters to his book on Socialism—as a retort to my criticism last spring that he suggested no alternative to capitalist enterprise plus political democracy. What his proposals will be we do not know; we imagine the same crazy combination, foolish thinking and brilliant expression, that so often nullifies his underlying wisdom. So far as other Socialists are con-

[1] Prince Paul Troubetzkoy. The allusion is probably to the life-size statue in the National Gallery of Ireland. [2] Catherine Wells, second wife of H.G.

cerned—more especially fellow Fabians—the best policy is to ignore him—to smile benevolently on his sparkling wit and look away. He intends making a great pronouncement at the last Fabian lecture—it will be a nine days' wonder among Socialists—will please one or two die-hard Tory politicians and West End clubmen and then go the way of so many of G.B.S.'s passing aberrations—on to his own private dust-heap. But we shall have some little difficulty in avoiding futile and exasperating discussion, and the more uneasy he gets about the validity of his new views, the more he will try to compel us to agree with him. The silent and somewhat contemptuous rejection of his "new model" will inevitably hurt his feelings and may lead to a refusal, on his part, to lecture again for the Fabian Society—which will be a blow to its finances, though perhaps a benefit to its reputation for sanity and sincerity. "If you won't accept me as a leader, you shall not exploit my genius," he may say in effect. That would be a repetition of the *New Statesman* episode, 1913,[1] when he insisted on writing unsigned leading articles on current events—so that he should virtually decide the policy of the paper—and when Sharp refused to accept his articles without his signature withdrew from the venture.

I am grieved about the storm in the Fabian tea-pot—I have a real affection, as well as admiration, for G.B.S., and he certainly is the only person, other than myself, whom Sidney would seriously miss from the world he lives in. If only G.B.S. could get started at another play, the mood might pass from him. It is writing this d— Socialist book, whilst living a luxurious life in the midst of a worthless multitude of idle admirers, that has upset him: a somewhat similar experience to that of a Nonconformist Minister concocting his Sunday sermon in the intervals of gambling in a low public-house! . . . Imagine the hot indignation and withering wit with which the meagrely-fed Irish journalist of the eighties, writing in his dark lodging, would have chastised the rich world-famous dramatist of 1927 defending the pitiless cruelties and bombastic militancy of the melodramatic Mussolini. The rack-renting landlord of *Widowers' Houses* would appear as the victim of circumstances beside the self-made and self-styled saviour of modern Italy. It is not wholly irrelevant to remember that it was after the first years of enjoying a large income that G.B.S. turned the corner in the character of Undershaft in *Major Barbara*. For the first time he glorified the ruthless use of physical force in order to get efficient wealth production and abolish poverty.

October 28th.—G.B.S. has made an inglorious retreat in his column answer to Salvemini[2] in the *Manchester Guardian*; two-thirds of it

[1] See Webb *Diaries, 1912–24*, pp. 70 and 75.
[2] Gaetano Salvemini (b. 1873); historian and anti-Fascist writer.

being an explanation that he was not talked over by flattering Fascists in the luxurious hotel at Stresa—the remainder of his letter almost unintelligible; the reader being left in doubt whether it is an attack or a defence of Mussolini's methods of government. What G.B.S. is repeating, in season and out of season, and what he will, I assume, develop in his Fabian lecture is, "I do not believe in Democracy." Whether he merely means that all the people cannot decide all the questions all the time—which is obvious—or whether he has some alternative to "voting" as a way of getting that consciousness of consent from the governed, we do not yet know. But why have dragged in Mussolini for special commendation as a desirable and practicable alternative to British Parliamentary institutions? It is a joke in Great Britain, it may easily lead to tragedy in Italy.

The Laskis brought W. H. S. Thompson, the counsel for Sacco and Vanzetti—a distinguished criminal lawyer who took up the case without fee and at the cost of lot of time—to stay the night here. A tall good-looking New Englander—conservative in opinion and pleasantly English in manners. He entertained us with a vivid account of the last stages of the great American tragedy—more especially the mean behaviour of Lowell[1] who presided over the final enquiry into the "fairness" of the original trial of seven years ago. If this account is true our old acquaintance stands out as a muddle-minded professor, a moral coward and snob—paralysed by the poisonous atmosphere of fear and hatred of the Russian Revolution. About the state of the American soul, Thompson is very pessimistic: the present overwhelming prosperity has standardised a low type of conventionality and insincerity; a spirit of arrogance towards other cultures and other countries, especially towards Great Britain. The U.S.A., he says, is working up for a war for world dictatorship—she is beginning to think that *she* is the natural heir to the British Empire and that sooner or later she will have to assert herself and take over the mismanaged property from the aged and senile relative! What with the melodramatic Mussolini at Rome and the Business Bosses at Washington and the Proletarian Fanatics at Moscow—each and all intent on extending their respective sphere of influence by arms or by propaganda, poor little England with her far-flung empire, her class-conscious political parties and her diminishing trade, is going to have an anxious time of it. But I doubt whether Thompson is right in assuming that Western Europe will be against Great Britain. It is the U.S.A., the universal and self-righteous creditor—who is concentrating on herself the suspicion and fears of old Europe; even the coloured peoples of India and Africa (leave alone independent Japan) would not

[1] Abbott Laurence Lowell (1856–1943), President of Harvard and writer on law and government.

relish exchanging the easy-going tolerance and administrative experience of Great Britain for the crude insolence and racial contempt of
the American governing class. Also the South American States of
Spanish and Latin origin are beginning to suspect the capitalist autocracy of the U.S.A. of predatory intentions. In one way or another
Great Britain will manoeuvre herself into the position of the Defender
of the Faith against the onslaughts of a new barbarian World Dictator.
But she won't quarrel with her powerful and contemptuous child if
she can help it—and I doubt Thompson's forecast of war with
America. He is not only an Anglophil: he is a traditional loyalist to
the English Crown, and when he built a small place of worship near
his home somewhere in New England he invited an Anglican clergy-
man to officiate and called it "His Majesty's Church"! He told me so
himself. If I had heard it from Laski I should not have believed it!
This American lawyer, however eminent he may be in his profession
and however public-spirited and enlightened in defence of these
particular alien anarchists, is an oddly naïve—Haldane says bluntly—
a "stupid man". But whenever poor men, with impossible ideas,
defy the great guns of a powerful state, Haldane becomes the last word
of Hegelian sophistication. Why did that old friend of ours join the
Labour Party? He says, "because the Labour Party is the most
idealist of the three parties". But he is always contemptuous of the
way they express their idealism and even of the ideals themselves, and
he abhors all the Labour Party's specific proposals—alike in home and
foreign affairs. At bottom I think there is a generous desire to help
on the young and inexperienced and unendowed party to find its feet
in the world, stimulated by a keen enjoyment in having a finger in this
new-fangled pie. Our great ones in the world's esteem, Haldane and
G.B.S., H. G. Wells and to-day Philip Snowden, are showing unmis-
takeable signs of scuttling from a ship manned by so disorderly and
half-trained a crew. The only answer is that the mean age of the
great folk is nearer 70 than 60. Dethrone the aged? say I, though I
am verging on 70.

November 14th.—Sidney and I are both suffering from "suppressed Lecture"; he gives his Kingsway lecture on Wednesday—an
explanation and defence of modern democracy—and I give my Sidney
Ball Foundation lecture at Oxford on Monday—a somewhat elaborate pronouncement on the past, present and future development of
the Poor Law. So work on the book stops and we are both feeling a
little below our common task. . . .

Out of curiosity I attended the Shaw lecture on "Democracy and
Delusion". An utter failure, evoking in the high-brow Kingsway
audience of some 2,000 persons no response except a polite attempt to

appreciate the few levities he threw in to lighten up a dull and wandering dissertation of one hour and twenty minutes. He opened in a lively fashion by twitting the five preceding lecturers with their scepticism about the reality of democracy, even insisting that Sidney's elaborate description of the multiform character of modern democracy was only another way of saying that democracy did not exist. Then he laid down his own definition of political democracy as "Government by the People", which he interpreted as the referendum, the initiative and the recall—to which he added oddly enough "P.R." As all these devices were found to be mischievous and to lead to anarchy or absence of efficient government, democracy was proved to be a failure. From that point he proceeded to defend dictatorship and the Efficient Tyrant in an extraordinary rigmarole which was almost unintelligible. The capacity for successful violence was the only road to successful use of benevolent power. Because the Irish had failed to get Home Rule by constitutional means and had acquired it by bloody rebellion, therefore all constitutional action under all circumstances would fail to attain its ends. There had to be a bloody revolution in order to get a dictator, for without a dictator nothing would be done. In the Irish analogy he entirely overlooked the question of national self-government as distinguished from political democracy. Obviously racial minorities, whether Jews or Irish, black or white, can be tyrannised over by an overwhelming majority of another race even if the minority have and are allowed to exercise their votes! He also put forward the dogma that all political democracies are negative and resist the increase of governmental action—whereas the exact contrary is true of modern democracy in Australasia, Scandinavia, Great Britain and Belgium. He hammered and hammered on absolute equality of income and compulsion to work as the be-all and end-all of social organisation. This could only be brought about by a dictatorship. He might have made more of the necessary connection between mechanical equality and despotism; because no democracy would tolerate it and the compulsory work that this type of equality involves.

The audience became more and more bewildered and when he sat down at ten o'clock—in order, as he remarked, to avoid any questions —there was the feeblest clapping I have ever heard at Kingsway Fabian lectures—and a hurried and silent departure of depressed men and women. He himself seemed downhearted and observed that he must "give the lecture a good many times" before he could make his points clear. If he does he will not add to his reputation! Poor Charlotte looked gloomy and suggested that we should discuss the subject with him when we go to Ayot for next week-end. But it will be useless: he is too old and too spoilt by flattery and pecuniary success to listen to criticism. He has the illusion that he is and *must* be right, because *he* has genius and his critics are just ordinary men. He wants to *impose* himself as a dramatist. What effect will it have on his self-complacency when he finds his ideas simply ignored? Fortunately there is a convention of courtesy and kindness to aged but distinguished persons.

November 30th.—I am enjoying life far more this autumn than last or the one before. I am in better health, at work with my beloved at a big book which we both think will be useful; no one, we think, could do the job as well as we can. Like G.B.S. we suffer from senile vanity! I am settled in this cottage as my home; I am relieved from the expense and constraint of a resident secretary; my household works smoothly and though I have no intimates in the immediate neighbourhood, all my relations with the neighbours—especially with the poor neighbours —are pleasant and friendly. My only trouble is about dear old Kate —alone in London—for whose ease and happiness I feel responsible— but I manage to see her once every week, sometimes twice. Then there is this delightful country-side for long walks—wireless music and occasional amusing talks—with the voices of friends and acquaintances coming over; I passing rapid judgment, as to their relative merits as broadcasters in tone and substance; occasional concerts at Haslemere and in London, and the weekly book from *The Times* Library. Of these books—Emil Ludwig's *William II* and *Bismarck*—I did not appreciate his *Napoleon*—Masaryk's *Making of a State*, Sir Henry Wilson's *Life* with its malicious picture of Lloyd George and other statesmen—have been entertaining studies of human nature at war and at peace. Of course I should prefer to have Sidney always by my side, but so long as he is in Parliament we *must* be separated most of the time even if I were living in London. Hence I am every day more satisfied that so far as health, happiness, and continued work at our own trade—the making of books—is concerned we did right in shifting our daily life from London to the country. Our good fortune has followed us into old age, and when we begin to sink into weakness and perhaps into pain we must remember with gratitude our past blessings. I doubt whether one would long survive the other one— we have grown together. . . .

PART V
1928

JANUARY 1928—DECEMBER 1928

January 2nd.— . . . A happy new year alone with Sidney (the Tawneys spent Christmas with us) working well at the book. In another fortnight we shall have roughed out two more chapters of Vol. II.; only the last one—"The Last Twenty Years of Poor Law Administration", and "Conclusions" yet to do. Certainly we are self-complacent about the book—owing to our all-round knowledge of the subject it is a sound piece of work. It may be a trifle over-elaborated—our friends who have read the proofs don't think so. But few will buy these ponderous volumes. Who to-day is interested in the question of "Poverty in the midst of Riches"? The rich seem to be more callous than of old; fear of Communism, of increased taxation and diminished privilege—have become their dominant emotion; pity for the misery of poverty is dead, indeed there is a certain resentment at the rise in wages following the rise in prices, and also at the "Dole". So if we are not seriously out-of-pocket in the printing of the work at the end of the year of publication we shall be content. Anyway we delight in this continued work together—one perpetual honeymoon day after day, year after year. Alas! in the course of nature, one will be left to struggle through the last days of life alone. The thought of the imminence of separation adds a certain intensity to our love-making. "Ridiculous old souls," we say to one another as I curl up on his knees in the firelight!

February 14th.—Sidney reports the Parliamentary Labour Party discouraged—they are not making headway in the country—Trade Unionists are, it is said, voting Tory; and now owing to Lloyd George's superb energy, the Lancaster win[1] has given the Liberals a fillip. Without superior brains, money or a press, it is a marvel that Labour continues slowly to increase its membership—but the increase gets slower and slower, and one wonders if it is not reaching its limit. MacDonald, Sidney says, looks a broken man; and his heart is no longer in his job. He asked Sidney where he could go for Easter. He wanted to get out of England: he is arranging to go to Canada in the summer as ex-P.M. and as the Canadian Government's guest, a set-

[1] Lancaster election result: R. P. Tomlinson (L.), 14,689; H. Ramsbotham (C.), 12,860; B. R. Davies (Lab.), 6,101.

off to Baldwin's official tour this last autumn. It was characteristic that he told Sidney that he had a *personal* invitation from Lady Londonderry to her official party the night before the meeting of Parliament and he obviously would like to have gone! Imagine Lloyd George feeling that way. The official Labour gathering—some five hundred, mostly the clerical staffs of the Labour offices—was a deadly affair and no wonder MacDonald with his artistic sense hankered after the gorgeous company of "the Haves" in their splendid show-rooms. Poor MacDonald: it must be mighty uncomfortable to be a façade to such an ugly building. And the worst of it is that he is the best we've got to put in our shabby shop-window! Either the Conservatives have a very long term of power before them, or some sort of fusion of Labour with advanced Liberalism will have to come about, involving a change of name (*Labour* cannot be a long-lived epithet, it smells too flagrantly of sectional interest) and a change of leadership, and a Fabian programme. In many ways it would be good business for Lloyd George and J.R.M. to disappear; perhaps all ex-Cabinet Ministers, Labour and Liberal, would be a good riddance. Anyway we are doing our best for the situation by Sidney retiring, leaving a safe seat for a younger man. Our old eyes do not see the younger men fit to oust our present governing class—the aristocrats and the *bourgeoisie* —but they may be there for all that! The crucial difficulty is uniting zeal with knowledge—in Labour leaders the two do not often go together—the zealous tend to be ignorant, those who know are apt to be indifferent to the sufferings of the Poor.

February 29th.—I was in a devil of a funk as I walked along the Embankment to Savoy Hill—in fact my heart and brain were so queerly affected that I wondered whether I was going to be too ailing to get through the job. The extraordinarily restful atmosphere of the B.B.C. mansion set my mind and body at ease, I was comforted by a sense of my own unimportance. I was kept waiting by the Custodian, at the entrance, whose business it was to deal with intruders! A queer little man, who seemed to be a performer of sorts, was being located in the schedule: "Show Mr. — to Room No. —" said an official, turning to me automatically. I gave my name and intimated that I had "to broadcast at 9.15". He looked at his schedule and, satisfied, he motioned me to the lift "Room No. —", he whispered to the lift attendant. "*Silence*" was posted up in more than one place and all the attendants moved about like robots—motion taking the place of words. You were not even scrutinised, much less spoken to! I waited in the "Artists" room—one or two men with instruments, and another with a photographic apparatus, wandered through this passage apartment. About nine o'clock there entered a tall, fair-haired, clean-shaven gentleman, in evening dress, (was it Reith?) who greeted me coldly. "I am sorry the loud-speaker has been removed for cleaning; you might have heard the Terry Programme,"[1] he observed. This enabled me to explain my early arrival—I *had* wanted to hear the famous broadcast (which was *not* true—I was early because I was desperately nervous of being late!). "You may like to hear the news bulletin," and he led the way along the silent passages. I tried to enter into some sort of relation to him—but he barely answered me. We entered the padded chamber; he took up the phone to see whether the Terry programme was finished: "Just about finished," said he; discussed an item of news with the announcer and left the room. The announcer, without even looking at me, sat down at the table over which hung the microphone, and in a mechanical voice read out the news, pausing between each item and keeping his eye on the clock. At 9.15 sharp he rose slowly out of his chair, remarked in the same impersonal tone to the microphone that "this evening Mrs. Sidney Webb—economist and social historian— will give a Talk on Herbert Spencer," made way for me, again without looking at me, and left the room. Once seated at the table and thinking myself alone I started off with little or no nervousness—indeed I rather enjoyed myself—it was like rehearsing in one's bedroom—I had hardly any consciousness of being listened to, so private and quiet was the place one was in. As I came to the last page of the MS., I was conscious of someone just behind me getting restless—I looked at the clock and saw that I was two minutes over my time—I refused to hasten and finished off on a good round note—with a pleasant sense of successful achievement. When the red light went out, I made some harmless observation to the attendant youth. "Anyone could hear *you*; but what a terrible life the poor man must have had," was his informal retort. The red light flared on again; "London will take a little music while the Daventry takes the Shipping News." Then he hurried out of the room, and I made my way through silent empty passages to the entrance and out into the Strand.

What struck me about the whole business was the amazing change it must be for the professional performer accustomed to the stimulus of audience and footlights and the noisy comradeship of the theatre company, to be bereft of any kind of personal contact—pleasant or unpleasant—no opportunity for praise or blame—just silence except for your own voice—no one to see, and no one to see you. I found the conditions most agreeable and attractive, and I gather from friendly listeners I did my job well, and compared to the ruck of talkers in first-rate fashion. All the same I doubt whether the value of my talk

[1] A broadcast programme of homage to Ellen Terry on her eightieth birthday.

to the listeners equalled the cost to me in nervous exhaustion. I was horribly tired not by the talk but by the long drawn-out fear of it. How can one do justice to anyone's life and work in fifteen minutes? Poor old man: he would not have been satisfied. . . .

March 5th.— . . . This morning Sidney and I started on the last lap of our English Poor Law History—the story of the last twenty years of Poor Law Administration.* For the previous period we had all the material gathered by the Royal Commission of 1905-9: for this we had nothing done—and not much that we could do in the way of research—for owing to the War and to peace, official reports are scanty. Six months ago we started one or two investigators getting the facts of to-day about the able-bodied, up and down the country—we ourselves have no longer the energy to carry out a roving enquiry. We have decided to draft the chapter on the material we have, and then fill up gaps by interviews with inspectors and clerks to Boards of Guardians. But I doubt whether it will be a well-finished book. Sidney is preoccupied with Parliament and I am not strong enough for sustained day-by-day drudgery—the most I can do is to add architectonics to his more massive knowledge. And to interrupt our few mornings' work together there comes a fashionable portrait painter to construct a picture of The Webbs for the Founders' Room at the L.S. of E. Though flattered by Beveridge's insistence that we must be staged as the recognised founders, I disliked the procedure of his "dunning" people for their names and their guineas—it is against both my principles and my sense of good manners. But we both felt it would be ungracious to refuse—so we acquiesced. My one and only experience of being painted, at dear old Kate's request, by an artist who did a charming portrait of her but an ugly one of me, made me loathe it—the product as well as the process! Why not be satisfied with the superior authenticity of a photograph? I rather suspect Beveridge has secured the guarantee of G.B.S. and that the signed appeal which is to come will not carry the matter very far. However, G.B.S. can afford it, even if he be "let in" for a few hundred pounds! We tried to persuade him to have Charlotte painted as one of the Founders— but she demurred—"It would not be me but my shell," she wrote in her final refusal. That is about what I feel. All that one can say to oneself is that it is not worth the fuss of refusing.

March 14th.—J.R.M. told Sidney that as he and Baldwin were waiting in the entrance of Buckingham Palace (after the State dinner

---

* This chapter was *not* the last lap ("Guardians on the Defensive"). The last lap —100 pages—is "The Recrudescence of Able-bodied Destitution". And after that the Epilogue. [B.W.].

to the Afghan ruler) for their motor-cars they saw standing at the top of the stairs Lloyd George, Winston and Birkenhead. "The future Coalition," the P.M. dryly remarked—and he said it as if he really thought it and not as a joke. J.R.M. agreed that the chances were that that, if any, would be Lloyd George's political destiny. Those three like each other—they are emphatically "birds of a feather"! With the possible exception of Snowden, Lloyd George has no friends among Front Bench Labour men. . . .

March 31st.— . . . The dinner of the Fabian Women's Group— some old associates and adherents to a common cause, was a genuine and a rather jolly affair—unpretentious and overflowing with good comradeship between the Aged and the Young.

Meanwhile we are realising that this last part of the book, including our considered conclusions, cannot be finished by the autumn—and that we must delay our holiday until early next year. In a sense, this book embodies our social philosophy, and therefore must be as effective as we can make it. Sidney would get on faster without me; but he is agreed that the Partnership will produce a better product than "The Other One" alone, so he is content to go at a slower pace. I am no earthly good unless I am allowed to plod and plod and plod until I have covered the whole ground open to me; then I *may* get a flash which illuminates the end we are seeking. We are devoutly grateful that, at seventy years of age, we two can still work—and apparently work effectively together—and that *Our Partnership* is still a honeymoon. . . .

April 18th.— . . . A gathering of nephews and nieces at "Aunt Kate's"—a sort of gathering the dear old lady delights in. The hundred and fifty odd nephews and nieces, grand-nephews and nieces and now great-grand-nephews and nieces are a mixed lot, of whom I only know, at all well, about a score. It is a mixed lot—very representative of English society—the older generation pre-eminently a company of business men and their wives, the younger generation being more professional—lawyers, medical men, Civil Servants, university dons. But among the lot there is an ex-chorus-girl, an ex-Duchess, half a dozen Peers' sons, a baronet, an out-of-work actor, a shorthand typist, an old curiosity dealer. In so large a group—in which males predominate—it is odd that there should be only two professional soldiers, no sailor of any sort or kind, and only one Minister of Religion—and he only a Unitarian who gave up his ministry when he married our niece; and was killed in the War. There is one suicide and one lunatic in the first generation and one suicide and two mental defectives in the second. Otherwise the family group is distinctly above the average in health and capacity. But there is no great personal distinction—not so much as in the group of parents, the 9 Potter girls and their 10 mates. Among the great-nephews and nieces there are one or two who *promise* distinction—the Cornishes, Mayors, Clays,[1] especially Andreas Mayor, who seems a prodigy child. The only *friend* we have is Barbara Drake—a Fabian, a writer on economic questions, a member of the Education Committee of the L.C.C., a lover of music and a charming woman. . . . My relation to all of them is "dutiful" not affectionate, and unless they want to see us, or I think they do, I certainly don't want to see them. Kate is the real centre of the Richard Potter family life—in so far as it has a centre—she is herself fond of her sisters' children and very generous, in her timely donations on all sorts and kinds of occasions. . . .

April 27th.—I listened over the wireless on Wednesday night to Wickham Steed's lively account of the Budget Speech and last night to Winston's vividly rhetorical representation of his own case. Except that his voice is harsh he is a first-rate broadcaster—his message has all the atmosphere of intimate personal conversation—there was, of course, a peroration! The Budget is certainly constructive—containing a new principle of taxation and forecasting a complete reorganisation of local government alike in constitution and in function, and also in relation to the central authority. The whole financial scheme is definitely capitalistic—reconstruction through the capitalist—leaving the profits of efficient establishments automatically increased, without any effort of the management. What the local government plan will turn out to be we don't yet know. The Boards of Guardians are to be swept away—and the County Councils are to become the predominant authority—it is odd that he did not mention the municipalities. The prospect of this big reform being explained and passed during the *winter* confirms us in postponing the publication of the two volumes of *English Poor Law History*, 1832–1918, until early in next year and delaying our building here until the spring months. . . .

May 2nd.— . . . At the Russian Art Theatre performance with Barbara Drake last night, watching that amazing Russian acting, the effect heightened by the musical though unintelligible language. A few rows behind us, on the other side of the gangway, I noticed a

[1] Lawrencina Meinertzagen, daughter of Georgina, the fourth Potter sister, and named after her aunt, the eldest sister, married Hubert Warre-Cornish and had two sons and a daughter. Her sister Beatrice married Robert John Grote Mayor (1869–1947), Civil Servant and Principal Assistant Secretary to the Board of Education, and had a son and two daughters. Andreas, the son mentioned in the text, became a classical research worker. Rachel Hobhouse, daughter of the sixth Potter sister, Margaret, and Henry Hobhouse, married Sir Felix Clay (1871–1941), the chief architect to the Board of Education; they had two sons and three daughters.

short commonplace smilingly self-important man, well groomed and in immaculate evening dress; at his side a pale dark-eyed woman also the last word of correct clothes for the occasion. They were looking at *me*. Their appearance roused no memory and my eye passed on seeking out possible acquaintances. During the next interval the man crossed the gangway and I became conscious of an out-stretched hand and a warmly intimate greeting. The fat featureless face still puzzled me, but I recognised the voice—a singularly attractive voice—it was an old friend, Granville Barker.[1] Clearly he was pleased with himself and prosperous.

There has been an event lurking in the background of our life—intensely interesting but unimportant to us personally—the break-up of the Christian Church in Great Britain. The rejection of the revised Prayer Book by Parliament and the consequent unseemly controversy which has raged among the ecclesiastics—the revelation of an indifferent and almost scornful public opinion—has awakened the English public to the fact that the English are no longer Christians in any real sense of the word. No one troubles to assert this fact, and no one denies it. What is becoming something near a public scandal is the paucity of candidates alike for the Anglican priesthood and for the Free Church Ministry. Meanwhile Dean Inge openly advises, in the pages of a profane journal, that no candidate for orders now believes in the supernatural element in the Christian faith—or in any of its specific doctrines; all that is needful is that he should be a mystic—that he should have a sort of an idea that there is a Force that makes for righteousness at work in the Universe. How long this queer state of mind, the Church, with its creed and its rites, its pomps and its ceremonies, can continue part and parcel of the British Constitution is difficult to foretell! But the rotting away of this ancient structure, in sight of curious and contemptuous citizens, is ugly and distressing; Dean Inge, acting as a cynical guide among the crumbling ruins, adds a touch of ironic humour to the melancholy picture.

I often think of Mandel Creighton.[2] When he lay dying in Fulham Palace did he realise the passing of a Christian faith? No man of the intellectual calibre of Creighton or Inge will again appear among Anglican Bishops. Dean Inge will stand out as the last of the intellectuals of the Anglican Church Establishment—and will be portrayed in history as opening the gates of the citadel to a mob of kindly but bewildered sceptics. (The metaphor, I fear, is mixed. What are men called who clear away collapsed buildings?) . . .

---

[1] Harley Granville Barker (1877–1946), Fabian and playwright; author of *Waste*, *The Voysey Inheritance*, etc.

[2] Bishop of London, 1897–1901. A very old friend of Beatrice's—see *My Apprenticeship* and *Our Partnership*.

May 14*th.*—A combination of greed and good nature has induced us to let our bungalow to Lord Arnold. Six months ago Arnold stayed a night here and was enchanted with the quiet and beauty of the place. He amused us by solemnly and shyly asking me "a great favour". Would we instruct our executors to give him the refusal of the property at our death? "A long while to wait," said I laughingly. "I'll do better than that; if *I* die I will instruct Sidney to offer you a partnership in the housekeeping." (More than once I have thought that if I *did* disappear this place would not be suitable for Sidney the whole year round and that it would be better for him to share it and spend part of the year in London.) But my words took root and a week or so ago Arnold begged Sidney to let him have the one-roomed bungalow. We dallied with him; it would not be possible for him to have it until we had enlarged the cottage—we should be building next spring, etc. etc. But he pressed all the harder. Meanwhile I was thinking that if we could get a £100 a year for the bungalow and an extra income for Mrs. Oliver it might be worth doing. Was it not unreasonable to pay a hundred a year for accommodation for a secretary for two days a week for about 8 months of the year? We had a second sitting-room in the cottage—seldom used except at week-ends. Also it *might* be pleasant to have him there: certainly if I *were* to disappear it might be good for Sidney. On the other hand, it was a complication in our life—his presence might turn out boresome—we might want the bungalow for a resident secretary or chauffeur and then not like to turn him out. As Sidney was in favour of it greed and good-nature overcame inertia and exclusiveness—reinforced by the general principle of making the fullest use of one's house accommodation and one's income. Arnold agreed gladly to £100 a year, remarked that that was exactly the sum he thought of offering and the experiment begins this July—unless he backs out of it—on the whole I should be relieved if he did so. . . .

May 28*th. Whit Sunday.*—The Snowdens lunched here to meet the Hendersons who are staying a long week-end with us . . . Henderson and Sidney agreed that if J.R.M. disappeared Snowden was the best man for the Party leadership. "Why not 'Uncle Arthur'?" said I. A conclusive *NO* was the answer.

Henderson is convinced that Baldwin will lose his majority and that the Labour Party will be called to office however short may be their tenure. Sidney still believes in, or hopes for, a small Conservative majority and the non-success of the Liberal campaign. Henderson, I was interested to note, assumed that if the Labour Party took office Sidney would go to the H. of L. "I shall obey orders," Sidney remarked, "but quite sincerely I should prefer not." To which I added "Amen."

Seeing that some Front-Benchers assume that Sidney would be required in the Lords he and I, of course, have discussed the prospect. I should very decidedly prefer *not*—it would involve the troublesome task of taking the office and refusing the title—this could be done but it would be unpleasant doing it. Also, as the salary would be short-lived it would mean expense—he would have to continue to serve in Opposition until disabled by old age. On the other hand, I think *he* would like the continued political activity under pleasant conditions—it would be an agreeable reason for going to London and a good club to go to. So the simplest way out of the difficulty of deciding is to do what the Party wants—to let the leaders know that we shall not be in the least hurt or disappointed if the question is not raised but that *if* they honestly *do* want him he will "do his best". But we still think that the occasion will not arise in the remaining few years of health and strength. It is amusing to note that we unhesitatingly agree with Henderson in dismissing Haldane, Parmoor, Olivier and some other of our contemporaries from consideration as possible Cabinet Ministers!!

The younger members of the Parliamentary Labour Party—not to mention the rank and file in the country—would certainly add Webb to the superannuated group. Meanwhile Henderson and Sidney are conspiring to hand over the safe and cheap seat of Seaham Harbour to "our leader". Who would have thought that the embittered vendetta of former years would terminate in such a model manner!

May 30th.—Clear to us that the chapter we began on March 5th will not be finished before we leave for our holiday. The portrait, a succession of week-end guests, my fagged brain have combined to prevent it. However long it takes, this concluding chapter or chapters have got to be as good as we can make them. What troubles me is that we do not yet see our way to get off the horns of a dilemma. How can we show up the disaster of unconditional outdoor relief to able-bodied persons with seeming to justify Chamberlain's callous application of the worn-out principles of 1834? His present policy means semi-starvation to thousands of *bona-fide* workers (and their children) for whom no work is available within their reach, however willing they are to do it. Here in the exquisite country-side, living in comfort and ease, surrounded by friends and social consideration—out of sight of poverty—are we not certain to fall into accepting a morass of misery which is at once cruel and preventible? I am arranging to go to South Wales on our return and see for myself what exactly is happening in those derelict mining villages. Some way out *has* got to be discovered and laid bare. What depresses me is the probability that it needs more virile and more adventurous brains than ours to discover the way out of this social jungle. . . .

June 15*th.*—Watching a well-known portrait painter at work has been instructive. He has taken an incredible time over me owing to the wrong scheming of the picture in the first instance. I have been painted in and painted out half-a-dozen times—now at last the figure satisfies him and is quite good enough for me—rather too young and good-looking—but that fault is inevitable in a woman's portrait.

William Nicholson has been a pleasant companion and has seemed to like us. But it has been an irritating business; wasted time and dissipated strength—all the material for our last chapter getting into a dismal mess, which *must* now be cleaned up in the few days of the Shaws' visit here. . . .

July 5*th. Val d'Isère: Savoy.*—Not for years have I enjoyed a holiday as I have this fortnight here: the long-houred walks up the villages by rushing glacier streams, resting among the rocks, larch and flowers, watching the glorious intimacy of mountain, cloud and sun—all the time honeymooning with my beloved! Also I am glad to discover that I can still walk for five hours or more and even climb three thousand feet in broiling heat without serious strain.

As a holiday task I have read right through—30 or 40 pages at a sitting—G.B.S.'s thick and closely printed volume—just to see what I really thought of it. Owing to his immense prestige the book will be *read*—whether it will be "learnt marked and inwardly digested" I very much doubt. His indictment of gross inequality of income, as it exists today, and of the anarchic use of capital without any deliberate consideration of social welfare is, of course, effective—though not as verbally brilliant as his other prose works. But the book has no backbone of consistent thought—it is a patchwork of observation, personal experience and hearsay; and it offers no practicable or even conceivable alternative to the present system of society. Everything he explains or proposes, in practical detail, is just the old Fabian stuff—measures which certainly have no necessary connection with his dogma of Equality of Income and Compulsory Labour—the income and the work to be wholly unconnected with each other. This strange dogma is nowhere justified. Whether or not such a redistribution of wealth be desirable, the reader is left completely uninstructed with regard to the changes in social institutions or the new "sanctions" requisite to bring about this Utopia. Hence I fear that no competent critic will take Shaw's "Bible" seriously. So far as thinkers and administrators are concerned it will fall dead. The one good effect may be that it will *advertise* among the rush of readers the ideal of economic equality and thus lead to a larger measure of that most desirable principle being accepted in the working out of our social life. But I wish G.B.S. had not got involved in the writing of it—he lacks the necessary equipment alike in the knowledge of facts and in the power of thought. The ill-repute of the book among statesmen and experts will be a source of annoyance to him and of a possible embitterment: an anti-climax to the international prestige of *St. Joan* and growing appreciation of his earlier works. "The less we discuss the book, either with G.B.S. or with others, the better," Sidney and I summed up. In Socialist circles this kindly "passing by" is what is going to happen. I doubt whether our adversaries will discover anything in the book which they will understand how to use against us. After all what a brilliant dramatist says is not evidence of what a political party thinks or proposes— especially when it is delivered in 400 odd closely printed pages! As a matter of fact the Maxton-Cook[1] sentimentally revolutionary manifesto has completely submerged the Shavian pronouncement as an electorally sensational document. But that slosh will merely act as a foil to the Greenwood-Tawney Labour Party programme[1] published last week.

August 21st.— . . . Haldane's death was no shock—we saw it coming; no friend could regret it, he was not only powerless—he was wretched. But it is a sorrow to think that our oldest and most constant friend has passed away. It was Haldane who created and fostered the flattering "Webb myth" that flowered so agreeably and advantageously for us and our schemes in the first decade of the XXth century. Even when the idealised myth withered and was replaced by a caricature, Haldane was one of the few who, in spite of a certain disillusionment, remained faithful to an old friendship. . . .

What bound us together as associates was our common faith in a deliberately organised society—our belief in the application of science to human relations with a view of betterment. Where we clashed was that *he* believed more than we did in the existing governing class— in big personages whether of Cabinet, City or Court, whilst we held by the common people, served by an élite of unassuming experts, who would appear to be no different in status from the common men; but about his personal disinterestedness there can be no doubt. He loved power—especially the power of the hidden hand or shall I say of the *recognised* hidden hand: but he frequently sacrificed his own prospects, if he could thereby save a friend or promote a cause he believed in.

Obituary notices stress the subtlety and range of his intellect.

[1] This *Manifesto*, bearing the signatures of James Maxton and Arthur Cook, had appeared in June. Its main purpose was to attack the "Mond-Turner" proposals put forward jointly by a group of employers headed by Sir Alfred Mond and the General Council of the T.U.C. (of which Ben Turner of the Textile Workers was chairman) for peace and collaboration in industry. The *Manifesto* denounced all forms of class-collaboration, and demanded a national campaign to fight capitalism on all fronts; it was accepted by the I.L.P.; but "Mond-Turner" carried the T.U.C. by a large majority. (Continued overleaf.)

About this I have my doubts. Capacity for sustained intellectual toil he undoubtedly had. . . . But about the *high quality* of his thought I demur. Compared to Bertrand Russell's logical reasoning, Arthur Balfour's dialectic, Bernard Shaw's illumination, Haldane's mind seemed a blunt instrument—his conclusions were blurred, his logic lacked sharp outline and continuity and was by no means convincing. The impression left was muddleheadedness—though this very mystification of the issues was sometimes useful in paralysing stupid opponents. About men and affairs Haldane was not only wise but also witty; full of curiosity about motives, or judgment about faculties—it was this human side of his that made him excellent company. He had a real gift for manipulating his fellow men and for organisation—for getting the best out of his subordinates—partly because, whilst being somewhat cynical, he was always benevolent and considerate. Towards the multitude and the press he was tactless. It was the members of inner circles who loved him and loved him even when they failed to agree with him. If I had to write his epitaph it would be "A powerful and beneficent personality, a great citizen, above all a loyal and generous friend."

August 24th. Cardiff.—After 48 hours' continuous talking I am pretty well exhausted—too exhausted to write investigator's notes, so I might as well write a descriptive account in my diary: as, at any rate, I can there write legibly (?) owing to long habit. J. D. Morgan, with whom I am staying, is one of the least known but most distinguished local labour leaders—a well-to-do boot factor coming of good shop-keeping stock. His father was the son of a colliery manager and became an officer of the Salvation Army, afterwards opened a business but on the death of his wife turned to the S.A. J.D. began life as a devoted Salvationist: private secretary to the organiser of Hadleigh[1] and afterwards to General Booth—lost his faith in orthodox Christianity, joined the I.L.P., became an intimate friend of J.R.M. and Snowden, had no political or social ambition and now carries on his business as boot factor with his brothers, spending the income on advancing all Labour causes and entertaining all Labour leaders who come this way. The wife is a good little soul, devoted to her husband and his causes; there are no children and one servant who has her meals with the family and their guests. The little house is extremely comfortable and refined.

The Labour Party itself shelved consideration of the *Manifesto* by discussing, instead, the long document referred to below, which after the Party's Annual Conference took final shape as *Labour and the Nation*.

[1] The Salvation Army land settlement for destitute men; some Boards of Guardians, such as Poplar, paid for some of their paupers to be settled there.

The first evening a prominent Cardiff Labour man, Griffiths—the proprietor of a local hotel—an old colleague of Havelock Wilson,[1] came to tell me about the Cardiff Guardians of which he is a member . . . He gave me the Ministry of Health Inspector's Report and the Guardians' answer. Cardiff has a huge rateable value and rates are only 14/– in the £—they have no loans out—their administration has been lavish though there are only half a dozen Labour men out of 90 or so Guardians. But he said the Labour men by pertinacity got their way until Ministry of Health intervened and threatened to surcharge. So the Guardians passed a resolution against out-relief to single men and subsidy to men in receipt of unemployment benefit, and lowered their scale. He was in favour of outdoor relief as cheaper than institutional maintenance; believed in the Guardians of each district administering the relief to persons in their own district; said that he always took up the case of a person refused relief by Relieving Officer; so that the applicants frequently came to him first so as to get tips how to state their case. He evidently regarded himself as the advocate of everyone applying for relief in his particular district. He got into a hopeless mess about the distinction between "urgent and sudden necessity" and "exception" under Article XII of the Outdoor Relief Order.[2] What had frightened the Guardians from their lavish expenditure was fear of surcharge and the pressure of the taxpayers' organisation. The most successful part of the interview was the Report he handed over which I sent off to be copied and returned.

On Friday morning I had two hours' interview with James Evans,[3] General Inspector of M. of H., out of which I extracted little that I did not know before. His thesis was that the money allowance given by and after the war had accustomed everyone to payments in the homes; that the Labour Guardians were by conviction and also by class and family interest in favour of distribution of money in the homes, and that even when they had been in the minority, their superior capacity and determination as Committee men compelled the adoption of their policy. He said that, in Welsh Unions, relief on account of unemployment was given, with some exceptions, as

---

[1] Havelock Wilson (1858–1929), creator of the Sailors' and Firemen's Union. In his early days a fighting organiser, he became later a violent opponent of both the I.L.P. and the Labour Party.

[2] The Relief Regulation Order, 1911. Under that Order it was generally forbidden to give poor relief to able-bodied men except in workhouses or on condition of stone-breaking or similar tasks in "Labour Yards"; but Article XII of the Order enabled relief to be given in "exceptional cases", subject to Ministerial sanction; and during the post-war unemployment, which practically submerged the old meticulous Poor Law administration, hundreds of Boards of Guardians took advantage of this loophole without suffering official reprisals.

[3] James Evans (1868–1950), Chief Inspector for National Health, Welsh Board of Health, then Housing Commissioner for North Wales; later General Inspector of Poor Law for Wales and Monmouth.

"urgent and sudden necessity" and not deliberately under Art. XII, but that he was insisting that when this urgent and sudden necessity was recurring, the Guardians had to report the case for the M. of H. sanction. Bedwellty had to be taken over because the Guardians were defiant and could not be controlled: Merthyr Tydfil might also have to be superseded. Pontypridd was being curbed by the fact that it was short of cash: Cardiff had pulled itself up and was becoming satisfactory. Pontypool had got the same problem of relief, on account of unemployment; but owing to agricultural representation and to an able official—J. P. Holmes Watkins[1]—had kept its administration strict. When I confronted him with the testimony of the M.O.H. of Monmouth that the health of the children and mothers was deteriorating he cited George Newman[2] who had been down to investigate and had said that there was no evidence that it was so, and he implied that the Monmouth M.O.H. was a fervent socialist and not reliable.[3] (This was rather confirmed by Labour Chairman of Newport Board of Guardians.) He said Test Work had failed as it had been carried out on basis of short periods at T.U. rates and men had settled down to it as an easy job. Some Boards of Guardians (Bedwellty) had insisted on employing outside labour for painting and gardening in the institution.

As for Vagrancy there were three joint Committees in Wales—two of which were statutory. When a committee was statutory it was formed for 7 years, and could levy a rate over whole district, adopt children, take old vagrants into institutions, and take other common action on the lines of classifying vagrants and dealing with them according to their characteristics.

(I skip these pages by mistake so I will enter something I had forgotten when I wrote the account of the interview. I had been told by "Captain" Griffiths that Cardiff relieved the wives and children of the unemployed and not the unemployed themselves. When I mentioned this to Evans he seemed to think it was quite in order. But I pointed out that this was applying the Merthyr Tydfil judgment to involuntary unemployment for which it was never intended and that it was contrary to the Outdoor Relief Order; that relief to dependants

[1] T. P. H. Watkins, Clerk until his retirement to the Guardians of Pontypool, the Rural District of Pontypool, the Urban District of Pontypool, etc. Mr. Watkins writes: "In the Pontypool Union the Guardians without any legal authority in a strict sense organised the local authorities to undertake very extensive relief schemes, so securing Government grants, and relieved the situation to such an extent that they were able to pay the debt incurred before the County Council took over the administration of the Poor Law. The Guardians themselves contracted with the County Council and District Councils for public works exceeding £150,000 in cost."
[2] Sir George Newman (1870–1948), Chief Medical Officer to the Ministry of Health, 1919–1935, and to the Board of Education, 1907–1935.
[3] Sir David Thomas Rocyn Jones (1872–1953), surgeon and public health officer, Medical Officer of Health for Monmouthshire from 1908 until his retirement.

was relief to the men and the men could only be relieved under the exceptions of Articles X, XI, XII together with "Sudden and Urgent Necessity". This seemed to puzzle him and he turned the conversation. In talking yesterday with Jenkins[1] and Leacock[2] about Monmouthshire Guardians it seems that all Monmouth Unions now carry out the Merthyr Tydfil plan[3] and give relief only to women and children. As the men continue to live in the home it means giving inadequate relief to the whole family—it is in fact a deliberate return to what has been condemned as unconditional and inadequate out-relief to able-bodied men.)

From this interview Morgan took me over to lunch with Vaughan,[4] a builder, Labour County Councillor and Parliamentary candidate. . . . Here I met the Chairman of the Newport Board of Guardians, Sidney Watts,[5] who is Principal of the Technical College—an able and public-spirited self-important little person who was anxious to become a L.P. candidate on his retirement. He knew very little about the relief on account of unemployment, being entirely concerned in his scheme for children's homes etc. He understood that the relief was given for the women and children and that the men were not given relief and knew nothing about the obligation to report each case to the M. of H. Newport had had loans but was paying them off and lowering their poor rate. There had been no enquiry into their administration and no criticism to answer. He thought the Labour representatives on Board of Guardians poor stuff.

On Saturday we motored around, up the Rhondda Valley and called on Evans, a wealthy multiple shopkeeper, who was, with three others, administering the Lord Mayor's Fund. They had formed their own committee—(they had refused to use the District Committee set up by

[1] Arthur Jenkins (d. 1946). Vice-President, South Wales Miners' Federation, Labour M.P. for Pontypool from 1935; in 1945 Parliamentary Secretary, Ministry of Town and Country Planning.

[2] Will Lewcock (not "Leacock") was Labour Party agent in Newport, Mon. In 1932 he became District Organiser for the North-Eastern Region and later Regional Council secretary.

[3] In 1900 the Master of the Rolls allowed an appeal by the Powell Duffryn Steam Coal Company against the action of the Pontypridd Board of Guardians in giving out-door relief to men on strike. In this, the "Merthyr Tydfil judgment", it was laid down that no man could be relieved who refused to take work for wages until he became so weak as to be in danger of starvation; but that his wife and children, nevertheless, could be relieved. It was this confusing judgment which the Boards of Guardians, in the very different conditions of the nineteen-twenties, were trying to interpret, with the results mentioned in the text. For the full story, see S. and B. Webb, *English Poor Law History*, Part II, Vol. II, pp. 835 ff.

[4] D. J. Vaughan, building contractor and co-operator; Labour candidate for South Bristol.

[5] S. G. Watts (1871–1947), of Newport, was a member of the School Board and thereafter member and chairman of the Board of Guardians. He was head of the engineering department of Newport Technical College (not of the College itself) from 1915 to 1936.

miners) they were concentrating on boots and other clothing; they had received £25,000 for Wales and might get £40,000 as the Lord Mayor had declared that S. Wales was the worst area (total fund £90,000). The money was being spent on clothing and boots. He was bitter against the Communist element; told us that the sane Labour men on the L.E.A. had refused to feed children with no evidence of undernourishment; that Pontypridd Guardians were doing their work very well etc. After that we called at the Pontypridd Guardians' office. Evidence of shortage of staff; restriction of relief on account of absence of cash.

General impression: South Wales is a jumble of local authorities with no deliberate policy. Labour representation of poor quality and Labour movement broken up into various sections. The only Labour policy is to get as much for the workers irrespective of any consequences, Labour representatives feeling themselves to be on Local Authority for the express purpose. Bankruptcy of L.A. the main force compelling stop in present expenditure especially on preventive services. Only fair to add that there is no evidence in Cardiff and other districts of great misery in the devastated villages. The inhabitants look thin, strained and apathetic; but the houses and streets look clean and there is no sign of disorder. Up to now all is respectable and the relations between different classes of the community are friendly.

August 28th.—Interviewed Arthur Griffiths (Miners' Federation and member of Monmouth County Council), Warren[1] (Auditor of C.W.S.), Lewcock (Labour Party Organiser for S. Wales) and James[2] (Director of Education for Monmouthshire). A. G. clean-shaven, ascetic and fanatical—youngish man well versed in poor law. First tried to make me realise that Monmouthshire Guardians had either adopted or been compelled to adopt the plan of relieving the wife and children of unemployed men and not the men themselves—which I believe is contrary to the Outdoor Relief Order of 1911. Newport Guardians were anti-Labour but had a Labour Chairman, Sidney Watts (see previous interview), elected because he was the only competent man on the Board. Monmouthshire County Council was Labour and their officials, Jones M.O.H. and James Director of Education, were also Labour. Told me about dispute as to feeding of children and medicinal feeding. Arose out of Conference of M.O.H.'s called by Board of Education to consider state of health of children in

[1] H. L. Warren (1870–1949). C.W.S. Auditor, who retired after forty-two years' service, mainly in South Wales; did much to reorganise Co-operative activities in the area during a difficult period.

[2] Thomas Gwynfab James (d. 1936), born in Cardiganshire, was brought up to the Baptist ministry, became Director of elementary education for Monmouthshire in 1910, and in 1926 Director of Education for the county.

early part of year: led to George Newman coming down and Eustace Percy. James took him to see school feeding arrangements for children in worst areas, which James had managed many years ago (details to be sent). Newman dissatisfied with these arrangements, food too cheap (2½d. dinner) badly cooked and badly served. Many children suffering from malnutrition—apparently made alarmist report which James transmitted to Monmouthshire County Council. Whereupon Monmouthshire C.C. demanded interview with Whitehall to get 50% grant extended from provision of meals to provision of malt and cod-liver-oil to subnormal children (£25,000 mentioned). This was refused. Whitehall said either school meals or medicinal feeding—not *both*. George Newman went back on his report. James was a good-hearted and energetic man but with little judgment. He objected to medicinal feeding because it would reduce his 17,000 children to a mere fraction. The children were hungry and ought to be fed whether or not they were subnormal. He was very inconsequent. They had been feeding since 1925—whether the miners were getting good wages or not. He stated that miners' children had always had and were still having better food than the agricultural labourers' and small holders' who were not and had never been given school meals. Even the men on unemployment benefit were better able to afford good food than the agriculturist of Monmouth, who saved all he could and often made a bare £1 a week. He declared that they did not feed the children if they knew the parents had sufficient income; if medicinal feeding were adopted they would have to feed *all* subnormal children. Altogether he was not convincing.

Warren, a crabbed and reactionary Co-op. auditor, was not pessimistic about South Wales, the bad patches being the result of decapitalisation—a wholesome process—the coal trade would stabilise itself on a lower basis than the boom years and the population would adjust itself. The coal trade was not on balance declining but it was not increasing. He was very abusive of Labour and its aspirations—industrial and political.

Interviewed Blackister, Labour Exchange official—heavy dull man, recently come into the neighbourhood, but quite anxious to be helpful. Had no figures to hand as to number unemployed in his district and their distribution in Poor Law Unions but promised these. Three causes of unemployment—lapse of foreign trade, improved processes, and influx of men of inferior quality during war—thought South Wales trade would soon be stabilised and that there would be shortage of labour. Disused villages would become dormitories and cheap ones. Thought that as Unemployment Insurance was worked in Wales it had ceased to be insurance, owing to all the tricks to get men on benefit and faking work at wages; declared that they were connived at by Government to keep men quiet. Many classes did not come to Labour Exchange. They were doing considerable migration (1,500 boys). He assumed there would be a report of Baldwin's general post with opening of Parliament.* All sorts were being applied for. Only 10% of the boys sent out during last two or three months came back: mostly home-sickness from which the Welsh suffered usually. Was not at all pessimistic about future.

Motored to see Major Dixon, Appointed Guardian of Bedwellty and Chairman of Abergavenny. Rough man—good-natured. Bedwellty Board had run amuck handing out money right and left—insurance agents and tallymen following the Relieving Officer as he made his rounds. Families receiving £3 10s. a week. A good deal of petty corruption. Now only the family was relieved at the rate of unemployment benefit minus the 10/– for the man. About £200 a week was being spent on Out-Relief to unemployed (200 persons?). No single men were relieved. Parents preferred 1/– a week to school meals. Number took their names off the book and tried to qualify for Unemployment Benefit by working alternate weeks. Thought benefit abused but gathered that Govt. connived in order to keep things quiet. Did not doubt that the men shared with wives and children the Out-Relief given—probably the wife went without her share. In Abergavenny they had never had any trouble with the miners—they took what they were given and were thankful. The agriculturists who ruled the Board would not stand any nonsense and were not accustomed to large incomes. . . .

August (no date).—On my way to Noble[1]—interviewed Dr. Murphy,[2] District M.O.H. Clever and hardworking young doctor whom Colston Williams,[3] County M.O.H., thought well of. Ran maternity and milk clinic for mothers and expectant mothers and infants. Up to one year old they supplied milk to any person having less than the Unemployment Benefit; cost was not deducted from Out-Relief by the Guardians; and they would continue to supply up to 3 years of age. They spent about £800 a year. Thought the families were now suffering—rickets worse, tuberculosis worse—mothers suffering from malnutrition—M.O.H. trying to lower the income limit.

* This was, I think, Baldwin's appeal to employers in other parts of England to take men and boys from South Wales. [B.W.]

[1] William Noble (b. 1885) and his wife Emma founded in 1926–7 the Settlement of Maes-yr-haf in the Rhondda Valley, which recently celebrated its twenty-fifth anniversary as one of the best-known experiments for bringing new hope, occupation and culture to "derelict" areas.

[2] Dr. William Aloysius Murphy, then Medical Officer of Health to the Ogmore and Garw Urban District Council.

[3] Dr. Edward Colston Williams, doctor (retired). Medical Officer of Health for Breconshire and for Glamorgan from 1920 to 1943.

Yesterday afternoon James,[1] the remarkably able Superintendent Relieving Officer of Pontypridd gave me an hour's talk. He is a character, huge ugly man with cheery manner, warm heart and powerful personality evidently dominating the place. Pontypridd Guardians have had a lively history passing from reckless extravagance and good times to extreme penuriousness; now they are bankrupt, not from theory but simply because they have no money in the till. When he first started in 1910–13 there were no unemployed—liberal out-relief was given to non-able-bodied—but they could always point to a job if any man came along. But in isolated cases they always gave outdoor relief—the scale being the income of the lowest paid class in the mine—about £2 10/– a week. During the war men, however incompetent and idle, could pick up a good income by just "going down the mine and looking at the coal"—then came the boom after the war when colliers were earning £5 to £10 a week. In 1921 the depression set in, and then the strike. For the first three weeks of the strike the Guardians relieved every one, men, women and children—then they suddenly realised that they could not go on, and they relieved only women and children according to Merthyr Tydfil judgment. After the strike was over the district was still wealthy and there was plenty of money about and the Guardians muddled on giving good relief without much principle. Then came the great strike and they reverted to the women and children scale of unemployment benefit, 10/– for wife, 4/– for children *given only in kind*, and this is all they give to-day unless the Poor Law Medical Officer advises more. But any hard case they send to Poor Law Medical Officer and ask for a certificate of "unfitness to work". They temper their penury with mercy in individual cases. No one bears malice because it is widely known that they may any day stop payment altogether, owing to refusal of bank to give further credit. The same is true about the Rhondda U.D.C. with regard to feeding at school. The whole district is virtually bankrupt owing to non-payment of rates through poverty. James said that the spending income of the lower-paid worker after deduction was often lower than the allowance for wife and children from the Guardians. One man might be getting 28/– net and have to pay the landlord 8/–; the pauper would be getting 22/– worth of food for wife and 3 children and because he had no money would pay the landlord nothing and have more food to eat. They have two or three hundred unmarried unemployed in workhouses. James said that somehow or other the people were not starving, the children and mothers were well dressed and booted; the men looked down and out, but the boys were still gambling freely. All the savings were exhausted. Those men and

[1] D. T. James, employed by Pontypridd Board of Guardians from 1912 to 1930; thereafter by Glamorgan County Council until his retirement in 1947.

boys they had sent off were doing well. But they all cling to the valley. There were no soup kitchens in South Wales. There was malnutrition but no starvation. There was no "revolution" in the South Wales mines and never had been. During the war and immediately after the miners had a swollen head and the Government and employers got into a panic but there was no real fight in them. To-day they were hopeless and dully apathetic; as a mass they just accepted what happened whilst the more energetic men struggled to get away.

August 30th.—In the evening there came in the Chairman of Rhondda Labour Party—checkweighman, remarkably level-headed man of the old religious type, become enlightened. Bedwellty had run amuck; present administration was hard and heartless; Pontypridd Guardians were stampeded into penurious ways by their debt—he promised to get me the doings of Bridgend and Neath. To-day Noble motored me to Aberdare where we interviewed Manager of Aberdare Co-op, X, leading Labour Guardian, and ? Director of Education, [*sic*] and inspected the worst school. Merthyr Tydfil Guardians are still giving relief to unemployed married men with family up to 33/– a week with more for special circumstances. Ministry of Health had tried to bully them but they have stood out: "You can do the job", they always say, "and we'll clear out; but while we are here we shall relieve destitution." They have about 2,000 heads of families on list and they are half-a-million in debt. I must ask Evans why this distinction between Merthyr Tydfil and Pontypridd. On all the preventive services the present Government is severely restricting expenditure. Contradictory testimony about condition of children; physical exercise mistress declared that there was no deterioration, so do all the mistresses and masters. Many of the children looked thin and ill and some had sores and crooked legs which seemed to need attention. But certainly there was no apparent extreme poverty—except in boots and clothes. I have seen more neglected children in the East End of London.

September 1st. Passfield.—The Nobles who are running the settlement are a remarkable couple of "missionaries" of the finest type. Noble is the son and grandson and great-grandson of G.W. railwaymen —his forebear ran the first engine of the G.W.R. and his father was a foreman in the Swindon shops. Already as an apprentice he became interested in Trade Unionism and soon after he had passed out of apprenticeship he became a branch official, rising rapidly to the position of Chairman of the Federation of Craft Unions which he had organised. The condition of these shops was deplorable; the Unions were not recognised and the wages were low and settled separately with each man. Just before the outbreak of war a strike had been prepared and would have taken place, but when war was declared a compromise was agreed to. The G.W.R. management however bore him a grudge and two or three months afterwards gave him 24 hours' notice to clear out. All the shops refused to work and he was at once reinstated. From that time onwards Noble was the negotiator for the shopmen but continued to work at his trade until he and his wife went for a year to Ruskin Hall in order to improve his knowledge of economics. (They were very much disappointed with Ruskin Hall, finding the study badly organised and the tone unsympathetic; it was here that they joined the Friends.) They returned to Swindon and he to work. In 1926 he and his wife were selected by the Friends to take charge of the Oxford Settlement at Rhondda. Noble is an attractive and magnetic person, with a cultivated manner and charming voice—if you did not know otherwise you would take him to be a public school and university man—he has certainly no sign of being a proletarian. He is more of an organiser and negotiator than a student or thinker—he reminds me of Tawney (to whom he is devoted) except that he is more practical and less intellectually self-conscious—he is singularly selfless. His wife is less personally attractive—a thin rather sexless woman—angular and jerky in her figure and movements—and very distinctly the religious missionary—a devoted and able worker who deals efficiently and rapidly with case after case. They have two children and their family life or rather that of the settlement is gently and deeply religious, though absolutely without dogmatic intolerance or narrow-mindedness. They seem to me ideal heads of that sort of settlement: intensely interested in each individual case of hardship yet aware of all the larger general considerations. They are both ardent members of the Labour Movement, in its industrial and political spheres—but distinctly disillusioned about T.U. officials and Labour politicians—especially about the former. From all accounts the Nobles are getting a great position in these Welsh valleys—even the Communists are drifting towards them.

My general impression is that the Welsh miners, though not starving —there are no soup kitchens and the homes look clean and the people respectable—feel themselves to be "down and out". There is a grim silence in the streets and the little knots of boys and men look apathetic and slink about as if ashamed of the shabbiness of their garments. The homes are getting barer and barer and the food deteriorating in quality— there is little drinking and smoking. Though the school mistresses and masters tell you that the children are all right they certainly don't look so, compared to the children hereabouts. In one of the class-rooms at 3 o'clock in the afternoon the majority of the little ones were fast asleep as if they were thoroughly exhausted—the mistress explaining that it was the first week at school. In fact the Rhondda valley reminded me of the streets of Hamburg when we were there in 1923—the people were respectable and quiet but they looked terribly depressed physically and mentally. The Nobles say that the Communists are not gaining ground and the better of them (some of the men and women are the best in the place) are gradually drifting away from their leaders. It is significant that at a Communist conference in the valley the two leaders, Horner[1] and another, wanted to prohibit the members from attending classes organised by the Nobles but the members voted against them. The Chapels are losing their influence and the Church has never had any. The Catholics keep their people together as in Durham. The only ferment is political and economic and the Labour Party dominates the situation in the Welsh coalfields, alike in local and national politics. Hall[2] seems to be the most popular of the M.P.s, but they all live in their constituencies. . . . Mr. Noble says that the leaders lack courage; they lacked it right through the strike; they denounced Cook in private but they dare not denounce him on the platform! Good men, sensible men, "but they are afraid of their members" and "dare not oppose what seems to be popular at the moment", was the Nobles' verdict. Right through the miners' strike many of the miners' agents and M.P.s knew the miners could not win; but they let them drift on into disaster for lack of courage to say so. It has been the same story in local administration; they gave way to the spendthrifts and they are showing the same common lack of grit in not resisting the pressure of the M. of H. to cut down anything that can be cut down. The Nobles say that even those with Communist views are beginning to realise that the Welsh miners are not made of the stuff that makes revolution possible; the herd dissolves when it meets with any determined action on the part of other persons.

I returned to Passfield tired out. But I have stood the test well and the stuff I have collected and my general impressions ought to help us to write a better conclusion than we should have done without it. . . .

October 7th.— . . . Spending morning after morning, sorting out notes for Sidney's use and meanwhile trying to evolve definite conclusions. S. does all the writing of these last chapters of the work; and I come breathless after him, trying to catch him up and insert such illustrations or such qualifications as I may become aware of in my laborious pondering over our multitudinous notes. We have got at least a dozen

---

[1] Arthur Lewis Horner (b. 1894). General Secretary of the National Union of Mineworkers since 1946.

[2] George Henry Hall, Lord Hall (b. 1881). M.P. for Aberdare, 1922–46; Colonial Secretary 1945–6, and First Lord of the Admiralty thereafter.

large pamphlet boxes packed to overflowing with notes and news-paper extracts for this last chapter on the "Recurrence of Able-bodied Destitution". And every week end we have friends staying here: this Sunday, Robson and young Ponsonby,[1] a nephew of Noel Buxton: a charming youth—working hard at the School of Economics and looking forward to Labour politics later on in life. Meanwhile the Labour Party is doing well in the country: J.R.M. and Henderson and the Evolutionists have swept Communism and left-wingism out of the way, Maxton and Cook agitation has fizzled out and Liberal-ism shows little sign of being a powerful rival for progressive support. All's well for electoral purposes. Whether all is equally well for the business of government, if or when the L.P. gets into power is another question! It depends on the younger men of the party and the persis-tency of the British working-class and the self-devotion of the brain-working adherents to Socialist principles.

"My Life" by George Lansbury.

October 11th.—I note in Lansbury a curious likeness alike in body and mind to W. J. Bryan of U.S.A. Large-limbed, debonair, big-mouthed, with a splendidly resonant voice; in face, half handsome, half stupid—in appearance, voice and bearing far more impressive as a performer to great audiences than as a member of an inner council—is as true a description of Bryan as of Lansbury. Overflowing with public spirit and private benevolence—almost ostentatiously so; immaculate in family life, devoted husband, indulgent parent, non-smoker, teetotaller—even the same sort of simple-minded religious faith and personal purity—could be added to the list of their common good qualities. No brains to speak of—certainly no capacity for solving intellectual problems—and a big dosage of personal vanity and passion for applause are their common defects. Of course Lansbury has not played so great a part as Bryan did in the U.S.A.—he is hardly a great public personality. He is toned down alike in qualities and defects, to suit the smaller, more crowded and more fastidious political stage of Great Britain. In short Lansbury is not so powerful an orator, not so great a demagogic booster, not so big a fool as William Jennings Bryan was in the opinion of his enlightened compatriots.

Whether these Great Hearts with Weak Intellects (of which A. J. Cook may be taken as a living caricature) are on balance good or bad for the country's body and soul is difficult to judge; especially for a shallow-hearted intellectual like myself! Bryan decimated the Demo-cratic Party; if Lansbury had led or dominated the British Labour Party it would have been to-day in ruins. But he is only one among

[1] Gilbert J. Ponsonby, now Sir Ernest Cassel, Reader in Commerce, London School of Economics.

many, in some ways complementary to other leaders; he may have added warmth and emotional content to the hard grit of the Henderson-Snowden-Clynes-Webb combination, finished off as it has been in the thin glittering façade provided by J.R.M.

When he and I were colleagues on the Poor Law Commission we were the best of comrades; he was a model of loyalty and helpfulness. For some years—during the Minority Report campaign 1909–10—we remained friends, but gradually he began to doubt the wisdom of the Webbs; we never quarrelled but he instinctively avoided meeting us. The preacher of "Poplarism" as Guardian and Borough Councillor, his chequered career in the H. of C. and within the Labour Party, the turmoil of the Great War and the Russian Revolution, his occasional contact, as a prominent Labour leader and Labour editor, with states-men of the allied countries embittered his feelings and inflated his vanity. His benevolence to the world at large still flows abundantly; but intersecting this beneficence are various little trickles of malice towards other leaders in the Labour Party, together with an altogether exaggerated self-righteous indignation against individuals or classes who do not share his view of social welfare and political experience. But after all is said and done George Lansbury does believe in the common people and in their overwhelming right to a better place in the sun. Which is more than can be said of either of the other political parties, of many nominal members of the Labour Party and even of some labour leaders. . . .

November 15th.—I am still grinding at the last chapter of the book —"The Recurrence of Able-bodied Destitution"—pruning each section of padding, sharpening the points, adding illustrations. Mean-while the Guardians are being swept away without anyone else paying the least attention to their fervent protests. Francis[1]—the head of the Poor Law Department—who was staying the week-end here, says that there is no sign either at Westminster or in the constituencies of questionings or protests on this issue; every M.P. and every Local Councillor and official is "doing sums or getting sums done for him" with regard to the exact effect of the derating proposals. Doubtless their abolition will add centres of discontent and even fury against the present Government—indeed the unpopularity of the Conservative Government grows apace—but the Guardians are thoroughly dis-credited and even Clerks to Guardians are saying confidentially, out-side their boardrooms, that their boards are *not* fit to govern. Whether after the demise of the Guardians anyone will care to read our elaborate

---

[1] Herbert William Sidney Francis (b. 1880), entered Local Government Board, 1908; later Director of the Local Government Division of the Ministry of Health, and Secretary and Comptroller of the National Debt Office.

two volumes of history giving a detailed account of this particular form of Government from start to finish is seriously concerning us: how many copies to print, for instance? Our work will at least have the distinction of dealing with its subject matter completely and finally —according to the present assumptions. What the world will be thinking of Poverty in the midst of Riches, a hundred years hence— whether mass destitution will prevail in advanced countries, in Great Britain, U.S.A., Germany and France—no one now living can tell. The problem of relative equality may have superseded that of sheer destitution. Russian Communism points that way. The still greater question of the *right breeding* of the race—how many and of what kind? Elections (will there be elections?) fought on whether "Gentlemen prefer blondes" or ladies prefer blacks; whether we are able to aim at turning out athletes, aesthetes, aristocrats, artists and anarchists or on breeding bourgeois, bureaucrats, benevolents and brainworkers? will be more entertaining than the present issues. When these questions are uppermost the parts of the Old Poor Law of the 19th and 20th centuries which will be most canvassed will be the provision for the child-bearing mother and the treatment of the mentally defective— just the parts that we have paid least attention to in the last volume, for the very good reason that the babies and the mentally defective have been, in theory, and are being in practice, "taken out of the Poor Law" to be dealt with by the communistic services. . . .

November 29th.—I listened from the Ladies' Gallery to Sidney's 1½ hour speech on the Local Government Bill. To me it is a nerve-racking ordeal—I am far more agitated than if I were speaking myself. Any little imperfection in delivery or in the arrangement of his subject matter—any little slip in tact or unnecessary repetition of phrases—makes me wince as if my nerves were being cut one by one. But as it turned out the speech was a great success; delighted his own party and was attentively listened to by the opposite benches. In its criticism alike of de-rating and of the abolition of the Boards of Guardians without providing for the break-up of the Poor Law it was masterly: what it lacked was a good delivery and a quick understanding of the effect produced by each successive sentence. He is not "at home" in the House of Commons. Now that he is known to be retiring he is beginning to be appreciated as an odd but potent personality equally peculiar in his defects and his qualities, singularly unpretentious and obviously disinterested but without style or parliamentary gift. He is one of the "characters" of the House, and is always being caricatured as the enigmatic learned person, at once absurd and impressive, who, somehow or other, is trusted and followed by the Party of the Proletariat and who does not hide his boredom and contempt for the ignorance and indolence of the representatives of property and privilege. When the common type of Tory comes in after dinner, a little the worse for liquor, and finds Webb speaking, he jeers; in his sober moments he sees the sinister figure of an English Lenin who is bringing about Communism, not by force, but by underground manipulation of the democratic machine. Not an altogether unpleasant reputation. Anyway neither of us feel we have anything to complain of. Considering how low we have valued the interests and opinions of our own class we have been kindly treated—we have had a pleasant journey through passing events. What troubles me is where exactly we, as a nation, are going. Are we at the beginning of a long decline? Are we, perchance, on the brink of a catastrophic subsidence in physical comfort and mental development? . . .

PART VI

1929

JANUARY 1929—DECEMBER 1929

January 4th.—Exactly twenty years ago in 1908 we were putting the finishing touches to the Minority Report—I in a state of abject exhaustion. On New Year's Eve, 1928, we were writing the last words of the Epilogue to our lengthy history of the English Poor Law —recording the sentence of death passed by Parliament on the Boards of Guardians and the opening of a new era in the legal relations between the rich and the poor. These two volumes will be the last big work of research. They will have cost over £1,000 in printing and some hundreds in out-of-pocket expenses of investigation and typing— not to mention all the previous researches for the Minority Report without which this larger work could not have been undertaken. Of course this history is far too long—from a publisher's point of view —but Sidney insisted on making it cover the whole ground of the preventive services. The consequence is an unwieldly production. A few days spent on pruning the last chapter and I, at least, will be done with the Poor Law.

In order to straighten out our finances and make practicable our building operations here and our two months' tour abroad, we have speculated in sending the enclosed circular[1] to the 7,500 persons on the Kingsway Lecture List, to the Fabians and to selected persons in U.S.A. and in Great Britain. If it succeeds to the full amount of the 750 copies, we shall just pay our printers' bill so that all the published copies that are sold will be pure profit. We contemplate another venture. The only part of the book which will be directly helpful in the Labour world is the chapter on "Unemployment and Able-bodied Destitution" together with the Epilogue—in all about 250 pages out of the 1,000. This, we think, might be printed off separately and sold directly, by us, to the Labour world through the Trade Unions and the Labour Parties for about 2/6d. a copy—possibly 2/– to organisations if they took a large enough number and paid in advance. But we shall not proceed with this until we come back in June—or at any rate until the book is published.

There has been a certain exhilaration and self-complacency in the writing of the Epilogue because it is clear that so far as the Chamberlain Bill goes it does *break up the Poor Law* in respect of the non-able-

[1] Not preserved in MS.

187

bodied. Further it leaves the whole problem of unemployment in such a hopeless tangle that it is safe to predict that the second part of the Minority Report—"A National Authority for the Able-bodied"—is almost certain to be carried out. It is in fact in process of being formed in the Ministry of Labour. To be able to *make* history as well as to write it—or to be modest—to have foreseen, twenty years ago, the exact stream of tendencies which would bring your proposal to fruition, is a pleasureable thought! So the old Webbs are chuckling over their chickens!

January 12th.—Sidney spent 23 hours with William Graham and Tom Shaw at Snowden's, drafting a programme for a Labour Government for the first year of office. He said he was agreeably surprised at Snowden's energetic attitude—he had it all laid out and showed no inclination to be a stingy Chancellor. The four then hammered at it for about 8 hours and they are to meet again in London before handing over the draft to the Parliamentary Executive. S. suggested that it should then be broken up into different sections and given to sub-committees of two or three to work out in detail. P.S. said that Lloyd George who has been broken up in health was making up his mind to support Baldwin's Government rather than put Labour into office. Which bears out what E. D. Simon reported the other day that Ll. G. was hardening against advanced programmes from the Liberals. . . .

January 16th.—In the beautiful Founders' Room at the L.S. of E. there was a reception to see the Webb portrait hung over the mantel-piece—a really lovely picture—as a picture—whatever criticism my friends may make about my portrait. And a most friendly little gathering, mostly Fabians—the other subscribers not turning up. Beveridge made a gracious little speech—far too impressive about us—he is a very faithful admirer. Altogether our stock is up—or rather we have, through old age, ceased to have detractors—no one troubles about aged folk except those who respect and like them. Which adds to the pleasantness of life, though possibly also to its illusions. We are waiting, with a certain anxiety, the result of our offer of the special subscription edition of our book—if we don't get near to the 750 we shall look rather fools! We might even lose money over the extensive circulation. On the third day after the despatch of the first 2,000 circulars, we have received 19 orders and there will go out within the next fortnight another 9,000—to the Kingsway list and to the Fabians and some to the U.S.A. We are printing altogether 2,500 copies of the book. It is perhaps our own greatest literary adventure—in the end the edition will sell out—but *we* may not reap the benefit—we might be £500 out of pocket on the first year. We are still out of pocket on Vol. I of the English Poor Law History. This book *ought* to sell. The sensational and long continued unemployment—and the abolition of the Boards of Guardians and the transfer of their activities to the Counties and County Boroughs ought to bring custom? . . .

February 2nd.—The winter months have slipped past at great speed owing to the strenuous routine of our lives—every morning our cup of coffee before 8 o'clock, then the morning's work—S. at it continuously, I as long as I can stand it—lunch at 1 or 12.30; the hour's rest—a cup of tea about 3 o'clock, a walk and back again at work until the "news" on wireless at 6.15—perhaps a little music—supper 7.30—a little reading or wireless music—bed at 10 o'clock—each successive 24 hours exactly like the past ones. And this is the life I have been leading all our married life except for the two years on our travels round the world, and during the years spent on the Royal Commission of 1905–9, on the Minority Report agitation of 1909–10 and the Wartime Committees of 1915–18. An extraordinarily peaceful and interested life, one long day of loving companionship and joint intellectual endeavour—no anxiety about ways and means, no serious illness or prolonged ill-health, always free and able to do what we thought best. "We *have* been fortunate," Sidney often says.

And this brings me to a slight feeling of uneasiness whether this "thoroughly comfortable" state of being does not bias us to underestimate the cruelty and stupidity of the present treatment of the miners and other victims of trade depression and dislocation. Have we exaggerated in our *History*—especially in the last chapter—the evil of "proletarianism", and minimised the evil of strict administration insisted on by Neville Chamberlain?[1] Certainly, it is a public scandal that the Poor Law has *not* relieved destitution in S. Wales, and that it has had to be supplemented by this demoralising and inept appeal for charitable funds dispensed by hastily improvised local committees. As the little Prince says, it is a *Horrible Mess*. (I wonder whether that personage is going to "upset the Apple Cart". Which is the subject of G.B.S.'s new play.) And have we made our plea for a fulfilment of responsibility on the part of the community to provide work or maintenance under training really convincing? To stop adequate outdoor relief as it has been given by "proletarian Boards" without any other alternative but the workhouse or repulsive test labour at less than subsistence wage—may be the *worst* of two evils in its callous cruelty? All the same we must abide by the verdict of

[1] The reader of to-day, re-reading Chapter IX of the book, will probably agree with the misgivings of the author; the scales are heavily weighted against the Poplar Guardians.

our intellect as to what *actually happens*, and our readers must discount the bias. It is ironical that the bias attributed to us, by the ordinary critic, will not be that of the property-owner—but that of the Labour leader. In the depths of my conscience I see the *rentier* discounting the claims of the manual working-class. I work and vote for public expenditure, the propertyless class at the cost of the *rentier* and profit-maker, but should I be *personally* grieved if it did not happen? As against this self-accusation of *rentier* bias there is a haunting fear that by withdrawing capital from private enterprise the community may be checking the re-equipment of out-of-date industries with new machinery and new methods of production and new and more effective salesmanship. A retort to this demurrer is the exodus of British capital to foreign parts—France, Italy and South America—in search of cheaper and less regulated labour. The net result is Agnosticism— I simply *do not know* what is happening in national finance still less what *ought* to happen. . . .

February 20th.—Uneasy about G.B.S.'s state of mind! At Galton's urgent request he came to the social gathering of the Fabian Society the other night—in a devil of a temper. He struck out here there and everywhere—The Fabians were dull dogs, the new Tracts were unreadable, the reviews in *Fabian News* were contemptible—all of which led up to his real complaint. The most ignorant reviews of his book on Socialism had been by Fabians. (This was a hit at Laski's review and also at Ratcliffe's.[1]) He had just heard from Germany that Einstein, who, it appears, is a Socialist, was absorbed in his book. Who were the Fabians compared to Einstein? All this was a repetition of what he and Charlotte had signified when last we lunched with them a few weeks ago. What irritated G.B.S. is that his treatise has not been taken seriously, either by the Labour Movement, or by the opponents of the Labour Party. Winston Churchill, in his new book,[2] has called him the "Socialist chatterbox"; but that was in reference to his views about the War. In all the pre-election platform speaking, G.B.S.'s manifestos have not once been noticed. And now comes the newspaper rumour that he might be, or ought to be, made a Peer by MacDonald when Labour forms a Government. "A very sensible suggestion," he is reported to have said, "but I have not yet heard from MacDonald." This may be one of his little jokes; but I am not sure that he does not fancy himself upsetting the world from the benches of the Lords. He has a better chance of the O.M. from Baldwin than he has of a peerage from J.R.M.! Which will further aggravate the

---

[1] Samuel Kirkham Ratcliffe (b. 1868), Fabian Socialist, lecturer and journalist.
[2] *The World Crisis*, Vol. IV.

relations between the genius of the British Socialist movement and its humdrum leaders, and workaday rank and file. . . .

March 25th.—The sensational Liberal victory at Holland following on the expected victory at Eddisbury and the increased Liberal poll at East Toxteth,[1] may be the result of Ll.G.'s grandiose "cure for unemployment" (the expenditure of £200,000,000 in relief works—relief works they will be whatever those choose to call them). To the pure party man in me this turn towards Liberalism is annoying—I said Damn as I read the result at Holland. But from the standpoint of getting on with the job of social reorganisation I am not so downhearted. Sooner or later Labourites and Liberals will have to coalesce —Labour needs brains and money and Liberalism needs numbers and a sound working-class basis: if the Labour Party had inspired leadership, a leader whose whole heart was in his cause and who was also an attractive and gifted personality, we could have done without the Liberals. But J.R.M. has appearance but not reality in the way of leadership—he is a mere day-to-day parliamentarian and platform performer and not so particularly good at that with his poor health, incapacity to take counsel and wrong social affiliations. The only other front bench man with any attractiveness as speaker and thinker is Philip Snowden—he also lacks faith, and his wife is the last word of vulgar snobbishness. Jimmy does not pretend to be a Socialist and though certainly clever is common and low-toned in manners and outlook. There are many front benchers of sterling character, good manners and firm conviction. Arthur Henderson is a magnificent moral stalwart and a sound party manager—but he has no intellectual or artistic gifts—no imagination, he is dull and slightly commonplace; within the Party he is trusted and even loved, but outside the party he is a nobody. Graham, Greenwood, Alexander, Ammon—all excellent fellows and competent speakers—sensible and well-informed but again dull and lacking in any kind of personal magnetism. Dalton and Mosley are the only men of distinction in the second rank of the leaders. And this sound but dull Front Bench is flanked by the silly fools of the I.L.P. and eaten into by the equally silly, but, owing to their association with the Soviet Government, more sinister Communists. The worst of it is that Ll. George's schemes, though brilliantly conceived and advocated, are always unsound and turn out terribly expensive. And I doubt whether Great Britain can afford any

---

[1] Holland Division election, March 22nd: J. Blindell (L.), 13,000; G. R. Blanco White (Lab.), 9,294; F. J. Van der Berg (C.), 8,257; F. W. Dennis (Ind.), 3,541.

Eddisbury Division election, March 28th: R. J. Russell (L.), 10,233; R. G. Fenwick-Palmer (C.), 8,931.

East Toxteth Division election, March 19th: H. L. Mond (C.), 9,692; J. J. Cleary (Lab.), 6,523; A. O. Roberts (L.), 6,206.

more expensive remedies—like insurance for health and unemployment—which neither alter the environment nor cure the patient. However, on the whole, I am glad he has set the pace. Among the Front Bench Labour leaders there is far too much dull acquiescence in continued unemployment—Ll. George has made it certain that the next Government will assume some sort of responsibility for the prevention of unemployment and the maintenance of the unemployed. Assuming that Great Britain is not on the road to ruin, unemployment like illiteracy and sickness will be tackled on a national scale. It is only by actually doing the job that we shall discover how to do it. But it is a pity we can't learn by past mistakes; and that today we are repeating the devices of the '80's—a Lord Mayor's Fund followed by relief works—both devices condemned by the Majority and Minority Reports of the Poor Law Commission of 1905-9 after long and detailed investigations.

Sidney says that the Holland victory was largely due to local conditions and may not represent a swing towards Liberalism. . . . Miss Francis[1]—the woman organiser—told Susan Lawrence that the Liberal was winning ground—and before the election, J. H. Thomas said that Blanco[2] would be out by 500. But no one, not even the Liberals themselves, expected a 3,000 majority over Labour! Some of G.B.S.'s paradoxical sayings in the *Intelligent Woman's Guide to Socialism* were hawked about by canvassers: certainly the Labour Movement is caricatured by some of its own distinguished intellectuals! As we thought, the Shaw new play, *The Apple Cart*, is a savage burlesque of a Labour Government. In 1962 the governing class has gone out of politics, and the Cabinet is made up of Labour men and two Labour women (caricatures of Susan Lawrence and Ellen Wilkinson, G.B.S. told us). In character, intelligence and manners the Shavian Cabinet is very similar to the Harding administration as caricatured in *Revelry*. The only redeeming feature is that it is very good fun—G.B.S. at his cleverest and naughtiest—reflecting the outlook of the Astor set. The love scene, sandwiched in between the beginning and the end of the political crisis, is an obvious reminiscence of Mrs. Pat Campbell and her overtures and G.B.S.'s refusal to comply—a very brutal portrait—a tit for tat. His belated retort to her publication of his love letters some fifteen years ago. . . .

[1] Miss Gertrude Francis, Woman Organiser for the Eastern Counties from 1920 to 1953.

[2] George Rivers Blanco White (b. 1883). A Fabian lawyer of very long standing; husband of Amber Reeves and son-in-law of Pember Reeves, once Director of the London School of Economics. Now Recorder of Croydon.

General Election

May 30th. 15 Cheyne Walk.—The one outstanding characteristic
of the General Election is the identity of the programmes of the three
leaders: they all appear to be equally convinced that social salvation
depends on the utmost development of what *we* have called the
Framework of Prevention, at home; and of peace by international
law in the world. This identity of programme sounded almost ridiculous in the three broadcast talks of the last three nights. (Of the
three, Simon was the most and Baldwin the least effective.)

The heat of the battle of to-day is not between H.M.G. and
H.M.O., but between the two Oppositions. And rightly so. It is
comparatively unimportant either to Baldwin or to MacDonald or to
the causes and interests they represent, whether the Tories remain in
for another two or three years and get defeated at the next General
Election, or whether the Labour Party takes office this year and
gets defeated in a subsequent election. What is at stake is the continued
existence of the Liberal Party and the continued power of Ll. George.
If the Liberals fail to double their numbers at to-day's polls, they disappear as a political force; if they succeed in winning a hundred seats
or more they become a possible alternative government to the Conservatives, and the demand for the equalitarian state ceases to be the
main issue in politics.

Sidney's forecast is 8 to 9 million votes for Labour, 7 to 8 for the
Tories, 4 to 6 for the Liberals resulting in 270–80 members for
Labour and Tories respectively and 50–80 for the Liberals. That is
also the forecast of Tom Jones who was dining here last night. I
am inclined to rate Labour higher—there may be a landslide—there
are signs of it in the crowded urban areas.

Considering how the result may affect us personally we feel singularly unconcerned and detached. A decisive Labour victory or even
the advent of a minority Labour Cabinet would probably send Sidney
to the H. of L. and into the Cabinet. My own impression is that Sidney
would rather like to be in office again, and that I should dislike it—
I certainly disliked it last time. But I doubt whether the remainder of
our lives would be much affected. The spell of office would be brief
and once over it won't be repeated. We shall go on living the same
sort of life anyway; old people can't and don't change their habits—
physical or mental. From the public point of view what counts is the
presence of a powerful Labour Party, not its *taking office!* The *rate*
of social progress depends on the amount of good will and knowledge
among administrators and legislators—what is desirable is clear enough
and not seriously disputed—what is lacking is the heart to desire it, and
the head to work the process out. After all it was Ll.G. who forced
the pace on unemployment.

O

June 1st.—Sidney and I sat up with the Laskis till 2.30, listening to the flowing tide of Labour victories—almost hysterical at the prospect of Labour being in a majority in the House. Today the relative number of Labour and Tories has settled down near Sidney's forecast—its difference being that the Tories excel in votes, and Labour in representatives, instead of *vice versa*, as he had predicted. What has been accomplished is the final collapse of the Liberal Party. Considering their money, their press, their brilliant demagogic leader with his pledge "to cure unemployment in one year", the failure to add even a score to their numbers is decisive. They will never again reach their present number in the H. of C. How interesting it would be to look into Mr. Trimblerigg's soul yesterday and to-day. Baldwin will be smoking his pipe, philosophically enjoying the prospect of a rest from responsibility, certain in his own mind he will come back to office in a few years' time. J.R.M. will be enjoying the sensation of inflated prestige and weighing the advantages of taking or not taking office. But for Ll. George the future is blank. And yet he is too restlessly ambitious and energetic to put up with a blank wall; he will try to dodge round, under or over it. Futile scheming or stunt speaking are not attractive in a rapidly ageing man and I doubt whether the Liberal M.P.'s, now that he has led them to disaster, will follow him; each one will go his own way—some of them, before the end of this Parliament, will have gone definitely to the Right or to the Left out of the Liberal Party. On the whole we are satisfied with the result of the General Election.

June 4th.—Baldwin resigns. Informed public opinion—*The Times*, the *Evening Standard*, insisted that the wisest course was dignified resignation and acquiescence in the advent of a Labour Government. Also B. must have felt that this step gives the "go by" to Ll. George and the Liberal party; it deprives them of their casting vote—or of any bargaining power. The idea that Ll.G. would intrigue with Austen & Winston to keep the Conservatives in office "on terms" must have been supremely distasteful to Baldwin, who loathes Ll.G. So Baldwin makes way for MacDonald and virtually agrees to support him so long as he does not introduce Socialism by instalments. But when the Labour measures are proposed Ll.G. and his followers will not dare to defeat them since they are all in the Yellow Book![1] From J.R.M.'s statement yesterday, I gather that he, Henderson,

[1] The Liberal Yellow Book, issued in 1928, contained very trenchant proposals for home economic development and for public action to deal with unemployment and expand production—proposals much more detailed than anything in *Labour and the Nation*. It was not until the eve of the Election that the Labour issued a definite pamphlet with the title *How to Conquer Unemployment*. But the vigour of their research department did not help the Liberals with the electors.

Snowden, Clynes and Thomas settled to take office and hold on for 2 years, bringing in just as much reform as the present House will accept.

During the next few days *we* shall be uncomfortable and unsettled —we are out of a home—and I am in the midst of an exhausting job—distributing the belongings of Kate Courtney[1] among the nephews and nieces and friends. If Sidney gets caught up into the Labour Cabinet, I shall feel harried—if he is not invited, I suppose we shall both feel a bit flat! I am glad the decision is not with us, but with those who are better able to judge what is best for the party. Sidney has made it clear that he is not a *candidate* for office, that he makes no claim to it, but that he would not become a peer except as a necessary condition of office. There are hosts of persons who passionately desire office, who will be offended if they don't get it; there are quite a good number who are quite fitted for it; or are young enough to grow into it. The chances are, I think, about even—possibly slightly loaded in his favour, by the difficulty of getting childless men for peerages— J.R.M. objecting on principle to making hereditary peers. In a few days' time, before the end of the week, we shall know how we shall spend the next two years—it does not amount to more than that—if indeed the Labour Government lasts two years—which I very much doubt! If I examine my thoughts and feelings about it I find: entire approval of his absence of claim and willingness to serve; of his refusal to be a peer except as a condition of office; doubt of the new responsibility and new calls for a man of his age; and, on my own part, positive distaste for the social obligation involved, even a certain fear that my strength will give way under the strain. But in spite of these doubts and hesitation, there is the all-pervading *amour propre*—why is there no English word? If he were *not* asked he would feel, and I should feel for him, slightly humiliated and depressed: also he is still strong enough to enjoy the excitement as well as the enhanced prestige of high office. He *might* feel painfully "out of it" if he were, day in and day out, at Passfield without any particular reason for going up to London except a meeting at the London School of Economics. What would suit him best would be the chairmanship of an executive commission to settle some big reform.

The next entry will tell the tale.

June 5th. Cheyne Walk.—Barely six hours after writing the above entry, Parmoor and Marion called. Parmoor had lunched with J.R.M. at the Athenaeum, and had fixed up with him that he, Parmoor, was to be President of the Council and leader of the H. of L. and representative of the Foreign Office there—the Foreign Secretary

[1] Kate Courtney had died on March 27th.

195

may be a Commoner. After finishing his own business, he had asked J.R.M. what he intended to offer S. J.R.M. had been vague and had intimated a peerage and no office. With much circumvention and kindly flattery Parmoor pressed Sidney that, in the public interest, he should accept the offer. But Sidney with my energetic support was quite fixed in his decision not to go to the Lords *except as a condition of office*. We pointed out that there were many men who would gladly become peers and would do quite well as *strengthening material* for the little group of Labour peers; that he did not claim or even desire office, and that he would gladly remain outside and help in any way he could; but we could afford neither the income nor the energy, for attendance merely to speak and vote, on occasion, and that we should very much object to being "ennobled". "Don't press MacDonald to include Sidney in the Cabinet; he is not anxious for office unless he is really wanted. We fully realise MacDonald's difficulties in filling the limited number of places with a large number of claimants, some men of distinction, most of whom will find themselves excluded." Then Alfred said that the Admiralty was a difficult office to fill for Labour men. Sidney said that he would accept any office that it was in the interests of the party that he should accept. Alfred thought that J.R.M. had not understood that Sidney would not accept a peerage except as a condition of office. He would take means to let J.R.M. know this and was going to write a letter to Arnold to give to J.R.M. at the Labour Party meeting. We told him that Sidney had made his position quite clear both to Henderson and also to Arnold. But he would be glad if he would let MacDonald know his decision so that there should be no misunderstanding. And so it was left. Our own impression is that we shall not be part and parcel of the Labour Government of 1929. This conversation, which lasted about 3/4 of an hour, convinced us that Sidney's decision was the right one— though I think Sidney and I were a wee bit disconcerted by Parmoor's news that J.R.M. did not intend to include him in his Cabinet. Such is the weakness of human nature! Directly the Parmoors had gone, I began to wonder whether it would not have been better to have refused to consider going to the Lords *under any condition*. For our literary work, and for the working out of our ideas during the last years of life, being "out of politics" would be advantageous. And I hanker after a quiet life together, and days and nights for meditation, on past experience and the perplexing problem of social organisation. "So far as our desires are concerned," said I to Marion, "I think Sidney would *rather* like to be in office and I should *rather* dislike it: the couple is therefore indifferent. J.R.M. can do *exactly what is best for the party*; whichever way we shall be satisfied with his decision."

MacDonald's Second Cabinet.

Midnight: A violent ringing of the front door bell: I thought it was Maud Keary locked out; but found her coming down to answer it. "Must be a telegram," she said—I followed on—opened the telegram—"Phone me tonight: MacDonald." I woke Sidney who came near swearing, trying to discover—still dazed with sleep—J.R.M.'s telephone number. He is to be up at Hampstead by nine. "Wants to persuade you to accept a peerage without office," said I. "I shall not do it" said he, and returned to his bed. I have asked him to telephone to Passfield, whither I go to-morrow at nine o'clock, what exactly is the meaning of the midnight call. I begged him to assure J.R.M. that he does not *want* office—that he will help in any way that is useful *except* going to the Lords without office. However, it is a nine hours' wonder and will soon be over.

June 6th.—The interview ended in Sidney accepting a peerage in order to take over the Colonial Office. The immediate reason for this very handsome offer was that J.R.M., anxious to complete his Cabinet at once, had not complied with the constitutional requirements that there must be two Secretaries of State in the Lords. He immediately thought of Sidney for the job. Sidney was delighted with the C.O.: it is his old office as a civil servant, one about which he knows a good deal more than about some others. Meanwhile I was at Passfield awaiting the news by telephone amply disguised by code. An odd compound of satisfaction for him, of tiredness, on my own part, and of a rather morbid awareness of old age in both of us, came over me for the rest of the day. . . .

At six o'clock good little Arnold came in. He had voluntarily excluded himself from the Cabinet or paid office (Paymaster-General) in order to ease the task for J.R.M. and devote himself to business in the Lords, and to serving as a link for J.R.M., to whom he is personally devoted. He told us a lot of gossip . . . that Jowitt, K.C., the jewel of the newly-elected Liberals, had accepted the Attorney-Generalship and was joining the Labour Party on the spot. Jowitt said that 25 Liberals would support the Labour Government: many of them might cross the floor during this Parliament. . . . Jowitt's secession is a big event. And now I have to finish up this tiresome business of distribution, find servants, settle back into Passfield, before sitting down to consider how I can best fulfil my part of Sidney's job —entertaining his colleagues, Colonials and the rank and file of the P.L.P. We must spend freely from the £3,500 net income, and if my strength holds, create some sort of social centre for the Labour Party. . . .

June 9th. 3 a.m.—It is characteristic of English political life that within an hour of the officials of the Colonial Office becoming aware that Sidney was to be their Chief, Amery, the outgoing Secretary of State, followed him from Cheyne Walk .to Grosvenor Road in order to put him "*au fait*" of the personalities in the office. Yesterday the second day of his attendance at the C.O., Amery and Ormsby-Gore[1] (the Under-Secretary) paid him friendly visits offering to give him any information etc. Much the same procedure is going on at all the offices. The general atmosphere of friendliness is peculiarly present at this change over and is accentuated, I think, in Sidney's case—Herbert Samuel and Sydney Buxton[2] have both written with promises of support. The British governing class have been taken aback by the solidness of Labour's advances: the absence of losses, and the way in which one industrial district after another is roped in by Labour propaganda. And their reaction is not bitterness or abuse—but "let these fellows have their innings—let us show them that we are playing a fair game." . . .

I have been so absorbed in my job, that I have not heard any Labour gossip about those who have been left out or not promoted. Arthur Ponsonby is in a melancholy mood—he very naturally expected to be promoted to the Cabinet: instead he is Sidney's Under-Secretary for the Dominions (Lunn being U.-S. for the Colonies), a position of less interest and importance than his Under-Secretaryship for Foreign Affairs, 1924 Government. Ponsonby is an exceptionally attractive aristocrat—a charming *littérateur* with a scholarly temperament. But he is a sentimentalist and without horse sense—an amateur and dilettante in politics. And he stands aloof from the rest of the party—he is poor and can't afford to entertain, he is fastidious and does not care to associate with the T.U. element. . . . He will be far happier with Sidney as Chief, in the Lords, than with a Trade Unionist in the Commons; but neither he nor Lunn were S.'s first choice; he asked for Dalton (Henderson had taken him) then for Drummond Shiels[3] (Wedgwood Benn had snapped him up). Barring these two, he is well content with Ponsonby and Lunn. Sidney is enjoying himself. For him administrative routine has always been easy going; and having had a nine months' trial trip as Cabinet Minister in 1924, he has lost his shyness.

Round about all the new Ministers there is the agreeable buzz of congratulations together with the political deference of the English

---

[1] William George Arthur Ormsby-Gore (b. 1885), afterwards Lord Harlech.

[2] Sydney Charles, first Earl Buxton (1853-1934). Radical-Liberal M.P. and politician; author of the "fair wages" clause and of other important social reforms; held many Goverment posts and was Governor-General of South Africa, 1914-20.

[3] Sir Thomas Drummond Shiels (1883-1953). See p. 232. Later became Public Relations Officer to the General Post Office.

towards "men in power" or at any rate "men in place". Ll.G. alone is bitter and insulting: he orders the Labour Government to do what he knows they are about to do, and he tells them that if they apply "socialistic theories" he will turn them out and they will have to depend on "Tory votes". Seeing that the programmes of all the three parties abound in "the application of socialistic theories", and that Tory votes are just as good as Liberal votes, Ll.G.'s threats and taunts are silly. For the rest Ll.G. implores the Liberal M.P.s to *all* vote in the same lobby, on every occasion—what wrecked the party in the constituencies was the way in which they had scattered their votes in the last Parliament. "The country has voted anti-Socialist and anti-Conservative, the predominant public opinion is Liberal," shouts Ll.G.; and yet, he complains, Liberal M.P's are always found in both lobbies! Which is the inevitable fate of a minority in the middle—it has equal contact with both sides. Ll.G. is, I think, at the end of his tether and knows it. That accounts for his undignified and obviously futile rage.

The Refusal to use a title.

June 20th. 41, Grosvenor Road.—When first it was mooted that Sidney should go to the Lords the question of becoming "Lord" & "Lady" was discussed between us. My instinct was against the use of a title and Sidney, tho' feeling less strongly, acquiesced. But breaking a convention which all accept, needs something more than mere dislike, which may arise from distorted pride, subconscious superiority, self-advertisement or other forms of egotism. The test is always: would it be desirable for all other people to do it? In breaking the convention are you making it easier to sweep away an evil thing or create a good one? Moreover if the use of a title is not desirable why should you put yourself in the position of having to refuse to use it? Why accept a peerage?

This last question is easily answered. The British Constitution being what it is, short of a physical force revolution, there have to be Labour peers in order to form and maintain a Government. Whatever objection there may be to accepting a peerage, it is immeasurably less objectionable than the refusal to take over the responsibilities of governing the country. In short, the acceptance, by a sufficient number of persons, of peerages helps to sweep away what you believe to be bad, and to create what you believe to be good. So far as Sidney is concerned, assuming that he thought himself fit to be in the Cabinet, he was in duty bound to go to the House of Lords.

The second question—and one which is not so easy to answer is: Having accepted the position why make a fuss about the title? And here it seems to me, and also to him, a question of manners and not of morals; and a question which was different for the peer and for the wife of the peer. We object to a *caste* of peers, and to all that honour and glamour that surrounds this social caste—we want to destroy the prestige enjoyed by the "ennobled"—in order to ease the way for destroying the constitution of an hereditary House of Lords, as part and parcel of the British Government. In particular, we do not want this liking for the institution of nobility to spread in the Labour Party—we do not want members of the Labour Party to seek the social esteem at present belonging to this venerable institution. Now one way of undermining the respect for the House of Lords is to give up the use of titles attached to peerages *as far as this is practicable.* It is clear that Sidney himself having accepted a peerage is bound to use the title in his official acts—he has accepted office on this condition—he might just as well refuse to call himself Secretary of State for the Colonies. But this obligation does not extend to his wife; nor, I think, to himself when out of office or in an unofficial capacity. By refusing to [be] come one of a social caste—honoured because it is a caste—I make it slightly more difficult for other Labour men to succumb to the temptation. By merely passing over my right to use a title I help to undermine the foundations of British snobbishness. There is far too much snobbishness—far too much regard for rank and social status in the British Labour Movement. It is a good thing to set the example of not considering a title as honourable to the person legally entitled to use it. And it is exactly this fact that by refusing to use a title you discredit it, that may cause a good deal of resentment on the part of the "powers that be" and may lead to a certain amount of disagreeableness. Owing to our peculiar position of acknowledged veterans in the Movement, our example will carry weight. Hence it seems worth while to break the convention. The more gently I break it—the less annoyance I rouse in breaking it—the more effective will be this little attack on the social prestige of the House of Lords. An honour ignored is an honour deflated. What amuses me is that the only possible retort, as far as I am concerned, on the part of the Court and London Society generally, is social ostracism, and that, of course, is the one that will best suit me. I *want* to be dropped out of the Buckingham Palace list, because it saves me from having to consider whether I am justified in refusing to attend Court functions. I respect our King and Queen and I acquiesce in a Constitutional Monarchy—the British Monarchy is an anachronism but it is a useful anachronism, an institution for which it would be precious difficult to find an equally good substitute. But its social environment of aristocracy and plutocracy is wholly bad; and the less the Labour Party accepts this environment the more wholesome will be its internal life. The ideal I set before me is to refuse to accept what seems to me a false scale of values, without bad manners or discourtesy. Anyway it is an interesting experiment, and if anything happens, I will record it. My present impression is that nothing will happen—I shan't be fussy or pedantic about it; if I find myself called "Lady Passfield" on official occasions, I shall not protest; obviously any one has a right to call me by that name. But I shall persistently call myself Mrs. Sidney Webb—and when once Sidney is out of office my intention will prevail. There is only one rock ahead. My action might mar Sidney's popularity in the House of Lords. I allay my fears by remembering the indifference of the Englishman as to how other people—especially those belonging to other sets—behave.

June 21*st.*—Sidney is of course enjoying himself: it is agreeable to be treated with deference by a long procession of persons of importance; to have skilled assistance in every task and to give what seem to be your own decisions, on innumerable questions—especially when you happen to have an outstanding capacity for swiftly mastering new issues and intricate situations. And his lack of all pretension and his genuine kindliness and courtesy towards subordinates is bound to make his way easy in the office. Whether he will stand the unaccustomed strain of continuous responsibility, day after day, time will show. . . .

June 20*th.*—Susan Lawrence has got her deserts by becoming an Under-Secretary. Whether it was wise that she should be at the Ministry of Health is not so apparent. Perhaps when she is up against the hard facts her views will change. "Unconditional and liberal outdoor relief", to all and sundry, is one of the danger spots in the prospects of the Labour Government. Fortunately the L.C.C. and other County and County Boro' Councils will soon be in the saddle, and the cruder forms of demagogy will be impracticable, except in the few very fanatical Labour-ridden authorities. Susan is enjoying herself vastly, she loves the exercise of power; she has visions of glorious changes; and her only regrets are that as an Under-Secretary she must be "good", and that the Party, not being in a majority, can only carry out that part of their programme approved by the anti-Socialist majority in Parliament. How comforting must be that sheet-anchor of an anti-Socialist majority to the political soul of J.R.M. I wonder whether there are half-a-dozen of the Labour Cabinet who do not agree with the P.M.? It is ten days since Sidney first went to his office; I am so dead tired with domestic details here, at Passfield and at Cheyne Walk, that I could not attend the Party reception to-night and shall hear no gossip! If only I can get through the next fortnight in London without a really bad breakdown and can settle in at Passfield with two decent servants, I shall deem myself supremely fortunate. Amen.

June 29th. Ayot St. Lawrence.—The episode of "Mrs. Sidney Webb", wife of Lord Passfield, has passed off quite happily. The press have been quite pleasant about it. . . . To get it published was not my intention. But the publication has been fortunate as everyone now calls me Mrs. Webb. The Labour people I have seen are quite pleased. By the general public it has been accepted as "an extreme feminist gesture", not as a depreciation of titles—which might have caused resentment. No one has yet tumbled to the reason for Sidney's assumption of "Passfield" instead of Webb as his ennobled name. But now that I have got my name accepted, he will gradually drop the title in private life, whilst using it punctiliously in public life. And when he retires from office we shall manage to get the second step accepted—his resumption of the name and status of plain "Sidney Webb".[1]

The Bernard Shaws are in high spirits. He wanted to persuade us that the Labour Party must do some "window-dressing" and he was to be the dresser. The shows provided to amuse the people were first: a press law prohibiting, under heavy penalties, any glorification of war or any instigation of racial hatred; secondly the creation of a Ministry of Fine Arts (incidentally a post for Olivier); thirdly the creation of a Senate to replace the House of Lords. Also the need for the equalitarian state was to be taught in all the schools. Banks were to be nationalised; and small-holders and small master-men to be given extensive credits. Above all the Labour Government was to put forward arresting policies—seeing, as he said, *they would do nothing!* Then they were to go to the country. Impatience, impatience, and again impatience is G.B.S.'s frame of mind. He told us, by the way, that his gross receipts for royalties etc., in 1928 were £40,000.

What strikes me in watching Sidney at the C.O., is the perfect smoothness of the British administrative machine—in the changing from a Conservative to a Socialist Government. The Permanent Heads and the corps of discreet private secretaries see to that. I walked with Sidney to the C.O. yesterday morning to receive the Palmers[2] (last Governor of Northern Nigeria) and bid them God speed! When the Secretary of State passes through the door, a bell rings throughout the passages, and silent and attentive messengers spring up at intervals, ushering him into the large ugly room in which he sits. The rather stiff secretary, Edgcumbe,[3] announced the Palmers; and returned in exactly half an hour "to raise the audience". Everything is done to

[1] This did not happen, however; Sidney used his title to the end of his life.
[2] Sir Herbert Richmond Palmer (b. 1877), Lieutenant-Governor of Northern Nigeria, 1925–30; Governor of Gambia, 1930–3; and of Cyprus, 1933–9.
[3] John Aubrey Pearce Edgcumbe (b. 1881), civil servant. Private secretary to Sidney Webb from June 1929 to June 1930, then returned to Department of Overseas Trade.

ease the situation and maintain the dignity of the new chief. It is all very funny, very unlike the informal camaraderie of the Labour Movement. At the National Labour Club, where I usually lunch, there are to be found, sitting side by side, short-haired typists from the T.U. offices, M.P.s, Cabinet Ministers, all being served in strict order to their coming, and all chatting together indiscriminately. "Well, Mrs. Webb," said a porter to me at King's Cross, "I really don't think a live lord ought to travel third-class. I see you are not using the title," he added in a tone of approval. So we stood and chatted; one or two other porters joining in. A taxi-driver jumped down from his seat in Downing Street and grasped Sidney's hand. This consciousness of social equality among all ranks of the Labour Movement is a great asset to a political party—a precious possession which we must keep intact and foster as the party grows larger. Of course at the extreme ends—left and right, there is conscious or unselfconscious exclusiveness. The Clyde group keep to themselves and never attend Party receptions; and the aristocrats, less ostentatiously, do not associate *privately* with the proletarian or lower-middle-class M.P.s and candidates, except on public platforms, victory gatherings or possibly in their own constituencies. It certainly would not occur to Thomson or Ponsonby, the Mosleys or the De la Warrs, to come for a meal to the National Labour Club—partly because the food is not good enough— but also because they would feel ill-at-ease between the short-haired typists, or at a table alone with some burly official of Transport House. Henderson, F. O. Roberts,[1] and ourselves are probably the most democratic in our manners and the most accessible to the rank and file. They may tease Sidney by calling "My Lord"; but they think of him as Sidney and feel that he does not differ from themselves—except that he is learned.

July 6th.—I have won on the name and lost on the curtsey! At the C.O. there is a cleverly tactful official—Colonel de Satze[2] who acts as Master of Ceremonies and organiser of social gatherings for all those coming to Great Britain from the Dominions or Colonies, whether they be native potentates, or British Governors and officials, or merely travellers of distinction or persons who represent the various "interests" in the countries they belong to. He also keeps in touch with well-to-do Canadians living in England. It is *his* business to see that all these people are brought into contact with the King and Queen and the Royal family: with the Secretary of State and the Cabinet, if their

---

[1] Frederick Owen Roberts (1876-1941), printer, president of Northampton Typographical Association, Minister of Pensions in 1924 Government.
[2] Lieutenant-Colonel Henry de Satze, now Gentleman Usher to the Lord Chamberlain's office.

status warrants it; or, at any rate, that they are invited to receptions (paid for out of public funds) at which the Secretary of State and his wife receive the guests. In the first days of Sidney's official life, de Satze informed him of all the social functions already arranged and pressed for my participation. "Could Mrs. Webb be induced to present some dozen Colonial ladies at the forthcoming Court?" "No," said Sidney, "a woman of over seventy ought not to be expected to attend evening Courts. But my wife will gladly meet any colonial ladies who wish to see her," he added. "Then Mrs. Webb will no doubt be present at your reception of the Canadian Clubs on July 3rd; there are many women members who would like to see her?" blandly enquired the wily de Satze. Of course I agreed—all the more readily as, Sidney not being yet a peer, the invitation went out as from "the S.S. of the Dominions and Mrs. Sidney Webb"—a fact which was greeted by the press a few days later (Sidney having meanwhile become Lord Passfield) as a defiant announcement that I intended to keep my commoner's name. What Satze had not told us was that the Duke of Connaught and Princess Patricia would be present at a certain stage in the proceedings. This was suddenly sprung upon us when we were half way through the reception. Sidney was hurried away to receive the Royalties at the entrance of the University, while I was left to await their entry, with two or three hundred loyal Canadians standing behind me. Without a grave breach of courtesy there was no way out of the curtsey. The Duke is a kindly old man and as he hobbled up to me I had not the heart to disappoint him. "She curtseyed", recorded the Press correspondents in some of next morning's papers. I am told that this world-moving event was duly broadcasted that very evening. So that's that, and curtsey I must on all future occasions.

Meanwhile Sidney spends long days at the C.O. interviewing endless people. Just now his attention is concentrated on Kenya—about which the permanent Head—Sir Samuel Wilson[1]—has been enquiring on the spot—testing the conclusions of Hilton Young's report.[2] It interests me to watch Sidney again as an administrator—intent on discovering what is practicable in the direction of racial equality—in the prevention of oppressive policy on the part of White settlers. It is the dominant problem of Colonial administration outside the Dominions. In the latter department beyond inter-trade arrangements the issues are constitutional—relating to the tie between each and all, with

[1] Sir Samuel Herbert Wilson (1873–1950), Permanent Under-Secretary for the Colonies, 1925–1933.

[2] The Report of the Royal Commission whose chairman was Sir Edward Hilton Young, Lord Kennet (b. 1879) appeared in 1928—one of the many Government reports on East Africa. One of its principal preoccupations was the question of Native reserves and security of tenure in Kenya; and one of its results the introduction of a Native Lands Trust Bill.

Great Britain. Is the British Empire anything more than a voluntary federation of free states? is there and ought there to be one Supreme Court? ought the laws to be assimilated? It is the uncertainty as to the reality and toughness of the bond that is the main reason for all the entertainments lavished upon the pilgrims from overseas to the one little Island of the U.K. As the wife of the President of the Board of Trade I had no social duties; as the wife of the S.S. for the Dominions and Colonies I could spend all the hours of the day and every ounce of energy in entertaining and being entertained. An unpleasant prospect.

An odd parallel between two careers in which I have been specially interested. Joseph Chamberlain first entered the Cabinet in 1880 as President of the Board of Trade; he finally retired from Cabinet rank in 1903 as Secretary of State for the Colonies. Sidney Webb first entered the Cabinet in 1924 as President of the Board of Trade; he is again a member of the Cabinet in 1929 as Secretary of State for the Dominions and Colonies. When Mary Booth[1] came to congratulate me yesterday and embraced me with emotional enthusiasm I could not help suspecting that this dramatic coincidence with the long time-lag between the twin events was in her mind as it had been in mine. A few days ago Sidney met Austen Chamberlain at a dinner to the P.M. of Egypt.[2] After compliments to the new S. of S., Austen leant over the table and observed in a confidential tone "I wonder whether Mrs. Webb remembers my coming with my father to stay with Mr. Potter when she was acting as hostess? I was a boy at Cambridge. I fell desperately in love with one of her nieces," he added by way of explaining this reminiscence. It was during that winter of 1883, that Austen narrowly missed becoming the stepson of the lady who is to-day the wife of one who has succeeded his father at two Cabinet offices.[3] A curio [sic] in the play of destiny.

We attended the Thanksgiving Service in Westminister Abbey. What with the brass band and music of Military Tattoo type, the gorgeous vestments of the clergy and uniforms of the Court officials, the calm impassive faces of the diplomatic circle to the right of the Cabinet and ex-Cabinet ministers to the left, this ceremony seemed to me barbaric and unreal—a survival of a dead ritual meaningless to the majority of those present. . . .

---

[1] Née Mary Macaulay, cousin of Beatrice and widow of Charles Booth, shipowner and philanthropist, who gave Beatrice her first "social investigator's" job on his great *Life and Labour of the People of London*. The Booths disapproved of Beatrice's marriage; but were later reconciled.

[2] Mahmud Pasha. He resigned after the proposals for an Anglo-Egyptian treaty had been rejected by Nahas on behalf of the Wafd, and was succeeded by Adly Pasha.

[3] See Appendix.

July 12th. Passfield Corner.—My first night spent in our little home since I left it to hurry back to Kate's deathbed—over four months ago.

It is exactly five years since I settled down here after we had made the small cottage fit for our every-day home by building on our study, two bedrooms and a servant's bedroom. Sidney was then in office, and I was down here a good deal, working at *My Apprenticeship*. To-day we settle down again to a far more attractive abode—no longer a cottage but a rather perfect little house—fit for a peer to live in!

I have no book on hand: and I look forward with a certain nervous dislike to this spell of official life. Our plan to write a manual of social study is clearly impracticable. It may be that after six months of social life mainly in London, I shall begin to collect the material for *Our Partnership*. Whether I could be as frank about our married life and joint career as I was about my girlhood is doubtful! the narrative might have to be far more objective and less personal. It would depend on whether I write for publication during our life-time or merely prepare the separate episodes for our editors' use. Also I should have to consider Sidney's susceptibilities. What I yearn to do is to sum up my experience of life—Have I come to any conclusions? What troubles me is our own good fortune—a superlative good luck, a good luck which is almost ridiculous in its completeness, contrasted with the daily grind of human life, as it is lived by the vast majority of men. Added to this general cause for mental discomfort, there may be, during this period of Sidney's high office and forced association with great personages, a way of life which will bring with it uncomfortable consciousness of inconsistency and insincerity towards the Labour Movement. If we were really single-minded about the equalitarian state, ought we to be living a life of relative luxury and social prestige? Ought we to have a flat in Whitehall Court? Ought we to buy expensive clothes? and participate in extravagant entertainments? Puzzling over these questions gives me a kind of mental nausea which is very upsetting. One longs to get back to the peaceful student's life—and yet one has moments of sly enjoyment of the other—leading in its turn to tiredness and depression. Is it wrong to spend far more than would, under any equalitarian regime, be practicable for one married couple, in making a home for oneself and one's friends—or is it a question of compromise between two desirabilities—the desirability of an equal sharing of the available services and commodities on the one hand and on the other the desirability of charming homes—especially for those who are doing important work? Was the former owner of Chequers quite right in setting it aside for the P.M. rather than using it as a home for children or for scholars or for tired and impecunious teachers? Ought there to be such places as Chequers—these places would not have arisen unless there had been a class of persons with the wealth and the leisure to create them. Those members of the Labour Party who have taken the extreme ascetic line—C. R. Buxton, Stephen Hobhouse,[1] have not thereby increased their usefulness. Those members who have crossed over—Mrs. Snowden in particular—and mixed with the other camp—preferred the Conservative and Liberal aristocrats and plutocrats to the drab society of the Labour Party—have lost the respect of their old friends. We have tried to compromise—leaning heavily towards the simple life; and since Sidney has been in politics, refusing to associate with the other camp. But then we are old and blasés—it is easy to resist temptation with these disabilities. On the whole I am not inclined to criticise any variety of behaviour in these matters—the rights and wrongs are too uncertain.

July 22nd.—Sidney tells me little of what goes on in the Cabinet and I ask no questions. About his business at the office I hear more, but through lack of knowledge it means little to me. The members of the Cabinet seem to see little of each other: each Minister is taken up with the multitudinous issues of his own administration or of the Cabinet Committees upon which he sits. A few days ago the P.M. with Arnold joined Sidney at lunch at the United Services Club (this Club has made the P.M. and Secretary of State Hon. Members for term of office). He asked S. whether he had been to Chequers: S. said no. Then with some awkwardness he explained that the Trust Deed did not permit or, at any rate, did not encourage the holding of week-end Cabinets there; but Chequers was meant to enable the distinguished occupier to *get away from his ministerial preoccupation.* The idea was thrown out by J.R.M. of an afternoon party at Chequers for the Ministers and their wives, which Arnold and S. welcomed as a way of the Ministers getting the desirable acquaintance with Chequers without depriving the P.M. of his weekly rest. . . .

July 26th.—My doubt whether it was wise to send Susan Lawrence to the Ministry of Health as Under-Secretary rather than to some other office about which she felt less strongly looks as if it were likely to be substantially justified. Last night hearing that she was unwell I looked in on my way up to bed, and S. joined me presently. She was obviously in a state of suppressed excitement; her features disturbed and her voice strained. She began to mutter threats of catastrophe to the Government: "I have seen the Ministry of Health Minutes for tomorrow's Cabinet; no Housing, only slum clearance; no relief of distress—Chamberlain's policy virtually continued; no 'work or

---

[1] Her nephew, Stephen Henry, son of Henry and Margaret Hobhouse; Quaker, conscientious objector and prison research worker.

maintenance'; none of the promises fulfilled." She intimated that she had resigned or intended to resign. We tried to soothe her, to persuade her to be patient. But she continued to describe, in tones muffled with emotion, how she had got this or that inserted into the programme: these proposals were not being carried out—she could no longer be responsible. With a parting word from Sidney: "Sleep over it—take the week-end to consider it," we left her. Her participations in the debates during the last week have been brilliant, and her resignation would be a shock. All the same a Cabinet could hardly tolerate a threat of resignation from an Under-Secretary a few weeks after her appointment on the ground that the Cabinet's privately circulated tentative proposals for the forthcoming session did not satisfy the conscience of an Under-Secretary—that he or she must have *his* or *her* promises immediately fulfilled by Cabinet decision or resign office! This would be virtually a claim to be not only *in the Cabinet* but to have a decisive voice in deciding its policy. It might well be that the P.M. would say, "The sooner she resigns the better for us. To-day her resignation would be considered absurd and unreasonable; to-morrow, or the day after, it might coincide with a big revolt on a critical occasion and bring real discredit if not defeat." And I think I should agree with him. Susan Lawrence, when she is under the sway of some appeal to her emotions, loses all sense of proportion—all consciousness of what is due to other people to whom she has obligations. . . . Her passion for power reinforces her pity or affection for this or that person or class—and she becomes wholly unreasonable. That frame of mind makes a dangerous colleague. Sidney admires her fine intellect and undoubted disinterestedness and zeal; but he would not take her as a subordinate and he would prefer not to have her as a partner in any difficult or delicate undertaking. Tho' she and we have continued friendly to the end and shall part a few weeks hence on the best of terms, I should certainly not start on another venture with her. Arthur Greenwood is, I expect, cursing his own good-natured courage in selecting her—and wondering whether he had better not forestall future trouble by accepting her resignation. If she goes to-day her chance of future office is closed. But as a rebel she might help to bring down the Government sooner than it would otherwise go. And about this I feel singularly indifferent. In home affairs I doubt the zeal of the P.M. and Snowden and the capacity and courage of Thomas, Greenwood and Margaret Bondfield. In foreign affairs it may be that this Cabinet is vastly superior to the last. But I know too little about foreign affairs to feel responsibly concerned. All we can say, at present, is that this Labour Cabinet of 1929, unlike the one of 1924, is a "pukka" Cabinet resting on a firm foundation in the country. If J.R.M. and Henderson make a striking success abroad, its moderation at home—assuming that trade revives—will not retard the march of Labour to power—probably not at the next General Election but at the one after the next. But will any leader in social reconstruction appear? At present there is no one who has at once the heart, the intellect and the personal magnetism for such leadership. There is no sign of any *group* of men who combine these qualities. . . .

July 27th.—Sidney and I made an analysis of the representative character of the present Cabinet. It is made up of representatives of three of the main social classes of the British people with the fourth represented in the outer circle of Under-Secretaries. I classify the members of the Cabinet according to the home, the schools in which they were raised together with the first men of England [*sic*].

	Ci-devant manual workers mostly represented by Trade Unions	*Intermediate*	*Lower middle class brainworkers*
In Cabinet	6	2	5
	Henderson	Alexander	Webb
	Clynes	Bondfield	Greenwood
	Shaw		Graham
	Adamson		Snowden
	Thomas		MacDonald
	Lansbury		

	Upper or upper middle class: old governing class of the 19th century	*Intermediate*	*The Social Caste of Aristocracy*
Not in Cabinet but in outer circle of Ministers and Under-Secretaries	6	1	4
	Trevelyan	Mosley	Russell
	Buxton		De la Warr
	Thomson		Ponsonby
	Parmoor		Lady Cynthia
	Wedgwood Benn		Mosley
	Sankey		

Note that the *brains* of the Party are in the lower middle class section. This shows the predominant element is Proletarian: manual or brainworkers (but all the proletarians have become professional brainworkers), with a third from the old governing class of the nineteenth century, and *in the outer circle* of the Government 3 or 4 *bona fide*

209

P

aristocrats: 18th century governing class. There are no professional profit-makers. Wheatley was the only profit-maker in the first Labour Government. Lansbury retired from business some time ago.

Non-Cabinet Ministers and Under-Secretaries

Manual Workers a poor lot!	Lower middle class brainworkers	Old governing class
9	3	8
Ben Turner[1]	Morgan Jones[5]	Susan Lawrence
Shinwell	Drummond Shiels	Hugh Dalton
Lawson[2]	Johnston	Lees Smith
Lunn		Addison
Short		Pethick Lawrence
Ammon		Jowitt
Montagu[3]		Melville[6]
G. Hall		Aitchison[7]
W. R. Smith[4]		

Note the "second eleven" show the old governing class out-numbering and out-shining the lower middle class.

Summary of Government

Class I Manual Workers	Class II Lower Middle Class	Class III Old Governing Class	Class IV Aristocrats
17	9	10	4

=40

What interests me about this analysis is that the presence of the Labour Party as an alternative Government makes it practically certain that neither the Conservative Party nor the Liberal Party will have working-men Cabinet or non-Cabinet Ministers.

[1] Sir Ben Turner (1863–1942), General President of the National Union of Textile Workers (wool), M.P. for Batley. Secretary for Mines, 1929–30.

[2] John James Lawson (b. 1881), Durham miner, M.P. for Chester-le-Street. Parliamentary Secretary to Ministry of Labour, 1929–31, and Secretary for War, 1945–6.

[3] Frederick Montagu, Lord Amwell (b. 1876), journalist, member of S.D.F., M.P. for West Islington. Under-Secretary for Air, 1929–31; Parliamentary Secretary, Ministry of Transport, 1940–1, and to Ministry of Aircraft Production, 1941–2.

[4] Walter Robert Smith (1872–1942), boot operative, M.P. for Norwich. Parliamentary Secretary to Ministry of Agriculture, 1924; and to Board of Trade, 1929–31.

[5] Morgan Jones (1885–1939), teacher, M.P. for Caerphilly. Parliamentary Secretary to Board of Education, 1924 and 1929–31.

[6] Sir James Benjamin Melville (1885–1931). M.P. for Gateshead. Solicitor-General, 1929–30; resigned owing to ill-health.

[7] Craigie Mason Aitchison, Lord Aitchison (1882–1941). M.P. for Kilmarnock and Lord Advocate for Scotland, 1929–33; stayed with MacDonald in 1931.

July 27th. Passfield Corner.—Susan came down yesterday morning at Grosvenor Road overwrought and tragic. She had told Greenwood, Henderson and Lansbury of her proposed resignation unless she could get assurances—and now she was going to tell J.R.M. She explained what I had not realised before that as Chairman-Elect of the Labour Party she had to give the Presidential address early in October. She must either be in the Government, or out of the Government, ploughing her lonely furrow. She clearly contemplated carrying out, then and there, her intention of resigning *unless she got assurances that certain parts of the programme were going to be carried out in the next session.* But resignation she knew meant the end of her career as a politician looking to office; it meant, probably, the loss of her seat. But it might compel the Labour Government to do more than they at present intended to do—even if they refused to give her satisfaction. There was really something distinctly heroic in her attitude—for she knew that she was sacrificing her own love of power. I kissed her and wished her well.

When Sidney returned in the afternoon he said that she could not have seen the P.M.—he had been closely engaged all day. A few minutes before we left Grosvenor Road Susan appeared. She was satisfied (I assume by Greenwood) that affairs were better than she had thought—she was going to discuss it again to-morrow. We warmly congratulated her and departed. Perhaps she has done good. The Cabinet wants some ginger on Home affairs and the resignation of the ablest and most popular of the Under-Secretaries would be a fall in prestige which the P.M. would avert if he could. Susan, by the way, when she thought she was going, assured me that she would not join the H. of C. malcontents in "yapping at the heels of the Front Bench". She would devote all her energies to propaganda in the country. However I think for the present the crisis is over and I am inclined to like and respect her the more for it. There was more honest fervour than egotism in her protest.

I am quits with the Court. Ethel Snowden told me that the King and Queen were seriously annoyed—(she said "hurt"—which was meant to be appealing!)—at my refusal, in spite of seven years of invitations, to present myself at Buckingham Palace. I replied that it never occurred to me that my absence would be noticed. But that if it were resented I would, of course, go whenever I received another command. (I had already settled in my own mind that a S.S.'s wife had court obligations unknown to an M.P.'s wife—or even to the wife of a President of the Board of Trade.) The invitation came to "Lord and Lady Passfield", and we attended the Garden Party. The organisation of this super-fête seemed defective. The refreshments for the ten thousand were heaped up in one marquee and no one without an active young person in attendance, ready to push through the crowd, could get service. The dense semi-circle of gazers at Royalty seated or standing round the Royal Enclosure as if it were a show was ugly. The manners of the crowd, mostly upper-class, were not kindly leave alone courtly. There was a scarcity of seats and these few were grabbed by men, for themselves as well as for their womenkind. One man, who occupied two, rudely refused to remove his hat when I humbly enquired whether he was reserving the second for a lady. Sidney had to present Colonials; whilst I wandered about in the crowd—quite amused by this private view of Buckingham Palace Gardens; chatting with old and new acquaintances. At the end of Sidney's presentations the Queen asked "Is your wife here?" "Yes, M'am: she is in the crowd out there. I am afraid I could not easily find her," he added. "That's a pity," said the Queen, "I should like to talk to her." "Thank you, M'am," said Sidney, and retired. It was past six o'clock and the Queen and her cortège passed into the Palace. Seeing that I was not told that I was to be presented or invited into the Royal Enclosure it was not my fault that I came away from Buckingham Palace without being presented to H.M. But in deliberately going there, I have done my duty and need do no more!

July 28th.—Arnold and Lees Smith dined here to meet Olivier who is staying the week-end. Arnold is in a great state of discontent with J. H. Thomas's incapacity as organiser of employment. Oswald Mosley and Lansbury, his lieutenants, report that Thomas does not see them; but he is in the hands of that arch-reactionary, Horace Wilson[1]—my old enemy—whom he calls "'Orace" and obeys implicitly. That he refuses to sit down and study the plans proposed and therefore cannot champion them in the House. That he gets "rattled" and when not under the influence of drink or flattery is in an abject state of panic about his job. Arnold thinks he might any day break down in health as he has done in temper. "If only he could be moved to other spheres." A Governorship in Australia, Arnold suggests. The more sophisticated Dominions—like South Africa or Canada— prefer Royalties—and would not put up with anything less than a big British peer of undoubted wealth and lineage. The P.M., oddly enough, is attached to J. H. Thomas—who amuses him, accepts the position of inferiority and spices it with affectionate familiarity and wit. Also, Thomas is popular with the other side. In spite of his bad

---

[1] Sir Horace John Wilson (b. 1882). Permanent Secretary to the Ministry of Labour, 1921–30, and Head of the Civil Service, 1939–42; in that capacity acted as chief adviser to Neville Chamberlain in the years before the war. The cause of Beatrice's "enmity" is not recorded in her diaries; it arose probably in connection with her work on Government enquiries owing to the war. See *Diaries, 1912–1924*.

language, his coarse wit and his more than doubtful City transactions, no word of scandal or disparagement appears in the capitalist press. To the suburban Conservative "Jimmy" seems the one redeeming personality in the Labour Government. He is undoubtedly *Labour* because he drops his H's and is common to look at—which panders to their sense of social superiority. And yet he disowns Socialism in public and scoffs at the programme of the Labour Party over his cups. Snowden appeals to the banking world; the P.M. is popular in refined aristocratic circles and at the Court. Certainly Susan is justified in beginning to sniff! But the resignation of keen reformers who have also brains would not improve matters. They have got to stick it and fight *within* the party and within the Cabinet for all that is practicable. The trouble is that the Cabinet is so taken up with day-to-day routine, and the Ministers are so absorbed in departmental work, that unless the P.M. were to make a point of conferring with groups of Cabinet Ministers, there will be no such consultations. But the P.M. prefers to spend his spare hours otherwise: he does not *like* his colleagues. There is something wrong with the British Cabinet as a supreme organ of government—the Cabinet does not govern. It broke down during the War and had to be superseded by the "War Cabinet". Some such inner circle is needed for carrying out the War against Poverty.

Ponsonby came over to meet the Hope Simpsons.[1] He was full of praise of the new Labour members and the general spirit of the Party and delighted with the success of the Lloyd[2] debate, perturbed about "Jimmy", and I think reconciled to his non-Cabinet office. He reports that the Conservatives are furious with my refusal of the title and regard it as a mischievous attack on the prestige of titles or an insult to the "fountain of honour". . . . He thinks my example will be followed—I am not quite so optimistic! He said that the question whether I had any moral right to frequent the Peeresses' Gallery had already been raised. So it is fortunate that I have already decided not to do so and had gone to the Strangers' Gallery when I went to the H. of L. the other day. What those who object to my action would like to do would be to "social-ostracise" me. But as I don't accept the invitations that are sent me, and wish not to receive any more—*and they know it*—that way of expressing their disapproval is not available. For this reason I think I shall hear no more about it—and "Lady Passfield" will pass into the oblivion she deserves. Lord Passfield will linger longer on the stage—but even he will fade out after the fall of the Labour Government some 18 months hence. . . .

[1] Sir John Hope Simpson (b. 1868), Indian Civil Servant and colonial expert. Chairman of the special Government mission to Palestine, 1930.
[2] Arising out of the dismissal of Lord Lloyd, High Commissioner for Egypt and the Sudan, by Arthur Henderson as Foreign Secretary, for refusing to carry out the Labour Government's policy.

August 13th.—Gentle-natured Parmoor motored all the way here to relieve his mind of anxiety about Snowden's pugnacious defence of his country's coffers[1]—which would, so P. thought, endanger the pacification of Europe and good relations with U.S.A. He had even written to J.R.M. that such an attitude might mean his resignation. Snowden was playing up to the vulgar international individualism of Chamberlain, the Jingo Press and the City—with the object of superseding J.R.M. We calmed him down—tho' whatever Snowden's wares may be worth I sympathise with Parmoor's dislike of Snowden's clientèle. One can understand the fury of the Left as they watch the Labour Government gaining popularity as good plain sensible men, just as likely to be in favour of "their country right or wrong" as the other fellows, and far more forcible and direct in their blunt English than Austen was in his acquired French. Ought one however to distrust a policy because it rouses the enthusiastic approval of wrong-headed people?

On Friday we stayed the night with Lord Lugard[2] to meet Oldham[3] and his wife and talked Kenya. When we stayed with him in Hong Kong in 1911 we singled him out as the wisest and most humane Governor we had known. He is a Conservative in politics; but sympathetic to the Labour Party's beneficent intentions with regard to "natives". He is pressing Sidney to do something to curb the naïvely barbaric capitalism of the White settlers in Kenya or elsewhere. The policy these settlers are carrying out is to deprive the natives of land ownership and subject them to taxation in order that they should be at their mercy as wage-earners. The wrong turn was taken when the White settlers were given self-government and freed from the control of Whitehall. The sympathies of the British Labour Party—far from the scene of the racial conflict—have been and are overwhelmingly on the side of the exploited coloured wage-earner. The White settler cynically remarks that the South African Labour Party who are "on the spot" support their policy. Indeed part of the difficulty is that the South African Dominion, whether represented by Smuts, Hertzog or Creswell,[4] demands that the whole of Africa up to the confines of

---

[1] At the Hague Conference. One of Snowden's first charges, as Chancellor of the Exchequer, was to take part in discussion of the Young Plan for German reparations, which replaced the Dawes Plan of MacDonald's first government. Snowden thought the share proposed for Great Britain inadequate, and fought furiously, successfully, and as it turned out, disastrously for a larger cut at the expense of France. At the time, however, he was immensely popular in financial circles and was made a freeman of the City. See Viscount Snowden's *Autobiography*.

[2] Frederick Dealtry Lugard, Lord Lugard (1858–1943), the great Colonial administrator and expert; Governor of Hong Kong, 1907–12.

[3] Joseph Houldsworth Oldham (b. 1874), missionary and Colonial educator; member of the Advisory Committee on Education in the Colonies, 1925–36.

[4] Colonel Frederick Hugh Page Creswell (1866–1948), Member of South African Parliament, 1910–1938; Minister of Labour, 1924–5 and 1929–33.

Abyssinia ought to be under the South African flag, and should adopt the policy of a land-stripped native proletariat under the autocratic government of a pure white oligarchy of British or Dutch or other European descent. And this policy has the backing of international capitalism. So it is not easy to turn back and withdraw the self-government of the Kenyan White settlers. The apparent alternative is to supersede or curb that power by other machinery of government dependent on Whitehall without rousing too overwhelming a re-action—or without involving too long a delay. "You won't have a Labour Government in power for long," says Sidney—"get the most you can now—even if it is not all that you want—before the S.A. Dominion joins up with a reactionary British Government."

(According to Oldham, Smuts is worse than Hertzog.)

The same question of how to apply the principles of self-government to mixed populations is the question arising in Palestine and Cyprus—countries in which two races of more or less equal status are struggling for the control of a particular area. Lugard suggests the traditional policy of the C.O. of finding some section of the inhabitants to whom to grant self-government is wrong; that wherever the inhabitants are broken up into communities whose economic interests, religious faith or manners and customs are irreconcilable there should be no self-government granted; but the ultimate control should be retained by the proconsul representing the far distant and disinterested Empire, supplemented by strong advisory committees representing the rival races or communities. Of course there is the alternative of withdrawing and leaving the inhabitants to fight it out among themselves with or without the help of some other far or near, interested or disinterested, Empire. Sidney keeps an open mind, in regard to the relative advantages of partial self-government or bureaucracy tempered by advisory councils, but altogether objects to Great Britain withdrawing and letting things rip (I am not so sure). One of the difficulties, in granting what is called "self-government", is that it means a Legislative Council engaged in criticising and refusing supplies, but not itself administering anything. The right to criticise and reject without the right to construct and administer seems a demoralising form of activity and inevitably tends to dull and inert governments. In the new constitution which is to be granted to Ceylon[1] (said to be the work of Drummond Shiels) the representative council is to administer as well as legislate on the model of a County Council. But then the population of Ceylon is more homogeneous than that of Kenya, Cyprus or Palestine.

[1] The Donoughmore Report. Shiels was a member of the Commission, which began its sittings in 1927.

I pick up all these disjointed thoughts from Sidney as he sits in his armchair and tells me about his day's work at the C.O. I wonder what they think of him there? A super-civil servant added to the C.O. staff? His main activity is to pick the brains of all and sundry, selecting from or harmonising conflicting or divergent policies. Not quite all and sundry, by the way! His would-be visitors are censored. "Not desirable that you should see Philby;[1] he has been most troublesome to the office fomenting discontent over there," said his official adviser. And S. did *not* see him. "Why not meet him casually in the Fabian office?" said I, on behalf of the rebel, who happens to be a Fabian approved by Galton. "Perhaps," replied Sidney, doubtfully. (Oct. 2. He did.)

August 18*th*.—Snowden's amazing press—"God be thanked for Snowden" is the refrain—is a revelation of the deep-down and ever-growing resentment against the gross and cynical self-seeking of France, accentuated by envy at her continued prosperity. In parti-cular, Sharp in the *New Statesman* glorifies Snowden in three separate articles and the *Daily Mail* suggests that he be given a national welcome from all parties when he returns successful or unsuccessful from The Hague! France is in fact accumulating ill-will from Great Britain, Germany, Italy and even from her old friend U.S.A. Whether these accumulations of ill-feeling mean much in the life of nations—Great Britain suffered from this ill-will during the Boer War and Germany before the Great War—unaccompanied by specific crises I am not so sure. Ill-will is so frequently a symptom of fear, and fear arises from re-spect for the power of the hated one. All the same, in the case of France, there are specific causes of ill-will; Germany wants revenge, Italy wants territory, U.S.A. wants disarmament, and we want gold.

Meanwhile Philip Snowden stands out as the champion of the moneyed classes—and is denounced as such by Brailsford in the *New Leader*. What is the P.M. thinking I wonder. I doubt whether the two ever discussed the business at The Hague, before Snowden left London. The substance of Snowden's case is good; but there is too much of the big stick in its form to please Sidney. And S. would have preferred the obstinacy manifested on a bigger issue than a couple of millions more or less in Great Britain's share of reparations. But then Snowden would not have had the enthusiastic backing of John Bull for any finer aim than cutting down the War Debt at the cost of the "other fellow"*

---

[1] Harry St. John Bridger Philby (b. 1885). Fabian, Indian civil servant; explorer and expert on Near East; strongly pro-Arab.

* S. tells me that Snowden informed the Cabinet that he would be rigid about the debt and that after general approval the degree of rigidity was referred to Henderson, P.M. and Snowden to settle. [B.W.].

August 30th.—A day of unusual excitement: our first flight in the air. . . .

The flight, each one alone, in a Moth, off the Brooklands aerodrome, was arranged and provided by our old friend, Horace Plunkett,[1] at whose house we had stayed last night. This fragile and, we always thought, hypochondriacal old man—four years my senior—has suddenly found salvation from insomnia in becoming a pilot of his own machine: he is actually applying for his certificate—which he will not get. Having failed to persuade the Shaws to fly, he tried it with us. I did not need any pressing as I wanted to break down any hesitancy by experience so as to be willing to fly whenever this was the best way to get to and fro in the world. Sidney, with some reluctance, agreed to follow suit. A very delightful jaunt it was: I suffered neither from nerves, noise or sickliness. Sidney said he had "quakings", but was satisfied that he could stand the ordeal of a journey through the air if required. . . .

September 2nd.—One of the few advantages of old age is that having no future before you, you have nothing to gain and nothing to lose and therefore tend to be detached and disinterested. Otherwise Sidney's life at the C.O. might be harassing. Roused by the tragic happenings in Palestine[2] there have buzzed around him Jews and the admirers of Jews, great and small, in a state of violent grief and agitation demanding revenge and compensation. It is noteworthy that no representative of the Arabs—not even a casual admirer of the Arab— has appeared on the scene. What one gathers from these excited persons is that the British officials on the spot are held to be perniciously pro-Arab—not because they love the Arab but because, for one reason or another, they hate the Jew. . . . Is there any principle relating to the rights of peoples to the territory in which they happen to live? I admire Jews and dislike Arabs. But the Zionist movement seems to me a gross violation of the right of the native to remain where he was born and his father and grandfather were born—if there is such a right. To talk about the return of the Jew to the land of his inheritance after an absence of 2,000 years seems to me sheer nonsense and

---

[1] Sir Horace Curzon Plunkett (1854-1932). Senator in the Irish Free State; the great promoter of Irish agricultural co-operation and founder of the Horace Plunkett Foundation.

[2] The Wailing Wall in Jerusalem was supposed to be the last remnant of Herod's temple, but it was also part of the external wall of the Islamic Mosque. On August 15th, the Jewish fast of Av, the followers of Jabotinsky went in procession to the Wall and held an anti-Arab demonstration; the Moslems responded next day with a similar demonstration at the Mosque. On the 23rd anti-Jewish riots broke out and spread to Hebron, Jaffa and other places. Troops and warships were called out, and after some time the Shaw Commission was appointed and arrived in October. This was the start of the "Palestinian troubles".

hypocritical nonsense. From whom were descended those Russian and Polish Jews? The principle which is really being asserted is the principle of selecting races for particular territories according to some *peculiar needs or particular fitness.* Or it may be some ideal of communal life to be realised by subsidised migration. But this process of artificially creating new communities of immigrants, brought from any parts of the world, is rather hard on indigenous natives! The White settlers in Kenya would seem to have as much right, on this assumption to be where they are, as the Russian Jews in Jerusalem! And yet exactly the same people—for instance Josiah Wedgwood—who denounce the White settlers of Kenya as unwarranted intruders, are hotly in favour of the brand-new Jewish colonies in Palestine! But I wander from my original remark. Sidney annoys the agitated ones by remaining in both cases rather cold. Obviously order must be maintained in Judea; and the responsibility for the looting and murdering must be fixed and proper action taken to prevent recurrence. But the case for the Arab has not yet been heard; whilst the case for the Jew has been vehemently and powerfully pressed on the Government. The Zionist Movement, and the mandate for a National Home for the Jews in Palestine, seems to have originated in some such unequal pressure exercised by the wealthy and ubiquitous Jew on the one hand and the poor and absent Arab on the other.

Sooner or later the League of Nations ought to work out some principle of conduct with regard to the relative rights of the native and the would-be immigrant, and as to the type of emigration to be promoted. Whether this new code would recognise the "2,000 years ago" inhabitance by some mythical ancestors as a valid plea, on either count, I very much doubt. If it were recognised it would be because there was also Superior Fitness. But how does this high-sounding principle differ from the old Whig doctrine of free migration throughout the world and Devil take the hindermost, whether he takes them by slaughter, or imported drugs, or civilised disease? Shall we come, in the last resort, to a scientifically planned distribution of this planet's surface among different races according to relative fitness standardised by a controlled birth rate, and a national minimum of civilised life for each race—coupled with anaesthesia for all unwanted infants. Then, perhaps we could afford to be benevolent to all living Humans; we might even encourage variation of species, and experiment in breeding the Human Race.

At present, our colonial administration seems a queer hotch-pot of conflicting aims and competing aspirations. . . .

September 14th.—. . . Alexanders here for week-end. He was promoted to the Cabinet because he was the ablest of the Parliamentary representatives of the Consumers' Co-operative Movement. For this wide-flung organisation of working people is held to be a constituent part of the Labour Party. He is forty—a vigorous and masterful personality; with good physique, alert mind, straightforward manner; but without charm or brilliancy. Somewhat of the Arthur Henderson build and temperament. The son of a blacksmith, brought up by a widowed mother who brought up four children entirely on her own earnings, he began to earn his livelihood at 13 years of age as an office boy; attended evening classes and graduated into a boy clerk; entered the service of the Somerset Education Authority, and rose rapidly in the office hierarchy. He became a captain during the War and was detailed for educational work among the troops at home. He entered public life as Secretary to the Parliamentary Committee of the Co-operative Movement, chiefly C.W.S. work. In 1922 he became one of the members for Sheffield. He is married to a pretty little wife— an ex-elementary teacher; clever and a good manager. . . . Of course this admirable couple are being courted by the Sea Lords and other personages and are enjoying themselves hugely. At Admiralty House they will entertain so far as £3,000 net income will permit. He, certainly, is too sterling a character to be led away by London Society. In political creed, Alexander is more of a Co-operator than a Socialist; he himself believes the Consumers' Co-operative Movement is the biggest step towards the Socialist commonwealth. He is, in fact, a centre-man like Henderson and Clynes—perhaps even less of a theoretic revolutionary than either of these. With him and his wife we have always been friendly, and this is their second visit to Passfield.

All Saturday there were telephone calls about the Anglo-American naval negotiations between here, the Admiralty and Colonial Office. The handsome Admiral Fisher[1] dashed down to dine and back again with papers! leaving Sidney and Alexander telephoning to the P.M. till 12 o'clock at night. Our little home became for a few hours the centre of the British Empire and the English-speaking world! What a comedy of manners is this sudden shift of personal power from one class to another—this almost ridiculous change-over in relative social status and degrees of mutual deference between aristocratic admirals and working-class organisers. Incidentally these negotiations between U.S.A. and Great Britain may mean the advent of a world-state dominated by the U.S.A. and Great Britain! Foreign affairs have gone with a swing since the Labour Cabinet took office. If J.R.M. brings off a working plan of universal disarmament—even a very little one—and trade revives, the Labour Party will be in for a long spell of office— not necessarily continuous, but stretching off and on over the 20th

---

[1] Sir William Wordsworth Fisher (1875–1937). Then Deputy Chief of Naval Staff; subsequently Commander-in-Chief in the Mediterranean, 1932–6.

like the Liberal Cabinet did over the 19th century, and like the Liberals giving to the country a dominant political creed. And our friend Alexander will be a member of these successive Governments —long after Sidney and I have passed away.

September 23rd.—Russell and Thomson here for the week-end, with Ponsonby, Arnold and the Snowdens intervening. The Snowdens were here for three hours: Mrs. Snowden and I retired to talk over entertaining the Parliamentary Labour Party. She is bitter about J.R.M. and by no means cordial about Henderson—almost implied that Snowden was tired of the job of working with such colleagues! The Snowdens had spent yesterday with the Connaughts; and the day before with the Balfours at Fisher's Hill, and had been received by Arthur in his bedroom.

Thomson was alarming about J.R.M.'s visit to U.S.A. Both the Admiralties were smiling at each other across the ocean—they had both got more than they asked for. J.R.M. had been led into a maze of figures by Fisher—and he had no head for figures. He would come back after a magnificent reception in U.S.A., with absolutely *no* reduction of expenditure on naval armaments. France and Italy would scoff and refuse to appear at the Conference; Japan would insist on her quota; she was already suggesting that she might not feel inclined to affix her signature to an agreement which meant *an increase of expenditure.* Lloyd George was "on the pounce", and he and Snowden would explode the bubble of the P.M.'s reputation. I observed that the Tory press might boom the P.M. if they were cynical and did not want a General Election. Thomson also told me that J.R.M. was perturbed by anonymous letters, warning or abusive, and added, "I don't know whether he has anything on his mind." General Dawes[1] had observed that MacDonald ought to have someone with him who "understood America". Altogether Thomson is no longer a MacDonald man—he was turning to Snowden or to Henderson. Sidney, to whom I made Thomson repeat his indictment of the P.M.'s handling of the negotiations with U.S.A, maintained that *any agreement* with U.S.A. was a step forward towards international regulation of armaments. Russell took no part in this somewhat denigrating political discussion: he is completely absorbed in the Transport Ministry and helping Morrison—I liked him much. About the validity of Thomson's criticism I am uncertain—as Air Minister he is biased against the Admiralty. And for one reason or another he has ceased to respect, or even to admire, J.R.M. What is only too clear is that the inner

[1] Charles Gates Dawes (1865–1951). Author of the Dawes Plan for German Reparations, 1924; Vice-President of the United States, 1925–9. Ambassador in London, 1929; President of the Reconstruction Finance Corporation from 1932.

circle of the Cabinet—the P.M., Henderson, Snowden, Thomas and Clynes—are not working together with any mutual confidence or personal sympathy. The P.M. invites none of these colleagues to Chequers—but he does invite smart society dames whom he meets casually. Again the disastrous consequence of radically wrong social environment for a Labour Cabinet—it throttles the brain of theLabour Movement. The leaders ought to live with each other and among their own people—they ought to remain a tight bundle of sticks. As it is the bundle is dispersed and each stick broken on the lap of luxury and social prestige. . . .

Thomson, in appearance and manner, is a stage aristocratic officer, exactly as Admiral Fisher is a stage Admiral and H. A. L. Fisher a stage scholarly statesman: oddly enough they all have French blood of the *ancien régime*. Tall and elegant, with pretty hands and feet, conventionally aquiline features, large grey eyes, clear skin, dark hair simply brushed across an increasing baldness, very "classy" pronunciation, and ideas, fastidiously "correct" in little personal habits (he has "success" with women) Thomson seems singularly out of place in a Labour Party. Distaste for the doings at Versailles and the ways of Denikin's[1] White Armies in Russia in which he served as military attaché—a certain superficial revolutionary idealism—possibly a touch of personal pique or personal ambition—brought him into the British Labour Movement. He knows how human nature works in the "Services" and in diplomacy; he is a much-travelled and a disillusioned man, familiar with the ways of the governing cliques in most countries, and his anecdotes and observations about these high spheres of human activity lend interest and spice to his conversation. Owing to his elegance and pleasant talk he attracted J.R.M. With the De la Warrs and the Mosleys he belongs, or *belonged*, to the P.M.'s chosen associates within the Party. But except for these external characteristics I have not the remotest idea what sort of fellow Thomson is—it is possible that there is not much inside him, good, bad or indifferent. When one talks on one's own subjects one soon gets to the end of his intellect. He slides off at the shallow end—without any break one is again gossiping about personalities. His chief use in the Labour Cabinet (beyond being the best available Air Minister) is as a watchdog of the expenditure of the other and older and more expensive war services—especially the Navy. His pacifism is however slightly blurred by his fervent faith in the doctrine of air reprisals. "Make them convinced that their own capital will be destroyed half

[1] Anton Ivanovich Denikin (1872–1947), White General in South-West Russia, operating from Rostov-on-Don. He had some success against the Bolsheviks in 1919, and nearly succeeded in joining Koltchak in the following year. But the behaviour of his troops, and his declared intention of restoring the land to the landowners caused his armies to collapse.

an hour after they have bombed yours," would certainly mean expenditure on aircraft. "A relatively small fleet of aeroplanes and ships, but a perfectly up-to-date one in machines and men: excel in quality but not in quantity," is Thomson's dictum.

September 29th.—Our last twenty-four hours in the little house overlooking the Thames, where Sidney and I have spent, off and on, near forty years of married life—an amazingly happy and full life.

I, certainly, feel relieved to be rid of it—or rather of the small part of the house which was still our possession. The untidy dingy dining-room, the long tramp up three flights of stairs—59 in all—to the two little garret bedrooms, and the dreadful noise, back and front, made the old home an unpleasant lodging for me on my occasional visits to London. For Sidney with his preference for the habitual—it has served well. . . .

Goodbye, little house on the Thames.

I doubt whether you will outlive the Webbs!

October 2nd.—Settled in our costly furnished flat in Whitehall Court (14 guineas a week including service!) which we have taken for six months to enable us to entertain, in return for our salary, the Parliamentary Labour Party and colonials. Whether we should not have chosen better if we had paid the thousand pounds we shall spend during the year in that way into the party funds and saved my health and strength is a moot question—perhaps we will do so in the second year of office if there be one. Meanwhile whilst Sidney will spend five days a week in London I shall still live mainly in the country.

We spent the week-end at Brighton at the headquarters of the Labour Executive and attended one day of the Conference. The P.L.P. has the air of being thoroughly established; all the Ministers are self-possessed and self-confident and just at present purring over the popularity of their government—not quite all, I imagine, as the absent Margaret Bondfield was much more abused than she was defended and J. H. Thomas has not yet established his parity in popularity with Snowden, Henderson and the P.M. There will be ructions during the next few months between Snowden, representing the Treasury, and Thomas, egged on by Mosley and supported by Henderson, representing a forward policy on unemployment. Also the Hatry collapse[1] and the rise of the bank rate have brought about a demand for a public and expert enquiry into currency and credit which can hardly be resisted.

[1] Clarence Hatry was convicted of extensive commercial frauds and sentenced to fourteen years' imprisonment. The press excitement—and the severity of the punishment—were due to the fact that financial houses concerned had been so trusting in the first instance; confidence was therefore badly shaken.

J.R.M. AND U.S.A.

I watched Henderson and Greenwood trying to persuade Pethick Lawrence to be favourable to such an enquiry.... What interested me was the submerging of the Trade Unionist and the growing prominence of the old 19th century governing class—Dalton—Mosley—Noel-Baker—Usher[1]—the Lawrences, Susan and Pethick—in the Parliamentary Labour Party. The Left was not in evidence—the Communists have been effectually excluded and the I.L.P. discredited as an impracticable faction without constructive force by the Maxton-Cook fizzle last spring....

October 15th. A feat of endurance and a triumph in political activities has been J.R.M.'s visit to U.S.A. Whatever other defect the second Labour administration may have its doings have not been dull! Whether Henderson will be able to follow up the P.M.'s magnificent rendering of a friendly neighbour and uplifting statesman by a practical success in limiting expenditure on navies at the Five-Power Conference, remains to be seen. But I am inclined to think that Sidney was right when he replied to Thomson's pessimism that *any* binding together of Great Britain and U.S.A. was better than the continuance of the covert hostility of the Chamberlain régime. The U.S.A. and Great Britain have *got* to develop a common international policy if the peace of the world is to be maintained. War between the two *would* mean the beginning of the end of Western Democracy—there Trotsky was right. How he and other Communist leaders must loathe Ramsay MacDonald's emotional embrace of Hoover. A Union of Hearts and a Pooling of Power between the two greatest capitalist States—Great Britain the pioneer of the capitalist system and the U.S.A. its outstanding modern exemplar—must seem to Soviet Russia the final betrayal by the British Labour Government of the world revolution as conceived by Karl Marx and staged by Lenin.

October 20th. Sidney has for the moment settled the affairs of Palestine and Iraq: his daily preoccupation is now Kenya and the conference of "experts" on the constitution of the B.C.[2] About Kenya he is confronted with three known alternatives: the *status quo,* the Hilton Young Report and the Wilson Report.[3] The latter, which does not pretend to be more than a statement of what the White settlers would

---

[1] Hubert Brough Usher (b. 1892) civil servant, Labour candidate for South Leicester in 1924 and 1929; personal secretary to the Prime Minister, 1929–35.

[2] i.e. British Commonwealth. The reference is to the long discussions arising from the recommendations about equality of status in Commonwealth relations made by the Imperial Conference of 1926. A special conference of Dominion and home experts was summoned under Webb's chairmanship and produced, eventually, a series of conclusions which, after discussion at the Imperial Conference of 1930, became the Statute of Westminster.

[3] Sir Samuel Wilson, see *ante.*

accept as satisfactory, is denounced by everyone in the Labour Party who is interested in the native question. The H.Y. Report contradicts itself in more than one respect; the *status quo* is condemned by all parties! So he has to pick his way warily to some compromise which would safeguard native interests as far as they can be safeguarded with the White settlers in possession of land and capital. Anyway he will be denounced by idealists and no one will be satisfied.

The other task—guiding the conference of legal experts through the mazes of law, agreements, nationalist aspirations, Buckingham Palace fears, with the aid of the Attorney-General and Colonial Office officials—is more to his liking. The Irish Free State and the South African Commonwealth want independence, and the Canadian and Australian Dominions want the best of both worlds. He seems to be doing the job well. About such questions as the succession to the Crown, the Judicial Committee of the Privy Council (whatever the High Court of Appeal may be called in future) the Navy Prize Court —he seems to have secured the consent of the experts to the understanding that no change can be made which is not concurred in by *all* the Governments—which means that the British Government can negative any alteration of the Constitution! . . .

October 27th. "Tell Oldham", said I to Tawney, "it is useless to wire-pull an old-hand wire-puller, it arouses derision." Ever since the Wilson report about Kenya came out, Sidney has been receiving letters from men of eminence and goodwill, frequently forwarded by other Cabinet Ministers, which, to his experienced eye, all come from one source. He has done the same so often himself—but I trust with more skill! But watching a Cabinet Minister at work makes one realise how situations are prepared for them by those who manipulate public opinion so that they feel impelled to go this way or that. Thus when Virginia Woolf exclaimed "How thrilling it must be to watch actual decisions being made—decisions which alter the life of nations," I retorted that it is "outsiders representing interests or enthusiasm who make the decisions", or "permanent civil servants"—Cabinet Ministers are relatively unimportant—which of course is a paradox —only partially true. Which brings one to an analysis of the working of democracy. Personally I see no objection to what is called "wire-pulling"—it cannot and should not be avoided. The great mass of citizens are uninterested in some or other—many of them in all—these current political issues. Wire-pulling is only the way in which those who *are* interested and have a certain knowledge of particular questions bring their experience and will into the common pool. Perhaps we ought to invent more direct and acknowledged channels for that influence—but, so far, that has not been done. All G.B.S.'s railing at democratic government comes from some naïve notion that democratic *theory* involves *the equal participation of all citizens in every act of government*, and that anything short of that is a sham. . . .

November 2nd. Sidney reports J.R.M., who summoned his Cabinet Ministers to meet him on his arrival at 10 Downing Street yesterday, is immensely pleased with himself and says that he has done more for Hoover than for Great Britain—converted Borah[1] etc. The Labour Cabinet is still in its honeymoon. But dark thunderous clouds are arising among our own people—coal and unemployment; for the public at large, increased expenditure. . . . Meanwhile E. F. Wise has made a brilliant début. Cynthia Mosley has charmed the House. The Labour Party is no longer as *dull and ugly* as it was in 1924—on the contrary its *appearance* to the outside world is brilliant—it is not the window-dressing, it is the stock behind that is in question! Baldwin and Lloyd George, neither of them have control of their followers; and their followers have no desire for a General Election. There will be a tacit conspiracy to keep the Labour Government in until it has become unpopular with its own people—and with the man in the street. The old governing class has lost faith in itself—it has no creed. When Neville Chamberlain objected to increased pensions and allowances as "giving something for nothing" and therefore demoralising to character, the charming Cynthia retorted, in her maiden speech, that she herself and most of the Honourable Members opposite had been brought up "on something for nothing"; were they all demoralised? There was no answer. "No Liberals and few Tories will dare to vote against the Widows' Pension Bill," sums up Sidney. And yet pensions for young and able-bodied widows during their widowhood seems to me about the worst form of public provision—whether in the effect on wages or on sexual morality.

November 4th. Wedgwood Benn, his wife and Elizabeth Haldane for the week-end. If it were not for an unusual alertness of manner—an almost brilliant rapidity of response—which would make an outsider wonder who the devil the man was—the Secretary of State for India would appear an insignificant little person—a city clerk perhaps? He is short and slight in figure, going bald and grey, clear-skinned, clean-shaven, small-featured, and *very* neatly clad; he is gifted with a sunny smile often breaking into a pleasant laugh. Markedly unpretentious, puritan in habit, but open-minded and tolerant towards other people's self-indulgences and vanities, he is universally liked by the Party he has joined, and respected by the Party he has left. But no one could say that Benn was a great statesman or a distinguished

[1] William Edgar Borah (1865–1940), the U.S. Senator.

thinker. His opinions—one can hardly call them convictions—sit lightly on him; always a democrat he changed over from economic individualism to political collectivism without any more reasoning or searchings of heart than detestation of Ll. G. and a shrewd idea that the Liberal Party was doomed to extinction. In spite of this slightness of texture he is a thoroughly successful politician and so far as one knows, a good administrator—not likely to be rattled, either by reactionary panics or revolutionary threats, which is what the Secretary of State for India is going to get from the right and left during the next few months.

For *Dominion Status* has been promised to India over and over again during and after the Great War. But in how near or how distant a future? Next year or fifty years hence? And how can any one kind of uniform status be given to the whole of India, broken up, as it is, into native states and British India, with different races, languages, castes and religions. The problem seems to be to put the several ruling native cliques and communities into the position of refusing instead of claiming powers from the British Government; to make those who claim to govern India on behalf of the people of India distrust their capacity to combine in order to do it so as to delay self-government—until some sort of common will has been evolved.

The two protagonists in the battle to-day are the present and the late Viceroy—Irwin[1] and Reading—the one a simple-minded Christian nobleman, who believes in keeping your word, the other a hard-grained self-made Jew whose business it is to drive a hard bargain. One happens to be a Conservative—the other a Liberal—which is convenient for the Labour Government. The position is complicated by the Simon Commission. . . . W.B. has no liking for Simon and Simon despises Benn—which is unfortunate for the settlement of the constitution of India. They may well upset each other's apple cart. The Cabinet, so S. tells me, is firm on Irwin's policy, and public opinion among Indians is singularly unanimous—made more so by the opposition of Reading and the aggressive hostility of John Simon. "We have the right cause and, what is equally important, we have the *right enemies*," chirped little bird Benn, cocking his eye at me. In parting he teased me by calling me "Lady Passfield"; I retorted with a swift tap on the left ear!

Meanwhile poor Sidney with the help of the Attorney-General struggles day after day with his conference of legal experts seeking to re-define the legal constitution of the British Commonwealth of Nations—a re-definition of Dominion status which has a bearing on the situation of India. The Irish Free State, the Union of South Africa, want no limitation in their power to change their individual

[1] Now Lord Halifax. Lord Reading died in 1935.

legal relations to the British Commonwealth as they think fit—even to altering the law of succession—i.e. to choose another king. This means in fact—not the right to secede—for here Might is Right—but the right to alter, to their own advantage, the present ties between the Dominions. It is clear that one party to an existing agreement cannot claim to alter it without the consent of all the other parties. He may denounce it. But then he risks reprisals—out of which might arise war. As a matter of prophecy I don't believe the British Government would fight either the Irish Free State or the South African Commonwealth—there would be milder methods of making our little neighbour hesitate before risking even economic reprisals. Reconquering South Africa is beyond our power even if the other Powers and our own working class would allow us to repeat the South African War.

November 9th. . . . Significant of the internal life of the Parliamentary Labour Party is the continuous contact of the Cabinet Ministers with the rank and file of the P.L.P. and even with members of the party in the country. This takes place, not only in the frequent meetings of the whole of the P.L.P., but in the smaller meetings of the Departmental Ministers, with the little groups of enthusiasts and experts—mostly enthusiasts!—interested in particular aspects of Governmental policy. Sometimes these are convened by the Minister himself—(Sidney has asked his critics to tea here on two or three occasions); more often on the initiative of the Consultative Committees on special questions revolving round the Eccleston Square office of the National Labour Party. Last night, for instance, S. was summoned by the P.M. to come to his room at the H. of C. at 9 o'clock. He left a little dinner we had here for the purpose, returning about 11.30. This deputation, consisting of C. R. Buxton, Wedgwood and Scurr[1] wanted to press their policy regarding Kenya on the P.M.—a policy of enfranchisement of the natives and the refusal to give to White settlers the dominating voice in the Legislative Council, therefore maintaining intact the official majority. The P.M. listened to their plea and asked Sidney to answer—while continuing to read his correspondence. Sidney and the deputation retired to Lunn's room to continue the conversation which lasted for over two hours. The rank and file tend to be always on the side of the under-dog, whilst the Minister argues in favour of some middle course which will secure the consent of those concerned who are outside the Party and thus enable the policy to be carried out. Of course the usual accusation brought by the outside enthusiasts is that the Minister is the tool of the Civil Service and that the Permanent Heads of departments are always

[1] John Scurr (1876–1932) M.P. for Stepney, 1923–31. Mayor of Poplar after Lansbury; went to prison with the other Poplar Councillors. See p. 9, note.

against progress along the lines of political democracy and social and economic equality. S. does not find that his Permanents are reactionary: they were indignant at Smuts's lecture declaring that it was the White settlers who were the God-sent protection of the natives and that the civil servants and missionaries counted for much less as agencies for the uplifting of the native races. But then the South African Dominion is anathema to the enthusiasts of the Left and vice versa.

November 15th. Looking through Robson's typed work on Local Government—especially Part II giving his reconstructive proposals—it flashed across my mind that the day is passed for cutting up so small a country as England into separate local areas as units of administration. It has been some such subconscious conclusion that has, in fact, prevented us from continuing our investigation into English Local Government, in order to lead to definite conclusions. What is needed are functional units, with indefinite areas, instead of definite areas with variegated and largely indeterminate functions. To-day it is as easy to communicate with towns, hundreds of miles distant, as with your own village, and not so very much more difficult to go there! When Arthur Greenwood was lunching with us at our weekly M.P.s' lunch I half seriously suggested this obsolescence of local government. "Certainly my experience during the last month's official work, inclined me to that outlook; it solves many of my problems," he quickly answered. Of course there will be no sweeping away of the great municipal corporations or even of the smaller local authorities by one Act of Parliament. What will happen is the setting up of new national bodies, with diverse constitutions, and not mainly composed of elected persons. It is in these bodies that we shall see the principle of constituency elections superseded by persons selected for their knowledge or experience. The difficulty is that these sort of bodies are apt to become stale and rent with intrigue. Meanwhile the irrelevance of local areas to modern problems, tho' not as yet recognised, adds to the disinclination to change areas for the very good reason that no plan of reform seems to anyone but its author to make matters better. That was the gist of my reflection on Robson's proposal to increase the number of County Boroughs and create regional indirectly elected bodies for such services as water, transport and town-planning. Why not have *national* bodies straight away, England, Scotland and Wales—if racial self-government be desired? And here I think might come in our conception of highly-paid representatives of local areas who might serve on all these national bodies as a sort of framework into which might be fitted the expert element selected for professional knowledge. . . .

November 28th. On Tuesday when Sidney came back to me at Whitehall Court late for dinner he was mildly excited. The P.M. had decided that the proposed report of the Conference of Experts as to Dominion status was far too serious for one political party to decide, so he invited Baldwin and Ll. George to a consultation at H. of C. The consultants were P.M., Sidney and Attorney-General, Baldwin and Amery, and Lloyd George. The Conservative Ministers agreed that the report, drawn up by S. and Jowitt, had to be accepted as the basis for discussion at the Imperial Conference next year; Ll. George sputtered and objected. He had "never been told in 1926 that the British Government" had given up the supremacy of British Parliament over Dominion affairs. Did it really mean that any Dominion could establish the R.C. church (!) Presently he left for lunch or another appointment. The conversation between the Front Bench leaders became completely amiable; Baldwin and MacDonald evidently like each other and dislike Ll. George whose appearance and manner S. said was distinctly unattractive. At the Cabinet on Wednesday, the Report was agreed to and Sidney hopes to get it finally ratified by the conference of experts. Sidney was much impressed by the P.M.'s wise handling of the situation.

About Kenya, Sidney had prepared an elaborate memo for the Cabinet, setting forth, in detail, what he believed to be a wise compromise between the Hilton Young and Wilson Reports—a Report which he suggested should be submitted to a Joint Committee of both Houses as the Cabinet proposals. But the Left Wing is in revolt— determined to have the blood of the settlers—to make them *feel* that they are beaten. So the Cabinet decided that the document submitted to the Joint Committee should not be a scheme of reform but a memorandum *discussing* different proposals, and that the Joint Committee is to be left to decide which proposals it will agree to. Here, again Sidney thought J.R.M. handled the situation with great skill, whether in discussing Kenya with deputations of enthusiasts, or with him, or in the Cabinet. Certainly he has been very considerate to Sidney and appreciative of S's. efforts to get a solution of an almost insoluble problem. The difference between the Colonial Office and the pro-native enthusiasts is not in aims but in methods. "I told MacDonald not to bother about me and my views: I have done my best to get a workable scheme of reform—but it is so uncertain how things will work that I'm quite ready to leave the final decision to the Joint Committee."

As the Joint Committee will be a large one and is going to call evidence it is just possible that the eventual decision will be made by another Secretary of State—which S. will not altogether regret. Josiah Wedgwood, of course, is the prime mover in the revolt of the

Left partly because he is a fanatical believer in crude political democracy on a strictly numerical basis, and partly from a desire to upset
MacDonald's government—Wedgwood does not suggest that the
Arabs in Palestine shall be allowed to vote down the Jewish settlers.
He is just as angry at Sidney's lack of unqualified enthusiasm for the
case of the Jewish settlers as he is at Sidney's lack of unqualified hostility to the English settlers in Kenya. What Wedgwood demands is
fervent partisanship—unless you are a *partisan* you must be a scoun-
drel.

Sidney, on the other hand, seems to have no likes or dislikes for a
particular person or particular communities: about every project he
asks "how will it work, what state of affairs will it actually bring
about? how will all the persons concerned—for after all they are all
God's creatures—like it and benefit or lose by it?" And he is singularly indifferent whether or not *his way* prevails. If the Cabinet
decides to listen to other voices, then he will carry out their wishes to
the best of his ability. When he is acting in a responsible administration he is, in fact, an excellent civil servant—his instinct is to obey the
orders of his chief, and make the best of the business. Research and
propaganda are most useful pursuits and both require personal independence; but neither the one nor the other can be combined with the
work of administration. There is no time for research, and you queer
your own pitch by being a partisan of persons or movements over
which you have to exercise jurisdiction.

December 2nd. The Hendersons and General Smuts stayed here, the
Snowdens, Ponsonby and Arnold looking in for lunch, tea or dinner.

Henderson is enjoying his work at the F.O.—far more, he says,
than any work he has ever done. But he is also supervising the
National Labour Party office and preparing for the next General
Election and trying to lend a helping hand to the P.M. in Cabinet
business. Outside the difficulties of his own job, he is most concerned
about the collapse of Thomas, who is completely rattled and in such a
state of panic, that he is bordering on lunacy. Henderson reported that
the P.M. feared suicidal mania. The joy-ride to Canada has brought
no result—except discredit. Meanwhile Thomas is too neurotic to
take counsel—won't even listen to it—regards all suggestions as accu-
sations of failure. Henderson is now suggesting to P.M. that he himself must take the subject in hand; that there must be a committee of
Home Defence against poverty, that Cole must be engaged if possible,
and a proper department started—and that Jimmy must be sent away
for a rest and Oswald Mosley installed, under the Council, to carry out
agreed plans. Henderson is also very critical of Margaret Bondfield,
who is entirely in Horace Wilson's hands and shows no tact in manag-

ing deputations. She broke out into a violent denunciation of the Miners' Federation before a meeting of officials (Henderson spoke seriously to her about it). The two other failures in the Cabinet, though they are more negative than positive, are Clynes and Shaw; Noel-Buxton too shows no imagination and the P.M. would like to send him to the Lords and get some one else for Agriculture. What worries Henderson is the lack of any organisation of Cabinet business especially with regard to finance. Ministers come, one by one, with demands for money to successive Cabinet meetings—There is no kind of survey of their respective demands with a view of discovering which of the proposals are most important! He blames the P.M. for meddling in the details of the F.O. instead of keeping himself for general management of the whole business of the Govt. He says that MacDonald sends for the officials of the F.O., even for H.'s private secretary, and discusses affairs with them without communicating with the Foreign Secretary. However Henderson considers that MacDonald is absolutely irreplaceable. "I could not work under Snowden and Snowden could not work under me." So that's that.

December 21st. Along with other Cabinet Ministers and their wives we attended the Guildhall ornate ceremony—the Mansion House lunch in honour of the P.M. and the Chancellor of the Exchequer. No Conservative Front Benchers and only Reading on behalf of the Liberals; no Labour Left-wingers. Otherwise it was a triumphant social event for our two great men. J.R.M. is, I think, the greatest political *artist* (as distinguished from orator or statesman) in British political history. His figure, features, colouring, gestures and voice "make up" splendidly—his phrasing, his metaphors and literary allusions, his romantic sentiments and moral axioms, are all admirably adapted to an audience of British citizens. Every now and again his sentimental stories—his yarn about his old Scottish schoolmaster for instance—grate on the more cynical listener as a wee bit shoddy—but his delightful voice with its Scottish burr redeems the tale as in the classic manner of Robert Burns. To some of those present Philip Snowden appeared a more distinguished *character* tho' less of a charmer; his diction is less flowing and there is greater personal dignity and sincerity in his appeal. The deeply lined pale face of intellectual effort in spite of apparent physical suffering, the two sticks and the slow drag of his disabled leg, is in picturesque contrast with his blunt insistence on England's rights and other countries' obligations—an insistence which might otherwise seem patriotic prejudice. Both these men were at the top of their form. J.R.M.'s handsome features literally glowed with an emotional acceptance of this just recognition of his great public service by the citizens of London: a glow which enhanced his beauty—just as a young girl's beauty glows under the ardent eyes of her lover.

In pitiful contrast to these supremely successful ones sat Jimmy Thomas in the front row gazing at the ceremony; his ugly and rather mean face and figure made meaner and uglier by an altogether exaggerated sense of personal failure. While we were waiting for lunch at the Mansion House I went up and shook him warmly by the hand and reproached him for not having answered my invitation to a Wednesday lunch. We sat down for a chat together. The poor man was almost hysterical in his outburst of self-pity; everyone had been against him and the "damns" flowed on indiscriminately. Margaret Bondfield and her d—— insurance bill, the d—— floods, the d—— conspiracy between restless Lloyd George and weathercock W. Churchill to turn out the Labour Government, and the d—— windbags of the Clyde responsible for his not fulfilling the d—— pledge which he had never made, to stop this d—— unemployment. There is honesty and shrewdness in his depreciations of the facile remedies of doles and relief work for the unemployed. But he took no counsel not even with Mosley and Lansbury who had been appointed to help, either about the appointment of his staff or about remedial measures. Then he lost his nerve and with it his strength. Poor Jimmy is egregiously vain and therefore subject to panic when flattery ceases and abuse begins. For years he has looked on himself as the future Prime Minister: to-day the question is whether he will be fit for any position at all in a future Labour Cabinet. In reactionary views, in his helplessness in the hands of an accomplished and hostile civil service, he is another John Burns. But he has not J.B.'s dignified appearance, literary tastes and puritan personal conduct. . . . So we rejoiced at the unquestioned refinement and personal charm of Labour's Prime Minister and Labour's Chancellor; sat and ate and drank the excellent fare and went home content with our outing.

December 23rd. Drummond Shiels and his wife and Kenneth Lindsay[1] for the week-end. D.S. is one of the middle-aged Hopefuls of the P.L.P.—verging on 50 years of age. He was chosen by W. Benn for Under-Secretary; he is now transferred to Sidney as Under-Secretary for the Colonies so as to make Russell an additional Under-Secretary in the Lords representing India. Sidney gave up Ponsonby who goes to reinforce the Labour Peers as Transport Under-Secretary.

Drummond Shiels belongs to Class II in my classification; he was born in poor surroundings. Before the war he assisted his father (now

---

[1] Kenneth Martin Lindsay (b. 1897), educationalist, originally Labour, but followed MacDonald in 1931. M.P. for Kilmarnock Burghs, 1933-45; and for the Combined English Universities, 1945-50.

dead) in a small photographer's business still carried on by his brother, and this business provides (so Drummond's wife told me) their "housekeeping money". After the war D.S. took advantage of the Government grant towards university training to qualify as M.D. But before he began to practise he unexpectedly won, in 1923, an Edinburgh seat. This Scot is a ponderous man alike in body and mind—six feet and proportionately big in limbs, head and features; with a hard strong voice and a hard Edinburgh accent with which he argues and tells facetious stories too plentifully. He takes no exercise, eats and smokes heavily and at bedtime takes copiously of whisky. He is conceited and regards himself, his opinions, and his future as important to the world's history. He is well read and tough-minded—he has an equal contempt for the revolutionary folly of the Clyde and the reactionary conservatism of Government officials—I suspect he looks upon himself as Sidney's guardian rather than as Sidney's subordinate. "I hope I shall be able to agree with your husband's policy: I *want* to be loyal to him in the H. of Commons," he added, as if in doubt whether Sidney would suit him as Secretary of State. A great contrast to the polished deference of the Colonial Office staff to the Chief! Perhaps a wholesome contrast. Unfortunately D.S.'s opinions, tho' held with a stiff obstinacy, do not show much coherence. What he wanted done in Kenya changed from one moment to another, as Sidney danced him through a complicated maze of pros and cons. From insisting on a High Commissioner with the powers of an Indian Viceroy over the Governors of the 3 East African territories he jumped to a High Commissioner who should be strictly limited to the management of the technical services under the direction of the said Governors, and ended by falling back on the *status quo*—the last resort of a man who cannot make up his mind ! . . .

December 27th.— . . . why I do not know, but my mind goes back forty years to the Xmas of 1889 spent at Box House with the Courtneys and the Playnes. Father we had thought was dying, but he was slowly recovering consciousness, and I was getting back to my writing of the first chapter of my book on the Co-operative Movement.[1] The weather was dark and gloomy as it is this week and I was feeling discouraged by not having the material I wanted—and living without companionship—struggling on day by day alone in the world. "Why not go back with Leonard for a week's change," Kate had suggested, "there is Browning's funeral at the Abbey on Saturday the 2nd— you can go with Leonard." Rather a grim diversion, thought I, but

[1] See *My Apprenticeship*, p. 347. Margaret Harkness was a second cousin of Beatrice's, with whom she was friendly in the early days when she worked with Charles Booth. According to *Our Partnership*, however, they became estranged after Beatrice's marriage.

I could go to the British Museum and get what I want—I will get Margaret Harkness to introduce me to some one there who will put me on the track. And it was in her little lodging opposite the B.M. that Sidney and I met in that first week of January 1890. And now at the very tag end of our joint life together, he is again at work in the Colonial Office—not as a Clerk but as Secretary of State and a peer. So far as we are concerned it has certainly been a topsy-turvy world— but the top has come last. Yet just because it has come last—it does not seem a top at all—only a step on one side from our own way in life which has been the way of research and the writing of books. . . .

PART VII

1930

FEBRUARY 1930—DECEMBER 1930

February 14th.—John Wheatley came to my Wednesday lunch. He has deteriorated mentally and physically since I knew him as a member of MacDonald's 1924 Cabinet. As a Cabinet Minister he was a brilliant success—alike in his department and in the House. As a rebel in the Party he has been a failure. His expression is sullen, his words are bitter; his lips are blue and his complexion is patchy—and he closes his eyes at you. He says that he has lost his faith in political democracy: the common people have no will of their own: they are swayed backwards and forwards. He would be a Communist if he were not a pious Catholic. As it is he has no consistent position and will, I imagine, drop out of politics. In the U.S.A. he would have succeeded as a local boss. He is a good mob orator and would have revelled in the intrigue and corruption of the "Machine"; he would have been acute and good-natured in dispensing offices and bribes among followers. But he lacks the sanity and honourableness needed for success in British politics. During lunch he unbent—he likes me and I like and admire him—though I do not respect him. I suggested, much to his delight, that his real rôle was to be the first Papal Ambassador to Moscow, to arrange a concordat between the secular and ecclesiastical dictatorships. This vision of the Soviet Communist Government in alliance with the Roman Catholic Church and he in the centre of it, settling down to govern the 120 million Russians, pleased him immensely and he chuckled over it while we trooped up to the Founders' Room.

February 20th.—Dwight Morrow,[1] his wife and daughter stayed the week-end with us. I had sat next this distinguished American, financier, diplomat and statesman, at the Naval Conference banquet and liked him much. On further acquaintance, he is not exactly attractive as a personality. His conversation, though sensible and well-informed as well as public-spirited and unegotistical, is somewhat dull, without wit or imagination or any original philosophy of life except the usual American optimism about all things American. Also he

[1] Dwight Whitney Morrow (1873–1931). U.S. Senator, member of J. P. Morgan and Co.; Ambassador to Mexico, 1927–30; in 1930 delegate to London Naval Conference.

believes that the tide of unemployment and depression will turn presently even for England. He has an outstanding reputation as a uniquely qualified Ambassador to Mexico, who has not only put the relations of the U.S.A. and Mexico on a sound footing, but also has solved the problem of Church and State tension as the impartial friend. His wife is an able, intelligent, public-spirited little woman, much mixed up with American university women's life; and the daughter has trained as a teacher. They also had ugly voices; and talked much. For the first few hours their voices got on my nerves. But Dwight Morrow is the very best type of American public man; on the same level of capacity and character as Hoover and far more sympathetic and humane in his outlook. Probably he would grow on one if one worked alongside him. He is in all respects a plain man—first-class as citizen, husband and father, as professional worker, in finance, law or diplomacy. But no one would call him a magnetic personality or a social charmer.

The Russian Ambassador[1] and the lady who is acting as his wife (it is said there is no legal tie between them) dined with us in our little flat and met the Shaws, Ponsonby and Noel-Baker. Neither of them could talk fluent English, but owing to G.B.S.'s wit and Noel-Baker's French, we had a successful evening. A young man, with a naïve faith in Communism as the last word of science; studious and ascetic—a veritable puritan—non-smoker, did not drink his wine; one would say belonged to the best type of young workman of good character in quest of knowledge. He may develop personality; his expression and behaviour gives an impression of sincerity and honesty. His attractive little wife is an author—was correspondent of the *Izvestia* in China and has published a book on the women of the French Revolution. They spend most of their leisure in the British Museum reading-room. Certainly they are strange members of the diplomatic circle. The Ambassador would be more at home as tutor in the W.E.A. As Ambassador I should imagine he would be at first at any rate a nonentity. Probably some other members of his staff are sent to look after him. But in their simplicity and unpretentiousness the two were an attractive couple and we shall see more of them. The only Embassies who have hitherto noticed them are the German and the Turkish. Will she be presented at Court, I wonder?

February 25th.—The life I lead is displeasing in its restlessness. Always week-end visitors chosen for political reasons—which means

---

[1] Gregori Jokovlevich Sokolnikov (b. 1888). Bolshevik leader from the Ukraine; Soviet People's Commissar for Finance, 1921–6 (when he became one of the "Right Opposition"). Ambassador in London, 1929–32. Tried for high treason in 1936 and condemned to ten years hard labour. (This entry is the first indication of Beatrice's interest in the U.S.S.R.)

talk, talk, and again talk—often interesting, but always exhausting. Then two or three nights in London: lunches, dinners, afternoon parties, press interviews and occasional social functions of a more pretentious sort. These I avoid like the devil; they have to me a ghostly flavour. Last night at the F.O. reception, where I went from a dinner at 10 Downing Street, as the wife of the Secretary of State for the Colonies, there arose a memory of my first F.O. reception: I had come from the dinner at which I first met Joseph Chamberlain forty-seven years ago! At Admiralty House, a funny picture emerged, of a flirtation in a corner of the great reception room, with an Admiralty clerk in 1876—the year I "came out"—over half a century ago. It is uncanny this looking backwards through vistas of bygone figures—great personages or interesting but little-known individuals—all dead and gone. Then I turn and gaze at the new crowd—more especially at the younger men and women—still in the stage of Hopefuls struggling to the front; not more than one or two will arrive—the others will recede, further and further and be lost among the multitude of "might have beens" who no longer count. When Lloyd George came and shook hands, after an interval of 11 years, he seemed a ghost from the middle period of my life. Thirty years ago he and his wife used to dine with us at Grosvenor Road—he a bright young M.P. on the make; his wife a homely little body in a high black silk dress with curls. In another fifteen years, he had become the central political personality —not only in his own country, but in Europe, his only rival, as a world celebrity, being President Wilson. Now Wilson is dead and largely discredited; whilst Lloyd George hovers uneasily in the wings of the British political stage; unable to come to the front, but unwilling to step out of the way of MacDonald and Baldwin. As I watched these three men, within a few yards of each other, Lloyd George seemed to be saying to himself, "One or other of those two must be tripped up, and that before long," and he looked at Baldwin. These shifting scenes, actual or imagined, would be amusing—if the background were not lowering with a sense of national decadence—mistaken pessimism perhaps, but also in other observers and these not the least experienced. "The Japanese, Italian and French delegates," said Maurice Hankey to us during his week-end visit, "are convinced that our desire to limit armaments is based on our feeling down and out." And now comes the Empire Free Trade Party headed, not by accredited politicians, but by the two great newspaper magnates,[1] building their hopes on Baldwin's honest incapacity, and the Labour Party's sensational failure to stem the rise of unemployment. These shout and shriek day by day, in heavily leaded columns of the most-read newspapers, Great Britain's impending doom, unless a wholly impracticable

[1] Lords Beaverbrook and Rothermere.

customs policy is immediately set on foot. If a general election were to come to-morrow—and it may come any day—all the three parties are so rattled that no one could predict what would happen—which party would suffer most from the lethargy induced by general disillusionment? I would gladly ascribe my own impression to senility—old people so often rail at imaginary contemporary disasters. But the young and the middle-aged seem even more disgruntled with the world than some old people. Indeed, Sidney remains unperturbed and says that most of the pessimism is "calculated". It may be that the "decay of capitalist civilisation"[1] which we prophesied and described ten years ago, is actually taking place and that some new and better forms of social life are struggling through in ways we fail to recognise. After all, the political world with its wasteful game of ins and outs, its curious tangle of personal ambition and conflicting creeds, though it feels itself to be the Boss concern, may be merely surface movement, reflecting or covering hidden activities—activities which do not change with changes of government—which may even be the cause and not the effect of what happens at Westminster and in Whitehall. "I am beginning to think we politicians are all flies on the wheel," said John Wheatley to me the other day. . . .

March 7th.—Yesterday we had to dine, in our little flat, three attractive Tory M.P.s—all I think destined to be Cabinet Ministers —Major Elliot,[2] Ormsby-Gore and Oliver Stanley,[3] together with Tom Jones, the convener of the meeting. We met to discuss the proposed separation of the machinery of government for home and foreign affairs respectively. It was an odd little party (we dined in my bedroom and sat in the sitting-room)—queerly unconventional. For why should these three Hopefuls of Conservatism—two of them frontbenchers—wish to consult with the Webbs and the Webbs with them? The motive in both cases was, I think, simple curiosity about the other personalities as well as a desire to fathom the practicability of the idea of two parliaments and their executives.

The Scot was the dominant figure: a big loosely made man trained as an M.D.—not altogether unlike Drummond Shiels, but with good manners and personal charm—an ugly but pleasing face—homely but well-bred manner. The youthful Stanley was tall and graceful, perfectly turned-out, apparently modest in spite of his delightful good looks and tactfully deferential manner. Ormsby-Gore—small and Welsh in appearance, did not impress me—partly, no doubt, because he quite clearly did not like me. . . . It was a freakish party—but I think

---

[1] *The Decay of Capitalist Civilisation*, published in 1923.
[2] The Rt. Hon. Walter Elliot.
[3] Oliver Frederick George Stanley (1896–1950). Conservative M.P. for Westmorland and West Bristol; Colonial Secretary, 1942–5.

we all enjoyed it—not least Tom Jones who sat and "listened in" —with a broad smile on his intelligent and good-natured face. Tom Jones like Maurice Hankey has had a record experience of associating with distinguished personages and being mixed up in overwhelmingly important public affairs. But this being at the very epicentre of political power—wherever this power happens to be located—seems to make the favoured observers quite superficial, alike in their knowledge and their judgments. One cannot see Hankey or Jones discovering how to reorganise parliamentary government or how to prevent unemployment or treat the unemployed. It is always the next moment's situation—the next moment's clash between personalities—that they are trying to ease or straighten out. Never the problem itself: which is only another way of saying that they are expert at this particular job of a skilled secretariat and have neither the time nor the brains to be expert at anything else. Indeed to have ideas of their own would be to put sand into the machine by taking the side of this Cabinet Minister or that. The neutrality of the secretaries to the Cabinet or to an international conference is essential to their efficiency.

What interested me in this discussion with leading young Conservatives was how easy it was to *assume* that we all desire the same end— the total absence from the argument of any reference to fundamental differences of opinion. And yet it is clear that those who desire to extend governmental action and those who desire to restrict it would try to make the machine fit, and fit only for the job they desired it to do. Which again raises the question—Do the Conservatives of to-day desire to limit the work of government? Many of their proposals —customs duties and unity of the Empire, agricultural policy—are all extensions of governmental action. And Elliot suggested that customs were to be considered as one among many ways of bringing the commerce and industry of the country under control. *Laisser-faire* is, in fact, as dead as ditch-water and stinks in the nostrils of all politicians. . . .

March 30th.—For the second time Sidney has found crucial questions referred, not to the Cabinet for consultation and decision, but to a suddenly-called meeting of the two ex-Prime Ministers, the P.M. and himself. The first was the Dominion Status question which will dominate the autumn Imperial Conference. To-day it is the Palestine Report which turns out to be far too pro-Arab for the P.M.'s taste.[1] The Commissioners, with a demurrer from Snell,[2] after adjudicating

[1] The Report of the Special Commission appointed "to enquire into disturbances in Palestine", under the Chairmanship of Sir Walter Sidney Shaw (1863–1937) the Colonial Judge.
[2] Harry Snell, Lord Snell (1865–1944), Fabian Socialist and lecturer to the Ethical Society; first secretary to London School of Economics; M.P. for East Woolwich, 1922–31.

on the immediate occasion of disorder in August, deliver *obiter dicta* on the impracticability of a National Home for the Jews without ousting the Arabs—which course they deprecate as inconsistent with pledges under the Mandate—the Mandate is, they imply, self-contradictory and ought to be revised. The P.M. was much perturbed. What was to be done before the Report was published? The first step was a lunch given by Sidney, at the P.M.'s request, at which the P.M. met the leading Zionists, then in the afternoon a private meeting between Baldwin, Lloyd George, Herbert Samuel and Sidney. The decision was to employ General Smuts accompanied by Sir J. Campbell[1] of the Colonial Office to report on the Mandate. So straight away the P.M. wires to Smuts and arrangements are made with Baldwin to ask the appropriate questions in the House of Commons.

The P.M. after further thought decided against Smuts as too Zionist and allowed Sidney to engage Hope Simpson to enquire into the land question. Meanwhile the Cabinet has not seen the Report leave alone considered Sidney's memo! As for the Parliamentary Party and the H. of C. as a whole neither one nor the other comes into the picture. . . .

April 3rd.—The last evening at 2 Whitehall Court—"A rich man's slum" as it has been nicknamed by contemptuous millionaires! Our little furnished flat at the extravagant rent of 14 guineas a week including service, on the gloomy but quiet side of the building, has served us well. It has been near the Colonial Office, convenient for most of the places of our resort; in its way well-appointed, in spite of its indifferent fare at absurd prices. But it is unpleasant living economically in an expensive establishment and we shall be glad to get into Artillery Mansions, where everyone has modest means or wishes to live modestly.

I have finished up entertaining the P.L.P. for this first year of salaried office. I have invited all the 292[2] M.P.s to lunch (over 200 came) and given a reception to them and their wives, and Dominion and Colonial personages, at Admiralty House—all being successful. Our own entertainments have been varied by official dinners and lunches—sometimes made up of wives (boresome). All evening receptions refused. Altogether my rather queer position in the political social world has been stabilised. And now I am going to rest from this distressful pursuit of social life for the Labour Party and try to concentrate on working out some practicable scheme of parliamentary devolution. Having broken up the Poor Law, why not break up the

---

[1] Sir John Campbell (1874–1944). Indian civil servant; economic and financial adviser to the Colonial Office, 1930–42.
[2] Most reference books give 287 or 288 as the number, according to classification.

*Beatrice Webb in the
'thirties*

*Sidney Webb in the
'thirties*

Beatrice Webb, 1942. *The last picture*

British Constitution? Maroon the House of Lords without reforming it; create an Assembly and Executive that can really set about re-organising British society—leaving the ancient H. of C. and the Cabinet to build up the World State and maintain the British Commonwealth of Free Nations (or at any rate bring it decently under the foundation of the world state).

April 5th.—H. G. Wells, whom we had not seen for some seven years, turned up for lunch on his way to Churt to collogue with Lloyd George. "He uses me as a super-press man," he jovially re-marked. H.G. has grown super-fat and wheezy—almost rivals Chesterton. This fatness accentuates the piglikeness of his features. (The pig face is uncommon in England—English are mostly dogs and birds—less often horses, cats and apes—but still fewer pigs. Mary Macarthur was a really attractive pig—the only one I have seen.) Wells has acquired the habit of monologue—badly. In old days part of his charm was his intellectual curiosity and the rapidity of give and take in conversation. To-day he was wholly uninterested in what we were thinking—probably he thought he knew it all. But he was curious to see how the old Webbs were wearing and what sort of home they had made for themselves. "This is a charming room," he re-marked as if surprised. I was glad to see the genial old sinner—a *revenant* from the middle period of our life when we were all pals to-gether. He has the poorest opinion of Parliamentary institutions in general and of the late and present Government in particular. In his forthcoming novel[1] he is said to have caricatured the lot of us. There is something likeable in his frankness and lack of solemnity about his own life, his bubbling egotism, his comradeship with the younger scientists, his insistent determination to educate his fellow men on all aspects of life—from the organisation of industry to the relation of man to the universe. How he and Lloyd George will enjoy themselves abusing the Labour Government, inventing slogans for the next general election. . . .

May 8th.—I gather from the constantly recurring newspaper para-graphs—*especially in the 'Daily Herald'*—of Sidney's approaching resign-ation, that there is a group in the P.L.P. whose wish is father to the thought. There is Hartshorn[2] who, when the Simon Report[3] is finished, expects to be put back in the Cabinet and there are the pro-

[1] Probably *The Autocracy of Mr. Parham.*
[2] Vernon Hartshorn (1872–1931), M.P. for Ogmore and President of South Wales Miners' Federation; Postmaster General in the first Labour Government and Lord Privy Seal after Oswald Mosley's resignation.
[3] The Report of the Indian Statutory Commission (1927–30) presided over by Sir John Simon. Vernon Hartshorn was a member.

natives who think that Sidney is too hard-faced and official in his native policy; and there are those who think that his appointments are far too *bourgeois*—that Labour men ought to have had a governorship. "What's the use of having a Labour Government if Labour men do not get the offices and salaries?" But so far as he knows neither the P.M. nor the Cabinet wish him to retire. So he sits tight and says nothing. All the same it is unpleasant and upsetting. Especially when your age would seem to make retirement not otherwise than desirable for yourself and others. But then he is younger than Parmoor and Lansbury and far abler!

I am getting plenty of criticism of my scheme—from Laski, Robson, Delisle Burns, M. Amos,[1] Finer,[2] Ponsonby and others—mostly unfavourable. But I am going to work this vein out; if it does nothing else it will start people thinking. Our Parliamentary institutions have to be changed to meet the new demands—the more competitors bringing forward specific schemes sufficiently detailed to be examined and judged, the more likely we are to get a feasible plan. And all this discussion interests me—it is a stimulating game to play—and if it does nothing else it will clear the issues—state the problem which needs to be solved.

May 10th.—The Sankey brother and sister here for the week-end. The Lord Chancellor—an impressive personage to behold—is far more winsome than that phrase would imply. He is the finest type of professing Christian—large-hearted, modest, wise—in the best sense of these terms. In many ways he is the exact antithesis of the first Labour Lord Chancellor. Not that Haldane lacked beneficence and wisdom; but it was a cynical beneficence and a wordly wisdom. Intrigue, manipulation and sophistry are altogether "out of bounds" for Sankey's pious soul. He has a direct intelligence expressing itself with slow sincerity: he is no respecter of persons, he is not impressed by, indeed he is largely oblivious of, the great people of the world—whether they are of the Court, of the City, or of the newspaper press. A fine presence, delightful voice, perfect memory and a certain emotional eloquence, proved him to be, in his first speech in the House of Lords (on the Coal Bill) a considerable orator. As a conversationalist he is slow, even a trifle ponderous; he has none of Haldane's wit and clever characterisation of men and women; he has no intellectual subtlety, no comprehension of metaphysics, no liking for abstruse science, techno-

---

[1] Sir Maurice Sheldon Amos (1872–1940), K.C.; judicial adviser to Egyptian Government, 1919–25; later Professor of Comparative Law, University College, London, and British delegate to International Committee of Experts on Private Aerial Law.
[2] Herman Finer (b. 1898), Reader in Public Administration, London School of Economics, 1940–2.

logy or scholarship; neither does he claim to be a lover of music, or art, or poetry. He is just a plain man with goodness and sweet reasonableness writ large in his thoughts and feelings, in his words and acts. Perhaps of all the members of the Cabinet he is the most trusted, and the least feared by his colleagues; he may be ignored by some, he is not disliked by any. No one ignored Haldane! But not a few suspected him of being a hostile force in the Movement he had joined. . . .

May 21st.—The Government narrowly escaped defeat—15 only —on reduction-of-Thomas's salary-unemployment-debate—a defeat which would I think have entailed a General Election and goodbye to the Labour Government. Thomas made the same old speech— just the sort of "statement of policy" which might be made by any slow-going conservative employer who happened to be in Thomas's position.

Mosley resigns.[1] If the Government survives the summer it will be by the tacit connivance of the other two parties who are not ready for an election. Also public opinion is against it on the ground that Great Britain must not show division of opinion now it is confronted with revolution in India.

May 29th.—Mosley's speech in the second attack on Thomas is acclaimed as that of a distinguished parliamentary orator, wholly admirable in manner and style, however opinions may differ about the practicability and desirability of his plan. The P.M. promises to place himself at the head of the Cabinet Committee for dealing with unemployment. It is interesting to note that he has never once mentioned the question to Sidney. Who is he consulting? The question has not been referred to the new research department—on the contrary, it has been expressly warned off on the ground "*that it is the specific job of Thomas's 'department'*". And yet we all thought that this new departure in the machinery of government was devised because of the breakdown over unemployment! Has MacDonald found his superseder in Oswald Mosley? MacDonald owes his pre-eminence largely to the fact that he is the only artist, the only aristocrat by temperament and talent in a party of plebeians and plain men. Hitherto he has had no competitor in personal charm and good looks, delightful voice and the gift of oratory. But Mosley has all these with the élan of youth, wealth

[1] Early in 1930, when the figures of unemployment were beginning to go up steadily, Sir Oswald Mosley produced a policy, called the "Mosley Memorandum", for combating unemployment. This policy involved the expansion of home purchasing power by means of credit policy, control of banking and exports, bulk purchase, increase of pensions and allowances, etc.; but it conflicted head-on with Snowden's orthodox economics, and was rejected by the Cabinet. Mosley thereupon resigned. (See G. D. H. Cole, *History of the Labour Party from* 1914, pp. 235 ff.)

and social position added to them. Like Mosley, MacDonald began
as an Utopian, but to-day he is a disillusioned Utopian whilst Mosley
has still a young man's zeal—and is, I think, more able to use other
men's brains. Whether Mosley has Mac's toughness of texture—
whether he will not break down in health or in character I have
doubts. . . .

May 31*st*.—On the night of our departure for the Channel Isles
Sidney reported an interview with MacDonald who is struggling out
of the depths of difficulties with the Party. Sixty members had signed
a demand for the dismissal of Thomas, and the P.M. was considering
how to find a way out for his old friend and colleague. Sidney played
up and offered to clear out of either of one or of both his offices as
Secretary of State for Dominions and Colonies. The P.M. expressed
his appreciation, but two Secretaries of State would still be needed in
the House of Lords. There was, however, the possibility of appointing
a new Secretary of State for the Dominions leaving Sidney as S. of S.
for the Colonies—giving Thomas the Dominions. Indeed this division has always been contemplated. Sidney acquiesced; told Wilson[1]
and Harding[2] to prepare for the division of the office as best they could
and came off for our fortnight's holiday in excellent spirits. He
reports MacDonald as "disgusted with the Party and professing indifference to continued office", and very angry with Mosley. Whether
Thomas will agree to this confession of failure and whether the King
and the Dominions will approve of this way of shelving a discredited
politician we shall see during the next week. But "Jimmy" is a
favourite in the higher circles of society. . . . There must be something
loveable in this ugly and low-down specimen of humanity—he has a
sort of genius—a pungent and appealing personality?—and above all
a gift of intimacy so insistent that it overcomes MacDonald's
intensely secretive mind.

But saving Jimmy's face will not save the situation.

A Socialist Government cannot take up the attitude of *non possumus*
to all schemes for making the lot of the workers secure against the
ravages of unemployment—either remunerative work must be found
or maintenance on tolerable conditions alike of mind and body must
be given. Such an aim may for lack of inventiveness be unfulfilled for a
generation; but it must be attempted and again and again attempted
with undaunted courage until this intolerable state of affairs has become
exceptional, like typhus is to-day in the big cities of the world. It is
absurd to assume that with the present enormous powers of production

[1] Sir Samuel Wilson.
[2] Sir Edward John Harding (b.1880), civil servant; Assistant Under-Secretary
for the Dominions, 1925–30, and Permanent Under-Secretary, 1930–40.

we cannot so distribute the services and commodities available as to insure to all men a sufficient livelihood. If the requisite services and commodities *could not be produced* with the existing means of production we might have to starve some in order to supply others. But the ironic fact is that in Great Britain and Germany, in Italy and U.S.A. and Japan, the immediate cause of workless and wealthless persons is an over-production of commodities and services! The Soviet Government by killing capitalist enterprise has not abolished poverty—all it has done is to distribute poverty, due to *under-production*, equally over the whole population. That at least makes the burden of poverty less demoralising. But it does not lift it off the life of the people. The U.S.A., by giving free play to pecuniary self-interest in a new country, with unlimited sources of unearned wealth, has distributed a greater measure of services and commodities among the mass of the people. But it has left the lowest levels of the population more miserably destitute and oppressed than they are either in Great Britain or in Russia. And by the neglect of the moral factor it has increased violence among the lower orders and lawlessness among whole sections of the well-to-do. . . .

June 22nd.—Two first-rate books by Americans on Russia—*Humanity Uprooted*, Hindus, and *Soviet Russia*, Chamberlin, are challenging to the philosophy of the Inevitability of Gradualness. One is a psychological study, the other a plain statement of political and economic facts. Both authors are thoroughly versed in all things Russian: one born in Russia, the other an old inhabitant and married to a Russian. A wonderful testimony to the reality and depth of the Communist creed reckoned in an achievement unique in the world's history alike in suddenness and ubiquity. The Russian Communist Government may still fail to attain its end in Russia, as it will certainly fail to conquer the world for the Russian brand of Communism. But its exploit exemplifies the Mendelian view of sudden jumps in biological evolution as against the Spencerian vision of slow adjustment. And the wonder of these sudden jumps of the common people from a state of abject oppression under the Czar to a state of supreme power under the Soviets, from the grossest inequality of circumstances to virtual equality, from the lowest type of magic to idolisation of science, from the most primitive methods of tilling the ground to mass mechanical production—is a wonder which unnerves observers accustomed to the slow and halting social reform characteristic of the western political democracies. As I contemplate the very attractive little house I have built up out of the considerable salary enjoyed by a Labour Cabinet Minister in 1924 and 1929–30 I doubt the superior virtue of the British over the Russian Socialism. As I read *Look at Chicago*, the record of vice, corruption and lawless violence, and compare it with the American journalist's account of puritan Moscow, one doubts the superiority, in law and order, and social manners of the American over the Russian city. In sincerity in faith and zeal for public welfare as well as in personal self-control the Russian ruling class seems superior to the Anglo-Saxon. A humiliating thought for the two English-speaking races! Our one retort is that however lacking we may be in spiritual grace, the everyday material condition enjoyed by the English and American workers is, as yet, far higher than that of the people of Russia. If and when that circumstance is reversed Russian Communism will be well on the way to conquer the democratic world in its aims if not for its methods.

June 30th.—Sidney showed me a remarkable report from Ovey,[1] the British Ambassador at Moscow. The gist is that Soviet Communism is firmly established and increasing its hold day by day in the medley of peoples making up the Russian empire. Communism he holds is analogous to the Mohammedanism of mediaeval times, it is a potent religion which is sweeping through continents—and like Mohammedanism and all other religions will sweep on until it finds its margin of cultivation. And he believes the Communist Party will succeed in destroying the capitalist system within its territories and will bring into practice a way of life based on common property, equality of incomes and the supremacy of the workers' interests. Autocracy is indigenous in Russia and will survive in the Soviet Republic as a political constitution. What has been revolutionised is the *purpose* of government, which is, under Communism, to bring about a millenium through the transformation of the motives of man —only in *this* world and not in a mystical after-life. Clearly this acute diplomatist—a professional diplomatist—has been converted to the general outlook of Russian Communism as a practical creed and one the rest of the world will have to tolerate if not to adopt. . . .

July 9th.—Cabinet meetings twice a day on urgency business: India, food taxes, and safeguarding, votes of censure, which it is rumoured Lloyd George is prepared to support; the Lords' Amendment on the Coal Bill, mounting unemployment—altogether the Labour Government is among the rocks and may any day be wrecked. A good deal depends on the Norfolk by-election[2] into which Beaverbrook has thrown himself with a naïve fanaticism—which is almost attractive. Lord Elibank—an enthusiastic supporter—says the Empire

<hr />

[1] Sir Esmond Ovey (b. 1879), the diplomatist. Ambassador to Moscow, 1929–30.
[2] North Norfolk by-election result: Lady Noel Buxton (Lab.), 14,821; T. A. Cook (C. and Empire Free Trader), 14,642. (A narrow squeak.)

Free Trade candidate will win by 1,000. Henderson feels fairly confident of the charming Lady Noel Buxton's success in keeping her husband's seat. Baldwin, in his letter to the Conservative candidate, surrenders to Beaverbrook. Alfred, whom I saw yesterday, is much fussed by Jimmy's promise to discuss Empire Free Trade at the Dominion Conference and theatens resignation. He is angry that the disreputable Jimmy was given the Dominions and still more angry (he intimated on Sidney's behalf) that *he* should have been replaced by J.H.T. Sidney himself does not object either to J.H.T.'s announcement that Empire Free Trade would be *discussed*, or at his own supersession by the General Secretary of the N.U.R. "Thomas had to be provided for and it is obvious that the Dominions Office was the best way of doing it." Also he finds the Colonial Office more than sufficient for his energies.

A most tiresome and rather odious ten days in London entertaining and being entertained during the Colonial Office Conference. My four lunches of about 24 persons each, at the London School of Economics—Governors and their wives to meet distinguished strangers—were most successful. But going to official dinners and other people's gatherings—though it satisfies curiosity—is, in this hot weather, almost unendurable. Also I detest the social atmosphere, especially when Royalties are present—the cringe before these admirable automatons—and the self-importance of everyone concerned. At the opening of India House, by the King and Queen, there was added the ironic background, in everyone's consciousness, of the grim upheaval in India—the elaborately decked-out native rulers, and the picturesquely clothed Indian ladies, seemed to make them traitors to Indian nationalism. Baldwin and Lloyd George were whispering together, Simon intervening now and again. . . .

What is as clear as noonday is that though the Indians may not be able to govern themselves they may make it wholly impracticable for Great Britain to govern them—if the non-resistance movement persists and spreads. Neither Great Britain's means, nor her public opinion, would permit any Government to reconquer India by force of arms. We failed to maintain law and order in Southern Ireland, with three million people, and close at hand; with three hundred million people, far away, the idea is tragically absurd! And we are up against a saint with his *soul force*—a force which seems potent to destroy the existing order but impotent to create the new. Rather like Tolstoy in the pre-war Russia. . . .

How I loathe London Society in all its aspects. The last fortnight has made me more than ever content with bourgeois status and absence from social functions. What I detest most of all are my own reactions to it—the stimulus it gives to latent personal vanity contemptible in an old lady of seventy-odd! Old age does not diminish personal vanity—if anything the decay of intellectual faculty and will-power increase the temptation to dream silly dreams about oneself. Perhaps the palpable absurdity of it, this secret vice, becomes more apparent— the indignity of it. Then there is the perennial perplexity about a rule of conduct for members of the Labour Party: *ought one or ought one not to associate with the Court?* I have tried to compromise: I have declined to go to the evening Courts and I have not been presented to the Queen. But can I avoid dining at Buckingham Palace if I am now invited, when I have dined at York House?

When once Sidney is out of office I shall be quit of the whole business—in any case I intend to give up entertaining at Christmas and save the remainder of our official salary lest worse befall old England and our own little income. Again the desire to be "thoroughly comfortable" in one's old age! Personal vanity curbed by greed! Alas! for human nature. I am of the old opinion still: I do not *like* human beings. . . .

August 3rd.—The Soviet Ambassador and his wife here for a day and night—a singularly sympathetic man and woman—in the prime of life—the man the son of a wealthy physician now dead, the woman the daughter of another medical man of a lower grade and a member of the Communist Party. Since the revolution Sokolnikoff has been in the financial department of the U.S.S.R. and recently the professor of finance in Moscow University—the lady has been a "publicist" of sorts and they have one little girl aged seven. They are refined, and admirably-mannered—quiet, dignified, straightforward and pleasant—not aggressive but very staunch in their upholding of Bolshevism in a hostile world. Of the two, she is the most outspoken—they had been in Glasgow and she observed the dull depressed attitude of the people in the streets—in Moscow everyone was excited and neurotic —England was healthier to live in but not so interesting. Certainly the tone and temper of these two—their outlook on life seemed to be calm reason and goodwill—doubtless there is a strain of fanaticism —an undue certainty in their opinions compared to the cultured scepticism of Western Europe about all things human and divine. But can there be organised movement without faith? Philip Snowden lunched here to meet them—directly he arrived the Soviet Ambassador asked whether he might have a talk with him about credits—which was arranged. He impressed Snowden favourably. Sitting after lunch in the loggia and discussing the Five-Year-Plan, Sokolnikoff described the enthusiasm with which the Communist workers were accepting low wages and a relatively hard life in order to save money for capital improvements. "That's sound," said the British Chancellor of the Exchequer. "I sometimes despair about the working-class—next week I have to meet the General Council of the T.U.C.; they want more wages, shorter hours, greater expenditure on social services —here and now—when we, as a community, ought to be saving in order to bring our old-fashioned plant up to date." "Ah! Mr. Snowden," said I, "you will never get the British workman to work harder on less wages when he sees the employing class enjoying leisure and large expenditure. It is the equality of income that enables the Soviet Government to ask and obtain increased energy and sacrifice from the manual working citizen. The workers know they are working not for other people's children but for their *own* children."

Snowden was, I think, impressed by our Russian friends. But most of his arguments and illustrations might have been those of a West End clubman or prominent manufacturer. In the afternoon we took them to Ponsonby's charming mediaeval home. Whatever else our Bolshevist visitors thought and felt about us, they signified that they appreciated the comfort and charm of the English home. "But why the title of The Labour Party?" I seemed to hear them enquire. . . .

September 5th.

The Times

The Prime Minister

The Prime Minister left Dunrobin Castle yesterday, after his visit to the Duke and Duchess of Sutherland, for Loch Choir, near Lairg, where he will be the guest of the Marquess and Marchioness of Londonderry. It is understood that he will return to Lossiemouth today and will go to Balmoral tomorrow. The return journey will be made on Monday, and it is understood that he will leave Lossiemouth for London on Tuesday.

Alas! Alas! Balmoral is inevitable; but why the castles of the wealthiest, most aristocratic, most reactionary and by no means the most intellectual of the Conservative Party? "Because," J.R.M. would answer if he laid bare his heart, "I am more at home with them than I should be with you or with any other member of the Labour Party." Considering that he represents Seaham his friendship with the Londonderrys almost amounts to a public scandal. This silly little episode will do the P.M. untold damage with the non-commissioned officers of the Labour Movement. He *ought* not to be more at home in the castles of the great than in the homes of his followers. It argues a perverted taste and a vanishing faith.

September 6th.—A week-end at the Viceregal Lodge and three days with Lion Phillimore—a visit arranged when Sidney was Secretary of State for the Dominions. Should I or should I not, curtsey? intrigued my mind as we drove with the A.D.C. from Kingstown to the very royal residence of the titular head of this very little kingdom. I gathered during my stay that the smart folk curtsey—somewhat derisively, and the humble folk do not curtsey—somewhat bashfully. I compromised, curtsied on arrival and at the "state" dinner party, but not otherwise. "Their Excellencies" and the splendour of the Viceregal establishment (27 indoor servants, 15 gardeners) seems an expensive anachronism for so small a community and will, I imagine, be dropped—the institution is clearly not popular with the citizens of Dublin. Republicans and Labourites refuse to recognise the Governor-General, and Belfast boycotts and is boycotted. In appearance and manner the McNeills[1] are admirably suited to their difficult role. McNeill is an ex-Indian official, tall, discreet, and dignified; she is thirty years younger—a teacher by profession—a graceful and accomplished woman, who is rapidly moulding herself to be a great lady according to a very definite conception of the role of "Her Excellency". (In voice and manner she reminded me of Ethel Snowden.) Which of course excites the derision of clever little women like Mrs. Smiddy, the High Commissioner's[2] wife, and amused recognition, by deep curtseys, from those aristocrats patronising the "King's representative" in Dublin. At the Viceregal Lodge we met the leading politicians, judges and foreign ministers. At Lion's we saw the Cosgraves[3] more intimately. The able group of young men now governing the Free State struck us as similar in speech and personal conduct to the Viennese municipal administrators —they certainly had much zeal and no "side". The quiet efficiency of their administration made me ashamed of the long struggle for Home Rule culminating in the disgraceful episode of the Black and Tans. The most notable impression left on my mind was the heavy hand of the Roman Catholic Church. In no other country have I become aware of the spiritual oppression of the common people by the fear of Hell —one almost began to feel this fear oneself! McNeill is formally a Catholic; his wife a fervent fanatic. Cosgrave goes to mass every day—with others, Catholicism is part and parcel of the nationalist creed—indeed there is supposed to be a tacit understanding between the ultra-

[1] James McNeill (1869–1938), Governor-General of the Irish Free State, 1928–32; married Josephine Aherne of Fermoy, Co. Cork.
[2] Professor Timothy Smiddy (b. 1877), of University College, Cork. High Commissioner in London for Irish Free State, 1929–30; married Lilian O'Connell of Cork.
[3] William Thomas Cosgrave (b. 1880), President of the Executive Council of the Irish Free State, 1922–32.

republicans and the priests to support one another. The second impression was the queerness of this pretence at a Court, with foreign ministers in attendance, in so small and poor a community. What did the Viceregal Lodge represent? The independence of the Irish Free State or the tie to Great Britain? It is said that De Valera, when he succeeds to the Government by the swing of the pendulum, will abolish the Governor-Generalship and stop the land annuities. Whereupon the British Government may retaliate by a trade boycott expressed in tariffs, prohibition of Irish emigration into U.K., and deliberate boycott by the mercantile fleet.   There is much bitterness about the separation of Ulster—"The Irish will never forgive, until that is put right," one Cabinet Minister said to me. "Sooner or later we shall fight for it," he added. They feel that they have been "done" by wily Englishmen. Meanwhile at the Dublin Horse Show the English team had a grand reception—the McNeills said it came from the Ascendancy crowd, but Thomson and Lion maintained that it was from the ruck of Dublin citizens. For some reason the Viceregal party is not popular; when we entered the Abbey Theatre there was no kind of welcome or even interest in the Governor and his guests; and when we were walking down the mountain road, with endless Dublin citizens coming up and down, not a single individual saluted the Governor-General, though many must have recognised him. At the Horse Show, so Lion said, he got no cheers from the crowd. Do the inhabitants of the Free State object to the office, or do they want, in that office, a distinguished personage or wealthy magnate? It is characteristic of the Dublin crowd that the two individuals said to be favourites for the succession to McNeill are, on the one hand, the wealthy, vulgar and "showy" ex-tenor McCormack[1]—with his papal title, and, on the other, the great British nobleman and Court official the Marquess of Granard.[2] Throughout our visit we were accompanied by an armed escort—an armed guard slept in the house with us when staying with Lion. Cosgrave's house was heavily guarded, and everywhere he went he was attended by armed detectives.

September 9th.— . . . It is probable that the Labour Government will be out before Christmas on unemployment or India. Lloyd George is clearly working for a quarrel with Snowden over the Loan, so as to be able to run his little Party as more advanced than the

---

[1] Count John McCormack (1884–1945), naturalised an American, 1919; raised to the Papal peerage by Pius XI, 1928.

[2] Bernard Arthur William Patrick Hastings Forbes (1874–1948), eighth Earl of Granard (an Irish peerage) and Baron Granard in the British hierarchy; Master of the Horse, 1907–15 and 1936–45; a Deputy-Speaker of the House of Lords, with a long list of foreign decorations.

Labour Front Bench (which so far as Lloyd George is concerned is probably true—he would have done more, wise or unwise). Meanwhile Baldwin must wish to hurry on a General Election before he is dismissed by Beaverbrook and Rothermere. The Labour Party will be decisively beaten at the polls—and, I think, J.R.M. will cease to be leader, and Arthur Henderson will succeed him. Great Britain will become protectionist under Neville Chamberlain's premiership. A new and more virile Labour Party will grow up with a sterner creed— the alternative being a post-election coalition between Labour and Liberal, as the official opposition, with perhaps a defiant "independent" left-wing party, preaching out-and-out Socialism. But I doubt this complete break within the Labour Movement happening—the British working-class, largely owing to universal suffrage and the much abused dole, are too comfortable and too conscious of their power at the polls for revolution: they are also too innately deferential for rebellion. With two million unemployed there is, as yet, not the remotest sign of *urgent discontent*, no unemployment demonstrations, no soup kitchens, no newspaper agitation, no frantic appeals for money, no growth of the Communist Party. What exactly is happening, one asks, in the devastated districts of coalmining and cotton manufacture? Is the prophesied shortage of new labour beginning to tell or have large bodies of men become reconciled to an idle life on a *secure* but low level of consumption? To those who are weak from insufficient food, doing nothing on very little food may be a pleasanter prospect than getting a new job under competitive conditions—so long as the very little *is secure*. It is a disturbing thought that whole sections of our fellow countrymen are losing their faculties and diminishing their desires—slowly becoming a harmless but worthless mass of low-grade humanity. The patriotic American may say that he prefers the annual crop of 12,000 murders and the sight of armoured cars dashing through his cities on private business!—facts which denote energy, even if that energy be misdirected. And we have India we can no longer hold and dare not give up. Whoever else won the Great War, Great Britain lost it! . . .

October 4th.—A spate of high-class social functions this week—I avoided two dinners and reception at Lancaster House but got through two lunches and an afternoon gathering in a little over 24 hours, and a Buckingham Palace state dinner on Friday, returning here for the middle of the week to rest and write letters. . . .

The Buckingham Palace dinner centred round the delegates from the Dominions and their wives—it was part of the web of imperial destiny and well wrought. The ceremony and its settings combined dull dignity with refined magnificence—there was almost a religious atmosphere as the 120 guests trooped up the stairs into the sumptuous range of reception rooms, each guest bending over the hands of the two Idols, on the way to the inner temple of the Banqueting Hall—with the golden plate and crimson-clothed attendants. What spoilt the pageant was the dowdyism of the women guests, in marked contrast with the superb garments and jewels of the Queen and her aristocratic Court ladies—I, for instance, though I appeared as The Lady Passfield wore a high-necked long-sleeved grey chiffon velvet which I have been wearing for six months at every dinner I have attended: Mrs. Lunn, the Under-Secretary's wife, had donned a conventional black satin, obviously bought for the occasion from the local Co-op. Ethel Snowden, with a paste tiara and a cheap fashionable frock, was the intermediate link between us humble folk and the court circle. At the table the Royalties sat, in a heap, opposite each other; close beside them the Dominion representatives, each man or woman being tenderly looked after by some great lady or nobleman attached to the Court. It was amusing to watch these charming women, sparkling their eyes and softening their voices to fascinate Scullin,[1] Forbes,[2] McGilligan,[3] and Bennett[4] (if I remember right Bennett's sister being placed on the other side of the Prince of Wales; Hertzog was honoured by a minor Princess) whilst their male counterparts bent over the Dominion ladies with a like solicitude. The British Ministers, Delegates and Opposition leaders and other official personages were not so well pleased by finding themselves lumped together. I sat between the Speaker and J. H. Thomas; Ethel Snowden looked bored between Benn and Byng[5]—finally at the horse-shoe ends straggled the minor delegates, permanent officials and household officers. After dinner the Queen stood in one of the large reception rooms and we ladies grouped ourselves round the walls—a few being picked out and led up to the Queen by the Duchess of Devonshire for two or three minutes' perfunctory talk—I being one of them. The Queen is a fine figure of a woman, she holds herself well and is magnificently apparelled and bejewelled. . . . After the uncomfortable ceremony most of the ladies slid out of the Queen's presence into the Gallery. I gossiped with old acquaintances—Mrs. Churchill, the Attorney-General, the Hankeys and Sir F. Ponsonby, who said he remembered

---

[1] James Henry Scullin (1876–1953). Leader of the Australian Labour Party, 1928–35, and Prime Minister, 1929–31.

[2] George William Forbes (1869–1947). Prime Minister of New Zealand, 1930–5.

[3] Patrick McGilligan (b. 1889). Minister for External Affairs in Irish Free State, 1927–32; Minister for Finance, Eire, 1948–51.

[4] Richard Bedford Bennett, Lord Bennett (1870–1947). Leader of Conservative Party in Canada, 1927–38, and Prime Minister, 1930–5. Removed to Britain and became member of House of Lords, 1941.

[5] Field-Marshal Julian Byng, Lord Byng of Vimy (1862–1935). Commissioner of Metropolitan Police, 1928–31.

me as Beatrice Potter![1] About 10.30 o'clock the King and Queen and other Royalties walked through the Gallery and the King stopped in front of me and hoped "that you are not too tired?" to which I mumbled some amiable reply. So ends my first and last appearance at the Court of St. James's!

October 6th.—A bare week ago Thomson was here for the week-end, and only a week to-day and to-morrow I met him at successive lunches. Oddly enough it flashed through my mind, "Shall I meet you again?" In the few words he said to me, and in his expression there was something that made one uneasy—probably the awful event[2] has magnified this dimly remembered presentiment. His death is a real loss to the Labour Cabinet and I feel it more than I should have foreseen. He was an attractive colleague and friend; antagonised no one, and amused and interested all of us: the one trait I did *not* like, and which still puzzles me, was his apparent intimacy with the P.M. and yet his constant deprecation of him. Though Sidney and I have never been intimate or even on terms of personal friendliness— we always found ourselves standing up for our leader against Thomson's low opinion of his character and intellect. And it was not a habit in Thomson to run down his colleagues; he had a great admiration for Henderson, whom he wished for leader, and a liking and respect for Snowden. The inner circle has lost one of its very few charmers— indeed, barring the P.M. is there any other *charmer* in Government circles? The forty odd ministers are a drab company! And the P.M. does not charm me. . . .

October 20th.—Mr. and Mrs. Scullin and Desmond Fitzgerald[3] here for week-end. Scullin is an ex-teacher and inferior journalist, of unattractive appearance and manner. He seems honest in speech and is reputed honest about money. He is certainly very unlike a political boss of the U.S.A. type—no sign of magnetic personality or dema-gogic power, or capacity for manipulating men—just an ordinary behind-the-counter citizen in some small provincial set of lower middle-class persons. His wife is much the same sort, except she is more genteel. They are both devout R.C.s. Sidney reports that Scullin is self-assertive and dull-witted in conference, but not so objectionable, because not so arrogantly pretentious, as Bennett of Canada. Here, Scullin was sensible and very eager to talk—he dislikes the T.U.

---

[1] Sir Frederick Ponsonby, afterwards Lord Sysonby (1867–1935), elder brother of Arthur Ponsonby and Treasurer to the King.

[2] The disaster to R. 101.

[3] Desmond Fitzgerald (d. 1947). Sinn Feiner, participated in the Easter Rising. Minister for Defence in Irish Free State, 1927–32.

element in his party—and threw out the suggestion that Australia would be better without Trade Unions! One was left wondering why exactly he was Labour Premier of Federal Australia—unless as a cover for the attractive and gifted Theodore[1] who has come a cropper. . . . I doubt whether Scullin will last long—some more vigorous, maybe less respectable person will push himself to the front of Australia's Labour Party.

Desmond Fitzgerald retrieved the liveliness of the week-end party —a pleasant literary-minded Irishman—reminds me of Desmond McCarthy as a conversationalist—but with less intellect and with a more romantic and heroic past behind him. All three disliked Bennett and admired Hertzog. (S. says H. is as good as gold in the Conference.) D.F. admired Snowden and wanted to have a talk with him. But I doubt whether Fitzgerald counts for much in the Irish delegation. Sidney reports that the Irish are isolated in the Conference. Altogether the Conference does not seem likely to lead anywhere in particular—except to the further disintegration of the Conservative Party— Baldwin, having first come out with a loud endorsement of Bennett's proposals, has now shuffled back into the old refusal of food taxes, and is being cursed by the two press lords. All I hear from Sidney about the Conference leaves the impression of disintegration—certainly not of any tightening of the ties between the U.K. and her sister Dominions. Possibly a common dislike of the U.S.A. is on the credit side —a distaste which is growing among the nations of the world—no doubt partly envy, partly the war debts. So far as I have talked to the delegates and their wives—which is not much—there is a general feeling that Great Britain is to be lectured, not listened to—rather the attitude of children in the prime of life toward an ageing mother— she has been too domineering in the past and has now to be told that she must do as her children tell her or be ignored. I rather doubt the wisdom of having started this Imperial Conference! It would have been better to have had each Dominion's deputation separately and treated them handsomely but evasively. The less the relationship is defined the more likely it is to endure. However if the world forces are against the survival of the British Empire no amount of wise manipulation of powerful individuals would have kept it alive, though the process of distintegration might have been slowed down. On the other hand, if the various Dominions find that owing to a British connection they are represented in the World State twice over, first as individual communities and secondly as component parts of a world power, they will remain attached together in some sort of union. But I doubt this latter forecast.

[1] Edward Granville Theodore (b. 1884). Premier of Queensland (1919-25), Commonwealth Treasurer, 1929-30, and 1931.

October 26th.—Sidney, by the publication of the Hope Simpson Paper,[1] and the *Statement of Policy* accompanying it, has involved himself and the Labour Government in a storm of anger from Jewry throughout the world. What interests me about all this ferment over Palestine is the absence from first to last of any consideration of Palestine as the cradle of the Christian creed—as the Holy Land of Christendom. I have never felt the lure of the Holy Land—but then I am not a Christian. But imagine the awful shock to the mediaeval crusaders if they had foreseen the Christian Kingdoms of England, France and Italy withdrawing Jerusalem from Islam in order to hand it over to the representatives of those who crucified Jesus of Nazareth and have continued, down all the ages, to deny that He is the Son of God. Has the glorified romance of Jesus of Nazareth, of his birth, of his life message, of his death and his resurrection from the dead, vanished from the mind of man? Is the promised land, for the Jewish Home, yet another sign of the rapid decay of Christendom? Lloyd George in his speech denouncing the *Statement of Policy* ends his peroration by urging the claim of the Jews to "the land which their ancestors made famous for all time". The Christian tradition of the infamy of the Crucifixion is ignored. An additional touch of irony to this ill-doomed episode lies in the fact that the Jewish immigrants are Slavs or Mongols and not Semites, and the vast majority are not followers of Moses and the prophets, but of Karl Marx and the Soviet Republic.

But this, after all, is a mere side-light and has nothing to do with the bargain between Balfour and the Zionists. At the time of the Balfour Declaration the one and only consideration was the relative power to help us to win the war of the international Jewish financiers on the one hand and on the other the Arabs in revolt against the Turkish empire. The man on the spot gave promises to the Arabs; the British Cabinet gave promises to the Jews—always qualifying the promise of a Jewish Home by the perfunctory condition of the well-being of the Arab inhabitants. After ten years it is clear to all who study the question that these promises were and are incompatible—either the Jew or the Arab, or partly one and partly the other,

[1] The Hope Simpson Report (Cmd. 3686) made proposals for land settlement, immigration and development in Palestine. It was published with the Government's own White Paper (Cmd. 3962), which endeavoured to sum up the political and economic problems of Palestine, and indicated the Government's policy, including special consideration for the settlement of the poorest landless Arabs on new land made available by drainage or irrigation. It was this provision which caused the storm to blow up; and its effect on the position of the Colonial Secretary was more serious than is disclosed in the *Diary*. Virtually, Palestinian affairs were taken out of Webb's hands, and put in the charge of a Committee, on which the Foreign Office was strongly represented. Many men would have resigned at this snub: Webb, though he is said to have considered it, did not—to the regret of some of his assistants.

will have to be deterred from getting the full value of those promises. Owing to the superior wealth and capacity of the Jews, it is the Arab who has suffered damage during the last ten years; the Jews would answer that the Arab has not been forcibly driven out of the land and that *in buying him out* or rather in buying his landlord out they have been acting in the normal way—in the way that any man might have acted under the laws of civilised peoples. To-day they are furious with the expressed intention of the British Government to protect the Arab cultivator from being expropriated and becoming a landless proletariat. This protection of the Arab is not only justified on grounds of justice but on the ground of expediency. Unless Great Britain is prepared to keep an army of occupation in Palestine indefinitely she cannot prevent the old and new Jewish settlements from being periodically raided by the neighbouring Arab states as well as by the resident Arabs. The British Cabinet have also to consider the feelings of the Mohammedans of India, not to mention Egypt. The responsibility for this débâcle lies with the fatuous promise of a Palestinian Jewish Home which if it meant anything worth having for the Jews meant a Jewish Palestine from which the Arabs would be gradually extruded by economic pressure.

Meanwhile Sidney remains unperturbed. He has done his best to hold an even balance. *The Statement of Policy* has at any rate served as a lightning conductor for the Hope Simpson report—upon which action will have to be taken. (The *Statement of Policy*, by the way, is a badly drafted, a tactless document—he ought to have done it himself. But so far as the Jews are concerned that betterment of form would not have made it more acceptable.)

Probably future Governments will be only too glad to have had the ice broken and the Jews forced to be more considerate and reasonable. What seems to me probable is that when the Jewish authorities realise the anti-God and communist character of the new settlers they will gradually give up the idea of a Palestine Jewish State and possibly even of a Jewish Cultural Home. But this latter might endure with the consent of the Arab inhabitants—what it could *not* survive would be the jeers of an advance-post of Soviet Russia with its rival culture of scientific materialism. That is perhaps the reason for the very moderate and even British attitude of the Principal of the Hebrew University at Jerusalem. . . .

November 12th.—We lunched on Thursday at the Soviet Embassy —a princely mansion in Kensington Palace Gardens—with great reception rooms and large garden—its occupants looking, according to ordinary diplomatic standards of style and expression—strangely out of place. Indeed, it was impossible to distinguish the Ambassador, his wife and staff from those serving them in what is here called a "menial" capacity—ideas, manners, and mutual relations being the same all through. This expression of the equalitarian state was unique and to me pleasing. We lunched in a relatively small room. Besides the Sokolnikoffs there was P——, the wily and fluent counsellor, and Gillett[1] the Under-Secretary from the Board of Trade, and the lunch was wheeled in and served by a pleasant-looking girl who might have been a relative of the Ambassador. The conversation was not exciting —His Excellency does not yet speak English fluently—but the little company was on easy terms and we chatted and chaffed each other without any constraint. I gathered from Madame that they lead isolated lives and are not called upon or invited out by the British governing class or by the diplomatic circle. In one of the large rooms, a collection of striking photographs, descriptive of life in Soviet Russia, destined to be exhibited in London, were being silently arranged by one or two of the male members of the staff, but whether they were secretaries or servants it was impossible to infer from their clothes or their behaviour. The Sokolnikoffs encouraged us to go to Russia— altogether denied that we should find it expensive if we arranged the trip through their Tourist Agency—whilst I agreed to try to get G.B.S. to open the exhibition of photographs some time in December. What a contrast to the swagger luncheon of the Palmstiernas to the Sthamers[2] which we attended some weeks ago. Communism *is* a religion to the Soviet Embassy to-day—very different from the Krassins or the Rakowskys, who were *converts* to Communism and really accustomed to bourgeois expenditure. These people have been bred in the new behaviour, they have not merely adopted it, as a political badge. And for that reason they are far more convincing as Communists and be it added far more objectionable to the diplomatic circle in London society. However long they stay, and however quiet and unaggressive they are, they will never be accepted, even by the well-to-do members of the Labour Party. We are the only "Cabinet" Members who have consorted with them—the Hendersons do not "know" them socially—nor the P.M.

November 17th.—Out of the six Fabian lecturers this autumn— to an audience well over 2,000 (only about one-third Fabians) three are over seventy! Not a good index to the vitality of the Society! But so long as this course yields the Society £600 profit, it is difficult to shut up the booking office for good and all. Meanwhile the Fabian

[1] Sir George Masterman Gillett (1870–1939). Banker and Quaker, M.P. for Finsbury. Secretary, Department of Overseas Trade, 1929–31; took MacDonald's side in 1931.

[2] Sthamers, German diplomatist, became a Nazi and served under Ribbentrop; negotiated tri-partite pact between Germany, Italy and Japan.

myth has its perennial recrudescence in this entry from the *Evening Standard*:

Government by Fabians

Many Labour members are talking about the dominance in the Government of that very academic body, the Fabian Society.

I find that many people believed that this organisation, through which many intellectuals entered the Socialist movement, had ceased to exist.

But it goes on with a membership, small but influential—some 5,000.[1]

Yet practically every recent appointment, either to high or low office, in the Labour administration, has been made from the membership of the Society, the latest examples of which are the new Air Minister, Lord Amulree,[2] and the new Solicitor General, Sir Stafford Cripps.

Civil Servants

I am told that at least 90 per cent of the members of the Government are on the rolls of the Society, and that, contrary to regulations, so are a good many highly placed Civil Servants.

The Civil Servants would probably defend themselves by saying the Society is more intellectual than political.

This ascendancy is, of course, due to the all-powerful influence of Lord Passfield and his wife, Mrs. Sidney Webb, with whom the Fabian Society has been the passion of their lives.

About one half of the Government—eight Cabinet Ministers and some ten non-Cabinet Ministers, I think—are Fabians. But this is explained by the fact that the Fabian Society is the easiest entry into the Labour Party; and aspirants for office, or those who have accepted office, without being members of a local Labour Party, apply for membership. Thus Jowitt, directly he had decided to leave the Liberal Party and join the Government, sent post haste for an affiliation form for the Fabian Society! It is needless to add that we personally had no part in bringing about the appointment of Amulree or Stafford Cripps. But the Webb myth to-day is in the ascendant; to-morrow we shall be dismissed as "Old Hats" and feel none the worse for it. . . .

---

[1] An exaggeration. The Fabian Society of 1930 had a national membership of 1,862, with a further handful in the provinces. This, however, emphasises the point of the article.

[2] William Warrender Mackenzie, Lord Amulree (1860–1942). Government arbitrator and conciliator and member of many Commissions. Secretary for Air after Lord Thomson's death in R. 101.

December 14th.—Sidney came back from London depressed: "People will say," he sadly observed, "that your husband has not been a success as a Minister." The P.M. is cross about Palestine: the Shaw Commission and Hope Simpson, with his report, both nominees of Sidney's, have been too pro-Arab; a White Paper (which the P.M. saw and approved) was "tactless"—indeed he allowed Lloyd George, in his virulent attack on the White Paper, to assert that "the P.M. has not seen it"—which was mean of MacDonald. Then Thomas comes along and wants to go to Palestine accompanied by Malcolm Mac-Donald and spend Christmas there, to which Sidney demurs as he knows Chancellor,[1] the Governor, would dislike Thomas's intervention. The P.M. lets Sidney know that he thinks him "fussy"— why should not Thomas go? In a minor matter of N. Rhodesia, Thomas again intervenes, and Henderson has taken over the negotiation with Weizman, Sidney in attendance. Sidney would like to retire, but as there must be two Secretaries of State in the Lords, that would put MacDonald in a difficulty; and it would be taken as a victory for the Jews over the Arabs and might lead to trouble in Palestine. Also Sidney thinks that if J.R.M. sees another year or more of office for the Labour Party he will prefer to go to the House of Lords as Foreign Secretary and leave Henderson as P.M. to face the anger of the left and meet a General Election. MacDonald would fancy himself as the Earl of Lossiemouth! That ending to his career, though conventionally correct, would be immensely damaging to the spirit of the Labour Party. . . .

December 28th.—Two books we have read during the Christmas week are significant because they light up the world's two centres of greatest activity—Adams' *Searchlight on America* and H. D. Harben's privately printed *Diary of his Russian Tour*. Adams despairs of U.S.A.; Harben has faith in Russia. The two reports are of unequal value; Harben's is a mere traveller's tale cleverly told; but its hopefulness is catching and then its conclusions about the success of the Five Years' [Plan] are borne out by the reports of Americans who have been contractors and technicians over there. Adams summarises the experience of a life-time, spent in business and study. Though he is clearly no Socialist his book is a startling indictment of capitalism as practised in U.S.A.—a terrible indictment—not from the standpoint of the toiling masses whose high wages he grudges! but from that of the professional middle class. Whether this preoccupation with the interests of the intellectual aristocracy be justified or not, the indictment itself leaves

---

[1] Colonel Sir John Robert Chancellor (1870–1952). Governor of Southern Rhodesia, 1922–8: High Commissioner and Commander-in-Chief in Palestine, 1928–31.

the reader under the impression that the U.S.A. will crash into some form of civil war or forcible dictatorship through sheer incapacity of its democracy to maintain law and order and to check corruption and blackmail in public services and private enterprise. On the other hand Russia may succeed in building up a disciplined and purposeful equalitarian State at the cost of a period of terrorism with the loss of intellectual freedom. Certainly the daily life—whether of work or recreation—of the Russian Communist has become intensely serious and public-spirited, whilst that of the U.S.A. citizen is becoming increasingly dominated by pecuniary gain and frivolous pleasure. Great Britain, meanwhile, remains orderly and apathetic—there is a sort of deadness in the air—is it industrial coma? The whole of Europe seems in a backwater relatively to these two vast continents of the U.S.A. and Russia. With these melancholy thoughts, I greet 1931.

PART VIII

1931

JANUARY 1931—DECEMBER 1931

January 22nd.—My seventy-third birthday: a basket of flowers from the Soviet Ambassadress, a bunch of carnations and lilies from the Countess of Warwick—a few telegrams, one from Cynthia and Oswald Mosley. The trend of my reputation is clearly to the left and not to the right.

Three days and nights in London; a disappointing 300-persons dinner given by Alwar,[1] to which I went in the hope of seeing the Indian Princes in jewelled coats and turbans—but through jealousy of Alwar only half a dozen turned up. Otherwise the usual high politics affair—the Baldwins and Wedgwood Benns, Reading, Zetland,[2] Peel[3] and Sankey, but no P.M. General congratulations about the Conference. Baldwin dragged in by Alwar (toasting his wife's birthday) to make a noncommittal speech.

The P.M.'s farewell to the Indian Conference a gorgeous success— what an artist the man is, how admirably he thinks and feels about external affairs—whether foreign or Dominion—[he] has enormously increased his prestige. Also Sankey comes out as a potent personality, and Wedgwood Benn played up, in his modest and zealous fashion, to the two principal actors. According to current talk the I.C.S., in attendance on the Conference or on leave, have let it be known that India cannot be held against the will of its people, and if we fail to yield our raj by agreement we shall be crushed by undercurrents of fanatical force, figuring as passive resistance.

Sidney and I had an evening in our little flat with Laski; he is bubbling over with delight at his own importance, which takes the form of graphic and amusing stories, some true and others invented, about his dealings with the Zionists—especially the American Zionists, and with the Indians in order to smooth the way of the Labour Government. He is a devotee of Sankey's, and has been used by the great man as an assistant negotiator running between various groups of

[1] H. H. the Maharajah of Alwar (1882–1937). Alwar was an Indian State of 3,125 acres and 750,000 population; its ruler was a Colonel of the British Army, a polo and racquets expert who was believed to have progressive leanings.
[2] Lawrence John Lumley, Marquess of Zetland (b. 1876). Governor of Bengal, 1917–22, and Secretary for India, 1935–40; at that time member of the Indian Round Table Conference.
[3] William Robert Wellesley Peel, Lord Peel (1867–1937). Held many Government offices; at that time member of the Round Table Commission.

Indians—Mohammedan and Hindu. The intimate talks he reports with "Mac" (so he says he addresses him) about appointments and policy are, I think, "imaginary conversations": there was a curious hesitation as to whether they were at Downing Street or Chequers. But it is all very good fun; he is never malicious or mischievous, but the tales he tells, if they are not all true, are vivid anticipations of what might have happened. What I fear is that he is dissipating his power of thought, in all these personal comings and goings, among personages of all sorts and kinds so stimulating to his own great fault—personal vanity. His appearance is just a trifle too smart for a professor of Socialist opinions. . . .

The visit to London ended with my Admiralty House reception: some 700 guests—mostly Labour, tempered with London School of Economics lecturers and their wives, Colonial Office officials at home and on leave, nephews and nieces and a few odds and ends of friends and acquaintances, one or two diplomats—among them were the Soviet Ambassador and his wife and two of his officials, the Japanese Ambassador and his lady and our old friend Palmstierna. It was a jolly affair, rather uncouth and unconventional—a notable lack of style in clothes and manners. One youth came in an open flannel shirt with bright-coloured tie, the only relief from universal drabness being the stately form of the Countess of Warwick and "Eddy" Marsh's[1] well-groomed presence. I doubt whether Admiralty House has ever seen such a democratic party as the reception of "Mrs. Sidney Webb", which I kept out of the Press as I find it best to do. The Labour Lords were strongly represented, but Labour M.P.s were mostly engaged watching the defeat of the Labour Government by the R.C. group[2] of rebels and their sympathisers. Everyone expects the Cabinet will be out before the Budget; it will certainly not outlast the session. Official and semi-official gatherings will know me no more, whether as guest or hostess; they have been an experience of mixed amusement and pleasure; an anachronism in the social environment of the Labour Party—because of the admixture of London Society in most of them, and the rather absurd background of the Royal Robots and their Court ladies and gentlemen which makes the whole business as unreal as the Beggar's Opera. . . .

February 4th.—"I should not like to say it to anyone else," Sidney observed last Thursday morning, "but I wish we had been defeated

---

[1] Sir Edward Howard Marsh (1870–1953). Civil Servant, art collector, author and connoisseur; private secretary to several Ministers; editor of *Georgian Poetry* volumes.

[2] On an amendment to the Education Bill in favour of Catholic and Anglican schools. The whole Bill was thrown out by the House of Lords in March, and Charles Trevelyan, the President of the Board of Education, then resigned.

last night." This is partly due to being tired of his job; but it also arises from the lack of any kind of plan in the Labour Government's treatment of the unemployed—just a drift towards more doles, in the autumn of 1929, and then a reaction against this liberality in 1931. The proposed curtailment of unemployed benefit, which Sidney says is contemplated by the Prime Minister and the Chancellor of the Exchequer, will complete the disintegration of the Labour Party. The time seems to me to be coming very near when Great Britain, Germany, Australia and any other capitalist country will be compelled to repudiate a large part of its debts, internal or external, or to lower its standard of civilisation for the whole of the people; Government will also have to decide which discipline is to be enforced—the whip of starvation for the manual workers or the communistic discipline applied to all sections of the inhabitants equally. We in Great Britain are trying to do without either form of discipline; the U.S.A. is verging on starving and terrorizing the poor; and Soviet Russia is enforcing with great brutality the subordination of all to the common will expressed in a General Plan for the enrichment of the whole country. Australia is talking about repudiation. Germany, France and Italy have already repudiated through inflation a large part of their internal debt and some of the foreigners' investments in their funds. Great Britain for the ten years since the war has been governed *exclusively* in the interest of the *rentier*; tempered by unconditional outdoor relief. That is why we and our like are so well off! Ramsay MacDonald and Snowden and many other Labour Front Bench men, in their heart of hearts, do not wish a *change in policy*. It is an absurdity that the Labour Party, as at present constituted, should be in power. The Labour Movement had better be referred to its studies. In home affairs it (the Labour Party) has no policy—it has completely lost its bearings.

What I am beginning to doubt is the "inevitability of gradualness", or even the practicability of gradualness, in the transition from a capitalist to an equalitarian civilisation. Anyway, no leader, in our country, has thought out *how to make the transition*, without upsetting the apple-cart. Sidney says "it will make itself", without an acknowledged plan accepted by one party in the state and denounced by the other. We shall *slip into the equalitarian state* as we did into political democracy—by each party, whether nominally Socialist or anti-Socialist, taking steps in the direction of curtailing the tribute of rent and interest and increasing the amount and security of reward of labour. But this cannot be done without transferring the *control* of the savings of the country; and I don't see how that is to be done gradually or without a terrific struggle on clearly thought-out lines. And no one is doing the thinking? So we shall drift on into some sort of disaster as we did into the great war. Sidney says, "All I know is that I don't know how to do it." When in doubt about the future describe the past. Meanwhile we shall have to be economical or we shall find ourselves among the new poor.

February 12*th.*—Snowden's speech in answer to the Conservative vote of censure bore out the previous description of his attitude—the end of it was cheered by the Tories and received in deadly silence by the Labour back-benchers. The long continued conversations of the Prime Minister and other Labour leaders with Lloyd George and his group of followers, in and out of the House of Commons, looks like a definite concordat against the Left. The likelihood of the Government being turned out by their own followers supported by the Tories is growing greater every day. When we visited the Snowdens the other afternoon Ethel said they did not intend to fight another election and intimated that Philip would go to the Lords—which Sidney welcomed as enabling him to drop out, if the Government goes on. But Sidney still thinks they will be out before the end of the session. The Trade Disputes Bill[1] will be mangled past Trade Union recognition, and if the allowances to the unemployed are also cut down, a large section of the Party—I.L.P. and Trade Union—will revolt against the Front Bench.

Another "hungry thirties and forties" will not end in a fiasco for the working-class as it did in the last century: it will end in a social revolution and I think eventually in the Communist direction. It may be brought about by the constitutional method of the vote—or by the general strike—or by a combination of the two—it may be defeated by a Fascist dictatorship of the Lords and Commons. But I doubt whether dictatorship for the defence of the property-owners could succeed in Great Britain: the workers are too well-educated and there are too many intellectuals who will gladly serve them. In the last resort the sailors and the soldiers would be on their side. Snowden and MacDonald, one or both of them, will be in the House of Lords, defending the existing order. If we were twenty years younger we should be drawing up a constitution for the rebels—more likely our ashes will be buried under the roots of the ash tree which I love to look at, in its winter leafless tracing, out of our study window. What troubles me is not the impoverishment of the minority of property-owners, but how far liberty and equality are compatible with each other? Under the capitalist system the property-owner has liberty to

---

[1] A Bill to amend the Trade Union Act of 1927 was announced by the Government when it came into office; but it passed its Second Reading by twenty-seven only, and was so mangled by Liberal-Conservative opposition in Committee that it was withdrawn. The Act endured unamended until 1946, when it was repealed outright.

do what he likes—the workers have not—even the amount of personal freedom given by what is called the dole is not practicable for long periods. Under Russian Communism everyone has to obey orders—and yet with increase in productivity it *ought to be possible to give to all* complete personal freedom over the larger part of their time and their energy, as well as plenty of opportunities to enjoy the nobler pleasures of life. . . . ,

February 25th.—An amazing act of arrogance, Oswald Mosley's melodramatic defection[1] from the Labour Party, slamming the door with a bang to resound throughout the political world. His one remaining chance is to become the He-man of the Newspaper Lords in their campaign against Baldwin's leadership of the Conservative Party. But Mosley's egotism would presently clash with Beaverbrook's and they would part company. As an orator—as a platform performer in a political circus he would be pre-eminent. A foreign journalist at the Labour Party Conference nicknamed him "The English Hitler". But the British electorate would not stand a Hitler. Mosley has bad health, a slight intelligence and an unstable character—I doubt whether he has the tenacity of a Hitler. He also lacks genuine fanaticism. Deep down in his heart he is a cynic. He will be beaten and retire. In the chaos of our political life to-day there will be many meteors passing through the firmament. There is still Winston Churchill to be accounted for. Have there ever been so many political personages on the loose? Mosley's sensational exit will matter supremely to himself and his half-dozen followers but very little to the Labour Party. It may even consolidate the bulk of the Labour Movement against all rebels—queer the pitch for any secession of the I.L.P. from the party organisation.

March 1st.—The Mosley Manifesto is an able document—its argument in favour of a general Plan, and there is much reason for it, is well done. But its proposals are as grandiose as they are vague. From the standpoint of propaganda it is a failure; it falls dead in the No Man's Land between those who wish to keep and those who wish to change the existing order. By its proposal to "insulate" the British Empire and its trade it offends the dearest aspirations of the Labour Party and

---

[1] During the months following the "Mosley Memorandum" Mosley had campaigned continuously in support of his views, and had come very near to success. At the Party Conference in October a motion calling for a full report on the Mosley plan was narrowly defeated, and Mosley himself elected to the Executive Committee, beating J. H. Thomas. Mosley then tried to get his views adopted by the Parliamentary Labour Party; failing, he issued them as a pamphlet, *A National Policy*, resigned and announced the formation of a New Party to carry them out. But besides his wife, only three Labour M.P.'s followed him. (W. J. Brown, though expelled from the Trade Union group of M.P.'s, did not join the New Party.)

invades the field of foreign affairs in which Labour statesmen have been signally successful. The proposal to establish Import and Investment Boards attacks the very stronghold of capitalism. The suggestion of an inner Cabinet of Ministers, without portfolios, to dictate policy to their colleagues with departments at their disposal, makes the whole scheme look absurd in the eyes of experienced administrators, whether politicians or civil servants. There is, in fact, nothing in the programme that will *grip* any section of the population—the curious assortment of reforms do not hang together; they are based on no political philosophy; they have no emotional appeal—they excite neither love nor hate—and they are far too pretentious and ill-thought-out to convince the commonsense citizen. The Mosley episode is another instance of a little knot of *clever* and inexperienced young men talking themselves into an impossible project—exactly like Mellor, Cole and Co. did about Guild Socialism. The "New Party" is another bubble on the surface of political life. Though the Cole-Mellor group left the Fabian Society they did not leave the Labour Party—those who did drifted into the service of Soviet Russia. I regret the loss of Mosley—he was the only orator in the Labour Movement, except MacDonald. But I am afraid he has slammed the door behind him and not even Uncle Arthur will be able to let him in again, not even as a prodigal son! Except that it means the loss of five seats, the other resignations— John Strachey, Dr. Forgan, Oliver Baldwin and W. J. Brown and Cynthia—are of no importance to the Labour Movement. The New Party will never get born alive; it will be a political abortion. . . .

March 8th.—The two great successes in external affairs—Henderson's and Alexander's statement on the Franco-Italian Naval pact and Lord Irwin's talk with Gandhi—have revived the *morale* of the P.L.P. —the temperamental Jimmy immediately exclaimed: "In for six years!" Unfortunately death and disease are decimating the Government: Russell dead and Parmoor incapacitated—probably permanently —and Snowden struck down and threatened with a serious operation on the eve of the Budget speech—will put the Prime Minister in a difficulty and increase the impression of a rapidly dissolving party. Meanwhile Sidney and I took part on March 2nd in a House of Commons dinner, given by Henderson, who was in bed and did not appear, but organised by G. D. H. Cole to restart the Fabian Research Department[1] with the help of Stafford Cripps and Pritt, K.C.—the two new lawyer arrivals in the Labour Party—and backed up by

---

[1] This meeting led to the formation of the New Fabian Research Bureau, which during the next few years enrolled a good few of the younger intellectuals and in 1939 took over the rump of the Fabian Society and galvanised it into an effective organisation.

Lady Warwick's week-ends at Easton Lodge, our platonic support, and the participation of the London School of Economics group—Robson-Laski-Lloyd-Dalton-Noel Baker—and the T.U.C.—Pugh and Bevin, J. S. Middleton, Grant McKenzie,[1] Galton being present. "Loyal Grousers", Cole called the new body as distinguished from the seditious seceders. It was a very pleasant family party—and may lead to something. We have also been seeing the Arnold Toynbees, Siepmann[2] of the B.B.C., and Malcolm MacDonald—an unexpectedly refined and thoughtful young man—very creditable as are all the MacDonald children to their father and mother—singularly unspoilt for the children of a Prime Minister. All this lot of persons—so intimately connected with British political life, though they are very amateurish, are singularly free of the assumed evils of political life—they are disinterested, public-spirited and amazingly free from curruption and vice. If moral tone and open-mindedness would save Great Britain—her salvation would be assured! Compared to the pecuniary dishonesty of the U.S.A. political world and the fanatical brutality of Russian Communism, the Labour Party and, I think, the Liberal and Conservative party organisations are Angels of Light—but they are Angels at a week-end Party—discussing and not working! . . .

March 12*th.*—Sidney went to see Philip Snowden, who is rather seriously ill, but who expects to recover in time to bring in the Budget. Snowden repeated that he *was not going to fight another election* and expected to go to the Lords before the end of the Labour Government, an expectation which Sidney warmly encouraged, suggesting that Snowden should become Secretary of State for the Colonies, which would enable him (Sidney) to retire from office. Snowden acquiesced and they discussed together the time and manner of the reconstruction of the Cabinet which, if the Government survives, would take place in June, July or August. For which I shall be honestly grateful. The episode has been an honourable and lucrative one—but we are both of us weary of our continued separation. If we are ever again to work together it is now or never. There is one fear that haunts me—that Sidney may find the continuous monotony of studious life in the country—one day after another—deadening—after all the varied interest and self-importance of high office—but he says not that he finds the strain and separation [hard] and longs to be free of it. Any-

[1] Grant McKenzie joined the staff of the Labour Party's Research Department in 1927, becoming Acting Secretary in 1929–31. In 1940 he became Personal Secretary to Attlee, and thereafter served in the British Information Service in Washington, and on the British Electricity Authority.

[2] Charles Siepmann, on the staff of the B.B.C. from 1927–39; first concerned with adult education in the Talks Department, later head of Programme Planning.

way it is going to happen one way or the other—he still thinks, by the Labour Government going out of office this spring. Against this is the increasing friendliness of Lloyd George (Sidney met him calling on Snowden) with the Prime Minister and the Chancellor of the Exchequer, and the fractious state of the Conservative Party. . . .

April 18*th.*—Having an evening free at Artillery Mansions after interviewing possible gardeners, Sidney and I phoned to the Hendersons and found them also alone and free. Henderson was perturbed about the breakdown of the French-Italian negotiations owing to the intolerable untrustworthiness and greed for armaments of the French Parliamentary Committee—(how hateful the French Government is)—"the Italians had been as good as gold"; but otherwise he was in good spirits—thought the Labour Government would last out the year but not two years. He was depressed about the absence of able men—who was to be leader after "we have gone". Jowitt he thought the most promising—he was turning from law to politics. Sidney told him about his desire to retire and his talks with Snowden about his going to the Lords as the Secretary of State for the Colonies. "So that's what you have come to tell me," Henderson said—evidently amused that Sidney should have been settling it "on his own". He thought that J.R.M. ought to make a considerable reconstruction of the Cabinet—if they were to stay in for another two years and then be out of office for five. The younger men must be brought on. But he saw little or nothing of the Prime Minister—who did not associate with his colleagues. What a curiously contemptuous indifference Henderson and Snowden have for J.R.M. *as a man*—exactly the same feeling that I have for him—and to a lesser extent, Sidney has. "What is surprising," Henderson said, "is that MacDonald has dropped —almost *cut*—all his closest associates in the Labour Party—Arnold, the Buxtons, the Mosleys." He implied, as Marley[1] did, that the Prime Minister had consulted with *Londonderry* as to whom he should appoint as leader in the Lords. Londonderry had quite naturally suggested Ponsonby, a true aristocrat—to which Henderson had objected. Henderson dislikes aristocrats; he always distrusted Mosley. He wants some of the younger Trade Unionists in the House of Lords. The poverty of the Labour Party, *in brains*, is rather ominous for the future government of Great Britain. In this respect the Labour Party is inferior to the Tory and Liberal parties—which makes the absorption of the Liberals all the more urgent! The rally of the Liberals to the Labour Government and Lloyd George's beneficent attitude in the Conservative unemployment censure debate points in that direction. . . .

---

[1] Dudley Leigh Aman, Lord Marley (1884–1952). Under-Secretary for War, 1930–1. A neighbour of the Webbs in Hampshire.

May 1st.—Finished the first chapter of *Our Partnership* on the Trade Union Movement, and opened the second on Municipal Administration. Now that I have got over my domestic troubles[1] and the beauty of spring has arrived with the birds singing from early morning to late in the evening, I am working better and enjoying life, in my charming house. Also I am looking forward to a happier autumn and winter, with Sidney by my side and a holiday abroad. The last two years, in spite of the ostensible glamour—a glamour which does not exist for those who, by temperament and habit, ignore the London Society side of high official position, have been alternating drudgery and loneliness for me, drudgery in London, and loneliness down here. Some pleasant acquaintances we have made: but then we have had to neglect old friends and the young lights springing up in our own subjects and within our own sets of Fabians and relatives, School of Economics staff and younger intellectuals. . . .

May 31st.—S.W. wrote to Prime Minister on Sunday a quite definite but very courteously worded plea for retirement, as soon as it becomes clear what is to happen to Snowden; and an ultimatum that he, S.W., *must be released* by October—suggesting Ponsonby, if Snowden is invalided, as his successor at the Colonial Office. The P.M. expressed his "sorrow", and promises to consider the whole business of reconstruction in his Whitsun holiday. Meanwhile J.H.T. has started in the press reports that Snowden is going to House of Lords and Sidney is retiring—the press men told Mrs. Snowden that it *was* Jimmy who had let it out. Jimmy has one of two ambitions: first, he would like to succeed Snowden, or, if that is not practicable, he would like to have the Colonial Office added to the Dominions Office before he goes to Ottawa. I doubt whether he will get either. Sidney is really tired—is feeling the strain of the perpetual worry of one colony after another—perhaps he is a little sore about the P.M.'s treatment of him over Palestine and the constant press reports for the last year of his retirement put about by Thomas. Alexander and his wife came to tea with me on his way to Portsmouth. He wants to go to the Board of Trade: he is also perturbed about the P.M.'s protectionist leanings and dislikes and distrusts Jimmy; he objected to S.W.'s retirement as weakening the Cabinet. There is no cohesion in the Cabinet; Ministers rarely see one another, each living in his own department. Cabinet meetings are exclusively engaged in

---

[1] This refers to the dismissal for dishonesty of domestic staff of seven years' standing. Mrs. Webb, partly owing to her girlhood experience in running her father's household, did not encounter as many domestic difficulties as beset some other Labour women (for example, Mary Macarthur), and the Scottish maids whom she finally secured served faithfully until Sidney's death in 1947; but the *Diaries* record a few distressful occasions.

parliamentary and party matters: Henderson is absorbed in foreign affairs, and in his management of the party machine. Except for my Admiralty party, there have been no social gatherings of the Parliamentary Party and candidates, since the miserable fiasco at the Friends' Meeting House last autumn, organised by the P.L.C. and the 1917 Club[1]—the latter not being a Labour body. Constant discussions have taken place between the "big four" of the P.L.P. (P.M., Henderson, Thomas and Snowden) and Lloyd George and his inner cabinet—Lothian, Samuel, Sinclair; they meet every week or so, and it looks like the preparation for the appearance of Liberals sooner or later on the Labour Front Bench. Meanwhile the cleavage between the General T.U. Council and the Labour Party is widening, while the I.L.P. shrinks up into a little group of dissentients. When defeat comes, I think it will be by Labour abstention. And it may come before the end of this session.

May 25th.—A happy Whitsun alone with Sidney, he helping me with the book—the part describing his administration of the Technical Education Board and the London School of Economics. He is quite pleased with my biography! The writing of this book I thoroughly enjoy; it is comparatively easy; have I not got the diaries and bits out of other people's autobiographies to play with? I don't care a little damn what other people think of it, probably I shan't be alive when it is published; anyhow I am too aged to care, and also this job of arranging material and patching bits together is one I am rather good at. Finally it interests and amuses me to look back over our life together; it heartens me to realise that we have had a jolly good time of it and turned out some useful work, and that taken by and large we have carried out our general plan of life, almost without being aware of it. What I did not foresee was that S.W. would be a peer retiring from Cabinet office —at the age of 72—and that I should be still writing at 73. And still a honeymoon couple!

There are the two spare bedrooms, there are two loggias; but instead of the one lounge there are three sitting-rooms—a study and a guests' sitting-room, and a hall dining-room—an improvement because it gives privacy. And there is absolute quiet except for the birds; as I write these words at 2 a.m. I listen to the nightingale in the wood near by. An ideal country home. There remains to be practised the art of "etiquette" in "getting old". Aged folk are apt to be querulous, to complain of their infirmities. Kind friends and relations insist on asking them "How are you?"—to which the poor old thing has to answer "Oh! I am all right"—which is not true, or "As well

---

[1] Founded, as its name implies, in 1917, in Gerrard St., Soho, mainly by left-wing Liberals, Labour, and pacifists. MacDonald was one of its chief patrons.

as an old person can be," which is an obvious evasion—or to start off describing small ailments, which is intolerable, as the questioner is uninterested and assumes that an old person is, and must be, a sick person. I think the second answer is the least trouble; in our case it has at least the advantage of exactitude. I think S. and I *are* as well as old persons can be—certainly Sidney is, and I am not far off that happy state. Every year or so I have to cut off a mile from the habitual walk. Yesterday, *June 1st 1931*, I went round by Waggoners Wells, which is seven miles or more—but I was over-tired and could not sleep at night. I feel less and less inclined to leave my home—but *ill* I am not, nor do I suffer pain. My one and only trouble is that I am *always* physically and mentally tired. Tiredness—irrespective of effort—is the specific disease of old age? . . . .

June 19th.—I dictated the last words of the second chapter of the book which ends the period 1892–8. The two chapters together must be 100 pages—about a quarter of the Vol. I (1892–1912). At this rate I should finish the volume in another 18 months or two years; by that time I shall be $75\frac{1}{2}$—leaving me $4\frac{1}{2}$ years before 80 to write the last volume, 1912–1932. Meanwhile S.W. and I will have personally produced 2 or 3 books together[1]—Methods of Social Study, The Reorganisation of British Government, the last volume of Local Government material 1689–1835, and Heaven knows what else—perhaps a work by Sidney on the Cabinet for which he has been collecting material for the last year. So there's the plan for our dotage. I feel singularly light-hearted about it and regard it more as a way of keeping the old Webbs comfortably occupied than as an additional contribution to our output. A postscript to our message to the world we lived in. . . .

June 30th.— What interests me most about Hindus's new book, *Red Bread*, is not the now familiar tale of the success of the General Plan as a method of wealth production; but the reaction of this success on the scale of moral values among the young people. And for this purpose one has to separate the economic from the metaphysical creed—Communism from scientific materialism. For instance, so far as sex is concerned, the change from the religious taboos of Christendom to the complete absence of any notion that the sexual act is sinful, either in man or woman, or that the sexual impulse differs from the appetite for food in the rightfulness of its satisfaction—is common to-day to capitalist countries—Germany, U.S.A., Great

---

[1] The first of these, *Methods of Social Study*, appeared in 1932: the others were never written. *Our Partnership*, however, was left practically complete by Beatrice at her death.

Britain; except that in English-speaking countries there is still a *convention*, getting weaker every day, that the "best people" hold to, though they may not practise, Christian ethics in sex matters. Otherwise the only obligations to-day accepted by the rising generation relate to physical health, your own, and your lover's. The distinction between Soviet citizens on the one hand, and, on the other, American or German, British or French citizens, lies in their respective outlook on the mediaeval sin of *covetousness*—on the desire for personal property or profit in hand—a sin which was turned into a virtue by the economists of the Industrial Revolution. It is *greed*, pecuniary self-interest, that is the Soviet Devil—the source of all wickedness. And this bears on honesty: and honour in public affairs. In capitalist countries the desire for wealth, the love of money, toleration for the hoarder and for the gambler, are the distinguishing features in current morals; indeed it is said quite openly that unless a large proportion of the ablest and fittest have this love for money, unless they passionately desire the things which money will buy—the capitalist system cannot be carried on successfully. One of the reasons given for the alleged decline of Great Britain and her approaching doom, is that the Englishman has lost his love of money. Now it so happens that the Russians, whether rich or poor were before the revolution one of the most dishonest and dishonourable of peoples. Hence the terrific discipline enforced by the Communist Party—the summary shooting of officials who defraud or steal. Communism represents a frantic effort to make the Russian people honest and disinterested, punctual and assiduous in the service of the community—on these issues it is intensely and fanatically puritan. In this devotion to a State, Communist Russia is exactly opposite to U.S.A. with its amazing laxness and tolerance of fraud and self-interest in public officials. Even murder and robbery with violence are made almost reputable if these crimes are perpetrated for the purpose of making profit. The *millionaire* gangsters have become popular heroes; their funerals and their weddings are great public spectacles. And yet in spite of this contrast, the most sympathetic race to the Russian Communists are exactly the Americans. Why? Because both races are concentrating their entire energies on the production of material wealth; they are both engaged in the same technique though for different objects—the American intent on making *himself* rich and the Soviet citizen obsessed with the desire to enrich the community even if he himself has to starve. It seems likely that given the survival of this strange creed Russia will become the richest country in the world. What then? Communal riches will do little more for the *good life* than personal riches. Man does not live by Bread alone even if it be Red Bread. But the disinterested work by which alone communal riches can be obtained is a big moral asset.

The method of attaining the purpose is finer than the purpose itself, whereas in the U.S.A., the purpose is amoral and the method immoral.

July 13th.— . . . My 24 hours in London, opening with a lunch to the Anglo-American Historical Conference, at the London School of Economics, ended in lunch with Madame Sokolnikoff at the Embassy, planned to talk about her book and my preface to it; but owing to the presence of a wide-awake and self-assured young attaché and an attractive Russian professor of history, our talk ended in chaff and semi-serious argument about the relations of the Soviet Government to capitalist civilisation. The cry to-day among official Russians is not the spread of the Revolution, but self-determination for each country, to develop its own social organisation and let the world—or rather the proletariats of all countries—choose between them; the Russians to-day so confident of their success that they intend to win in the competition! And certainly the events of the last fortnight prove that Trotsky's fear, which he expressed to us, that capitalist civilisation had reached a "new equilibrium" does not look well-founded. It is significant that the only Embassy with which we are on terms of intimacy is the Russian; it is the only one at which I, at any rate, feel "at home". All the other diplomatists I meet, including our old friend Palmstierna, a ci-devant Socialist Foreign Secretary—seem to me swallowed up in luxurious London Society—living on the rotten crust of British aristocratic and plutocratic society, circling round the Court. I feel they don't like me any more than I like them! As we do not go to evening receptions I see little or nothing of the diplomatic world. Except, by the way, we had the Japanese Ambassador[1] and his wife down to Passfield—I do like them, they are simple and sincere people and too aloof from European politics to be either sympathetic or hostile to either side in any controversy. The Japanese Ambassador, however, told us that the *Communists* among the students in Japan are increasing and that the creed is attracting the best of them. "We Japanese always like the new thing, and, at present, the Communist faith is the newest we know of." The Japanese, like the Germans, would make a success of a "General Plan" on Communist lines; if they once get rid of their time-honoured Emperor, descendant of the Sun—they have the necessary self-control, technique, and devotion to the community they live in.

July 20th. Beachy Head.—Sidney came down for the week-end with J.R.M.'s letter in his pocket. "This means," said I after reading it, "that he goes to the Lords as Foreign Secretary.

[1] Tsuneo Matsudaira, b. 1877. Ambassador to Britain, 1929–35.

Very confidential   10 Downing Street,
                                              Whitehall.
                                              14th July 1931.

The Rt. Hon. Lord Passfield,
   Colonial Office,
      Downing Street, S.W.1.

My dear Passfield,
   I am so sorry that I did not know that yesterday was your birth-day. It is not much use wishing a man who is even approaching seventy 'many happy returns of the day', but the oldest of us can appreciate the hope that they may have many quiet days to enjoy the memory of their good works, and I hope most sincerely that that will be yours—although I am afraid you cannot regard me as one who has helped you very much in this respect.
   As you know, I am in a most awful difficulty about the House of Lords. You may think that I have been doing nothing, but as a matter of fact I have been working at it for week-end after week-end, and am in a complete dead end. We have not the material in our Party that we ought to have. The solution will have to come, I am afraid, by moves which will surprise all of you. I am still working at it however.
   The situation in Palestine gets worse and worse, and will not be improved by what is going on at Basle at the present moment. All my information goes to show that the appointment of Drayton will be regarded as a declaration of war. I shall very likely see Weizmann when he returns, but in the meantime I am trying to get Wauchope over before the Recess so that we may have a talk with him about the problems which he has to face.
                        Yours very sincerely,
                     (signed)   J. Ramsay MacDonald.

He will resign as P.M., and recommend the King that Henderson be sent for; which will involve the break-up of the Cabinet. Henderson will omit from his Cabinet Parmoor, Passfield, Amulree and probably Margaret Bondfield. It is a most desirable way out for you. And I think it will take place early in August." Sidney had not thought of this solution; he had been so busy with Colonial Office affairs that he had put the matter on one side till he came down here. But he agreed that this was the most probable explanation of J.R.M.'s letter. And it bore out what Henderson had told us last November, that the P.M. had said to him, "Either you or I must go to the House of Lords." It is clear that in the Party's interest and his own peace of mind, it had better be MacDonald; leaving Henderson to face the General Election. This chance of leadership will also give some hope of reconciling the insurgent elements within the Labour Party before the Scarborough Conference in October. And we shall be able to settle down comfortably at Passfield for the last lap of life together. With the threatened loss of interest on investments, it will have to be on an economical scale; otherwise we might not be able to continue to live at Passfield without sharing it with some other person; which would be a nuisance in one's old age! We do not want even the best of housemates. . . .

August 4th.—S.W. reports that the Cabinet held immediately after the return of the P.M. and F.S. from Berlin was a very "jolly and cordial" meeting. Henderson and Mac. were well pleased with themselves and satisfied with the results of the visits. The plain truth is that like G.B.S. in Russia, they have been the centre of admiring crowds, respectful great personages, and a good press. But the Cabinet is really *in a very tight place*. The report of the Economy Committee,[1] appointed by Snowden, made up of five clever hard-faced representatives of capitalism and two dull Trade Unionists, is a sensational demand for economy in *public* expenditure—not merely cutting down what they consider "doles"; but also Health and Education services. Luxury hotels and luxury flats, Bond Street shopping, racing, and high-living in all its forms is to go unchecked; but the babies are not to have milk and the very poor are not to have homes. The private luxury of the rich is apparently not *wasteful expenditure*. A Cabinet Committee has been appointed to consider it; and the matter will have to be dealt with during the first weeks of the October session. The best thing that can happen to the Labour Government is that it should be defeated in its refusal to carry out the report. But Snowden is responsible for appointing the Committee. And he is really in agreement with the report! So is MacDonald except that he is too indifferent to home affairs to have an opinion of his own about it. He is completely absorbed in foreign affairs and India and so he may well be! Cabinet Government under present circumstances is a tragically absurd machinery of government in its helpless inadequacy. However as there is among the little group who will decide the policy of the Government—J.R.M., P.S., J.H.T., Henderson and Graham (Clynes is dropped)—neither the enthusiasm nor the knowledge to cope with the economic crisis on Socialist principles, the absence of any

[1] The May Committee, presided over by Sir George May, retiring chairman of the Prudential. Snowden had appointed this Committee in February after a discussion in the House of Commons on methods of reducing national expenditure, persuading his colleagues to accept a Liberal amendment to a Tory motion. The Committee's Report, from which the two Labour representatives dissented, presented the country as on the verge of financial disaster; for the Government it was the beginning of the end.

machinery wherewith to do the job is of relative unimportance. S.W. would like to be out of the Government, not only because he is tired but also because he does not like to accept responsibility for a reactionary policy; he is inclined to think that Henderson will stop it and that the outside members of the Cabinet will back Henderson up against Snowden. In which case Philip may go straight to the Lords and let S.W. out of the Cabinet; or he may decide to remain on as Chancellor of the Exchequer and fight for economy. Meanwhile I have to prepare my evidence before the Unemployment Commission[1] and S.W. is helping me.

August 8th.—G.B.S. spent two nights here and gave his pleasant chatty address on Russia to the Fabian Summer School. He was tired and excited by his visit to Russia: carried away by the newness and the violence of the changes wrought: here is tragedy, comedy, melodrama, all magnificently staged on a huge scale. It *must* be right! The paradox of the speech: Russian revolution was pure Fabianism—Lenin and Stalin had recognised the "*inevitability of gradualness*"! Also they had given up "workers' control" for the Webbs' conception of the threefold state—citizens', consumers' and producers' organisations. What is not Webbism or Western is the welding together of all three by a *Creed* oligarchy of two million faithful, dominating a population of 120 million indifferent, lukewarm or actively hostile. That is the crux of the controversy between those who approve or disapprove of Soviet Russia. It is odd that it is this domination by a creed that seems so attractive to G.B.S.; he being that great destroyer of existing codes, creeds and conventions, seems in his old age, to hanker for some credo to be *enforced* from birth onwards on the whole population. G.B.S. owes his immense vogue—perhaps the greatest in the world of to-day —not to wisdom or wit—but to his fascinating personality. In his old age he is a supreme charmer—appearance, voice, manner, gesture —outlook on other human beings—build up a Perfect Old Man— to be adored by the multitude.

August 18th. 3 *a.m.*—The Snowdens, who lunched here yesterday, were full of G.B.S.'s speech and his more careful letter in *The Times,* which reacted violently [*sic*]—"it was a wickedly mischievous

---

[1] The Royal Commission on Unemployment Insurance was appointed in the spring of 1931, like the May Committee, in response to Opposition pressure. In June it presented an interim report which resulted in the passing of the Anomalies Act, the most hated act of the dying Labour Government, which struck a large number, mostly women, off the register of beneficiaries. The commission continued to sit, and to report, after the fall of the Government; its final report was issued in 1934.

speech" Philip muttered—whereupon we and they had a hot dispute over Sovietism: they denouncing it as a cruel slave state and we upholding it as a beneficent experiment in organising production and consumption for the common good. It was significant of our completely different outlook on life. Without being conscious of it Philip Snowden has completely changed his attitude towards the organisation of society—(I doubt whether Ethel ever had a standpoint)—from being a fervent apostle of Utopian Socialism, thirty years of Parliamentary life and ten years of Front Bench politics, has made him the upholder of the banker, the landed aristocrat and the Crown. The Snowdens are an extreme case. But all the Front Bench including ourselves find our sympathies with the unemployed smothered under our own comfort and personal freedom. We just don't think about them. Except when we have to prepare official memoranda on the subject! Which Sidney and I have done during the last fortnight of his free time. It is a portentous document; but I could not criticise the present lax insurance scheme without giving my alternative—in the way of treatment, and *hinting at* the conclusion that unemployment cannot be prevented under competitive profit-making capitalism. To which it might be objected that British production has been so disturbed by a haphazard development of a huge export and import trade, that we can't replace it, without risking disaster, even if we could persuade the British people to do it. It is a black prospect.

It was noteworthy that though I suggested that Philip and Sidney should talk together in the study and Ethel and I retire to the sitting-room, the Chancellor of the Exchequer did not welcome the suggestion. He did not take the opportunity of telling Sidney anything whatever about his own proposals, he did not ask for S.W.'s views of the situation. Sidney did not resent it as he feels he is a retiring member, that he is old and that he is not representative of the two big organisations that can make or mar the Labour Cabinet—the T.U.C. and the Labour Party Conference. But we gather that there has been no direct consultation by the Big Five with any other member of the Cabinet; whilst they have been talking with the leaders of the Opposition. It was a calamity that the Labour Government was not turned out last spring—but whether the calamity was to the Labour Party only—I am not quite sure! We are swinging down the slope so rapidly that the disposition of parties is a very minor matter. It is almost worth living on in one's dotage to see what will happen. How will the T.U.C. and the L.P. Conference react to the financial policy of the Big Five; assuming this is that of the City or only a slight modification of it? Will any members of the Cabinet—Alexander, Morrison, Johnston —the livest among them—protest? And if they protest would they have any clear idea of an alternative policy?

August 22nd. 4 a.m.—Sidney came back from the Cabinet meeting, August 20th, which had sat all day and was still sitting at 7 o'clock when he left to catch his train, tired and depressed. He goes up this morning for another long day of critical meetings. The financial plight of Great Britain, whether because of the incompetence of the governing class, political and industrial, or because of the mischievous depreciation of its resources by its enemies in other countries, or because of the inherent weakness of its financial-industrial situation in 1931, is very serious and certainly does no credit to the Labour Government in general and to Philip Snowden in particular. At any rate, the Budget of last spring looks now a fatuous device to save the present taxpayer at the cost of the future solvency of the country. Snowden was very ill at the time. But to think that none of his colleagues knew what the Budget was to be, or the facts on which it was based, or the arguments which induced P.S. to make such a Budget, *until the day before its introduction*! The only excuse for the Labour Cabinet is that no other group of men—whether politicians, business men or academic economists, whether Tory, Liberal or Labour—seem to understand the problem. No one knows either, what the situation is, or, assuming that it is bad, the way out of it to sound finance. Even the fundamental facts of the situation are unknown. . . . Sidney observes, sadly, that he would have resented being excluded from the consultations of the inner Cabinet about the financial position if it were not that he feels that he knows no more than other people about the real situation of the British people in the world welter, and he has no clear idea of the way out.

At the Cabinet it was suggested that the "transitional class", 500,000 of them, should be struck off the dole and simply transferred to the Poor Law. Sidney stopped that by a vigorous protest. The Free Traders were beaten over the revenue tariff on manufactured goods—an humiliation for Philip Snowden (they were only six—Snowden, Lees Smith, S.W., Benn, Parmoor, Alexander). Yesterday S. did not go up for the 8.30 p.m. meeting held, after the conference with the Opposition leaders, [with] the T.U.C. and Labour Party Executive. He is deliberately swinging rather loose from the Cabinet—as he wishes it to be understood that he is retiring on the first opportunity. If there were to be any resignations he would be among them. But he does not want to give any useless trouble to his colleagues. It might end in a coalition government. Which would break up the Labour Party for many a long year. Anyway it is a sorry end to the second Labour Cabinet. Whether they have been "flies on the wheel" of world welter or not, they will leave the state of England worse than it was when they took office. And it is difficult not to conclude by the increasing laxity of the Insurance Act of 1930 and the Budget of

1931—not to mention their drifting backwards and forwards about public work for the unemployed—they have quickened the pace of sliding down the slope of a discredited British people. . . .

August 22nd.[1]—S.W. came back from London yesterday after five hours' Cabinet meetings to receive reports of the interviews with Opposition leaders, the Labour Party Executive and the T.U. General Council. "The General Council are pigs," S.W. said, "they won't agree to any 'cuts' of Unemployment Insurance benefits or salaries or wages. They are referring their conclusions to T.U.C. meeting September 7th." The Conservative leaders refuse to consider more than 25 % increased taxation—if that. The Cabinet is now unanimous against tariffs: they stand on 50/50 in 'cuts' and 'taxes', representing "equality of sacrifice". Parliament is to be summoned on September 14: the Government expects to be defeated; and the Conservatives will take office. "No resignations," urged J.R.M., and no general election till the budget is balanced. But just as S.W. had finished telling me this, the phone rang up to tell him that there was to be a Cabinet 9.30 today; so off he went by 8.12 train this morning. He is serious about the financial situation. The bankers have let us in for it by their 150 million long-term credits to Germany, whilst accepting short-term deposits of 200 million from other countries. The German credit cannot be withdrawn, whilst the other countries are withdrawing their deposits because British finance is not solvent! And the British people are not solvent because of the dole!

He thinks J.R.M. has behaved in all good faith over the whole business. The discredit of Great Britain abroad is said by other Labour leaders to be absurdly overdone; it is the result of the sabotage of British credit by the Yellow Press to bring down the Labour Government. The so-called "governing class" has been deliberately and insistently pessimistic about the "waterlogged" condition of British money owing to the dole. What with the sabotage by the capitalists of Labour Cabinet administration, and the sabotage of British industry by Trade Union pigheadedness, the prospect is extremely disturbing to public-spirited citizens. We have reached a state of hidden class war, conducted with good manners and tolerance of each other's opinions, resulting in a disastrous stalemate in industrial and social reconstruction. Both parties refuse to "play the game". Anything may happen. This time last year the Cabinet was refusing to think about home affairs because it was absorbed in Dominion affairs and India. To-day it has forgotten the Dominions and can

[1] *Sic.* The MS. is slightly confused here, and it is not very clear what meetings Sidney did or did not attend. The two entries under this date must have been written at different times of the day; but there is no further indication.

give no thought to India—largely because it refused to take home affairs seriously for the first two years of its administration.

August 23rd.—S.W. reported that at the Cabinet yesterday morning the Prime Minister stated that the Conservative and Liberal leaders refused to accept the Labour Cabinet proposals and demanded 75% cuts mainly in the dole and 25% taxes. The Cabinet refused to compromise to that extent and the King was informed by telephone and decided to return to London from Balmoral. J.R.M. raised the question of a Coalition Government: some of the Labour Cabinet Ministers remaining in office. This, he intimated, was what the King desired and might propose. This proposal Henderson and other members hotly rejected. The impression left on S.W.'s mind was that J.R.M., Snowden and Jimmy *might consider it*. "A good riddance for the Labour Party," I said. They rose at 12 o'clock under the impression that it was settled that the P.M. would resign and Baldwin would take office. However in the luncheon hour J.R.M. and Snowden met the Opposition leaders again and suggested another compromise— (S.W. said that J.R.M. was not authorised to do it)—which Chamberlain accepted *assuming that the City agreed*. It was left to the Bank of England (Vice-Chairman) to consult the Federal Bank of U.S.A. whether they would back such a governmental policy and their decision will be reported to-day (Sunday) when the Cabinet meets at 7 o'clock.

So it is the financiers, British and American, who will settle the personnel and the policy of the British Government. Sidney hopes that they (the American and British bankers) will decide against the Labour Cabinet remaining in office and hand over the government to their friends the Conservative and Liberal leaders. It certainly is a tragically-comic situation that the financiers who have landed the British people in this gigantic muddle should decide who should bear the burden. The Dictatorship of the Capitalist with a vengeance! Henderson blames the P.M. for spending so much time in negotiation: he thinks it would have been far better to have settled really what the Labour Cabinet would be prepared to do in economies and resign if it were rejected by the Opposition, assuming that it was not possible to await the decision—owing to the action of the international financiers —of the House of Commons on the 14th. It seems that owing to the run on the banks by foreign financiers (*which has not been reported in the press*) the policy had to be settled straight away; otherwise there would have to be a moratorium on Wednesday. Graham thinks that the City is bluffing the Government. The Labour Cabinet ought to have "stood up" to the financiers. Let the Tories come in and stand the racket: and that is S.W.'s opinion. The plain truth is that the

Labour Prime Minister, Chancellor of the Exchequer, together with the ineffable Jimmy, are converted to the capitalist creed and would be quite contented to carry it out if the party would agree to let them! If the Cabinet decides to break off negotiations with the Opposition these three might decide to join a Conservative Government, which would leave the Labour Party free to reorganise on sterner lines. . . .

The Fall of the Labour Government 1929–31

August 24th. 6.30 p.m.—Just heard over wireless what I wished to hear, that the Cabinet as a whole has resigned, J.R.M. accepting office as Prime Minister in order to form a National Emergency Government including Tories and Liberals: it being also stated that Snowden, Thomas and alas! Sankey, will take office under him. I regret Sankey: but I am glad the other three will disappear from the Labour world—they were rotten stuff: each one of them for different reasons. A startling sensation it will be for those faithful followers throughout the country who were unaware of J.R.M. and Snowden's gradual conversion to the outlook of the city and "London Society". Thomas has never been a Socialist and will probably cease, like other ci-devant Trade Union leaders, to be even formally on the side of the Labour Movement. So ends, ingloriously, the Labour Cabinet of 1929–31. A victory for the American and British financiers—a dangerous one, because it is an open declaration, without any disguise, of Capitalist Dictatorship; and a brutal defiance of the Labour Movement. The *Third International* will gloat over the "treachery" of MacDonald, Snowden and Thomas. It's worth while living to watch the reactions at Bristol and Scarborough to this declaration of class war from the financiers of U.S.A. and Great Britain. Henderson will, I think, be the right leader in this dramatic episode. S.W., who is staying in London overnight, is, I assume, consulting with the other dissenting ex-Ministers with regard to the statement they will issue to the press or make to the Wednesday meeting of the Joint Executives as to their reasons for refusing to accept the terms of the U.S.A. and British financiers, and thus co-operate with the two capitalist parties of Great Britain in putting the cost of the sins of capitalism on to the manual workers' livelihood. British credit may be temporarily saved but internal peace is jeopardised for many a long year. The first result of J.R.M.'s defection may be the consolidation of the Labour Movement, political and industrial, under Henderson's leadership—with a sterner outlook, a more disciplined behaviour and a more scientific programme.

The danger in front of the Labour Movement is its deep-seated belief that any addition, under any condition, to the income of wage-earners is a good thing in itself. That was why it was so fatal to start state-subsidised insurance, it was bound to end by becoming unconditional outdoor relief—and that "addition" to the livelihood of the poor was certain to increase the area of unemployment. It is a most demoralising form of voluntary idleness. Under capitalism the wage-earner's life is often so hard, and the wage-earner is so irresponsible, that idleness, with a regular pittance, is comparatively attractive to large bodies of men—they won't accept and won't keep work they don't particularly like and are not accustomed to—and when they do accept it, they are not overkeen to bestir themselves. And yet the typical Trade Unionists—though when administering their own out-of-work benefit they insist on all sorts of conditions—resent these conditions being attached to the state scheme. That is the danger of the Labour Government, and always will be, as far as I can see. The sins of capitalism become excuses for the sins of labour, and the sins of labour become the justification for the sins of capitalism. Politics becomes a question of reprisals, each party or class trying to damage the other—to sabotage each other's institutions. In the U.S.A. there is another interest intervening, organised crime; fortunately Europe is not yet afflicted with that type of "big business".

August 25th.—S.W. came back early in the afternoon of our second Fabian Garden Party. He was exhausted and rather upset by the queer end of the Labour Cabinet—but delighted to be out of it all. At the seven o'clock Sunday night Cabinet meeting J.R.M. brought back an inconclusive answer from the U.S.A. and British financiers to the revised Cabinet scheme of economies, indicating that more cuts in the insurance benefit would be required to satisfy the U.S.A. financiers. Whereupon nine members of the Cabinet, headed by Henderson, revolted and stated that they would not go so far in cutting the dole *even as J.R.M. had done on their behalf.*[1] Whereupon the Prime Minister left for Buckingham Palace and adjourned the Cabinet for 12 o'clock on Monday. At that meeting he announced that he had accepted a commission to form a National Government—his colleagues listened with the usual English composure—Henderson intimating that discussion would be out of place; after which the meeting proceeded to wind up the formal business about documents etc.; passed unanimously a vote of thanks to the P.M. proposed by Sankey, and without further leave-taking left the Cabinet room. Whereupon Sidney joined up with Henderson and Lansbury and some six others and went off to lunch at the Office of Works to discuss the situation. There was a certain relief that their association with Mac-Donald was at an end, and a very distinct opinion that he had meant to come out as Premier of a National Government all through these

---

[1] According to a note in the *Diary*, the seven others besides Webb included Addison, Alexander, Clynes, Graham, Greenwood and Lansbury.

latter days of panic and confusion. Whether MacDonald had already arranged with Snowden and Thomas some days ago no one knew, but it is assumed so. What is in doubt is whether MacDonald himself, and the Conservatives and Liberals with whom he negotiated, expected a considerable group of Labour members to follow him? If he or they did, they will be grievously disappointed! One of the good results of the National Government under Mac. is that it unites, as no other event could, the whole of the Labour Movement under Henderson in determined opposition to the policy of making the working-class pay for the mistakes of the financiers. . . .

August 27th.—Arnold reports that Lansbury told him that J.R.M. spoke to him casually at the end of July after the issue of the May report, as to the desirability of a National Government if the financial position became serious. Lansbury rejected the notion as impossible and J.R.M. dropped the question. By the light of this incident the P.M.'s letter to S.W. July 14, which puzzled us, seems to indicate some such solution, put forward tentatively. "You may think I have been doing nothing," he wrote, "but as a matter of fact I have been working at it for week-end after week-end and am at a complete dead end. We have not the material in our party that we ought to have. The solution will have to come, I am afraid, by moves which will surprise you all. I am still working at it however." I don't believe that Mac. deliberately led the Cabinet into a trap: *tried* to get them into agreeing to economies in the process of bargaining with the U.S.A. financiers, all the time intending to throw his colleagues over and form a National Government—but *he drifted into doing it*—largely because he is secretive—he never *can* be frank—yet he will let the cat out of the bag in a moment of queer indiscretions to someone who is a comparative stranger like Sidney or even an enemy like Lansbury. I trust the Labour Party is quit of him, finally and completely, and I wish him well among the Dukes and Duchesses: if it cost me nothing I would endow him with an adequate income for his position as Earl of Lossiemouth on the condition that he made no kind of attempt to veer back to the Labour Movement. What I should advise is that the Parliamentary Party should assume that he has left the Party out of conviction and proceed to forget him and go forward on their own lines as an Opposition without troubling to denounce him as a traitor. Who can judge the heart of man? If you don't like his behaviour, block his way if you can: if not, get out of his way—but in any case cast his presence out of your consciousness. . . .

September 2nd.—A shock to public opinion, at home and abroad, the swift, cold and practically unanimous repudiation of MacDonald,

Snowden and Thomas by the entire Labour world—by their colleagues in the Government and all but three peers and two ex-Liberal lawyers —by the Parliamentary Labour Party (even by J.R.M.'s devoted friend and biographer, Mary Agnes Hamilton). The next few days discovered four followers, beside his son, Malcolm MacDonald—Sir Ernest Bennett,[1] Gillett (Overseas Trade), Holford Knight,[2] Lovat Fraser[3]—all, except Gillett, of no consequence (Gillett is a banker— foreign acceptance house)—by the Labour Parties in their own constituencies, by the Trade Unions and Co-operators—without a single protest, or dissent, or moment of indecision. How different from Joseph Chamberlain's break with the Liberal Party in 1886, carrying with him not only a group of distinguished M.P.'s and the majority of Liberal peers, but a solid block of nine Liberal constituencies in the Midlands, which he kept to the end of his life! The last touch was put by the contemptuously silent "showing of the door" to Thomas by the N.U.R. The Labour Party emerges stronger—far stronger and more united than they were three weeks ago.

This spitting out by the Labour Party of those they hated, with a gesture of getting rid of some poisonous substance, is, of course, partly due to the dramatic issue—are the sins of the capitalists to be borne by the mass of the workers?—and partly to the class-consciousness of a political party based on the Trade Union Movement. But it is also intimately bound up with MacDonald's aloofness from the Labour world, his quite obvious dislike of Labour men and women and almost insulting refusal to associate with members of the Labour Party except the De la Warrs, the Jowitts and formerly Lord Thomson and the Mosleys and poor little Arnold—now discarded. . . .

September 10th.— . . . The personal question is how to use one's remnants of wits? Last spring I was working happily at *Our Partnership*, a pleasant easy job, selecting entries from my diary, and composing the explanatory paragraphs. Then came the calls from outside, the demand of the Royal Commission on Unemployment Insurance for a Memorandum with a view of giving evidence; and the pressing request from the B.B.C. to give talks in the course on "The Changing World". With Sidney's help I have prepared an elaborate memorandum on unemployment and for my own edification I have been reading up the recent reports—May, Macmillan,[4] Insurance evidence,

---

[1] Sir Ernest Nathaniel Bennett (d. 1947), M.P. for Central Cardiff, 1929–45.
[2] Holford Knight (1877–1936), lawyer and divorce reformer, M.P. for South Nottingham, 1929–35, afterwards Recorder of West Ham.
[3] James Alexander Lovat Fraser (1868–1938), barrister. M.P. for Lichfield, 1929–35.
[4] The Report of the Treasury Committee on Finance and Industry, appointed 1929 with Lord Macmillan as Chairman.

together with a lot of pamphlets and books. All these essays in contemporary industrial and financial affairs, with the endless disputations
and dialectics—about credit and currency and tariffs and the level of
wages—all the doctors disagreeing with each other as to remedies,
surgical and medical, for the dire diseases which afflict the production,
distribution and exchange of the nation's income of commodities and
services—raises the deeper issue of whether we believe in a society
based on the acquisitive instinct or on one based on public service.
For what all the pundits and practical administrators are discussing is
"How can we make the profit-maker behave in the public interest?
How can we lure him on to virtue?" But supposing we don't want the
animal?—and are better without him? Moreover, while we dispute
and wrangle, the real issue will be decided over our heads. In the
course of a decade we shall know whether American Capitalism or
Russian Communism yields the better life for the bulk of the people;
which of these "cultures" wins, we in Great Britain will have to
"follow suit". The position seems to me very similar to the struggle
from the 12th to the 16th centuries between Christianity and Mohammedanism for the soul of Europe. There was no third creed open to
the civilised world of those days; they had to follow Christ or Mahomet.

Now in view of this conclusion how shall we spend our old age?
Am I strong enough to go to Russia so as to give vividness to any line
we take? Can we master the intricacies of capitalist finance sufficiently to be able to expose its futility? For without doubt we are on
the side of Russia. . . .

September 20th.—The Hendersons came down on Tuesday night
—he depressed and tired, sad at leaving the F.O., and not enjoying the
worry and toil of leading the Labour Party and explaining the ambiguous attitude of late Ministers to economies. But, as always, Henderson is not rattled; he is not thinking of himself, or of J.R.M.'s tor-
tuous ways, but of the country first and the Party second. He dislikes
and intensely resents the way in which J.R.M. (all the time intending
a National Government) led his colleagues into a *cul-de-sac*; into
accepting, provisionally, some of the terms of the enemy without
having gained any equivalent concession. They were, in fact, first
compromised and then dismissed! Henderson is, however, not disposed to shut the door on any old colleagues—"I keep an open mind
as to what it may be necessary to do." He entirely exonerates Sankey
and thinks he was right to go on with his Indian business. He tells us
that before the crisis he had hoped to go on, as Foreign Secretary, in
the House of Lords, and devote himself to the Party machine; and had
never wished to be leader, but only the manager of the Party. He
deplores the loss of Mosley; but thinks that he showed himself without

judgment or character. He hopes to get Jowitt back. Jowitt felt bound by his personal friendship with J.R.M. but is very unhappy. Henderson is disheartened by the lack of possible successors: "Alexander, Morrison, Dalton in that order, are the most promising as possible leaders." To my surprise he was impressed with our Memo. on Insurance (I thought he would jib at Occupation Centres): we talked about the need of a new departure in policy created by the breakdown in City finance administration, and it ended in his appealing to us to draft a programme for the Labour Party so that he might have it in his pocket for the Labour Conference—which we have promised to do. But while he and we had been talking, talking, talking in our long ramble over Ludshott Common, things were happening on the stock exchanges of the world and in the late afternoon the telephone bell began to ring. The Hendersons had left after tea with Arnold to see the Marleys and Arnold's bungalow and Sidney and I were wandering in the garden. First it was Stevenson,[1] Editor of the *Daily Herald*, who wanted to speak to Henderson and spoke in default to Sidney. A conference of all the editors had been called for Sunday at 5.30 at 10 Downing Street. Half an hour later the private secretary of the P.M. wanted Henderson urgently. Then we heard, over the six o'clock wireless, that there had been something like a panic on the London Stock Exchange and that at Amsterdam there had been heavy selling of British securities. When Henderson returned, Stevenson told him that he (S.) assumed that the Sunday conference of editors would be concerned with a Cabinet crisis: the Liberals had sent an ultimatum to J.R.M. and demanded an answer on Monday morning. The Liberals in the Cabinet would resign at once unless he gave an undertaking that there would be no General Election until the financial crisis had been overcome (the drain of gold was going on as before, it was said). From J.R.M.'s secretary Henderson learnt nothing except that an important letter to him was on the way and that it was urgent that Henderson should get it on Monday morning—better on Sunday night. He (Duff[2]) would ring him up to-morrow. All of which left us completely mystified and awaiting further news to-day. Though this Government has been in office nearly a month the P.M. has had no consultation with Henderson as the leader of the Opposition. "If Baldwin had been leader Mac. would have been constantly colloguing with him." "He dare not face a meeting with you," said I, "for the simple reason that he knows that he has betrayed you and that you know it too." Henderson says that J.R.M. expected to take 100 members of the Parliamentary Labour Party with him; he only

[1] William Henry Stevenson, Editor of *Daily Herald*, 1931–6.
[2] Sir Patrick Duff (b. 1889), civil servant, Private Secretary to Baldwin and MacDonald; High Commissioner in New Zealand, 1945–9.

took eight, excluding Snowden and Jimmy and his own son! Moreover the P.M. and his two colleagues were either too certain of being rejected by, or too contemptuous of, their own party, to attend the Party meeting; only Sankey, the outsider and the specialist, attended to explain his reason for continuing office. No wonder the P.M.'s Liberal and Tory colleagues think that he has "done them" and are trying to make fresh terms: the Liberals wanting a period of steady government without a tariff as the only way of preventing the fall of sterling and the drain of gold, with or without a General Election. It looks like a big smash-up.

September 21*st.* 5 *a.m.*—While the Hendersons and we were walking round Weavers Down on Sunday morning Duff rang up to ask Henderson to come to London so that he might receive and consider the letter the P.M. had sent him. Ponsonby and Marley came to lunch: Marley reports that Sankey had told him that at a Cabinet on Thursday the date of the General Election had been fixed, the Liberals dissenting. Apparently the Party met on Saturday and sent the ultimatum to the P.M. The letter from the P.M. is presumably a request to Henderson to persuade the Parliamentary Labour Party to help the National Government out of the difficulty either by joining or supporting them until there could be a General Election. Henderson is quite determined that he will do nothing without the approval of the three Executives and the P.L.P. Otherwise he will keep "an open mind". There is a wild rumour that, in return for a tariff, the Conservatives are willing to give up the economies on wages, salaries and the dole. But such a surrender is inconceivable and from the standpoint of Continental and American opinion would be disastrous. It is one thing not to do a foolish thing; it is another to go back on it when confronted with "disobedience in the Fleet"![1] To the Continental statesman it would be like the first step in a revolution; rebellion in the Fleet being, after the German and Russian revolutions, the classic way of upsetting the existing Government. Henderson agreed that we had come to the end of an epoch and needed a new and striking departure in the policy put forward. "If you both could sit down and put into words what we have been saying, that's what I want," were his parting words.

September 23*rd.*—When, on the Sunday afternoon, two ex-Cabinet Ministers and two ex-Under-Secretaries were discussing the probable

---

[1] On September 15th certain units of the Atlantic Fleet at Invergordon mutinied against the cuts in the pay of ratings which had been announced in Snowden's autumn Budget; on the 22nd it was announced that the cuts to soldiers, sailors and teachers would be made less severe, and simultaneously Britain went off the gold standard.

character of the P.M.'s summons to Henderson to return to London, not one of them had the remotest inkling that the decision was "to go off the Gold Standard". The silly old Snowden had broadcast, the day after the formation of the National Government, the horrors—bankruptcy of all business and death by starvation of the working-class —implied by the "loss of the pound": no suggestion of giving up parity had been even mooted at any Cabinet meetings—the saving of the parity of the pound had been the very purpose of the negotiations with U.S.A. and France, the reason for ousting the Labour Government and forming the National Government. At the meeting with the T.U.C. Thomas and Mac had slobbered over the agony of "going off gold"—had vividly described the sudden and simultaneous disappearance of all luxuries and most necessaries from the homes of the workers. And now, having dismissed the Labour Government and exacted the "Economy" Budget and thrown the unemployed back on to the Poor Law, the bankers advise the Government to repudiate gold and go back to the prosperous pre-parity days of 1918–25. The plaudits of the press on Monday and poor Snowden's second broadcast explaining that the whole difference between disaster and a "new start for industry" lay in the fact that "the budget had been balanced"—a "scrap of paper" which the Labour Cabinet was quite willing to provide—was a comic and humiliating exposure of the consummate trickery of the financial world, when it feels itself menaced either in profits or power. It is also, alas! not a very complimentary sidelight on the financial acumen of the Labour Cabinet: that no one of them saw through the little conspiracy of the City. And at the cost to taxpayers of some 10 millions by the way of the fruitless loan. But one step forward has been secured. We know now the depths of the delusion that the financial world have either the knowledge or the goodwill to guard the safety of the country over whose pecuniary interests they preside. They first make an appalling mess of their own business—involving their country in loss of money and prestige—and then by the most barefaced dissimulation and political intrigue they throw out the Cabinet and put in their own nominees in order to recover the cost of their miscalculation by hook or by crook from the community as a whole. And the P.M. had the effrontery to state in the House of Commons that under threat of mutiny the Fleet can get some of the "cuts" revised, and under threat of political disaffection the police and teachers can have the Economy Budget changed. The *reduction of the dole* was a condition of the loan from the U.S.A. and may not be altered! Well, well.

It is certainly a striking coincidence—a flash of light on contemporary world politics—that the first Labour Cabinet fell because of the forged Zinoviev letter, implying Soviet propaganda in Great Britain,

and the second Labour Cabinet fell on the express and openly acknowledged ground that the Federal Bank of U.S.A. practically demanded
this dismissal of the Labour Cabinet as *a condition of their financial
loans*. It looks as if Great Britain is to be a pawn in the struggle between
the two great forces in the world of to-day—Russian Communism
and American Capitalism. And yet it is American brains and American
capital that are helping to make the General Plan of Soviet Russia a
success in return for handsome salaries to American engineers and pro-
fitable orders to American Capitalism. Imagine Russian Communists
trying to make American Capitalism a success! The distinction lies
between men ruled by the acquisitive instinct and those governed by
what might be called a religious motive—over-riding their personal
interests and impulses. . . .

Scarborough Labour Conference

October 10th.—Dull, drab, disillusioned but *not* disunited, is the
impression I got of the Labour Party Conference of 1931. There are
few women among 800 delegates; there is a marked absence of wives;
there are numbers of pale and listless men in the Conference—there
is an uncanny absence of laughter and mutual chaff—there is no anger
and very little sympathy with rebels—the I.L.P. were steam-rollered
by 2 million to 200,000 out of the Party.[1] The Communists and their
absurd little paper, the *Daily Worker*, are ignored. Henderson got a
great reception; there was singularly little attempt to call the late
Ministers on the platform to account; and little more than silent contempt for J.R.M., Snowden and Jimmy: these apostates seemed to
have no following in the Conference. There was, of course, an opposition: a very powerful though silent opposition—at the Conference—
the Citrine-Bevin-T.U. element—but it was an opposition that has
no intention of overtly opposing. The General Council is intent on
carrying on its own alternative policy, in the outside world, of industrial co-operation with employers, together with determined resistance
to any lowering of the money incomes of the working-class by cuts in
dole or "means test", etc., or reduction of wages. Thus "this crisis"
with its indirect lowering of the people's income has not converted
Citrine from his policy of co-operating with leaders of industry.

At Headquarters (Prince of Wales Hotel). The scene has completely changed from the last Conferences I attended, Margate, 1927,

---

[1] The I.L.P. had long been moving towards a split with the Labour Party. The
vote at Scarborough was on an attempt by the I.L.P. delegates to refer back the
section of the Executive Committee's Report requiring I.L.P. Members of Parliament to obey Standing Orders even against the decisions of their own conference.
Their defeat on this meant that the I.L.P. candidates at the General Election fought
without Labour Party endorsement; but the I.L.P. did not finally disaffiliate until
the summer of 1933.

and Brighton, 1929. The smart set that surrounded MacDonald, and gave the tone to Headquarters—Thomson, Mosleys, De la Warrs, Jowitts, Usher, etc.—have disappeared. Henderson's bodyguard of intellectuals—Dalton, Noel Baker, Laski, Colin Clark[1]—together with the younger Labour Ministers—Morrison, Johnston and Susan Lawrence—are very much in evidence. The most notable newcomer —one who is already acclaimed as *the future leader*—is Stafford Cripps. He moved among the younger men with ease and modesty—he is able and virtuous without personal vanity or airs of superiority—uncontaminated by "Society", a homely person—a distinguished intellectual and first-rate advocate, but not yet an artist like J.R.M. or Mosley. He is not to me, though he is my nephew, *personally* attractive. He has neither wit nor humour; neither subtlety nor artistry. But *if* he has sufficient physical vigour, he will go far, because he has character as well as intellect; he is pious in the best sense. Isobel is a good sort— and they are a devoted couple—the very essence of good bourgeois virtues, unworldliness and personal refinement. With all these younger men Uncle Arthur is on the best and most confidential terms. Whatever else is lacking, Headquarters for the first time is a happy family!

Of course the depressing feature of this representative conference of Labour is the absence of sufficient will and capacity to "run the revolution" whether it be peaceful or tempestuous. We have got rid of the rotten stuff from the movement, but we have not yet sufficient willpower and knowledge to take control of the big formless business of capitalist production, distribution and exchange which is now disintegrating before our eyes in Great Britain and apparently in U.S.A. and Germany and other countries. What seems now to be the prevailing spirit among the new governing group of the P.L.P. is a dour determination never again to undertake the government of the country as the *caretaker of the existing order of society*. They intend to lay down, on the first day of office, a positive policy of immediate legislation and executive control of the nation's income and investment of savings— with no damned nonsense about H. of Lords obstruction or Court objection! I do not yet see the men for such a job! But there is the *Will* present—in this little group at Headquarters—at any rate the Will to elaborate a plan whilst in *opposition*; and though in office they might be smothered in the complications of the business, they won't be throttled by the embraces of the Court, the aristocracy and the City like the "lost leaders" were. It is amazing this sense of relief, at having got rid of these three men, spreading right through the Labour Conference of 1931. The *relief* has almost cancelled the bitterness. No one wants to think about them. . . .

[1] Colin Grant Clark (b. 1905), the economist, afterwards economic and financial adviser to the Government of Queensland.

October 18th.—Snowden's broadcast last night was a model of lucidity, delivered with conviction, without the unctuous insincerity of Simon or false rhetoric of J.R.M.; admirably planned and phrased. It was a repetition of the old story that unless the poor consented to remain poor and even to become poorer, the capitalists, abroad and at home, would withdraw their wealth and reduce the country to universal bankruptcy and consequent starvation. The process, however, was described not in the terms of human beings whether capitalist or worker, but in the impersonal form of the behaviour of gold and credit—the catastrophe would in fact be the inevitable working out of "natural law". And Philip Snowden believed it, which Simon did not; he is too clever not to see the other side of the argument. As to J.R.M. he neither knows nor cares—the argument is just a counter to be used in the game. Of course P.S.'s contention, that the wealthy class will not play the game, *is very likely true*: we may have reached a period of revolution and counter-revolution. A most unpleasant prospect! As an aged *rentier* I *was* much touched by P.S.'s hidden plea that the division of the population into the few free rich and the many subordinate poor *must* continue unless all alike were to be put on "food cards"—another way of bringing about equality of income. Why disturb our present comfortable social order so far as the well-to-do citizens are concerned? The programme of the Labour Party was "Bolshevism not Socialism". The question arises: What was the meaning of Socialism to Philip Snowden, when he was a Socialist? The one note of insincerity was his reiteration of the claim to be still a Socialist. His real convictions are those of Ricardian economics; he has come to dislike and despise the working-class. The General Council of the T.U.C. has become the Devil—the source of all evil; the City and the Court the centres of light. Of the three deserters Philip Snowden is the most respectable: he is a genuine *pervert* to the other side: he remains a man of principle. If only he would confess that he has changed his outlook! We could forgive him! . . .

October 28th.—"The Commander-in-Chief of the progressive forces" may write the future historian "and his two leading generals, nauseated by the disorderly, disrespectful, disobedient and generally incompetent crowd behind them, escaped one night into the fortified camp of the defenders of privilege and property, bargained with them for pride of place, turned right about face and marched, with bands and flags flying, and massacred their old followers so that only fifty of them escaped with their lives. A comic incident marked this dramatic event. A little old man with his daughter, his son and one follower, watched from a lonely hilltop, this act of treachery. He yelled with all his might against the advancing army; nobody listened to him, nobody cared. For all remembered that thirteen years ago, as a great progressive leader, he had done exactly the same thing himself; put himself at the head of the men of property and the men of rank, and destroyed his old friends and associates: also under the plea of national unity and also at the cost of social progress."

Ponsonby and the Marleys and we two listened to the wireless from ten to two on Tuesday the 26th. Towards the end of the tale of Labour losses we became hilarious; the unfolding situation was so absurd! MacDonald, at once author, producer and chief actor, of this amazing political drama, had shown consummate art; he had been aided and abetted with acid malignity by Philip Snowden; a malignity which could only be accounted for by the reutrn of his recent illness. The Parliamentary Labour Party had been not defeated but annihilated: largely we think by the women's vote.[1]

On the Front Opposition Bench there will be only one ex-Cabinet Minister—George Lansbury; only two ex-Ministers of rank—Stafford Cripps and Attlee; with one or two ex-Under-Secretaries and Household Officers. This Parliament will last four or five years; and the Labour Party will be out of office for at least ten years. The capitalists will remain, for this fourth decade of the 20th century, in complete and unchallenged control of Great Britain, as they are of the U.S.A., France and Italy. They will, at any rate, be held responsible for all that happens at home and abroad. Meanwhile the Labour Movement may discover a philosophy, a policy and a code of personal conduct—all of which we lack to-day. The desertion of the three leaders was not the cause of our defeat; it was the final and most violent symptom of the disease from which the Party was suffering. Future historians will point out that the Labour Government of 1924 was hatched prematurely; it came into office, through a political episode which had no connection with the Labour Movement, no relation to the fitness of the P.L.P. to become either H.M. Opposition or H.M. Government. That episode was Lloyd George's smashing of the Liberal Party in 1918. The Liberal Party *did* represent, in its policy and outlook, the anti-Conservative element in the country;

[1] Results of General Election, 1931:
Labour *plus* I.L.P., 52 (a loss of nearly 250);
Conservative *plus* National Labour, i.e. the thirteen followers of MacDonald, 484;
Liberals of all wings, 72—these were split, even before the election, about equally into Simonites, who voted with the Conservatives, and Samuelites, with the tiny Lloyd George group standing slightly apart. There were also 7 "others", who have been variously assigned.
The total poll was 21½ million, less by a million than in 1929, though the electorate had risen by almost the same amount. The Labour vote fell by 1¾ million; and that of the Conservatives rose by 2¾ million. But about half of the 2¼ million Liberal poll must in fact be counted as Conservative, having been cast for Simon's Liberal Nationals.

and if it had not been for the Great War and for Lloyd George's post-war action, it would have continued to occupy the position, with the Labour Party as a left wing. Under MacDonald's leadership 1906–14, the forty members of the P.L.P. had never been more than a left wing made up of Trade Unionists and not very left at that! As we knew, J.R.M. was willing in 1911 to enter the anti-Asquith Cabinet that was being engineered by Lloyd George in league with Balfour; and he actually offered Henderson an Under-Secretaryship which the latter indignantly refused. The Great War and the world upheaval brought the Labour Party on to the Front Opposition Bench and transformed it into a definitely Socialist party. Two spells of office and the embraces of the old governing class converted the more prominent leaders into upholders of the existing order. Gradually becoming conscious of their leaders' lack of faith, the P.L.P. rapidly disintegrated. The dramatic desertion of the three leaders on the eve of the battle turned a certain defeat into a rout. But it revealed a solid core of seven million stalwart Labour supporters, mostly convinced Socialists. Whether new leaders will spring up with sufficient faith, will-power and knowledge to break through the tough and massive defences of British profit-making capitalism with its press and its pulpit, its Royalties and House of Lords, its elaborate financial entanglements of credit and currency all designed to maintain intact ancient loyalties, and when necessary, promote panics in favour of the *status quo*, I cannot foresee. Have we the material in the British Labour Movement from which can be evolved something of the nature of a religious order —a congregation of the faithful who will also be skilful technicians in social reconstruction? What undid the two Labour Governments was not merely their lack of knowledge and the will to apply what knowledge they had, but also their acceptance, as individuals, of the way of life of men of property and men of rank. It is a hard saying and one that condemns ourselves as well as others of the Labour Government: *You cannot engineer an equalitarian state if you yourself are enjoying the pomp and circumstance of the city of the rich surrounded by the city of the poor.* If we are to continue to accept the existing social order, in our own habits of life, it is safer and more wholesome that these institutions should be administered by men who believe in them and who represent those who believe in them. The Labour Party leaders have shown that they have neither the faith, the code of conduct, nor the knowledge needed for the equalitarian state. . . .

Christmas Day.—This day forty years ago I was at Box House; Father was dying and Kate and I were at his bedside watching the flickering out of his dear life. I had been privately engaged to Sidney for some months and I was awaiting the death of the dear one to tell my family that I was bound to another for the rest of my life; and both of us bound up in the vocation of continuous enquiry into social organisation. A life, it proved to be, of extraordinary happiness and some success. "I knew my little Bee would do well for herself," I could hear dear Father saying, with his beaming smile, if he came back to see. For he had a good opinion of my *business capacity* and matter-of-fact judgment. Others of his daughters had greater personal charm and good looks—"but for sheer common sense give me my little Bee!" he would have said. And I think he was right. "Beatrice," once said Leonard Courtney to Kate, "has great general capacity—she is not an intellectual—she merely applies this general capacity to certain problems of the intellect." And that is exactly what I want to do about Russia. Those who think about Russia seem to me to become hysterical—they either see red with hatred or see mythical virtues in the new social order.

The queer experience of being at the centre—or ostensible centre —of political power is now ended for Sidney and we can resume the old life; day-to-day thinking, reading, writing, walking—a delightful existence even in old age. The Labour Movement, as a force, has sunk very low in the capitalist countries—it hardly counts politically or industrially either here, or in the U.S.A. or in Europe or even in Australasia. The capitalists are, outside Russia, everywhere in control —not of the financial situation which gets worse and worse, but of the governmental machinery. But they are in a devil of a funk and have lost faith in themselves and their system. Russia and her General Plan is in the ascendant; but her activities are almost delirious—and her enemies still believe that she will blow up through some misdirection of her passionate energies in all directions—educational culture as well as industrial production. What is the value of this strange combination of science without free thought, and fanaticism without religion, which is possessing the Russian race?

For the next four months Sidney and I will be turning out a text book on *Methods of Social Study*—a good part of it written years ago. But our main task will be preparing our mind for seeing as much of Russia as we can afford strength and money to see. My next diary book will, I hope, tell the tale of our adventures and give our verdict on *What we can learn from Russia* by Sidney and Beatrice Webb.

PART IX

1932

JANUARY 1932—DECEMBER 1932

January 4th.— ... Why does the world to-day seem such a gloomy place to live in? I think it is because of the strange atmosphere of fear and hopelessness; everyone apprehensive and inclined to be timid, doing without things, retiring from the fight. Every kind of social organisation is on the defensive: capitalist enterprise is on the defensive; Trade Unionism is still more so; political democracy is on the defensive; the British Empire is very much on the defensive; Europe is on the defensive and the U.S.A., the big booster of prosperity only two years ago, is almost abject about its bankruptcies and deficits and empty tills; more uncertain and downhearted about the *American Way* than even we are about the *British Way*. Indeed the only ray of light for us, here in Great Britain, is that, whereas in the last few years the rest of the world have been telling us that we are decadent and "down and out", we can, to-day, look them all in the face and shout *So are you*!

This is especially comforting in the case of the U.S.A. The Americans are worse off than we are, whether measured in vital statistics, in employment, in home and foreign trade, in municipal and state deficits, and scandalously so in *crime*, and in the sudden death of its inhabitants by accident, suicide and murder. If only we could feel satisfied that FRANCE was in a bad way; (and we are beginning to think she is), our spirits would rise! All the same it is a doleful world when one's only consolation is that other people's misfortunes equal one's own; and are, perhaps, a trifle worse.

What, of course, is satisfactory to us, as Socialists, is that those who defend the present order of society, in the newspapers or over the wireless (the B.B.C. has been collared by the defenders of capitalist enterprise) are at their wits' end as to how they can explain the present world disaster—the worst collapse of profit-making enterprise the world has ever seen. There has been no failure of crops; on the contrary nature has been over-abundant; she has mocked men with her fertility; there has been no failure in skill and knowledge—man's intellect has been increasing his power over nature, has been decreasing the amount of necessary effort by fabulous percentages; 100% or even more in some cases. And yet in the midst of all this plenty—men are

297

workless and destitute. Nor can the pundits of private enterprise tell us *what* is the cause of this mad state of things: some say it is the stupid use of credit or currency, others war debts and reparations; others the denial of free trade and free exchange between countries, others too much spending or speculation, whilst a few attribute it to rationalisation and too little spending. The Devil is, according to Gerald Heard,[1] the advance in applied physical science without an advance in the art of life. If only we were less able and less inventive we should do better. Not one of these clever ones—not even Keynes—*dare* say that the game is up for profit-making enterprise. Even the continental Socialist parties hesitate to say it. Why? Because that way lies Soviet Russia. And Russia is the menace to the party organisation of the continental Socialists and the Second International. Will she become the Mecca? If so it will be the British Fabians who will show the way: not the continental Marxists. A pilgrimage to the Mecca of the equalitarian state led by a few Fabians, all well over seventy years of age, will bring about the world's salvation! Well, well; it is an exhilarating, even an amusing prospect, if only it were not so damned expensive! However we shall get a bit back by writing for the U.S.A.

What attracts us in Soviet Russia, and it is useless to deny that we are prejudiced in its favour, is that its constitution, on the one hand, bears out our *Constitution of a Socialist Commonwealth*, and, on the other, supplies a soul to that conception of government—which our paper constitution lacked. We don't quite like that soul; but still it seems to do the job—it seems to provide the spiritual power. Personally being a mystic and a moralist I always hankered after a spiritual power; always felt instinctively that there *must* be some such a force, if salvation were to be found.

On the first point: the Soviet constitution—the secular side of it —almost exactly corresponds to our Constitution—there is the same tripod of political democracy, vocational organisation, and the consumers' co-operative movement. And the vocational or Trade Union [side] is placed in exactly the same position of subordination that we suggested. Also the position of the separately organised consumers' co-operative societies is similar to ours. There is no d——d nonsense about Guild Socialism! But the spotlight of intriguing difference between the live creation of Soviet Russia and the dead body of the Webb Constitution, is the presence, as the dominant and decisive force, of a religious order: the Communist Party, with its strict discipline, its vows of obedience and poverty. Though not requiring chastity, Communists are expected to be puritan in their personal conduct, not

---

[1] Henry Fitzgerald Heard (b. 1889), author. Beatrice was probably thinking of his fortnightly broadcast series, *This Surprising World*, which ran from 1930–3.

to waste energy, time or health on sex, food or drink. The exact opposite of the D. H. Lawrence cult of sex which I happen to detest. It is the invention of the religious order, as the determining factor in the life of a great nation, that is the magnet which attracts me to Russia. Practically that religion is Comteism—the religion of Humanity. Auguste Comte comes to his own. Whether he would recognise this strange resurrection of his idea I very much doubt. Of course the stop in my mind is: how can we reconcile this dominance of a religious order imposing on all citizens a new orthodoxy, with the freedom of the soul of man, without which science—that sublime manifestation of the curiosity of man—would wither and decay? How can we combine religious zeal in action with freedom of thought? That is the question which we want to solve by studying Russia. . . .

January 17*th.*—Into our circle on Saturday afternoon came an old acquaintance, Professor Jevons,[1] recently returned from a professorship in India. He is a gentle intellectual, with a refined but rather hesitating mind, disinterested and public-spirited. He wanted to interest us in a society for promoting Co-operative Economics, which has the support of L. Woolf, Plunkett, etc. and is being engineered by the Russian, Barou,[2] who as a non-Communist had to leave the managership of the Narodny Bank. But the gentle professor had not made up his mind whether the dominant note of the new venture was to be *voluntary* organisation as against governmental; or consumers' control as against producers' or profit-makers' control. His support came from the voluntarists; his own leaning was towards consumers' control. We sent him away rather disconsolate: at our insistence that the only live issue at the present time was consumers' control, whether governmental or voluntary, and with a decided preference for the compulsory over the voluntary. If Soviet Communism succeeds it will be because its economics are *consumers' economics*; production for a known demand. What has to be worked out is this *Consumers' Economics.* Can we do it? . . .

February 20*th.*—Graham Wallas with us. It interests me that he and we are much nearer in opinion than we have been for many a long year. He has dropped his liberalism as a possible creed: he thinks that American capitalism will fail to give a decent and continuous livelihood to its people; and that Soviet Russia will succeed in doing it.

[1] Herbert Stanley Jevons (1875–1955). Political economist, Fabian, son of W. S. Jevons; Professor of Economics, University of Rangoon, 1923–30.
[2] Dr. Noah Barou (1889–1955), born at Poltava in the Ukraine, economist, sociological writer, authority on Trade Unionism and co-operation in the U.S.S.R. From 1925–30 a director in London of Centrosoyus and the Moscow Narodny Bank.

And though he fears the suppression of free thought in politics under Communism, the Soviet system has his sympathy in its anti-God crusade and in its subordination of the Trade Unions to the will of the consumer-citizen. It is strange how Graham Wallas has stuck, throughout life, to his leading antipathies—Royalty, the Priest and the Trade Union. But what interested me was that he had not re-acted more violently against the suppression of free thought, free press and free speech in Soviet Russia. Poor liberalism! Even aged Liberals are reconsidering their faith out of sheer disgust at the ways of profit-making capitalists, more especially in U.S.A. Bertrand Russell, recently in U.S.A. and here for lunch, agreed about Soviet Russia, but maintained that, in spite of all the corruption and violence of the U.S.A., its oppressions and cruelties, there was more hope for the future, there was more action and life in it than in Great Britain. Here the people were good-natured and tolerant; but action and thought were just petering out. He was violently indignant at the flunkeyism and treachery of J.R.M. and Snowden. . . .

February 28th.—Meyendorff[1]—ex-Baltic Baron (formerly landed proprietor in Latvia with a house in Petersburg); member of the Duma; belonging to the Russian aristocracy: since 1920 he has been lecturer in Near Eastern affairs etc. at the School of Economics. He has gone through two revolutions—an agrarian revolution in Latvia where he was deprived of his landed estate, except his share among the rest of the inhabitants, yielding him £20 in rent; and the other in Petrograd— October 1917—where his home and other belongings were confis-cated. Until 1918 he was employed in the Swedish Legation but in the summer of that year he and his wife were allowed to depart in peace. He is an old friend of Mirsky[2] and when the latter escaped from Denikin's defeated army via Greece to London, penniless, Meyendorff got him employed on various literary jobs and eventually he was taken on by Pares[3] at the School of Slavonic Studies at King's College. According to Meyendorff Mirsky is a born rebel and fanatic. As a young officer in the Guards he refused to drink the Czar's health and was dismissed the regiment; had an interval of university life, joined up in the war and distinguished himself for bravery and finished up as an artillery officer under Denikin, escaping to Athens, where his mother had taken refuge at the Court; from there to London

[1] Baron Alexander Meyendorff (b. 1869). Reader in Russian Institutions and Economics at the London School of Economics, 1922-34.

[2] Prince Dmitri Mirsky (b. 1890). Former Czarist officer, served in White Army. Changed sides and became lecturer in Russian Literature, School of Slavonic Studies, University of London, 1922-32; returned to Russia in 1932.

[3] Sir Bernard Pares (1867-1949). Professor of Russian History, University of London, 1919-36; and Director of the School of Slavonic Studies, 1922-39.

penniless and proud, with a notable literary gift. During the war he was married for six weeks; but separated from his wife, and "forgot to mention his marriage to his mother"—altogether a strange character with a Russian strain of mysticism and romance.

Meyendorff is a benign and attractive person; intellectually accomplished, more German than Russian, without any bitterness or animus. He is very grateful to the School for his £500 salary. His view is that Russia, prior to the war, was evolving into a modern capitalist state, with an increasing measure of representative government in the normal manner. The Russian peasant was not a competent agriculturist; he had no real love of the land; by temperament he was a "petty trader"; he was a temperamentally idle person and lounged through life. After the abortive revolution of 1905 the tendency was towards the enclosure of the common fields and the upgrowth of small energetic capitalist cultivators (Kulaks), who together with the big estates were by 1914 producing far more than the old system of semi-serf individual cultivators, or the wasteful strip cultivation of the *mir* (the first result of the emancipation of the serfs in the 1850s), a system which had its climax in 1880–5. In October 1917 the land was seized by the peasants and strip cultivation of equal parts was reintroduced with calamitous results. Lenin in 1923 reversed the process and encouraged the so-called Kulaks in order to get the food necessary for industrialisation. On Lenin's death this policy was at first continued by Stalin, in opposition to Trotsky, who demanded collectivisation and the "liquidation" of Kulaks. Then came the Five-Year Plan and the wholesale starting of collective and state farms. Meyendorff—with, I think, increasing hesitation—thinks that this movement will fail owing to the incapacity of the Russian peasant to use the machines and work regularly. "Russia will become a country of Pyramids—scrapped machinery and a famine-stricken population." Mirsky, on the other hand, has been converted, and has become a fanatical Communist. "We never meet now," Meyendorff said sadly; for apparently he has a real admiration and liking for the talented and wayward Mirsky; he rejected Kingsley Martin's suggestion that Mirsky's conversion was not sincere—it was all of a piece with his romantic career and his refusal as a young Guards officer to drink the health of the Czar and consequent dismissal from his regiment. Indeed he said that Mirsky was a little mad and was becoming madder—he feared that there might be some crisis.

The Court, by the way, according to Meyendorff, "did not count" in the years before the war, and he dismissed the Rasputin scandal as a mere incident in Court life. The predominant note of Meyendorff's conversation and of his book, *The Russian Revolution*, is that "Russia was going on quite well before the war". But then as he himself says,

"I am an old-fashioned individualist, believing in private property and bourgeois mentality." Meyendorff, in a long walk I had with him on Sunday, emphasised the erratic element in the Russian character: the idleness and vagrancy of the peasants, the vapidity and inability of the aristocracy, the unpunctuality of the students; he could not imagine that Russians would long submit to the terrible pressure of the Communist régime. But he admitted that the professors whom he had seen "on leave" said that the Russian student had changed in character; that formerly he was willing to question everything and disregard discipline—now there was a "stop in his mind", a sphere of thought, feeling and action in which he did not question, but obeyed, as if hypnotised. When would he rebel? I suggested that our population in the middle of the 18th century was as vagrant and disorderly as the pre-war Russian: drunken, licentious, working when it listed—but that as regards the mass of the workers it was brought to heel by machine industry and as regards the middle class "reformed" by the Wesleyan and other evangelical religions coupled with the desire to become rich. In Russia the same sort of "reformation of manners" was going on: with the difference that the workers were being educated —and stimulated by the idea they were conquering the world for themselves; whilst the intelligentsia were being put into the strait-jacket of the Communist creed. There was also the liberation of the intellect by the cult of science. I suggested that the Communist discipline coupled with the exhilaration of the proletarian faith was raising the standards of the mass of the people, whilst crippling the energies of the ex-bourgeois and non-party intellectual. The worst feature was, he thought, the suspicion and fear in which the brain-worker lived and had his being—the heresy hunt. Meyendorff could not understand why the British Socialists were so far more sympathetic to Russian Communism than the continental: he would have expected their cult of personal freedom would have made them less so. . . .

March 7th.—The Sokolnikoffs here for 24 hours. From our talks with them, S.W. and I gathered that Sokolnikoff was exiled in 1913 as a student of 20 to Siberia, escaped with a friend and found himself first in Berlin then in Paris during 1914, returned in 1917 to Petrograd, joined Lenin, was appointed manager of Moscow Bank in 1918, Financial Commissar and Professor of Finance and then Ambassador to London 1928. Madame joined the Red Army at 14 years of age in 1920, married in 1922, her child was born in 1923; then she became correspondent in China, Turkestan, Geneva and Paris for a Trade Union paper—suffered during the Civil War typhoid fever and famine, her child being born neurotic and delicate in consequence. He is of German-Jew extraction, a solid intelligence and character, with a sense of humour, a Marxian dogmatist—belonging to the intellectual bourgeoisie. She is an Eastern type, very sympathetic and talented— far more sensitive than he is—an artist in words. They are both deli- cate—giving the impression of bad hygiene and overstrain; and both puritan in morals. She is more critical of the Soviet system than he is —fears the effects of its intense excitement and stimulus on the young people—she objects to "collective" establishments and wants the individual home and family life. She has left her child in Petrograd partly because the English climate does not suit it, but also to save it from "bourgeois standards" as an Ambassador's child in London. The Sokolnikoffs are now getting many invitations to dine from Conservative M.P.s, etc; but the Diplomatic Circle is still stiff and aloof. At their last reception, which she said was a "brilliant affair" and "very useful", English political High Society was represented, which it had never been before, but not the Diplomatic Circle. "We have few friends in London," she said, and intimated that we and the Shaws were among the few. She is going back to Moscow "to work", and to be with her little daughter—she feels restless without anything "to do" in London and dislikes the little she has seen of London Society. When I asked her what was her impression of the English people, she said it was of politeness and good manners, tolerance, kindliness and honesty—"it would be so easy to introduce the Com- munist state here"! In Russia they had to deal with all sorts of races, many extremely gifted, but all barbaric and uncouth compared to the English people with their cold smooth manners and reasonable but dull minds—"the poor" she had seen in Glasgow "looked terribly depressed and lifeless". This was the general impression, *not* the literal expression of what she said. Sokolnikoff talked mainly with S.W., Malcolm[1] and Stafford Cripps. He speaks English badly and does not understand it well and he is very slow on the uptake— but everything he says gives the impression of candour. From his tone one would gather that the responsible governors of U.S.S.R. fear, more than anything else, war. They are straining all they know how to train the vast multitudes of their peoples into efficient machinists working regularly and skilfully at providing all the necessaries and many of the amenities of a civilised life, so that they may develop their equalitarian state into a fully-grown civilisation superior in strength and happiness to any other community. If this be done they believe that this type of social organisation will spread all over the world through the workers insisting on having it. . . .

Stafford and Isobel Cripps here for the first time for a few hours. In manners and morals, in tastes and preferences, Stafford would make an ideal leader for the Labour Party: he would be equally at home with

---

[1] Possibly Malcolm Muggeridge, her nephew-in-law, now editor of *Punch*.

the T.U. official, the Co-operative administrator and the Socialist intellectual. He has also sufficient personality—physical and mental—for leadership: tall, good-looking, with a good voice and pleasant gestures. But he is oddly immature in intellect and unbalanced in judgment: a strange lack of discrimination and low standard of reasoning, in picking up ideas—queer currency cranks or slapdash remedies—universal insurance against poverty for instance! and the latest currency craze—"disappearing money". He does not *know* his own limitations: he is ignorant and reckless in his statements and proposals. It is characteristic of this state of mind that he prefers George Lansbury as leader to Henderson—and would like to see the latter retire—the truth being that George Lansbury is intellectually woolly and uncritical and does not curb or check Stafford's advocacy of this or that new project picked up casually from someone. . . .

March 19*th.*—*Good Earth* by Mrs. Buck—the wife of a missionary in China—is the finest piece of sociological fiction that I have read since *The American Tragedy* (Dreiser)—far finer, regarded as literature. Perhaps I am biased by the way in which the hero's character and circumstances, from early manhood to old age, bears out my general impression of Chinese life when we were there in 1911 as a dead civilisation—a race, with a great past, but which has somehow or other lost its way—its art, its literature, its science, its religion, its hygiene, its aptitude for government. All that is left is tenacious industry and capacity for endurance; greed of wealth, together with certain conventions about family obligations, and a type of good manners—the last of dubious value because Chinese good manners are largely make-believe and "saving your face". Rich food, sexual indulgence, opium, and the social prestige of great possessions are the "good things" aimed at through lives of unremitting toil. The result, a low standard of livelihood and security: a wasted land, devastated by drought or floods, where man is cruel and nature uncontrolled; where "women are for use and boys for pleasure"; where superstitious rites are fading out, and religious emotion is non-existent; where war, pestilence and famine rage. There is a certain type of patriotism and national self-conceit which Japanese aggression *may* harden and Soviet Communism *may* enlarge into public spirit. What the Chinese need is a new culture, some humanistic faith fanatically held—that would inspire an altruistic code of conduct and a passion for applying knowledge to life. Russian Communism is the only hope for China. It is a tragedy that its propaganda began on the way of destruction instead of as an exemplar of re-construction.

But however wanting the Chinese may be in positive virtues they seem to have a curious kind of stamina—of reserve power—a pride of race?—which will make the 30 million in Manchuria precious hard to govern. Japan, I think, will fail to maintain her sovereignty in spite of the tacit support of Great Britain and France. Here again the relative success of American Capitalism and Soviet Communism as a social order will be the deciding factor in future Chinese civilisation.

What interests me in Mrs. Buck's book is that, though she is the wife of a missionary, there is not one single reference to Christianity from start to finish! (Sidney corrects me: there appears, in the crowded streets of the Southern City, to which the family is driven by the famine brought about by drought—a distributor of leaflets, with a picture of a man crucified—but as the recipients cannot read it means nothing to them!) . . .

April 5th.—S. and I are immersed in Soviet literature of all types and kinds—official reports and travellers' tales, of both of which there are many, a few novels, more memoirs. At present we cannot make our way to any settled estimate of success or failure, whether success or failure be partial or on a colossal and catastrophic scale. The experiment is so stupendous, alike in area, in numbers involved, in variety, in speed, in intensity—in technological change and necessary alteration in human behaviour and human motive, that one's mood alternates between the wildest hopes and the gloomiest fears. All I know is that I *wish* Russian Communism to succeed—a wish which tends to distort one's judgment. When one becomes aware of this distortion, one has "cold feet". To be for or against Soviet Communism is, to-day, a big gamble of the intellect. Will our pilgrimage to Moscow bring enlightenment or rightly measured judgment? Are events ripe for such an evaluation? . . .

April 28th.—I attended the sectional meetings and dinner of the British Academy of which I have been elected the first woman member. It is a funny little body of elderly and aged men—the aged predominating; broken up into sections—supposed to consist of the pundits of the several humanistic sciences as a counterpart to the Royal Society in physical science. The Society was started by Arthur Balfour, Lord Reay[1] and a few others—it is now presided over by H. A. L. Fisher—I belong to the Economic section presided over by Professor Scott[2] of Glasgow—the sectional meeting was attended by

[1] Donald James Mackay, Lord Reay (1839–1921). Governor of Bombay, Under-Secretary for India, and Chairman of London School Board. First President of British Academy, 1901–7.

[2] William Robert Scott (1868–1940), economist. Professor of Political Economy at University of Glasgow, 1915 onwards.

Bonar,[1] Clapham,[2] Bowley,[3] Foxwell[4] and Scott. There were some forty out of the one hundred and thirty members at tea and the same number at the dinner. The little crowd gave a lifeless and derelict impression—very Oxford donnish and conventional in culture and tone. It is a mystery why anyone agrees to pay £10 entrance fee and £3 3s. od. a year: I did it at Keynes's and Alexander's request as the first woman. It is typical that there is no section on Sociology—only Economics. Politics is assumed to be covered by History, ancient and modern. The main business is arranging a few annual lectures, publishing a few treatises, or biographies of deceased members, and, most important of all, canvassing for rival candidates to fill vacancies up the statutory limit of 150. The candidates up for selection included Bertrand Russell, Beveridge, Tawney and Graham Wallas. Our section nominated Robertson[5] of Cambridge. The aged Foxwell wanted Henry Higgs[6]—whom I remember as Leonard [Courtney's] private secretary at the Treasury—some fifty years ago! H. A. L. Fisher was very oncoming and wanted to see us when we return—I wonder whether he means us to meet Ll.G.? We are rather off the stage to be considered a way of approach to the Labour Party, but Ll.G. is badly sidetracked. Our availability is slightly increased by my auntship to Stafford Cripps, who is assumed to be the future leader of the Labour Party. It is certainly a strange family episode that there should have been two "R.P.'s" sons-in-law in the two Labour Cabinets and that a grandson should be the heir-apparent to the Labour Party's future premiership. Dear old Father would have chuckled over it: in spite of his Toryism. Mother would have been more gratified by my F.B.A. and triple doctorate. Her daughter the perfected *Blue Stocking*! and her own lifelong absorption in book learning amply justified—her ambition brought to fruition in one of the ten children whom she had, at the cost of her own career as an intellectual, brought into the world. Bless her. . . .

May 14th. 4 *a.m.*—Our journey put off for one week owing to ice in Gulf of Finland—thus prolonging the worry of our elaborate preparations—alike in bodily comforts and the tutoring of our minds.

[1] James Bonar (1852–1941), civil servant, economist, author and lecturer.
[2] Sir John Clapham (1873–1946), the economic historian; Professor of Economic History at Cambridge, 1928–38.
[3] Arthur Lyon Bowley (b. 1869), Professor Emeritus of Statistics, University of London.
[4] Herbert Somerton Foxwell (1849–1936), economist; Professor of Political Economy at University College, London, 1881–1928.
[5] Dennis Holme Robertson (b. 1890). Professor of Political Economy, University of Cambridge.
[6] Henry Higgs (1864–1940), civil servant, economist, lecturer and statistician; Secretary to Royal Economic Society, 1892–1906.

Continuously revolving and discussing hypothetical conclusions about Russia and forecasting our book. What amazes me is the originality and completeness of the constitution imposed, in the course of little more than a decade, on 160 millions, made up of different races, with different religions and languages, scattered over one-third[1] of the habitable globe, by a group of emigrés, without experience, carrying out the theories of a German Jew. Soviet Russia, in its political and economic constitution, differs from that of any other state, past or present. It is true that one of the constituent parts is a type of political democracy—a centralised democracy—based on the indirect election of a series of delegates, in successive meetings of different bodies, to a veritable hierarchy of authorities; the power radiating from the top and not from the bottom. But this political democracy does not stand alone, nor is it supreme: it has two partners—industrial democracy, representing man as a producer, and co-operative democracy, representing man as a consumer. The salient and distinctive feature of Soviet Russia is, however, the establishment of a Spiritual Power over and above the ostensible government, dominating all other elements, central and local. The Communist Party welds, in one united body, all the constitutions, races, creeds, languages, cultures, included in the New Russia. This Spiritual Power knows no boundaries; it claims, like the Roman Church, to be a world-power and opens its arms to all peoples who subscribe to its creed and accept its discipline. Almost without intention, on the part of its founders, the Communist Party has taken on the characteristic features of a religious order; it has its Holy Writ, its prophets and its canonised saints; it has its Pope, yesterday Lenin and to-day Stalin; it has its code of conduct and its discipline; it has its creed and its inquisition. As yet it has no rites or modes of worship. Will it develop ritual as did the followers of Auguste Comte? For the emotional thought underlying Communism is the Service of Man, and faith in his perfectibility. One of its main doctrines is that truth manifests itself in *action* and that active *participation*, on the part of the believer, in the task of perfecting humanity, is the test—the touchstone of faith. Finally it has a kind of collective confessional in the *self-criticism* which fills columns of the newspapers with detailed accounts of this or that failure, in the working of factories, government departments or of social services.

Now all this new structure and function in Soviet Russia would not be exciting attention among intellectuals and social reformers of all countries—notably, by the way, U.S.A. and Great Britain, if it were not for the material and moral collapse of capitalism. If prosperity were to return and the crime wave, in the U.S.A. and Germany, were to decrease, the manifest defects and breakdowns—the lack of

[1] One-sixth, according to the Dean of Canterbury.

luxuries, if not of necessaries in the U.S.S.R.—and more important than all the restriction on the personal freedom of the brain-worker—would enable a hostile world to write it off as a failure. But to-day there is the fact that this new social order is not only promising work and wages to all its subjects, but alone among states is increasing the material resources and improving the health and education of its people. Instead of the despairing apathy or cynical listlessness of capitalist countries there is enthusiasm and devoted service on the part of millions of workers in Soviet Russia. The one big drawback lies in the activities of the G.P.U., and even here the U.S.A. runs Russia very close—except that in the U.S.A. the well-to-do intellectuals and rebels are seldom denounced or persecuted; it is the destitute unemployed and sweated workers who may not think or say what they believe and wish others to believe. The other matter of difference is the absence of a wealthy leisured class and therefore of the refinement and comfort—perhaps personal charm—which wealth brings; which some will think an evil, and others a good consequence of Communism. Midas has been dethroned and his Court has been dispersed; the Webbs, for instance, would not in Russia have played their little game! All this I scribble down in order to record what I have gathered from three months' reading and note-taking and talks with Russians, red and white, in preparation for our tour. Anyway whether our study of Russian Communism results in anything worth publication or not, the old Webbs are finding it extraordinarily interesting—not to say exciting. "You must not become a monomaniac about Russia," S.W. warned me. "What does it matter what two 'Over Seventies' think, say or do, so long as they do not whine about getting old and go merrily on, hand in hand, to the end of the road?" I answer back.

May 17*th.*—S.W. and I drafted this as our hypothetical conclusion prior to our tour:

Soviet Constitution

The ostensible constitution of Soviet Russia consists of three separate institutions, all of them derived from modern Western civilisation, but taking on, in the Russian environment, differences amounting to new varieties, namely (1) Political Democracy based on indirect popular election by the whole body of productive citizens, and manifested in the hierarchy of Soviets.

(2) Vocational Democracy, represented in the analogous hierarchy of Trade Unionism including Factory Committees; and

(3) Consumers' Democracy, existing in the similar hierarchy of Co-operative Societies, with the addition of an extensive layer of

various forms of Associations of Producers among artisans on the one hand, and among agriculturists on the other, variously embedded between Consumers' Co-operatives and the political Soviets. Added to these, all of them well-known and tried institutions of 19th-century Western Europe, is another, of a different character, reminiscent of earlier centuries, having indeed, the nature of a Religious Order, definitely limited in membership to a specially selected minority, less than 5% of the population, having a creed, a discipline and a code of conduct, and the avowed and inflexible purpose of using all the resources of theoretical and applied science, in order to produce the state of society deemed most advantageous for Soviet Russia in particular, but also for the whole human race—in this purpose reminiscent of Auguste Comte's Religion of Humanity. It is this Religious Order, the Communist Party, pervading every part of the organisation and every section of the community, that dominates the whole of the ostensible constitution of Soviet Russia, and gives to that huge nation to-day its distinctive character.

Sprouting out of all these basic institutions, in their various strata, are multitudinous and varied voluntary associations and other connective tissue of the most varied nature of greater or less range and permanence.

To which I will add that the leaders of Soviet Communism have realised that production must be planned from the standpoint of the consumer; and the conditions under which the required services and commodities are produced must be decided from the standpoint of the workers, by hand and by brain—the assumption being that all men should produce according to their ability and consume according to their needs—objective needs, mind you, not appetites!

What terrifies me about the system is the strain put upon the industry and intelligence of the leading men and women by the amount of planning required; and the strain of the morality and enthusiasm of the ordinary worker, if pecuniary self-interest be largely eliminated. That is why Communism demands a new religion and a new discipline. Here again it is the catastrophic failure of the motive of pecuniary self-interest to-day, the *suicide of profit-making capitalism* as manifested by the world *depression*, that turns men's thoughts to Russia. If it does not pay either you or your fellows to pursue your own interest why not *all* of us serve our fellow men and have a pleasant time together?

And now I say good-bye to this book until we return from Russia —some eight weeks hence—let us hope—not seriously disabled from reaping the harvest of our seedtime in "reading up" Russia, seeing it, and scribbling about it in these pages. In spite of our old age, Sidney and I have had a delightful time together since he left office; and studies and thoughts about Russian Communism have added to the zest of our honeymoon companionship.

APPENDIX

Beatrice Webb and Joseph Chamberlain

It has long been known that there was at one time a possibility that Miss Beatrice Potter would become the third wife of Joseph Chamberlain, whose second wife died in 1875 when he was still only 39; but details were lacking. Beatrice, when she published *My Apprenticeship*, left out any reference, perhaps because members of the Chamberlain family were still living in 1926. It is now possible, from passages in the MS. *Diaries*, and correspondence preserved therein, to reconstruct in part, at any rate, the story of this abortive romance, which incidentally throws some interesting light both on Chamberlain and on the girl to whom he directed his attentions.

The opening is an entry in the *Diary* dated June 1883, which runs: "Interesting dinner here [probably Prince's Gate] on the 18th. A Whig Peer on one side of me—Joseph Chamberlain on the other. Whig Peer talked of his own possessions; Chamberlain passionately of getting hold of other people's—*for the masses*! Curious and interesting character, dominated by intellectual passions, with little self-control but with any amount of purpose. Herbert Spencer on Chamberlain: 'A man who may mean well, but who does, and will do, an incalculable amount of mischief.' Chamberlain on Herbert Spencer: 'Happily, for the majority of the world, his writing is unintelligible, otherwise his life would have been spent in doing harm.' No personal animus between them, but a fundamental antipathy of mind. In what does this originate? I understand the working of Herbert Spencer's reason: but I do not understand the reason of Chamberlain's passion. But the motive force which moves the man of action is seldom rational. Philosophers will influence but never rule the world, at any rate not until the human nature of the masses is fundamentally altered; and then I imagine the philosopher will have advanced on to a still calmer sphere. . . . How I should like to [word undecipherable] that man [Chamberlain]." This extract (without the final sentence) was reproduced by Beatrice in *My Apprenticeship* (p. 107).

Immediately thereafter the *Diary* is silent; but it is clear that Beatrice was thinking a great deal about Chamberlain, and may even have been meeting him. For in September, having visited a lady whose name she does not mention, she writes:

311

"More light on J.C.'s character. Coming from such surroundings, he surely *must* be straight in intention. He is one of the many minds who are all working for the same ends and choosing the same means, and yet all is darkness when I try to discover their reasoning. Much might be learnt in studying the life and thought of such a man."

Possibilities must have developed fast in her mind, for within a few weeks she was seeking counsel from her sisters. The next item is a letter (undated) from Theresa Cripps, the sixth Potter sister, who married Lord Parmoor, and became the mother of Sir Stafford Cripps.

"We were also much interested in your account of Mr. Chamberlain, the more so that we had been hearing of Mr. Chamberlain from Trevor and Bessie when we were at Dorking on Sunday though they (the C's) evidently did not know that we were connected with them. I think, my dear Bee, you must, if you go into the Lion's Den even for a few days, keep up a strong "scientific" bias, and if, as I hear from many quarters, Mr. Joseph is on the look-out for a good wife and one who would forward, as you could do, his most ambitious views, don't you be carried away by any ambitious ideas yourself, or any feeling that your life would be worth more in such a position than it is in the quiet pursuit of science which is *really* congenial to you, and in the quiet duties—devotion to Father's and Rosie's[1] lives which we are necessarily unable to give . . . in the same degree. Look at the *man* himself as a man, and if apart from his whole connection with the Radical party and politics he is not congenial and companionable to you in the highest sense, look at something or somebody else. Your life is one we are all much interested in and indeed it seems so satisfactory to me now as it is and without knowing this man at all there seem to be so many (perhaps superficial) counts against him that you must forgive my writing this. . . ."

The reader will perhaps detect in this letter some panic at the idea of Beatrice's upsetting what was obviously a comfortable family arrangement. The third sister, Mary Playne, was not, however, so apprehensive. She wrote, on October 11th:

"I return Theresa's letter, which interested me very much. Her advice is excellent, and I quite agree with her that it is the man and not the position that must be carefully studied." She goes on to write with lack of enthusiasm of the "quiet pursuit of science", and ends, "I think you are well suited for a married life where there would be considerable call on your powers"—but makes no comment upon the prospective partner.

On November 5th, in the course of some general reflections, Beatrice writes: "*If* I remain free (which also is a big "if"). . . . At present, in this phase of my work, my duties as an ordinary woman

[1] The youngest sister, afterwards Mrs. Dobbs.

are not satisfied with the pursuit of my private ends. I doubt if they would ever be, *if one chose to remain unmarried.* [My italics] . . . The next fortnight will show me pretty clearly whether or not I have the gift of social diagnosis, and the last entry in this diary will be the means of checking it."

The last sentence refers to her first visit, under Martha Jackson's auspices, to the Co-operatives at Bacup (see *My Apprenticeship,* p. 121 ff.) which proved so formative of her thought and life. She was at Bacup from 7th to 20th November, and what she saw there most certainly played its part in the events of the ensuing weeks. Nevertheless, matters were moving to a climax of some sort. On December 7th she writes:

"I began my account [of Bacup], but a practical problem has inter-vened, and I must keep all my strength of mind to deal with it. One thing *I will not* do. I will not give way to a feeling however strong which is not sanctioned by my better self. I will not desert a life in which there are manifold opportunities for good for a life in which my nature is at war with itself."

The next item is a letter in holograph from Chamberlain himself dated December 16th. It runs:

"Dear Miss Potter,

I do not despise dancing, and I have a great respect for King David who continued the exercise to a late period of his life—but what would the Tories say? Nero fiddling while Rome is burning would be nothing to a Sybarite President of the Board of Trade dancing on the ruins of his country.

I feel I must sacrifice my inclinations to the prejudices of the British Philistine, but I shall be very happy to avail myself of your kind invitation to visit you on Saturday and Sunday, 5th and 6th Jan.

With many thanks, and kind regards to Mr. Potter.

Believe me, yours very truly,

Joseph Chamberlain."

This somewhat ham-handed epistle (which survives by itself) could hardly be described as a love-letter; but it was certainly assumed, as the next extracts show, to be in some sort a "declaration of inten-tion".

There was a house-party at the Argoed from Christmas onwards, which included Herbert Spencer. On December 27th Beatrice, having recounted a talk with Spencer in which he apparently made his famous declaration that he could never have considered marrying George Eliot, for all her intelligence and sympathy, because of her lack of physical beauty, speaks of the depression of that Christmas, and says:

"Father was excited and really unhappy, tho' he did his best to appear genial and happy. Slight feeling of fear in the whole party, and consciousness of a wide difference of opinion on a possible *coming* question. When host and hostess are not at peace with themselves and the world there is not much chance of much geniality. However my tortured state cannot long endure. The to be or not to be will soon be settled."

Then, on New Year's Eve:

"It is indeed an Eve for me. Two distinct ways open to me, one of which, it seems inevitable, I must take. Herbert Spencer's last words, 'It is not only foolish, but absolutely wrong of you, not to publish your Bacup experiences. At the present time, a protest, founded on actual observation of the working man in his normal state, against the pernicious tendency of political activity, would be invaluable!!!! I shall arrange with B— about publishing an article from you.' And while the philosopher is discussing with the editor of the XIX Century the desirability of encouraging a beloved disciple to come into the literary arena, the same beloved disciple is entertaining with no untender feeling the arch-enemy, the very embodiment of the 'pernicious tendency'.

"And this horrible dilemma which appears to threaten me (principle versus feeling) renders all my thought egotistical. My own immediate fate stares me in the face wherever I turn. I seem to be moving onward amidst a company of phantoms, some pushing, others restraining, but both parties equally ghostly in their powers, equally immaterial in their influence of the result. I, too, seem to be as in a Dream, acting a part with my own family the audience—a part which *makes itself* as I go on, the final scene of which lies not within that healthy region of free-willing foresight. And as the time approaches I *dare* not *think*, but trust [erasure] that the energy stored up in days of *thoughtlessness* will suffice for the last struggle; or that perchance some current arising within the 'whirlpool' will drift me outward. This truly is my last hope; if I do hope for continued independence of mind and body."

And so to the end, the visit of Chamberlain to the Argoed on January 5th. The next entry is dated January 12th:

"Another small episode in my life over. After six weeks of feverish indecision, the day comes—House full of young people and the three last days past in dancing and games; I feeling all the while as if I were dancing in a dream towards some precipice. Saturday 5th: remainder of the ball party—chatting round the afternoon tea-table, the great man's son and daughter among them. The door opens. 'Mr. Chamberlain'. General uprising. I advance from amongst them, and in my nervousness almost press six pounds just received into his hand. General feeling of discomfort, no one quite understanding the reason of Mr. Chamberlain's advent. There exists evidently no cordiality between him and his host; for Father in a few minutes retires to play patience with an absent and distressed look, utterly disgusted at the *supposed* intentions of his visitor. At dinner, after some shyness, we plunge into essentials, and he begins to delicately hint his requirements. That evening and the next morning till lunch we are on 'susceptible terms'. A dispute over state education breaks the charm.

"'It is a question of authority with women; if you believe in Herbert Spencer you won't believe in me.' This opens the trouble. By a silent arrangement we find ourselves in the garden. 'It pains me to have any of my views controverted', and with this preface he begins with stern exactitude to lay down the articles of his political creed. I remain modestly silent; but noticing my silence he remarks that he requires 'intelligent sympathy' from women. 'Servility, Mr. Chamberlain,' think I, 'not sympathy, but intelligent servility. What many women give men, but the difficulty lies in changing one's master, in jumping from one *line* of thought to the exact opposite— *with intelligence*'. And then I advanced as boldly as I dared my feeble objections to his general proposition, feeling that in this case I owed it to the man to show myself to be absolutely sincere. He refutes my objection by *re*asserting his conviction passionately, his expression becoming every minute more gloomy and determined. He tells me the history of his political career, how his creed has grown up on a basis of experience and sympathy, how his desire to benefit 'the people' had become gradually a passion absorbing within itself his whole nature. 'Hitherto the well-to-do have governed this country for their own interests; and I will do them this credit, they have achieved their object. Now I trust the time is approaching for those who work and have not. My aim in life is to make life pleasanter for the great majority. I do not care if it becomes in the process less pleasant for the well-to-do minority. Take America for instance. Cultured persons complain that the society there is vulgar, less agreeable to the delicate taste of delicately trained minds, but it is infinitely preferable to the ordinary worker.'

"I suggest meekly that this characteristic of American Society does not appear to have any relation to the superior equalisation of conditions, brought about by American institutions. That no doubt the working-class are better off, but that that surely is due to the unlimited space and power of development of the American continent; on the other hand huge fortunes are accumulated and *seem* to be more limitless than in England and to wield more power. That in fact the plutocracy owing to the generally corrupt nature of American [?administration] is *said* to be more powerful than in any other country.

"And so we wandered up and down the different paths of the Standish garden, the mist which had hid the chasm between us gradually clearing off. Not a suspicion of feeling did he show towards me. He was simply determined to assert his convictions. If I remained silent he watched my expression narrowly. I felt his curious scrutinising eyes noting each movement as if he were anxious to ascertain whether I yielded to his absolute supremacy. If I objected to or ventured to qualify his theories or his statements, he smashed objection and qualification by an absolute denial and continued his assertion. He remarked as we came in, that he felt as if he had been making a speech. I felt utterly exhausted; we hardly spoke to each other the rest of the day. The next morning, when the Playnes had left, he suggested some more 'exercise'. I *think* both of us felt that all was over between us so that we talked more *pleasantly*, but even then he insisted on bringing me back from trivialities to a discussion as to the intellectual subordination of women. 'I have only one domestic trouble. . . . My sister and daughter are bitten by the women's rights mania. . . . I don't allow any action on the subject.' 'You don't allow division of opinion in your household, Mr. Chamberlain.' 'I can't help people thinking differently from me.' 'But you don't allow the expression of the difference.' 'No.' And that little word ended our intercourse. . . . Now that the pain and indecision are over, I can't help regretting that absorption in the peculiar nature of our relationship left me so little capable of taking the opportunities he gave me of knowing him."

The next reference, a passage reproduced in *My Apprenticeship* (pp. 108–9, Feb. 1884), is a vivid description of a meeting at Birmingham, and the appearance of the master of his town. It carries no rancour; it is indeed appreciative, though in parts critical; it seems that the wound, though sharp, had not gone very deep.

To-day's reader may read what he pleases between the lines of this record. When writing—without having seen the MS. *Diary*—my life of Beatrice Webb, I expressed the opinion that she was well out of the entanglement; I see no reason to revise it. But the whole episode goes far to account for the eagerness with which she accepted in the following year the offer of Charles Booth to enlist her in his enquiry into the Life and Labour of the People of London.

M.I.C.

INDEX OF PERSONS

Y

GENERAL INDEX